WORDS,

A Hermeneutical Approach to the Study of Language

Robert Lord

University Press of America, Inc.
Lanham • New York • London

Copyright © 1996 by
University Press of America,® Inc.
4720 Boston Way
Lanham, Maryland 20706

3 Henrietta Street
London, WC2E 8LU England

Library of Congress Cataloging-in-Publication Data

Lord, Robert
Words: a hermeneutical approach to the study of language / Robert
Lord.
p.   cm.
Includes bibliographical references and index.
1. Language and languages--Philosophy.   2. Word (Linguistics). 3.
Hermeneutics.   I. Title.
P106.L637   1995   401 --dc20   95-36387 CIP

ISBN 0-7618-0138-3 (cloth : alk: ppr.)

℗™ The paper used in this publication meets the minimum
requirements of American National Standard for information
Sciences—Permanence of Paper for Printed Library Materials,
ANSI Z39.48—1984

To Owen Barfield

Contents

Acknowledgments

I cannot thank enough those of my friends and colleagues who have assisted or encouraged me in the completion of this book. My greatest debt of all is to my wife Mak Yee Fun, who has many a time raised a flagging spirit and created temporary islands of tranquillity in an otherwise distracted existence. A different kind of debt I owe to my friends Charles and Shirley Barham, who allowed themselves to be inveigled into a close and critical reading of my final draft. Any flaws that remain are certainly not theirs. I wish also to thank Terry Gordon and William Righter, who were kind enough to read much earlier drafts, and wise (and tactful) enough to discourage me from attempting to publish in those "early days". For this reprieve I shall be forever grateful. My thanks also to all those who helped me with the typing and word-processing of earlier drafts, not least Sharon Yip, whose patience I must often have tried.

My debt to a host of writers and scholars will be apparent from the Bibliography as well as from the text itself. The quotations from Wallace Stevens and from W.H. Auden are included by permission of Faber and Faber, Limited.

Preface

This book will doubtless be seen as one of a small but growing number of publications calling fundamentally into question some of the preconceptions to be found in existing approaches to the study of language.

Yet my aim has been less to do battle than to attempt to find the true measure of language, language as it really is. This I have obviously not been able to achieve off my own bat. My debt to a wide range and variety of thinking and viewpoint is apparent on almost every page. Only the particular orientation, the new direction, is mine. At the same time a different but closely related purpose has been to grope my way towards reality, a question so many of today's writings, from science to religion, hold as their prime concern.

The first promptings of the need for a different approach to language, for me at any rate, came from phenomenology, an endeavour spanning the half century from Husserl to Heidegger and Merleau-Ponty, and subsequently from philosophical hermeneutics, more especially Gadamer and Habermas. All of these authorities have insisted on the centrality of words in human being and doing. Gadamer in particular has linked hermeneutics integrally to the phenomenon of language. It could even be maintained that, in Gadamer's thinking, language has occupied centre stage. Yet, oddly enough, none of these thinkers has paid more than scant attention to linguistics ("the science of language") as such. Any approach to language that is devoid of reference to the range of procedures and models developed within linguistics promises to remain insubstantial and incomplete. So, troubled by such theoretical and practical inadequacy, especially in the domain of what surely ought to be a prime concern – the lexicon – to the extent that without words only an insubstantial understanding of the nature and workings of language can be achieved, I have set out to bring together philosophical hermeneutics and various facets of linguistics, poetics, semiotics, and other "disciplines" within a single theoretical and pragmatic framework and, in so doing, to reappraise various current insights into the nature and function of language.

My particular intellectual complexion however stems primarily from two influences.

The first of these has been Owen Barfield, to whom this book is dedicated. Barfield whose life has filled the greater span of our nigh-expired century was for most of his working life a lawyer. From his university days in Oxford he became a close friend of C.S.Lewis, and became associated with a group of writers and scholars, known as the "Inklings", whose informal gatherings also included J.R.R.Tolkien, Charles Williams and David Cecil. The exigencies of his professional studies and routines notwithstanding, Barfield published several major works in the course a long and active lifetime, including (for me, and I am sure for many others) two seminal books – *Poetic Diction* and *Saving the Appearances* – as well as a study (written at an age when many academics have already quit the scene) of the philosophy of Coleridge. Along with these should also be mentioned a series of highly original essays all of which appeared in American publications while Barfield was (in his "retirement") a visiting professor at Drew University.

A second influence, dating from the time of my work on the Russian novelist Dostoevsky, is Mikhail Bakhtin. In those distant times when I was drawing attention to Bakhtin's quite astonishingly original ideas on Dostoevsky and the European novel in general, his work was virtually unknown outside Russia, condemned as he was by the "Stalinist years" to obscurity. Bakhtin's important later works, including his *The Problems of Speech Genres* from the nineteen-fifties and his previously unpublished "notes" of 1971-2, written shortly before his death, were unknown even to me at the time they were written.

Among my conclusions will be that linguistic and philosophical approaches to language have largely misconstrued its nature. I shall try to strip away some of the misconceptions, and argue that language has to be seen under two completely different, if crucially and uniquely interrelated, aspects.

The first of these aspects (I have called them "modes") finds itself rooted in our common awareness, in our feelings, thoughts, motivations, imaginations, values and perceptions; in short, in our human world, one that is shared by all human beings, and modified only by cultural, social and ideological factors.

The second aspect arises from our motivation as human beings to enter into spoken (and written) transaction and negotiable communication with one another. We have no need to communicate what is already present in our minds or inner worlds since all that is, as Merleau-Ponty pointed out, already shared. But we do need to achieve a life together, a "life-world", one that is productive and culturally tolerably secure, in communities. For this reason we have to be able to learn and develop as human beings, to assert our own identity and rights, to maintain sometimes longlasting human relationships, to communicate our precise feelings, opinions and wants, at particular moments and in particular situations. All this has made individual **freedom** and **creativity** possible. Human beings appear to have developed, as part of their genetic inheritance, a complex and specific sort of instrumentality, at present relatively poorly understood, but having to do with the functional complexity of our neurophysiology. Also, through our own mysterious organisms, more than through our minds, we have direct access to a hidden but semiotically active world, known in modern times as the Unconscious.

The word itself, I shall argue, is what brings these two otherwise unrelated domains of language together into a dynamic something that enables each one of us in our capacity as human beings to transcend and change, however infinitesimally, the received world in which we find ourselves; and above all, to make it possible for elements and goings-on in the unknown world that lies "out there" beyond our ken to make themselves felt in sign and symbol.

1. Language and Being: An Introduction

We assume there is such a thing as language. But seldom, if ever, do we stop to consider what language might be. In these pages we start to wonder from the outset. Luckily we do not need answers straightaway. But, during the course of what follows, the question of the nature of language will emerge in many different guises. Even if the particular line of argument and proposed solution should fail to convince, readers will at least have had the opportunity to take stock of their own thinking and, in the true spirit of inquiry, may even have been prompted to pursue alternative or more adequate solutions.

It seems no accident that "language" as a concept – language as something that defines human being, in contrast to a mere language among languages, the form of speech peculiar to a people or a region – turns out to have been a fairly recent historical arrival. It is only in modern times, and characteristically during the present century that, over an entire range of mind and sensibility, a scattered handful of our more inquisitive spirits have been exploring the predicament of our being in the world and the strangeness of the spoken and unspoken relation between individual consciousnesses. For a relatively short time Western Man has been working out the implications of the realization, perhaps not new as such, that speaking and thinking have their roots, mysteriously, in the unseen, unconscious realms of Self.

Attempts to attain objectivity, on the other hand, find themselves frustrated at every turn by the same enigmatic core of language and the demands, especially in our own time, this seems to make on us. Paradoxically, the more we try to attain an objective distance, the less likely are we to succeed. Merely to think about language is to be drawn back into it. Human beings, we now know, can think only **in** and **through** language (Gadamer 1967, 62). Like the legendary creature of the deep, with its inchoate awareness of the watery medium it shares with other creatures, modern man has been as if awakening to find himself immersed in the all-encompassing medium we now recognize as **language**. Not only are we spatially and contemporaneously immersed in a medium "across" which we appear somehow to communicate, in a way analogous to the seemingly instantaneous radiation of electro-magnetic waves across a notional space, but we are beginning to find that our whole network of temporal relations – the time dimension itself no less – is inherent in it. Husserl, the founder of modern phenomenology,[1] found a name for this phenomenon – **life-world**: the universe in which human beings interact, become interfused with one another, a "world in common" that involves their being, quite literally in certain respects, "inside the skins" of other people. Such a life-world is no mere community (many non-human species form communities) but a world of truly interrelated **persons**.[2]

Extraordinary as it may seem to us today, the creators of so much of our science, our aesthetic, our mental make-up, our ethos, and our distinctive world-view – the Greeks – had themselves no term for language as such. The word *glossa*, like its Latin congener *lingua*, was used only to refer to particular languages.[3] But the Greeks more than compensated for this seeming lacuna with their *logos*, a word enshrining a bewildering breadth of significance, including reason, reflection, discourse, meaning, law, as well as the ever-elusive Word itself. Aristotle it was who defined Man as the *zōon logon ekhōn*, a living being embodying *logos*. Here was something significantly more than a merely "logical", more than what might nowadays be styled a "discourse-oriented", being. Human beings, Aristotle reckoned, are distinguished from animals through their sense of futurity, their being able intuitively to tell right from wrong and, most of all, their capacity for making reference to and communicating as yet unmanifested situations and events. Oddly, human beings seem able to communicate everything they intend or need to communicate. They have created (not developed, it should be emphasized) meanings and concepts in common, whether in the intimacy of their personal lives or in their common institutional relations. All of this is implicit in Aristotle's disarmingly simple assertion that Man is a being endowed with language.[4] In a succession of Gnostic, Neoplatonist and early Christian writers, the subsequent *logos* tradition prepared much of the ground for present-day hermeneutical approaches to language.[5] But it is a tradition that has been bypassed by Western philosophy, most of all in the latter's more nominalist moods. Ever since Plato's *Cratylus*, with its whimsically Socratic observation that no sensible person would "put himself or the education of his mind in the power of names," language has tended to get in the way of philosophy. Only in our own time has the bias of Western philosophy against language as "something within which men are bound and frozen" (Gadamer 1991, xxiv) progressively weakened, at least partly on account of the swelling tide of continental European phenomenological and hermeneutical philosophy which has hailed language – far from being the bane it was once held to be – as our only sure access to the familiar world of everyday.

Modern linguistics, by contrast, for all its claim to being the science of language, has suffered in varying degrees from a myopia deriving in part from the linguist's particular range of instruments and conceptual yardsticks, with their origins in a blend of Late Classical and Medieval grammar, the Universal Grammar of the seventeenth and eighteenth centuries, and the paradigms of nineteenth-century psychology, sociology, and comparative-historical linguistics (the latter much influenced by pre-Darwinian natural history), as well as in part from a range of presuppositions about the kinds of data considered eligible for analysis.

In broad terms, linguistics has leant towards the notion of language as **system**, the interface of form and content, or meaning, on the one hand, and form and function on the other. The interplay of an alleged biplanar structure is believed by some to fulfil, through the linguistic sign and signification (as developed by Ferdinand de Saussure), a range of cognitive, expressive, social, communicative, and other purposes. Depending on their point of view and provenance, linguists quite often emphasize selected aspects of their legitimate domain to the virtual exclusion of all others. a trend justified by the precedent of the "harder" empirical sciences. Bolder and more radical exponents may seek to establish their own "systems", adapting and refining them in accordance with expediency, but without wanting to reexamine their premisses or presuppositions. Even those who, in their different attempts to focus upon language as a phenomenon in its own right, achieved a fairly thoroughgoing shaking of the foundations ultimately failed to find a route beyond the paradigms of earlier centuries.[6] Few indeed were those who grasped the full significance of the thesis advanced long before by Wilhelm von Humboldt, that language and world are inseparable, and that without language there could be no human being. The world, Humboldt had been saying, is verbal in nature:

> Not only is the world a world only insofar as it comes into language, but language too has its real being solely in the fact that the world is presented in it. Thus, the claim that language is human in origin means at the same time that man's being-in-the-world is primordially linguistic. (Gadamer 1991, 443)

No words, no world.

It had become too much to expect that we should ever attain a truly balanced conception of the many-dimensional skein of mind, *logos*, system, and creative imagination that in the past few decades have compelled the recognition of language as the fundamental irreducible category of human being. "Language" is becoming more than just an abstract object to be dispassionately investigated and analyzed, and is at last being recognized as something that we are actually **growing into**, something that has been as if revealing itself to us by degrees and in unseen ways, surreptitiously almost.

It is impossible to keep the whole of language before the mind's eye, because language is flush with the world in which we live, a world that is ours in that it has literally been somehow fashioned by us, a **life context** as opposed to a mere environment. Other creatures, other life forms undeniably share with us the physical and biochemical environment of our planet. But the objects, locations, times, events, the myriad phenomena that make up our life-world — not always the familiar things, but as well the alienness of frozen wastes, wildernesses and untravelled oceans, the glories of planet Earth herself — are already, or potentially, imbued with sensation, imagination, feeling, *mythos*: the very stuff of language. Without the perpetual bringing forth, the bonding and life-blood circulation that is language, the meaning of the world would dry up, and our life context would empty itself into a nonhuman alienness of raw unperceived environment. By moonlight a movement out there becomes transformed in my consciousness into a "badger". Without the word "badger" , or at the very least "creature" or "animal", the fleeting movement would have remained an unknown "movement or flurry".[7] Mikhail Bakhtin in a notebook entry of his last years made the tantalizing observation that the most important thing about human beings is that they are, as he puts it, "witness and judge":

> When consciousness appeared in the world (in existence) and, perhaps, when biological life appeared (perhaps not only animals, but trees and grass also witness and judge), the world changed radically. A stone is still stony and the sun still sunny, but the event of existence as a whole (unfinalized) becomes completely different, now that a new and major character in this event appeared for the first time on the scene of earthly existence – the witness and the judge. And the sun... has stopped simply being and has started being itself and for itself... as well as for the other, because it has been reflected in the consciousness of the other... This has caused it to change radically, to be enriched and transformed. (Bakhtin 1986, 137)

It is not simply that nature began to be aware of itself, to reflect itself, in living beings. If this had been so, existence would have remained passive and "solitary". A supra-existence had to emerge: a whole being who was not solely an ego but at the same time an **other**. It is the **sense** of the world that has changed with Man, not the materiality. Only in language, in the word, can this sense be expressed. Authenticity and truth inhere not in existence itself, but only in an existence that is acknowledged and uttered.

The coming to the fore of language in some of the more innovative thinking of our own time has nothing directly to do with "the widening of scientific horizons" or anything of that sort. Rather it appears to be the result of one of those subtle shifts in human consciousness that occur from age to age, a phenomenon not to be confused with the Kuhnian[8] change of paradigm (though it may have something to do with Thomas Kuhn's "shifts of vision"). It is something intimately bound up with the ways we are now able to look at language, and something that we, as human beings, had perhaps not previously been entirely ready for. Even now, as will surely be illustrated in the pages of this book, our human conceptual repertoire for coping with this shift in consciousness falls woefully short of what is requisite. The complaint is frequently heard that science and technology have outpaced Man's capacity to handle new knowledge and the consequent power he is endowed with. But when it comes to the inwardness of the human spirit and its rare but radical metamorphoses, human beings prove just as inept. They go on dissecting, constructing and trying out model after model, at a time when language has been bursting its bonds, leaving its exponents high and dry with their ever more ingenious deconstructions, instead of giddy at the marvellous vistas that beckon at every turn. On the other hand, language has already so permeated late twentieth-century consciousness, with its renewed vision of *logos*, that the more towering of our own century's poetic creations, many of which could never have been conceived at any time previous, are inevitably shot through with this same self-consciousness, itself now inseparable from the grandeur of the creations themselves. Even the modern reader's oft-times fussy disregard for the integrity of texts and writers' *oeuvres*, however trivially iconoclastic or "deconstructionist" it might look, is but a part of the landscape laid bare by retreating horizons.

A renewed awareness of the Word is opening up worlds that were previously – though all the time potentially within our grasp, as Romantic poetry, philosophy (Coleridge) and science (Goethe) only too vividly show – hidden from view. It appears to have been Nicholas of Cusa, the early Renaissance German cardinal and first to conduct a modern biological experiment on plants, who conceived of *logos* not so much as a gradual revealing of a pre-established order of things but as an autonomous creative principle, one that continuously creates and re-creates order through differentiation and recombination from the given stuff of existence.[9] Despite the endless diversity of modes of discourse, ways of saying things, and the impossibility of translation, there exists only one Word, one language, one revelation, somehow emanating from and through human being and depending on this baffling creature for its existence. A renewed *logos* has, so to speak, stolen upon us, unawares, announcing itself through a freshly deepened awareness of language. We have begun to discover not only **that**, but **how**, the "words" of language – every feature of discourse, every function of language, the unlimited resources of creativity and interpretation – are ultimately in harmony; not in any lifeless *Gestalt*, but in "the form in the instant" (Benveniste 1971, 285) in whatever idiom, known or imagined. Modern man's debt to sometimes remote ancestors in building a provisional world, not his as property, or even as heritage, but as something never finished, always open, growing and changing through the workings of *logos*, remains to be assessed.

It is an ancient view: that language (*logos*) endows human beings with the power to apprehend, relate, identify, classify, set apart and, even more fundamentally, **to enable things to be**. Language was conceived as being something more than a mere human capacity. It is what makes a person human. It has been said that it is *logos*, not Man, that speaks. In the words of Martin Heidegger:

> We always see the nature of language only to the extent to which language itself has us in view, has appropriated us to itself. We cannot know the nature of language – know it according to the traditional conception of knowledge defined in terms of cognition as representation. (Heidegger 1975, 192-3)

The special characteristic of Man is not that he can exploit vocal utterance, but that he is the only entity to have discovered the world as a unique predicament – a sense of "being-there", "being-in-the-world": *Dasein* no less.[10] Language is what I am made of. Flesh, blood, genes, temperament, nothing stamps me with my individual character so much as language. "Je suis langage" – "I am language" – Sartre once said. As a person I first attained consciousness through the form and agency of language. My life, insofar as I understand it, depends on language, and my death is already predicated in it. It is through language just as much as through the generation of a physical organism that a human being emerges into existence, unfolds, blooms, declines, and eventually – dies. My own individual consciousness is in a crucial sense a unique constellation of language, and the language that is me directs or frustrates drives and impulses, filters moods, delivers a version of me not only to others, but even to myself. I am thus preordained by language to forge a reality for myself, a life and a history. Words allow me to think, feel, remember, plan, anticipate, dream and play. I can even be said to be a function of the Word, one of its artefacts.

Language has gone on revealing itself as a something which not merely does things, enabling speakers to do and express things, but has declared itself, as it were, at the very core of the individual's life as a power intimately woven into their being; more than just an instrument to be switched on and off at will, more than a mere capacity to be invoked whenever there is something to be said or written, or whenever someone other has something to say.

More than anyone, perhaps more even than Husserl, Heidegger, Cassirer or, more recently, Gadamer, the "discoverer" of this fresh departure in human consciousness was Maurice Merleau-Ponty. Merleau-Ponty was also its poet. In an inimitable and sensuously metaphorical language Merleau-Ponty manages to convey something of the poignancy and immediacy of this modern metamorphosis of language, which is at the same time a metamorphosis of humankind.

In a remarkable essay *Indirect Language and the Voices of Silence* Merleau-Ponty suggests that language is "much more like a sort of being than a means". That is why language can perform so well:

> A friend's speech over the telephone brings us the friend himself, as if he were wholly present in that manner of calling and saying goodbye to us, of beginning and ending his sentences, and of carrying on a conversation through things left unsaid. (Merleau-Ponty 1964, 43)

Instead of being a mere assemblage of component parts, which our present-day mania for print and computer software makes it appear, and from which we seldom doubt we can select at will, language should be seen as an active individual organismic whole. Meaning embodies the "total movement of speech" and it is in language that our thinking "crawls along":

> Our thought moves through language as a gesture goes beyond the individual points of its passage. At that very moment language fills our mind up to the top without leaving the smallest place for thought not taken into its vibration, and exactly to the extent that we abandon ourselves to it, it passes beyond the "signs" to their meaning. (Merleau-Ponty 1964, 43)

The opaqueness of language, its obstinate reflexivity, its turning and folding back on itself are what gives it its potency. Language begins to look like "something of a universe...capable of lodging things themselves in this universe – after it has transformed them into their meaning."

Words were never mere counters – "lexical substitution counters" J.R.Firth once dubbed them, but in an untypically dismissive way – for the drift of our thoughts to play with:

> There is a power in words because, working one against another, they
> are attracted at a distance by thought like tides by the moon, and
> because they evoke their meaning in this tumult much more
> imperiously than if each one of them brought back only a listless
> signification of which it was the indifferent and predestined sign.
> (Merleau-Ponty, 1964, 44)

If speaking were simply a matter of tagging each thought with words
nothing could ever get said, nor would anything said ever be worth
saying.

Language "gropes around" what it wants to say, unguided by any
"text" save the one it is in the process of "writing". Availing oneself
of language is closer to feeling than ratiocination: an intuitive
unmasking of the endless possibilities of what might be said; quite
unlike running through an index, a library catalogue, or a computer
programme, and more akin to a sense of verging upon some
superhuman manoeuvre. The possible ways in which hoveringly
incarnate expressions might in some other possible manner have
"touched and shaken the chain of language" have to be felt, not
reasoned:

> In short, we must consider speech before it is spoken, the background of
> silence which does not cease to surround it and without which it would
> say nothing. (Merleau-Ponty 1964, 46)

To bring ourselves to a true understanding of language, Merleau-Ponty
suggested, we have to imagine what it is like to be deaf: "we must
pretend never to have spoken." We must "submit language to a
reduction without which it would once more escape us by referring to
what it signifies for us."

PART ONE

WORDS AND WORLD

2. The Shared Word

A little over a century ago, a heterogeneous group of historical linguists known to posterity as "Neogrammarians" saw that language has its roots not, as was earlier supposed, in some purely notional abstract world of grammatical and lexical forms but in the actual living breathing individual. Despite the proneness to analysis at any cost that has gone on bedevilling the linguistic study of language since their time, the view that language is to be sought in the living human organism, and not in theoretical constructs, persists.

There is, it has been claimed, perhaps nothing that could be called "language" in a universal sense but only "languages", the linguistic behavioural particularities of individuals; there being no such thing as a language even, except insofar as the verbal practice of two or more individuals overlaps [2] – an extreme view, and one that raises many more difficulties than it resolves, for it betokens not only Babel, but Babel to the nth degree.

It cannot be denied, however, that what little is known of the brain and the central nervous system points to a highly singular, in many ways unique, neurophysiological network of functions among which language is interwoven with character, cognition, memory, imagination and motivation. Would such evidence alone compel the conclusion that no two people speak the same language when it is all too obvious that language is also something shared, something in common? The words I use are at the same time the words used by others. Two friends stop for a breather on the ascent of a mountain. One turns to the other exclaiming: "An amazing view, isn't it", the other responding "It certainly is!". They might if subsequently pushed concede that, even though they are addressing the same object and situation, they cannot possibly be "seeing" the same view (their backgrounds, interests, and previous experience of "views" will ensure this). But they may not even be aware that they are drawing upon a concept – "view" – which could not possibly be more abstract. The only feasible explanation, in view of the apparently successful communication, is that their concept is shared. Solutions to this kind of paradox range from Bakhtin's 'supra-I'[3] to Chomsky's uneasy marriage of intrinsic linguistic competence – "the tacit knowledge of the native speaker" (1965, 20) – with the "creative" aspect of language use (1966, 46).

Caught on the horns of a dilemma, linguistics has been thrust into the uncomfortable role of arbiter. Saussure favoured the notion of language as a self-contained, self-regenerating "structure" with all of its parts intricately and precisely interlocking in the manner of some idealized Swiss timepiece. Instead of remaining what it had been in earlier times – a guide to correctness, an ethic – grammar underwent transformation into a self-maintaining rule-governed system, a "fixed code" capable of directing, not to say dictating, the language behaviour of the individual: aptly styled the hegemony of the "language machine"(Harris 1987, 95).

The metaphor of the language machine, never more than a metaphor until the time of Saussure, reached its apotheosis, it could be said, in Chomsky's "generative grammar". The ultimate in anti-prescription and linguistic de-restriction, generative grammar allows the (idealized) human speaker unlimited scope in the production of (legitimate) utterances. Grammatical "competence" – the capacity to produce a limitless range of utterances in accordance with consciously inaccessible rules – was thought to reside in the neurophysiological structure and function of the brain, which innately determined what are and what are not legitate linguistic structures. A mythical arbiter therefore permits "well-formed" sentences such as, for example, *It rains every day in Wonderland* (even though no such claim can be verified or is even likely), but rules out semantic "malformations" of the order *Colourless green ideas sleep furiously*, even though contexts can be found in which even so outlandish a formulation as this can find a niche. It might also justifiably be asked **where** in the brain are these internalized rules and where are they "represented". What possible identifiable form can such "representations" take? (Harris

1987, 131). And what can there be in common between the brain and rules?

Abstractions breed abstractions. If it is to be believed that the language potential of individuals is regulated by grammar, it is but an easy step to conceiving robot-like beings, signallers in the void, "encoding" and "decoding" "messages" to and from each other – speakers being presumed to be endowed with the capacity for transmitting and receiving verbal messages, signalled precisely by means of codes. Signals, we hardly need reminding, are best assigned to an (abstract, hypothetical) physical world, the domain of communication science and various related branches of physical science. This is not a matter to be brushed aside however, and its ramifications will be considered in later chapters. Meanwhile, there is no avoiding the conclusion that messages and other communicative transactions engendered by the "business of language" within a shared world are, paradoxically so it might seem, **internal** to our own life-world, that intersubjective, "supra-personal" world which you and I inhabit.[4] "Out there" is the realm of physical events; not directly knowable, even by the physical sciences. The old familiar, but naïve, picture is that of a speaker transmitting code-like signals somehow representing certain bundles of meaning or intent to a hearer-receiver who picks up these same signals and decodes them.[5] Saussure's editors (1959, 11) depict this process as two Tweedledum-Tweedledee-like replicas facing each other, engaged in a non-conversation and effectively satirized in a "characters-in-search-of-an-author" scenario entitled *Saying Nothing* (Harris 1987, 164ff). Clearly, no such "model" of the transmission-reception of spoken messages fits any world we can understand or describe.

In reality, our vocal and other bodily gestures are merely the outward signs of a much more truly remarkable and (as will be seen) clinically observable phenomenon: **intersubjectivity** – the matching of separate consciousnesses, the living confluence of physically separate human beings. Whenever communication takes place, a train of gestures, whether vocal, or imprints on a sheet of paper, or non-verbal body language is set in motion. In such a manner, the persons I am attempting to communicate with are afforded the possibility of literally sharing my private mental universe, through participating in a life-world which is both mine and theirs.

Communication is the outcome of a sympathetic resonance. Nothing passes between. Nothing is actually "transmitted" between individuals as such. It was Merleau-Ponty who categorically dismissed as illusion the phenomenon of two-way communication. No one, he insisted, would be able to comprehend even the most commonplace of utterances, make sense of the simplest of texts, if these did not arouse in us images, impressions, thoughts and sensations that are ours already. Or as Bakhtin (1986, 68) was to put it,

> when the listener perceives and understands the meaning of speech, he simultaneously takes an active, responsive attitude toward it. The listener adopts this responsive attitude for the entire duration of the process of listening and understanding... A passive understanding of the meaning of perceived speech is only an abstract aspect of the actual **whole** of actively responding understanding. (Emphasis mine)

In other words the listener becomes the speaker, and *vice versa*. Language has to be envisaged as something altogether different from a mere device for expressing meanings and exchanging verbal messages. In the words of Merleau-Ponty (1962, 184) "it is within a world already spoken and speaking that we think." Between utterance and what is expressed through the utterance no gap intervenes. The speaker or writer takes up a position within an already existent world of meanings. Language precedes itself, teaches itself, and cues its own decipherment (Merleau-Ponty 1964, 39).

Merleau-Ponty did not want to rest there however. He was keen to explore the phenomenological implications of a claim that might otherwise have remained unfounded. In his view Husserl's *Logical Investigations* had attempted a resolution of the dilemma (always a vexed question also for linguistics) prevailing between **language** as one of the "objects supremely constituted by consciousness" and actual **languages** as "very special cases of a possible language which consciousness holds the key to." Husserl had seemed to relegate language to a mere object among objects, an object of thought, a secondary means of communication, a mere accompaniment.[6] In Husserl's later writing though a rethinking of his earlier approach to language becomes evident. Language is now taken to be a fundamental, a corporeal entity even – "corporeal" in the sense of being intimately implicated in gestures and in the spatiality of the body – an entity through which thoughts that would otherwise remain private and inaccessible to others acquire an intersubjective value, rooted not in the individual speaker or hearer but in a historically real yet at the same time ideal existence. Language only becomes a reality for speaking subjects when they make use of language for the purpose of communicating within an actual living community. Thus, to express is to become aware. Communicating subjects say what they want to say, not merely to impart their concerns to others, but also to arrive at greater self-awareness as regards their own standpoints and intentions. There would be little point, except in certain restricted domains of pure communication, in expressing something that would result only in its replication in another's consciousness. The "significative intention" creates for itself, as it were, a body. The form and stuff of this body bring about "a certain arrangement of **already speaking instruments**" – the whole repertoire of existing, so to speak, "preprogrammed" conventionalized language features, from phonology and institutionalized vocabulary to discourse and speech genres – which arouse in the hearer the presentiment of a signification not previously registered. Expression thus makes use of these "already speaking instruments", causing them to enable something to be said that has not previously been said.[7]

Another figure to have come to the fore in recent years is Wilhelm Dilthey, a contemporary of the Neogrammarians. Not so many years ago, starting out from the seminal position of Dilthey, Jürgen Habermas opened up neglected territory.

Dilthey had drawn attention to the difference between the language of the natural sciences and the language of social and cultural communication. The former, he had observed, is an artificial idiom, a pure "language", whose functions are "exhaustively definable by metalinguistic rules of constitution", exemplified in logic and in the language of mathematics (Habermas 1978, 168). By contrast, the "language of social and cultural communication" is considered "ordinary" language. Dilthey's "ordinary" language calls to mind Wittgenstein's "language on holiday" (1963, I, 19), obeying as it does, if capriciously, the rules underlying and ordering "pure" language, achieving completeness only when involved in intersubjective interaction, in the corporeal forms of expression. "Ordinary" language abhors metalinguistic prescription, following exclusively its own dictates. It is **reflexive**. In other words, ordinary language is alive, responsive to the fluctuating situation in which it occurs; exhibiting all the quirkiness, intractability, ambivalence and unpredictability of real life. Above all, ordinary language permits reflexive allusion to what has remained unstated (Habermas 1978, 168). When a prominent actress opened in Shaw's play *Candida*, he is said to have cabled her: "Excellent, greatest." She apparently cabled back: "Undeserving such praise." Shaw then replied: "I meant the play." At which the actress retaliated: "So did I." Without a prior understanding of the potentialities inherent in such repartee, we should never know how Shaw, or his female equal in wit, really meant the first telegram to be "read". Many are the categories of allusion that have become conventions: whether in joke, wit, poetic diction, in the stylized forms of irony, understatement, innuendo, parody, in figurative language of every kind, or in a whole array of rhetorical devices, from euphemism to mockery and denigration.

"Ordinary" language, in the sense elaborated by Dilthey, seems even to flout the conventions of "pure" language. In pure, logic-driven language for example, a sentence in the form of a question should always be treated as a question, and answered appropriately. But what kind of question is the "ordinary" *How do you do*? The reply *I'm doing quite well, thank you* would seem untoward, since in English no *do*-reply is called for (except in the facetious or ironical *How do you do?*). Again, what kind of question is *What have we here?* spoken in the context of bewilderment or mild consternation? It is partly a direct question, partly a rhetorical question, partly an exclamation of surprise or other emotion, depending on context. *Stand up!* is an unambiguous command. But what kind of command could *Say when!* be, as uttered in the context of pouring someone a drink? These samples, along with an indefinitely large number of others, are likely to disconcert only those of the (metalinguistic) temper of Wittgenstein, but are all an indispensable feature of ordinary interpersonal communication.

It was Dilthey who first proposed that language is the ground of intersubjectivity, that no one who has never before set foot in the domain of language can even begin to form an objective view of themselves, whether in words, attitudes or actions. In the words of Dilthey "only in language does man's interior life find its complete, exhaustive, and objectively understandable expression."[8] Everyday language is the medium in which meanings are shared. To resolve the problem of the isolation of language in the individual – in effect no language at all until it becomes linked to the "languages" of others through this shared medium – Dilthey proposed the notion of "a community of life unities" (though not, it might be noted, a community of languages). It must be for this reason, Habermas suggests, that "ordinary language has a structure that actually allows what is individual to be rendered understandable through general categories in the dialogue relation" (Habermas 1978, 163). This structure of ordinary language, totally different from any proposed by modern linguistics, makes communicable, no matter how obliquely, that which remains "ineffably individual".

Whatever this structure might ultimately prove to be, it must exhibit the reflexivity identified by Habermas. It must be a structure that will accommodate all linguistic and all non-linguistic means of expression – the arts, music, mathematics, and much else besides. It must not only gear itself to the malleability, open-endedness, and constant self-adjustment within this newly conceived shared language but must also be able to incorporate vectors of change. The "grammar" of "ordinary" language will vastly outstrip the "grammar" of grammar, immensely complex though the latter is already reckoned to be. In the most general terms the whole of this (some would add, fortunately) will probably never be possible. And if we were to press our inquiry too far we might find, as Habermas indeed suspects, that ordinary language is its own metalanguage, there being no possible means of describing or explicating it in other terms.

Even more crucial to our concern is the position adopted, especially in the writings of his later years, by Bakhtin. It was Bakhtin who first drew attention to what should long since have been obvious to linguists and philosophers of language (though, as we all know, the obvious becomes obvious mostly in retrospect). On the one hand, says Bakhtin, there is the language that linguistics (and also to some extent the philosophy of language, it should be added) is content to investigate. This "language" consists of phonological, morphological and syntactic units, marshalled into phrase structures, sentences and propositions. The linguist takes the view that "our speech is cast solely in stable sentence forms that are given to us" (Bakhtin 1986, 81). Where the series of such interrelated sentences stops appears to be entirely subject to the whim of the analyst and to the vicissitudes of an entirely mythical "speech flow". In fact, as Bakhtin points out, the sentence as a unit of language (as conceived by linguistic theory) no authorship. It belongs to no one. From the linguist's point of view language is regarded, lopsidedly, as having only one speaker, without any **necessary** relation to other participants in speech communication (Bakhtin 1986, 67). The arsenal of tools and instruments created by linguistics may look impressive, but they are "absolutely neutral with respect to any real evaluation." Bakhtin takes the example of the word *darling*. Lexicology would have it that *darling* is as neutral as any other word in the lexicon. For the linguist the word is a mere "language tool". As such, it never rises above a potentiality for expressing an "emotional evaluative attitude towards reality." In this respect the word cannot be applied to any particular reality. *Darling* only becomes real language when it is swept up into actual live utterance, when it can become suddenly imbued with any of an entire range of affection, passion, humour, innuendo or, quite simply, social decorum:

> Words in themselves evaluate nothing. But they can serve any speaker and be used for the most varied and directly contradictory evaluations on the part of the speaker. (Bakhtin 1986, 85)

Further examples are probably unnecessary. Readers can recall scores of live ones for themselves.

On the other hand, there is what Bakhtin termed "living language": the **concrete utterance**. In concrete utterance language becomes alive; and, conversely, it is through the reality of such utterance that life enters language. Live utterance thus occupies a nodal position between the limbo-like realm of neutral linguistic forms and structures at the one extreme, and life and reality at the other (Bakhtin 1986, 63). The utterance, not the sentence, Bakhtin says, is the real unit of speech communion, or "shared" language.[9] By comparison, the "system of language", as represented in linguistics and linguistic philosophy, resembles a a pale repository, inasmuch as nothing new can enter such a system "without having traversed the long and complicated path of generic-stylistic testing and modification" (Bakhtin 1986, 65).

If real, shared language does not consist of grammatical structures and forms, then of what does it consist according to Bakhtin? An inopportune question perhaps. Real language is no objectively observable, fixed configuration. It is subject to the whim and wit of human beings who live through and in it. This living language is none other than the realm in which we as human beings exist; it is the fabric of our lives. Utterances areunrepeatable: neither their intention nor their context can ever be identical. However many times I say *I love you!* I can never exhaust the utterance's possibilities: my sentiment and intention may be anything from sincere, insincere, casual (in exchanges, for example between some North American parents and children) or cliché, to an extreme verging on possession or delirium. A sure way to turn such live utterances into "dead" sentences is to attempt to copy them or, alternatively, to enshrine them in language textbooks.

What then can be the linkage that binds utterances together into meaningful speech (or writing)? Bakhtin's answer is: the **speech genre**. The speech genre is the living mould in which our utterances are cast. It determines the degree of weight, nuance, cajolery, pomposity, humour, vacuity one's words may or may not express. It ranges all the way from workaday conventionally stylized discourse to literary worlds of such unimaginable complexity as Dante's *Divine Comedy* or Dostoevsky's *The Brothers Karamazov*. The speech genre enables us to distinguish between serious utterances and mere spoof. It allows us to know when an utterance has come to an end. Spoken interaction usually takes the form of dialogue. Most often (though far from always) the utterance stops at the point where the interlocutor takes his or her turn; a complex business though, as the ethnographer of communication has not been slow to point out.

Linguistics is flawed, says Bakhtin, in that it attempts to study the sentence and the utterance as if they were one and the same, and ends up with a "kind of hybrid of the sentence (unit of language) and the utterance (unit of speech communication)" (Bakhtin 1986, 75). Linguistics has confused true meaning with form and system. Its exponents have failed to notice and take account of the qualitative difference between the (hypothetical) units of grammar exhibiting their admittedly marvellous (superimposed) order – doubtless an indirect reflection of the even more marvellous information-processing capacity of the brain – and the vastly different domain of meaning, communication, style and context, all of which form an inalienable part of Bakhtin's speech genres. The two domains – system-oriented language and concrete intersubjective utterance – do have important interfaces, as we shall see. Not only can these interfaces not be ignored (so far they have not even been properly identified or discussed) but they probably reveal an important ingredient in the uniqueness of human being.

3. *Logos* and *Poesis*

Language, it is proposed, combines two separate aspects or modes.

The first is that aspect or mode which coincides with our concrete everyday experience. It is one that is so plain, so obvious, that everyone takes it very much for granted. We are scarcely, if at all, aware of it. It is that mode of language that might make us respond, on being asked what we think language is, with a shrug of the shoulders or with a verbal gesture: "What a silly question!" The only occasions on which we might stop to wonder might, for example, be when we are confronted with the problem of learning an "exotic" new language, or the novelty of the early utterances of our offspring, or the often strange manifestations of speech handicaps, or when as writers we happen to be struggling with the waywardness of words.

What people only seldom notice about this mode[1] of language is its **sharedness**, its **intersubjective** nature. It is this same sharedness that masks the extraordinary, even bizarre, nature of this common idiom, which ensures that we have essentially the same fund of images, impressions, sensations, feelings, values and attitudes, even when these are masked by "cultural differences". The universality of this idiom amounts of course to an imposition on individual freedom, but it is the price we pay for being able to understand and communicate with one another. Whenever much-travelled people utter the cliché "People are the same the world over" it is this same phenomenon of intersubjectivity, capable as it can sometimes be of surmounting the "language barriers", to which they are alluding.

The second mode or aspect of the model under discussion is that in which the human organism and the human individual "being" enter the picture; a mode that not only allows but, as it were, insists on our being different from one another. We have here the living "organic" aspect of language, making change, creativity and personality possible, but also inevitable. It is in this sense that language becomes synonymous in meaning with *poesis* "making". Being at odds with the first mode, this differential mode accounts for all the personal idiosyncrasies of verbal expression, whether in speech or writing, and for all individuality of style and utterance.

Even more than with the first mode, our lack of awareness of the presence of the second language mode is total. Any means I might possess for accounting for my desires and actions belongs to the first mode, which is also the conceptual mode: the "rules of grammar" or the dictionary will explicate only the first language mode, a hegemony becoming especially apparent in the presence of another, who by virtue of his or her presence alone seems to incarnate commonality and intersubjectivity.

The one entity wholly mine, unshared, is my own body, and especially my "heart" and mind. The body delivers my moods and motivation; the heart my strength, truth, will and imagination; the mind, underpinned by the brain, the means, the "tools" to maintain and even to develop my discrete existence as an individual. There is nothing mechanical or algorithmic about this second mode, inasmuch as it is infinitely responsive to the slightest nuance or shift in my environment, in others' gestures and body set,[2] in my moods and personal relationships; although among its principal tasks are its dealing in information and raw physical data, discriminating between what communication science calls "noise" and "signal" – identifying potential messages, that is, – comparing and discriminating between different possible scenarios of action, and strenuously and constantly projecting provisional perceptual schemata. In certain respects it appears to complement the metalinguistic prescriptions of the first mode and, although it does not itself "write" codes, it everlastingly tests their feasibility, making adjustments in accordance with the communicative demands of the instant.

A straightforward example of the relationship between these two modes should not go amiss. I have a close friend, let us say, and both of us are fond of listening to and discussing twentieth-century music. Over the years there has developed such an empathy in our personal view of things, that we are almost always "on the same wavelength", hardly needing to "say" anything to one another beyond emitting signs of mutual understanding (the first mode takes care of all this). But one day, when I am due to meet my friend, I find myself feeling not up to the demands of Boulez or Ligeti. Somehow I need to get across to this valued friend, without awkwardness or mutual detriment, that today I don't much feel like the session we had planned that evening, but for a change would rather listen to some Haydn or Mozart. It is at this point that the second mode of language comes to the rescue. I know **what** I want to say (mode Number One), but I need to be subtle about it, and my language (mode Number Two) has to be sensitive to the quality of our relationship.

It would be tempting to regard the two different modes as separate "languages", were it not for the obvious circumstance that the two modes must be closely interrelated and to a high degree interfused. In fact of course they have to be regarded as forming separate facets of a single whole. The difficulty only is to attain an understanding of the precise nature of an interface that fuses incommensurables.

The one dimension of extensive interface, for example, is the lexicon, actual words. It is through words especially, as I hope to demonstrate in my final chapters, that the two different modes enter into a common purpose and a single creative enterprise.

The first mode will be variously referred to as the **shared** or **intersubjective** mode. As must be already apparent, it is difficult to characterize this mode of language in a few words, and much of the remainder of this book will be concerned with it. This mode is the seat of *logos*, the Athenian Greek concept for which we moderns have no single word-equivalent. *Logos*, as we saw earlier, is the domain of reasoned argument, conceptualization, definition, form, relationship. All theory, even the dimmest glimmering, any description or analysis, however vague, belongs to this mode. It is the condition in which all awareness, clarity, truth and judgment are attained and attainable. In a word, the first mode is Bakhtin's "witness and judge". This shared, intersubjective mode is that facet of language which holds everything, including our selves, together. It brings our selves in relation to other selves, manifesting itself as meaning, insight, mutuality, as world conception, order, and classification, as predication and also predictability. Any metalinguistic operation furthermore, any "standing back" or "taking stock" finds itself anchored in this mode. Even the concern for, or neglect of, moral truth, cultivation (*Bildung*), values, every moral conceit, has its roots in this order of language. It is our human element *par excellence*, what it means to be "human", as opposed to some other (unimagined or unimaginable) state of being. Without this shared, intersubjective mode of language we might have been able to jabber away with utter fluency and, like chimpanzees and gorillas, might also have been able to manipulate tokens or icons, but we would be unable to say or communicate anything specific with any degree of sense or significance.

The most fitting term for the second mode would be **organic** (and quite often this term is preferred), were it not for the current practice of confining the use of the word to biological contexts. The Greek word *organon*, from which the word *organic* is derived, signifies an **instrument** or implement. So, besides "belonging to the organization of a living being", *organic* can still mean "done by means of instruments"; and both meanings happen to be directly relevant to the second mode. This second mode is **active** or **dynamic**, in ways that the first mode, always reliant on received frames of reference and stasis, cannot be. The second mode is also **differential**; a feature to be discussed later. It is coextensive with the individual as a biological-spiritual organism, and is therefore somehow dependent both on physical functions of the brain and central nervous system as well as on the imponderabilities of the principle of life and energy within the individual, or (to borrow that quaint but telling word) soul. At a pragmatic level, this second mode appears to be involved with orientation, spatiality (but not geometry), temporality (but not clock time), qualities (as opposed to values), quantities, percepts, and with information schemata of various sorts: that aspect of language which engages directly with what I am prone to call the world "out there". As an individual idiom varying from speaker to speaker it serves **instrumentally** as the means whereby individuals function actively as speakers (or writers) within language conceived as a whole, and are able, as hearers, to reconstruct what seems to be being spoken (or written) or addressed to them by others. It is a mode that manifests itself in such domains as acoustic phenomena, perceptual cues, kinaesthetic servomechanisms within the speech musculature, neural networking, as well as in all aspects of information processing. It is an information-processing mode, to the extent that it ensures that what in the first mode is in principle deliberated and "delivered" becomes in fact communicable. This second mode, above all, tunes in to the uncanny "things in heaven and earth" which by their "out there" nature have no place in the shared intersubjective domain of awareness. In passing, it might be noted that the "out there" is no static realm, but one whose contents undergo changes of *persona* with the changing consciousness of man. Three centuries ago demons and angels flourished; today we have neutrons, quarks, anti-matter, black holes and space-time.

Since I need to keep reminding myself that this book is about language, and words in particular, I shall confine my examples of the reciprocity between the two different language modes to linguistics.

The initial sounds (*t,d* and *th*, respectively), as sounds, in the three English words *tin*, *din* and *thin* are significant in that they establish three distinct meanings. To a speaker of English they "sound different". It is in the shared mode of language that this distinctiveness is registered, specifically of course among speakers of English. Linguists call these meaningfully distinctive units of sound "phonemes". They are systemic, and this systematicity is also reflected in English orthography, which is (or rather was, in Middle English) "phonemic".

But at the same time an indefinitely large number of different *t*-sounds, *d*-sounds, and *th*-sounds occur in English (as indeed in all languages) both within the same variety of English, and among the numerous different varieties, not to mention the vast diversity existing in the speech of different individuals. The differences are measurable, but are of interest mainly to the phonetician or speech scientist, who study the "mechanics" of human speech, as they are also to the communication engineer. All this plethora of diversity is discounted altogether by the shared mode. Speaker-hearers literally do not "hear" any difference. Yet, behind the scenes, as it were, in the second, organic mode of language these unperceived differences are playing a key role in the "management" and "negotiation" of information being channelled into and from the brain, that unseen but none the less crucially busy operator.

Different languages do not usually display identical "boundary demarcation" across the shared and organic modes. In English, for example, the shared mode of language recognizes only one *k*-phoneme. The shared mode in Arabic, by contrast, recognizes two phonemes. These latter *k*-sounds effectively divide the articulatory-acoustic range of possible *k*-sounds into two segments, distinguishable in Arabic spelling, as well as in the romanized *kalb* "a dog" and *qalb* "he cut". The shared mode of language among speakers of Arabic, one might say, appears to be in this instance (conventionally) geared towards recognizing phonetic features to which the speaker of English pays no conscious attention, solely because for the speaker of Arabic these phonetic features distinguish **meaning**. It can thus be seen that speech sound straddles the two different modes of language. The second mode deals only with physical (in this case, phonetic) quantifiables, modes of transmission, feedback circuits, and so forth, while the first (meaning-identifying) mode is concerned exclusively with signification and meaning.

These are, it might be objected, trivial examples. But when multiplied many times over they can be seen as parts, however infinitesimal, of the vast edifice known as language.

My third and final example, slightly less trivial perhaps, may also prove more accessible. In English a division is drawn between the personal pronouns *he*, *she* and *it* (and of course between *him*, *her*, *it* and *his*, *hers*, *its*). For the speaker of English this gender demarcation seems the most natural thing in the world. In Chinese however, no such demarcation (though it can readily be made if needed) is written into the overt language code. In speaking English for example, a native speaker of Chinese does not find it too difficult, while still making the odd "bizarre" and misleading mistake, to conform to the conventions of that language; only that the same speaker may find the convention fussy and unnecessary. Not only that, but English is not entirely consistent: dogs and eagles tend to be "he", while cats and wrens are usually "she"; a person may be either "he" or "she", but a ghost is "it"; named boats, large or small are "she", whereas unnamed rowboats, canoes, etc. are referred to as "it".[3] All the latter features are shared in English as part of the first mode of language. In Chinese, gender conventions do exist, but they form only a minor niche within the shared language; the burden of gender differentiation in Chinese falls heavily on the organic mode, whose "processes" remain virtually unknown and unexpressed.

In case readers have detected a suspicious resemblance between my bi-modal plan and Hjelmslev's biplanar expression-content dichotomy, the remaining pages of this book should disabuse them.[4] The two modes of language, so far identified, although interconnected in interesting ways, belong to entirely different worlds. Meaning and instrumental devices are as different as can possibly be imagined. The wonder is that the two worlds do actually interconnect, an actuality that seems to be telling us something of much wider import and scope about human nature. Perhaps the most original feature of the theoretical model of language currently being explored is that which has to do with the "phenomenology" of the **contact between** the two different modes of language.

4. Communicating and Relating

Communication hides a paradox. On the one hand, as Merleau-Ponty clearly saw, two-way communication is an illusion. Nothing passes between me and another when we engage in interaction. In reacting to another's speech and gestures I am responding to impressions, thoughts and feelings that are mine already. And yet, on the other hand, I do actually respond to an individual, a human organism, an other who is "out there", and whom I know nothing about except as some reconstructed simulacrum, some hopelessly inadequately conceived projection of myself. For example, there is a need I feel to communicate with you, the reader. That must be why I have written this book. I know, simply through the context of this dialogue (between you and me), that you must at this very instant be reading these very lines (If you had for one reason or another not reached this point, there would of course be no context and no dialogue).

Less trivially, even if your first language is other than English, you will have immediate access to the meanings of a very large part, perhaps all, of the language I have used (if not, you would already have put the book aside) and will probably not have paused even to consider this fact strange. Any significant barrier between us, if there happens to one, will more likely arise less from the extent to which you concur, or not, with the ins-and-outs of my argument, than from discrepancies between our different natures, approaches and outlooks; and these will be apparent to you on every page, even though it may not always be possible to articulate them. If you are not a professional philosopher (and perhaps even if you are) you may simply make a mental note of any bone of contention, and perhaps indulge any weaknesses or unsoundness in my line of reasoning (provided they do not become excessive, and provided of course that I am not found unduly abrasive, obtuse, verbose, idiosyncratic, or whatever). If authors are managing to satisfy their readers, they must possess a sound awareness, whether intuitive or more less conscious, of the shared mode of language; its traditions, its rhetorical possibilities, its prowesses. But they will also need to be intuitively aware of some of the manipulative potentialities of the organic mode. These include the ability to soothe, amuse, titillate, charm, mystify, provoke or dazzle their readers, whose organisms (nervous systems, emotions, sensibilities, moods, adrenalin levels) are reacting, and at moments over-reacting, to what is being said by the other, in this case the author. Writerly empathy engendered in the intersubjective mode, by contrast, will more likely result only in vague dissatisfaction or *ennui*.

This is the dialogic principle, highlighted by Bakhtin. Says one reader (inwardly) to a writer: "I can see, sort of, what you are driving at, but I find what I am reading tendentious and distasteful. Why should I be expected to accommodate such drivel as this?" Or, depending on the reader's inclinations, at another extreme: "I'm really impressed. That's exactly right. If only there were more books like this." What "turns" readers "on" is seldom the rigorous pursuit of reason, or even acute critical judgment, but "animal" factors, such as captivation, "magical" manipulation, the ability to evoke, the more irrationally the better, laughter or tears: catharsis, after all, occurs not in the bright light of the shared intersubjective life-world but in the dark unconscious recesses of the human organism.

The world "out there" – and this includes other people, other beings, each one a complex organism – what little we know of it, or them, demands continuous and sure interpretation by users of language. The internalized repertoire of the individual speaker – in either mode – must enable that speaker not merely to distinguish signals originating in another's utterances from random "noise" but must also simultaneously – not to say, instantaneously – interpret, as well as open up at least a corner of his or her personal world to the possible external ("out there") purport of those utterances. At the same time we constantly need reminding that everything of which direct and confident sense can be made goes on within our own luminous conscious world. No one can remain opaque. A human being is not after all a Leibnizian monad, but a complete incarnation of a world that is already shared with other "persons" presumed to resemble oneself in many respects.[1] Without such a life-world, there would be no understanding; even less, communication.

The persons subscribing to the shared intersubjective world of language are not, it is perhaps worth being reminded, simple multiple replications of onself. Bakhtin it was who threw into particularly sharp relief the role of the **other** in the personal language formation of the self. "It is through others," Bakhtin (1986, 138) claims, "that I first begin to realize myself." For the entire duration of my life, I live not in my own words but in the words of others. It is in other people's mouths, in others' contexts, serving others' intentions that the word exists. It is from others, like it or not, that we must take the word and make it our own (Bakhtin 1981, 294). All of my life is filled with complex interrelations with the word of the other. Discourse itself, says Bakhtin, is more than just a concatenation of utterances; it is the arena in which an endless and unresolvable struggle between my own and the other's word is taking place.

Even in my persistent attempts to overcome the resistance of objects, even to reach them, I must engage with the "fundamental and richly varied opposition of the other's word":

> Between the word and the object, between the word and the speaking subject, there exists an elastic environment of other, alien words about the same object." (Bakhtin 1981, 276)

The environment in which we find ourselves – a tension-filled environment of alien words, values and judgments, a shared world none the less – can be so hard to penetrate. The shared world is only comfortable, integral even, when it is for me alone. Once things start to **happen** in the interaction between organisms there is tension. If we have no desire to suffer this tension, we can try to exorcise it in vapid everday dialogue, which however may never be found to exist in pure anaesthetized form. It is in the living interaction with the other that the word is individualized and given stylistic character, or being.

It could be a long time before we have a completely adequate grasp of the sought-after ontological equation, bringing together the organic mode of language inherent in every biological-existential individual on the one hand and the language of shared experience on the other. The coalescence of these modes makes up my personal and interpersonal world, seen in the context of an unending dialectical struggle between my language and the language of the other. Together, these two non-complementary modes, through tension and struggle, share a common interest in bringing into being, maintaining and, above all, in **renewing** a world: one that is in part a life-world, but one that is also rooted in some mysterious dimension, in an opaque external presence with which I am compelled willy-nilly to engage. Various beginnings to this quest are apparent nevertheless, and it seems opportune at this juncture to consider in brief outline two albeit sharply contrasting avenues.

Starting out from ground already broken by Austin,[2] John R. Searle (1969 and 1979b) moved directly towards a position that "a theory of language" (in the sense of "grammar") must be part of a theory of action" (1969, 17). That most fundamental and agonizing of all questions: "How do words relate to the world?" Searle puts in the following manner:

> How is it possible that when I say "Jones went home", which after all is in one way just a string of noises, what I mean is: Jones went home... What is the difference between **saying** something and **meaning** it, and saying it **without** meaning it? And what is involved in meaning just one particular thing and not **some other thing**? For example, how does it happen that when people say "Jones went home", they almost always mean Jones went home and not, say, Brown went to the party and got drunk? (1969, 3) (Searle's emphases)

Old questions perhaps, and ingenuously put, but undergoing timely restatement: How **do** words stand for things and what is it that makes something said valid or true?

Speaking – that is **really** speaking, generating real utterances, as opposed to producing gratuitous strings of syllables, the ramblings of vacuity or mental disturbance, or the inanity of textbook "dialogues", so hilariously parodied in Ionesco's *Bald Prima Donna* – is, according to Searle, the performance of **speech acts**. Speech acts can be of many different kinds but, like the categories of grammar, are not limitless. They are, says Searle, the basic units of linguistic communication. When I take a series of noises or graphic marks to be instances of communication – messages perhaps – I have to assume they were produced by some human being and also that they originated in particular instances and kinds of intention. A placard planted on a level uninhabited islet in the middle of a lake and containing the warning "Mind the step" is clearly incongrous until it is seen to be some lame practical joke. The case underscores the speaker's awareness of the narrowness of the range of contexts in which a potential message can become actual. A different kind of utterance: "Do you believe in Santa Claus?" will be understood only in a cultural environment in which the term has (now, alas, largely commercial) currency, and normally the question will be asked only of small children.

"Whatever can be meant can be said" is central to Searle's philosophy, and one that he shares with the exponents of hermeneutical philosophy. This is not to imply of course that everything that can be said is meant. Often, people do not quite mean what they say, and as a guide to sure interpretation the shared mode is not all that reliable. People are recognized as liars through inconsistencies in their "story", from their facial expressions, manner, tone of voice, reputation, and so forth. Such factors are either circumstantial, or they are filtered through the organic mode of language. The performance of particular speech acts and the concomitant occurrence of appropriate utterances (I make a promise, and at the same time I say "I promise...") or gestures (I make a promise and nod my head as an indication) have their roots probably not, as Searle seems to suggest, in objectively real grammatical structures but in the differential strategies of the organic mode – utterance and action – which conspire to achieve a certain social outcome. Promising is a moral act, and the individual can employ any of a range of devices, some spoken (or written), others not, in making a promise. It is impossible however to distinguish a true from a false promise by applying the kinds of rules Searle proposes.[3] We can distinguish between true and false promises only by applying cultural norms (e.g."good faith"), by assessing a person's character, by taking a calculated risk, or by simply noting the end result (Was the promise actually kept, according to me, the witness?)

Approaching all this from a different perspective, Jacques Derrida seems more concerned with social fictions than with questions of morality. In some of his more recent work[4] Derrida has "deconstructed" the speech act altogether, dismissing it as a symptom of an authenticating presence, a readiness on the part of the issuer to honour the commitments entailed. Austin had discounted all speech acts which do not actually mean what they say. Excluded were instances in which someone says "Get out!" or "Hello!" or "Can you tell me the time, please" without the appropriate intention, except when that someone happens to be in a region in which English is not normally spoken, or is mentally deranged, or is a non-character in a textbook dialogue, or for some other identifiable reason. Likewise, but for different sets of reasons, statements of the kind "You win!" or "I've got it!" can only achieve validity in a suitable range of contexts. By the same token, declarations such as "You're fired!" or "I fine you 100 dollars" can only become valid when the issuer is properly authorized. But all speech acts regardless, Derrida insists, are couched in theatrical overtones, involving role-play and strict convention.[5] We shall be returning to this question later.

*   *   *

Most people are unaware of the complexity of the language they use. For them language is never more than a device for making life more manageable and more comfortable. They remain quite unaware of the everyday miracle of linguistic communication, which Searle has characterized thus:

> If I am trying to tell someone something, then (assuming certain conditions are satisfied) as soon as he recognizes that I am trying to tell him something and what I am trying to tell him, I have succeeded in telling it to him. Furthermore, unless he recognizes that I am trying to tell him something and what I am trying to tell him, I do not fully succeed in telling it to him. (1969, 19)

All this happens through the interplay of two totally distinct modes of language which, however modest a person's role in life, make him or her in no trivial way god-like. The world is Man's plastic medium, as it were: by virtue of it he has become endowed, both through *logos*, and through the mysterious depths of an earth-given organism, with the power to modify, adapt, curb, enhance, impoverish, expand, reduce, exhaust, cherish, redeem. Through *logos* we inhabit each other, but in so doing we encounter the other, who disconcerts us but from who mediates our speech. Through the instinct-driven, intelligent organisms with which we find ourselves strangely endowed, we achieve existence in a world we experience as real and, along with this mysterious mode of being, the power to manipulate, thrive, survive, dominate, capitulate, endure.

On the other hand, all that has to do with imagery, form, sensation, meaning, content, imagination, understanding, feeling, cognition belongs to my subjective world. To yours also. In some inexplicable manner the life-world shared by us is an intersubjective, even transcendental, confluence between individual subjective worlds. This is no convenient fiction, but a reality. Language, in both its modes, plays a paramount role. Yet, so far in our line of argument, neither the individualized communicative doings of the organic, instrumental mode, partly instinctive, partly learned, nor the shared dimension with the inclusive ideational forms it projects into the supra-personal life-world that provides a common, integrating domain for our individual personalities have taken sufficiently into consideration the world "out there" and the opaqueness that bars our direct entry into that world. It goes without saying that there would be little point in taking up space in these pages speculating about the nature of the "out there". We may simply note that we can form no "idea" of it beyond what has been revealed by the physical scientist, the poet, artist, or visionary. Suffice it to mark however the significant if obvious fact that real space and time intervene between you and me, and this gap cannot be bridged by pointing out that "space" and "time" are artefacts of the *logos*-informed mind.

Although the immediate if fleeting glimpses of the "out there" are always internal perceptions, this uncanny zone possesses an independent reality, more real than anything we can conceive. Locke's reminder, that what is presented to the senses by "external objects" cannot be changed, remains an impasse. These external objects, whatever their nature, along with the external object that happens to be my own body, are not only important to me; they are vital. Under normal circumstances I have no difficulty in distinguishing the "imagined" things I perceive in dreams and daydreams from "real" things. But with access to the real world cut off or the very capacity to recognize it suppressed (as in certain modalities of mental illness), access to the life-world would be interrupted also, with all kinds of deleterious consequences. Yet these same external objects, although exciting the most vivid visual images in those whose eyes are unimpaired, and evoking sounds in those whose hearing is not deficient, are themselves lightless and soundless. Most crucial of all, this externality conveys the signals ("as soon as you recognize that I am trying to tell you something...") that provoke an awareness that someone – let us say, you – may be attempting to say something – for example, to me. The signals are "really there" and I depend on them absolutely in order to determine what "already speaking instruments", what meaning-bearing harmonics of our shared world are being invoked, and what message it may be that I am about to "read". Any marked "distortion of the "signals" is going to reduce the chances of my "receiving" a message in order to "read" it.

In addition then to language, composed of two mysteriously conjoined modes – the one active, individual, probing, and organic in its nature and function, the other intersubjective, shared, and flooded with meaning, but neither mode being really separable from the other, and together shaping the contents of the whole of my conscious awareness and experience, shaping the shared life-world – there exists a real world "out there", of which we know by inference rather little, except that its existence is not only a fact, but also a lure, challenging us to unceasing effort, what at times seems a Sisyphean enterprise. The *prima materia* doggedly guards its secrets. The artist – whether sculptor, painter, composer, or craftsman – works at his or her material, which does not readily allow itself to be transformed into the human, into creative achievement, always in the direction from "out there" to "in here". Science makes persistent inroads, but hard-won gains are instantly converted into "knowledge" (which of course is no longer "out there"). The world "out there", as Dr. Johnson graphically reminded his contemporaries, is no solipsistic illusion. Moreover, our attention and motivation are engaged by it ("just because it's there") at every turn. All communication takes place across it. But from a scientific point of view the physical realm "out there" appears to be virtual emptiness, apart from an incomprehensible (outside mathematics) diffusion of infinitesimal particles and "waves" of energy.

Do we in fact know anything worthwhile about the ways in which our language engages with the world "out there", or about how we establish "contact" with each other across this most fascinating (because impenetrable) of divides?

Curiously enough, we do. Studies of the neurophysical processes in the brain support the notion that (in the organic mode) a creative activity goes on whenever sensory data is received from "out there", even at the most rudimentary stage of distinguishing (provisionally) between signal and noise.[6] An incoming message is no longer considered, as it once was, to be a discrete impulse registered by the brain and central nervous system, somehow waiting to be interpreted in an appropriate centre in the brain. The central nervous system has been compared, rather, to a complex banking system in which transactions take place in a definite sequence, each "transaction" modifying the original elements of the input. Thus, an incoming message undergoes constant modification and elaboration, by way of a circular loop-like process of mediation, involving a vast number of neuronal assemblies, all the way from reception to perception. The brain, it appears, goes rapidly and circularly through a series of matchings with an "internalized model", itself undergoing constant modification, until the many times modified incoming message and model merge, and perception and response are achieved. Furthermore, incoming speech is not merely "heard"; it has to be re-created kinaesthetically before it can be perceived, let alone understood. Using a variety of means therefore, the brain, so to speak, reconstructs for the hearer, recreates within one's organism's own perceptions the speech of the one who is speaking. Quite specifically, the claim has been made,[7] on empirical grounds, that speech is perceived by reference to the articulatory movements which physically produce sounds, and to their sensory effects, the mediators between the acoustic stimulus and actual perception. And surprisingly, speech can be perceived and understood even when the laryngeal muscles have been removed or anaesthetized, as in the case of an eight-year-old child who for reasons unknown had never been able to speak.[8] It has also been pointed out that it is perfectly possible to distinguish the phonemes of a foreign language before being able to produce them, a fact also borne out in children, who can respond to adult phonemic distinctions before being able to articulate them themselves (Jakobson and Halle 1956, 34).

From the ground so far covered in this as in previous chapters, and from our recognition that communication is already shared (and thus an inalienable part of the shared mode of language) it should come as no surprise that strategies geared towards speech comprehension can vary considerably depending on the situation or context, and that there are strategical hierarchies which, were they to be over-rigidly programmed, would inhibit both speech development and speech production. If there happens to be an acoustic input, all well and good. We can match our constructions against it. If not, this cannot be done, and alternative strategies are called for. Above all, we will be guided by our interests and motivations: we will tend to hear what we **want** to hear. The organic mode of language, ever-present as a key adjunct, aids us in our message construction, and desists only as motivation or energy wanes.

The human brain and its elaborate workings, making possible ultimately the construction (not the reconstruction, please note) of messages, must surely be one of the natural wonders among wonders. Even more astonishing though is the marvel of intricacy and tuning that constitutes a human relationship. Such a relationship is so finely crafted, so much like a work of art, that a slight shadow can, over a period, disrupt the balance of inherited temperament, libido, fellow-feeling, precision of awareness and judgment, social convention; in a word, the delicate ecology of social and environmental textures. Amongst them, a single damaged ingredient can transform a close friend or a loved one into a stranger, a close familial affinity into disaffection, a warm sense of belonging into chronic alienation, delight into depression, idols into pariahs, bonds into bondage.

With human relationships we are at the pinnacle of Man's attainment. Partly conscious, partly unconscious, the maintenance of such relationships is ensured by three different factors: firstly, the efficiency and split-second adaptability of the brain and central nervous system; secondly, the precarious, gossamer-delicate network of social relations, the moral and aesthetic perceptions; and finally, the contradictory blend of plasticity and stability that characterizes language as a whole, and particularly the lexicon. These three factors, along with, doubtless, a number of others some of which remain for the most part still below the threshold of our understanding, are bound together with all that constitutes being human. On them rests that supreme human faculty combining spirit, intellect and imagination that we recognize as consciousness.

In the natural state there is no such thing as either neutral communication or neutral social relations. As unseasoned early anthropologists and missionaries found to their cost: to approach a member of an unknown tribe, shake him by the hand, with a "Good to meet you" or some such, was not necessarily of course taken as the friendly greeting intended. A fair amount has to be known, or surmised, about the culture of a group or society before successful communication, verbal or otherwise, can be achieved. Neutrality calls for explicit coding and this, in turn, depends on a certain metalinguistic sophistication. The use of English, for example, as the internationally agreed language of communication among international airline pilots is such a code. A Russian pilot, for example, who would normally use this code (English) happens to know quite a bit of Japanese, and tries out his Japanese with the controllers at Narita Airport as the plane is coming in to land. They are caught off balance, pleasantly surprised in fact, and as a result the touchdown is not of the smoothest. All speech, gesture and body language as a whole is marked for medium as well as message (*pace* McLuhan). And each community has different perceptions of how communication should be structured. In English, a standard expected ("unmarked") reply to *Hello, how are you today?* might be *Fine, how are you.* Additional information about the state of one's health is uncalled for, unless, that is, the first speaker reiterates his greeting with a special emphasis or asks specifically for information about the respondent's health. Silence in response to such a greeting would also constitute unanticipated ("marked") communicative behaviour (Saville-Troike 1982, 13) and would in most circumstances be interpreted as surliness or rudeness. In other societies by contrast, a nil response might be the norm and unmarked in any way. Learning appropriately "fine-tuned" responses in one's mother society, let alone in a different society, takes years of observation, application and communicative prowess.

Nor is the role of language the same, or even similar, from one community to the next. Language can be used to identify or characterize social groups and categories, or it can be employed in the maintenance and manipulation of social relationships between individuals, or for effecting social control (Saville-Troike 1982, 38), or for none of these. Even so, the relationship is far from static, and the use and evaluation of linguistic markers feeds back upon and can affect the character and persistence of the categories themselves. Some societies, for example, require eloquence as an integral part of social doing; others emphasize role-play; others demand strict adherence to ritual. In not a few societies language helps perpetuate inequality between the sexes, to the extent that their languages and speech communities impose a different lexicon, morphology and discourse style on women. Likewise with caste and rank. Even among more "primitive" communities, communication can range, at one extreme, from complete informality, such as exists among certain pygmy groups in the Equatorial African rain forests, to extreme rule-adherence at the other extreme. At their first encounter, speakers of Navajo attempt without delay to establish to which clan the other person belongs. To carry on a satisfactory conversation, the Navajo has to be able to place that person within "the network of existing relationships, and to know how to behave appropriately, including how to speak and what terms of address to use."[9]

Speakers of English may be tempted to assume that English stands at the opposite end of the spectrum from such tedious adherence to custom. But studies carried out disconfirm this. It transpires that, even in ordinary two-party conversations, the two participants find it necessary to invoke "interactional procedures" in such a way that the second party finds it possible to collaborate and achieve "coordinated entry" into a conversation.[10] This is particularly striking in the case of telephone calls when, in Western societies, the obligation to speak first falls on the person who answers (For the person making the call to open the conversation is a violation of a strict communicational rule, a fact which has been experimentally proved but which can easily be tested independently by the reader).[11]

A global solution – to reduce all communication to a formula – might seem to be that of establishing symmetrical contrast in the use of language and non-language devices across different cultures. Unfortunately, this would prove impossible, since some cultures do not allow for any lines of demarcation to be drawn between language behaviour on the one hand and social behaviour on the other. Take the case of the Subanun, living on the Philippine island of Mindanao. Among the Subanun, requesting something is not simply a matter of being able to use the language effectively; one must also participate in the social ritual. If someone wanted to ask for a drink, for example, it would not suffice to know how to use the requisite grammar and lexicon. Efficient structuring of utterances "might elicit praise for one's fluency in Subanun, but it would probably not get one a drink."[12] For among the Subanun, drinking is social and communicative, and inseparable from "drinking talk".

In Burundi, to take a contrasting example, the ruling consideration is aesthetics. There people believe that the emotions are the source of all action and, as a direct consequence of this, speech behaviour is directed towards the manipulation of the emotions through aesthetic devices:

> Sensitivity to the variety and complexity of speech behaviour is evident in a rich vocabulary for its description and evaluation, and in a constant flow of speech about speech. Argument, debate, and negotiation, as well as elaborate literary forms, are built into the organization of society and the content of the world-view as means of gaining one's ends, as social status symbols, and as skills enjoyable in themselves.[13]

In Burundi, people would go to any length to avoid speaking bluntly or facing the naked truth, and would have at their command an arsenal of aesthetic means of avoiding explicitness in confrontation. "Whatever works is good", and aesthetic-emotive values are placed higher than logic or moral principles.[14] Much effort and planning goes into the speech training of older Burundi children, who are taught verbal formulas and styles appropriate to a variety of modulations of voice, eye-contact, posture, body language, and so forth. The most prized skill of all is the "speedy summoning of appropriate and effective verbal response in the dynamics of interpersonal relations."[15] People of humble status are expected to speak to superiors in a bumbling and hesitating manner, while in speaking to their equals they become fully eloquent, "their speech flowing gracefully and smoothly, their gestures fitting the words, and compliments framed in poetic figures of speech." This is in sharp contrast, to be sure, with the practice of the Senegalese nobility, who feel constrained to commit minor grammatical errors, inasmuch as in their language and community an emphasis on fluency and accuracy, or on performance for its own sake, would be considered inappropriate.[16]

The interface of words with social behaviour appears endless as well as highly entertaining. The samples chosen illustrate the regional-cultural variation in the shared mode of language which ensures that language, speaking individuals, and community are flush with each other. We have learned from them, however, nothing of the organic mode, precisely for the reason that the sources were focussing only on ethnolinguistic congruence. If to return were possible (and perhaps it is not, on the principle that one cannot enter the same river twice) it would be a profitable and intriguing undertaking to examine the junctures in these communities at which tensions enter the language, when shades of disharmony arise, as they must in every community for most of the time. Furthermore, there appears to be no taking account of the other: a complex web of manoeuvre that relies absolutely on the health and resilience of the organic dimension

My last piece of speech ethnography lies exactly at the point at which you and I are interchangeable. Known to linguistics as "shifter" pronouns – *you* and *I* – they are not only present in all known languages (shared mode) but are regarded as a pre-condition for a language to be accepted as a language. The sample should illustrate how highly precarious is the relationship between the self and the other, and I leave it in large part to reader's own ingenuity to consider what processes in the organic instrumental mode might be at work and the degree to which the bridge between them is maintained by the interplay of the different modes, and what roles you and I play in all this.

European and various other languages tend to have two, and sometimes more, ways of expressing "you". Modern English is exceptional in having only one form. Languages possessing more than one form make use of the different forms of course to distinguish between singular and plural, as *thou* and *you* once did in English. But, equally important, they may also use the alternative forms to distinguish between **formal** and **informal** address and/or between relations of "power" and "solidarity". In a language spoken by a community with complex kinship systems – as Franz Boas many years ago observed of the Vandau of Mozambique (1966, 391) – the latter distinction, again expressed by two different pronoun forms, can find itself distributed through the entire system of kinship relations, the speaker being under obligation to know and use the correct form in addressing a particular kin-relation.

In European languages, matters are on the face of it less complex. It has been claimed that the particular distinction of meaning attaching to the singular (T) and plural (V) forms can be traced back to the Late Roman Empire when under Diocletian there were two Emperors (in addition to multiple Caesars) who alone were addressed as *vos*. By the time of Pope Gregory I, the "power semantic", a non-reciprocal relationship in which the superior says T and receives V appears to have been well-established, giving rise to some literary curiosities. Centuries later, in Froissart, for example, God appropriately addresses his angels as *T*, but they address God as *V*; all celestial beings say *T* to Man and receive *V* in return. In Italian literature of the fifteenth century, Christians address Jews and Turks as *T*, but are addressed by them as *V*. In the France of Louis XIV, the *V* pronoun becomes a mark of elegance; even lovers addressed one another as *V*.[17]

The French Revolutionaries denounced *V* as a vestigial remnant of feudalism and insisted on the reciprocal use of *T* but, not long afterwards, the power-solidarity polarity was reestablished. Clearly, the French speech community has not always found the distinction an easy one, and has been particularly squeamish, especially in the egalitarian ambience of modern times, about the use of *T* between adults. The practice of addressing waiters as *T* was particularly condemned as a remnant of seignorial *mores*. In circumstances of intimacy however, *T* becomes normal and condoned. Even French-speaking mountaineers after they reach a certain altitude shift to *T*.[18] German, Italian and French informants all indicated that, once *T* is extended to the other it is seldom taken back, as this would become marked as insult; although the use of *T* can be conveniently encapsulated – as when in wartime Nazi Germany a prostitute and her client were said to have addressed one another as *T* in private, but resumed the mutually distant *V* in public. In Russian, partly on account of the less well-rooted use of *V*, the *T* and *V* distinction became complicated by several different factors, including not only age, rank and kinship status, and emotional solidarity, but also the topic of conversation, the context of the speech event, group membership and dialectal variation.[19] A good deal of switching between *T* and *V*, a sign of realigned discriminations, can be observed in various literary records of Russian speech; in particular the tendency to shift from the more distant *V* to more intimate *T*. The latter has been ascribed to "unconscious slips or outbursts", which did not however "reflect a mutual restructuring of the relationship" between speakers. Another, possibly more adequate, explanation would be the assertion of the organic mode over the overt shared mode of language, the former engaging in a kind of play with the more sober, orderly latter. The element of play is especially significant:

> Some mood, whim, or mental state could make the speaker play with or altogether ignore the usual rules, depending, of course, on his emotional makeup and social sensitivity. In such instances the [*T*]

pronoun often had latent or purely expressive functions.

Evidently, the Russian alternation between T and V was highly mobile as well as emotively critical, and Russian writers in general were highly conscious of the value of the contrast as a potent stylistic device, exploited to the full by the particular speech genre.

The V - T polarity is not confined to pronouns. A study made of English (in America) in the 1950s showed that if V is represented by title and last name (*eg*. Mr. Smith) and T by first name, identical non-reciprocal power-solidarity relations are reproduced. The only significant difference in the latter respect between English in America and French in France is that, in the former case, anyone in doubt "avoids the use of any sort of personal name and makes do with the uncommitted omnibus *you*."[20]

What passes then between speaker and hearer is not simply a ready message, a definite content, but a complex linguistic and social repertoire of strategies, an entire hermeneutic, bringing into play the potentially limitless domain of culturally shared language and the equally boundless array of instrumental means available within the individual, organic mode of language. Together, they can be represented as grammar, all the way from the most elementary sound particles to immensely complex lexical networks, as well as in the formidable apparatus of the central nervous system which, functioning in unison, albeit in their different modal domains, enable speakers to establish the probability of a message in the making and, eventually, to achieve a specific "understanding" between one another. Communication only occurs when the existential gap between the separate organisms of the speaker and hearer diminishes, a process reflected in the unimaginably complex cycles of neural activity, and reduces to vanishing point. We may not be solipsistically enclosed within our own mental and affective universes, but at the instant we address somebody we are, in a real if paradoxical sense, talking to ourselves. All our cognitive and aesthetic models and insights into others, as well as our relations with them within an ethical, social and cultural framework, are, we must accept, internal to our own organisms – **on this side** of all that goes on strategically within the organic mode – "language as the link between otherwise unconnected nervous systems" (Bloch and Trager 1942, 5) – even if their ultimate form is shaped within a shared life-world.

5. Semiotic Being

We can now begin to tackle an ostensibly nonsensical question: How is it that we as human beings exist in a shared world, in such a way that my world and yours, in spite of the difference in their contents, their "furniture", are not in essence distinguishable? How can our life-world be in common when we can "communicate" to each other specific differences in outlook, temper and vision, and thus from the outset recognize each other as being different, not to say alien, personalities? Paradoxes as radical as these cannot be ignored. To make secure headway therefore, we should consider a different route through terrain that may by now be familiar, and make a fresh assault.

Our initial guide will be Ernst Cassirer whose approach was grounded in Kant but also, and perhaps even more immediately, in natural science, especially the work of Helmholtz and Hertz, both of whom took as their starting point the post-Kantian view that science has no direct access to reality, external objects and concepts such as "mass" and "force" being fictions or "symbols".

Cassirer had reached the conclusion that language itself is (what he termed) a **symbolic form**, a category without which nothing real can become an object for intellectual apprehension. A symbolic form, according to Cassirer, is a particular way of seeing, an entity bearing within itself its own source of light. Things and processes, objects and events, are never in themselves prior to language as a substratum of fact. On the contrary, it is language itself that initiates and brings into being all objects and all phenomena, that gives form and articulation to our perceptions. Only that which is necessary for the integration and ultimate wholeness of our actions and lives is selected from the uniform flux of impressions, to receive what Cassirer termed a "special linguistic accent"; in short, a **name** (1953a, 38). But language is not the only symbolic form. In Cassirer's view, art, religion, myth, law and cognition reside in their own image-worlds, with their different symbolic forms, each constituting a particular facet of "reality", and each freely generating its own world of symbols, the true vehicle of their particular development (Cassirer 1953b, I, 78). More recently however, this view has been challenged by Gadamer, who holds that language should not be bracketed alongside art, religion and law, but should be seen as the sustaining medium for all of them (Gadamer 1977, 76).

A symbol is a moment of creation. Cassirer borrowed this notion from Humboldt, who from his wide-ranging and monumental descriptive studies (Humboldt [1836] 1971) concluded that language, at once the source and crucible of symbols, cannot be regarded as a something that is simply present, something to be apprehended all of a piece and used as a tool of communication. Rather, Humboldt saw that language has to be constantly **produced** and, while the rules and principles in accordance with which language is so generated can be determined, the scope of language and in some respects the manner of its production remain indeterminate. In a particularly telling metaphor, Humboldt conceives of language as mediating between the individual and nature, the latter working upon the former both from within and from without. Language designates neither the purely subjective nor the exclusively objective, but effects a fresh mediation, a particular "reciprocal relation" arising between the polarity. In the words of Cassirer "the two ends are joined, thus creating a new synthesis of 'I' and 'world' " (1953, I, 93).

For Cassirer, the wellspring of language, as of all forms, is the human spirit. Spirit, or however that principle may be designated, informs the whole of Cassirer's argument; equating with Humboldt's *energeia* – an intense and independent activity of human being – eternally recommenced: an *energeia* finding its embodiment in the act of saying. Words distil certain contents out of the flux of impressions, endowing them with a conceptual form that raises them above the mere immediacy of sensory data. Language is the only sure way by which we may pass from ordinary sensation to intuition and ideas.

How is it possible, one may well ask, for the raw data of the senses, a finite and particular set of data, to be so transformed, to become the vehicle of a general spiritual "meaning"? How can the "flux of contents" become fixed for the speaking subject in an enduring unity of form? How is it that when physical sounds, which consist of nothing more than pitch, intensity, duration, and other acoustical properties, form temporal sequences as word-forms, they can become the medium for the most refined distinctions of intellect and feeling? For some far from straightforward answers to such questions we should look to the **sign**.

Concern with the nature of signs, as with much else, has its origins in the thinking of the Greeks, and in particular in the writings of the early Stoics. Our own concern however is primarily with modern semiotics, and initially with the vistas opened up by Charles Sanders Peirce.

Echoing perhaps Leibniz's contention (Peirce 1931-58, II, 135) that the sign serves not merely to represent, but actually to discover hitherto undisclosed relations, to provide something more than a mere symbolic abbreviation for what is already known, and to open up new paths into the unknown, Peirce says simply that a sign is "something by knowing which we know something more" (1931-58, VIII, 211). Peirce concurs with the Stoic tenet that signs are no empty abstractions, but particles of human activity. A sign **addresses somebody**, creating in the mind of the person addressed what Peirce considered an equivalent sign, a replica. The sign thus stands intermediately between the reality it directly represents and the interpretant (the subject's replication of the sign). Although the relation between sign and object cannot be said to be direct or straightforward, there is nothing arbitrary about it either. On the contrary, this relation between sign and object is somehow an "emanation" of the object. For all that, the sign, it seemed to Peirce, in no way leads to a knowledge of objects, inasmuch as such knowledge can only be won empirically. Talking or writing about, describing, comparing or classifying objects will not extend our knowledge of them one bit.

So here was (yet another) paradox. As a way out, Peirce in the end developed a distinction between two species of object: immediate and dynamic. The former is that aspect of the object represented in the sign, whose emanation is the sign, while the dynamic aspect is reality itself, indicable but not expressible. The interpreter is left to find this reality by way of "collateral experience".[1]

Symbols, as Peirce well understood, are never static entities, despite their association with rule and convention. They grow. They have their source in other signs, especially icons. In this way symbols acquire that crust of mythology identified by Roland Barthes as "the signified of the sign", the sign itself in this instance having become a mere signifier.[2] Whatever theoretical approach one takes, all signs must be conceived as living, active things straddling several dimensions and ill-adapted to formal simplicity. Only at the level of hypothetical linguistic structure is it possible to think in terms of a simple binarism,[3] tidily accommodated it might seem within the Peircean symbol[1] but actually representing no more than a mere facet of it. Even Kant's Thing-in-itself, according to Peirce, is a sign. From the moment meaning makes its appearance there are only signs. We think and act only through signs.

Owing perhaps to his being first and foremost concerned with language, and not with semiotic as such, Saussure, a contemporary of Peirce, hit upon a conception that has exerted a profound influence on the thinking of our own time. So extraordinary was Saussure's discovery, that one is tempted to see it as yet another expression of the avant-gardist originality of his time, along with Cubism, Dada or quantum theory. There was nothing new in Saussure's claim that linguistic signs are arbitrary and conventional. What was unique was the realization that signs signify nothing. A sign (quite unlike that of Peirce) marks only a divergence of meaning between itself and other signs. Language, Saussure became convinced, is made of differences. The concepts and forms of language are

> **purely differential**, not positively defined by their content but negatively defined by their relations with other terms of the system. Their most precise characteristic is that they are what the others are not. ([1916] 1959, 117) (Saussure's emphasis)

One of the simplest illustrations of Saussure's differential principle at work can be taken from phonology, the systemic patterning of speech sounds within particular languages. For quite some time it had been suspected that the phoneme – the structural unit of perceived sound within the phonological system – is a composite entity, a simultaneously occurring "bundle" of distinctive sound features; and a number of studies had been undertaken with a view to establishing this.[4] In the years immediately following the Second World War strong empirical evidence in support of this approach came from a distinguished collaboration between linguists and an acoustical engineer.[5] On the basis of phonetic articulatory features, as well as acoustical and perceptual analyses, twelve distinctive acoustic-perceptual features were adduced. These were predicted as being likely to account for the phonology of many different languages and, with further fine-tuning, to become recognized as "phonological universals". In this differential scheme the distinctive features are represented by plus and minus signs – a "plus" indicating the presence of a particular feature; a "minus" the absence of such a feature. Inasmuch as phonology, as was noted earlier, straddles the shared and organic modes of language, information in the form of redundancy plays no small part in the contrastive play of distinctive features. Thus, a particular array of, say, seven pluses and five minuses in a particular order, tells us nothing of significance about the (consonant or vowel) sound in itself, but only about the way it **differs** from a sound immediately preceding or following it with, say, six pluses and six minuses (after discounting redundant features).[6] Although the meaning derived from the **interpretation** occurs within the shared language mode, the perception of these features is unconscious, regulated as it must be by other statistically representable differentials at the level of social relations and attitudes.[7] Thus, the particular interpretation is **semiotic** in nature, mediated by difference, which occurs within the organic mode.

Comparable, though sometimes considerably more complex, differentiation can be observed in every domain of language. All languages, for instance, divide the colour spectrum differently. Colour differences in language are never absolute, but always relative. All that can positively be said (as far as language is concerned) about the English term "brown", for instance, is that it is different from "grey", "tan", "beige", "red", "yellow", etc. The average speaker of English will fail to notice any transition from "brown" to "beige" (to take examples not occurring in the actual colour spectrum) unless he or she is especially interested in colour and has some basic experience of colour-shade differentiation, but no one familiar with the terms *beige* and *brown* and their use will move continuously from one to the other; they will make a quantum-like jump. In the linguistic colour spectrum, colours are distributed not in representable two-dimensional space, but in notional (semiotically and sociolinguistically regulated) "fields".[8]

In optics on the other hand the three primary colours and the seven spectral colours have come to serve as measures against which all colours and all colour perception can be calibrated. One curious side to all this is that physicists, although they can tell one the wavelength of yellow light, the colour "yellow" will not enter into their scheme of things (Schrödinger 1959, 88ff.). Furthermore, physics regards infra-red and ultra-violet as much the same kind of phenomena as any of the visible colours. Added to this: different wavelengths can produce the sensation "yellow". If waves of a certain wavelength evoking "red" are mixed in a definite proportion with waves registered as "green", then a colour indistinguishable from "yellow" will result. This is not of course because "yellow" is somehow halfway between "red" and "green" on the colour spectrum. A mixture of "red" and "blue" for instance gives "purple", which is not on the spectrum. In short, the sensation of colour cannot be accounted for by the physicists' distributive picture of light radiation.

The (physical) colour spectrum nevertheless has provided a useful model outside optics, perhaps especially in psychology, not least for the "objective" standard it offers, and the promise that arguments might be established on the basis of colour, in abstraction from contexts in which a colour is familiarly embedded. In more recent times the colour spectrum has loomed large in contrastive semantics and linguistic relativity.as well as in the study of aphasic disorders;[9] especially when it was found that, despite attested absence of colour-blindness, aphasics can experience profound difficulty in distinguishing readily between colours. It was especially studies of the latter kind that gave credence to the suspicion that colours, as represented in perception and language, are more and other than radiations of certain wavelengths; they must also be complexes of brightness, surface texture, and hue; but, even more important than that, expressions of personal and cultural attitudes and feelings.

The sensation of colour then is only partly dependent on light wavelengths. Any artist worth the name will confirm that colour is qualitatively complex. In surprising ways the sensation of colour is something inseparable from the life of the individual and community – the life-world – as may be observed in its poetry, ritual, taboos and social categorization. In English the word *black* early developed strongly negative connotations. In modern times this negative signification prevailed, particularly in racial prejudice, until such a time as all oblique reference could be stripped away (first *dark* or *negro*, later *coloured*) when *black* came once again into its pristine and positive own. Through political struggle and the work of powerful public personalities, *black* regained, though in a different guise, the charisma ("black is beautiful") it lost during the early Middle Ages, before which time the word *black* was cognate with continental Germanic forms meaning "shining, white".[10]

Towards the end of the 1960s, Brent Berlin and Paul Kay completed their influential and much discussed study of "basic colour terms" (1969). In this study evidence was provided in support of the claim that colour categorization in language is not random, and that the foci of "basic colour terms" – said to be eleven in number – are similar for all languages. In their investigations standardized colour stimuli were used. These consisted of a set of more than three hundred colour chips of forty equally spaced hues and eight degrees of brightness, together with nine chips of neutral hues, including white, black, and greys. The basic colour words over a selection of languages were elicited through informants, with as little use of an intermediary language as possible. Each subject was instructed to map both the focal point and the outer boundary of each of the colour terms on the array of standard colour stimuli provided in chart format.

Berlin and Kay claimed success in determining a set of rules governing the distributional restrictions that apply to colour terms across a range of different languages: a set of colour "universals", so to speak. It was discovered that all the languages included in the study had terms for "black" and "white"; but, if a language had only three colour terms, the third would be *red*. If a language contained four terms only, it would have a term for either "green" or "yellow", but not both; whereas, if there happened to be five terms, both *green* and *yellow* would be present. Only when a language had as many as six terms would "blue" make its appearance. "Brown" would only occur in a language with at least seven terms (1969, 10).

For all its elegance and originality however, the Berlin and Kay study is open to criticism on several counts. In the first place the range of languages chosen for their experiments was, some claim, over-restricted. Nor has their hypothesis that languages fit into an evolutionary pattern found support. Their method of eliciting colour responses takes no account of the fact that colour discrimination can be finely tuned, as anyone associated with the "rag trade" for instance can confirm, and a fairly specialized vocabulary tends to exist for this purpose (How many speakers of English can reliably recognize or distinguish between *maroon* and *magenta*?). If the language of the Dinka of the Sudan had been included in their study the experimenters, contrary to predictions, and given the fairly "low" "evolutionary" social level, would have found Dinka colour vocabulary – especially colour terms relating to cattle – to be extraordinarily rich. In Dinka life in fact, cattle play such a paramount role that their cattle vocabulary teems with terms for colours and shades of colour, in innumerable blends and configurations. Dinka visual vocabulary has been said to be virtually co-extensive with cattle colours.[11] If the Dinka were to be deprived of their cattle-colour vocabulary, they would at the same time be left with scarcely any means of describing visual experience.[12]

The conclusions reached by Berlin and Kay have provoked a critical and fundamental reexamination of the nature of colour as represented in the lexicon, and of the correspondence between colour vocabulary and colour perception. In an earlier culture-sensitive study of the Hanunoo of Mindoro Island in the Central Philippines, Harold Conklin found that colour (in the Western optical sense) is far from being a universal; and that the language of the Hanunoo in particular possesses no terminological colour equivalents to those used in the technologically more advanced West. In addition to spectral colours or hues Hanunoo draws on two further dimensions of colour: saturation or intensity, as well as brightness. Together, the three dimensions combine model-wise into a coordinate system in the form of a cylindrical continuum, a "colour solid". The axis of this cylinder appears to be achromatic, with one extremity "black" and the other "white"; "greys" being distributed along the circumference. The Hanunoo, Conklin claims, have so to speak four primary colours: "relative darkness/blackness", "relative brightness/whiteness", "relative presence of red/redness", "relative presence of green /greenness". With the exception of "green", which has no decorative value on account of the tropical surroundings, the other "colours" increase in aesthetic value as their separate focal points on the "spectrum" are reached. As colours they do not in essence contradict Berlin and Kay's findings; but there exists also an important secondary "spectrum" of numerous and overlapping colours. These correspond to colour terms in English used when greater specification is called for. What can easily be overlooked – a point that cannot be over-emphasized – is that the basic terms are not exclusively "colour" terms. To avoid confusion between colours a learner of Hanunoo would need to know that the four basic colours are inseparably associated with lightness, darkness, wetness, and dryness. At the same time he or she should be able "to distinguish sharply between sensory reception on the one hand and perceptual categorization on the other" (Conklin 1955, 344).

Further reservations about the uncontextualized investigation of colour terms come from a different direction: the study of early literature. A classic case is the language of Homer, first examined from a chromatic point of view by W.E.Gladstone (the British Prime Minister no less). Homer's language, Gladstone noted, was devoid of colour terms, beyond the stereotyped *wine-dark, copper-coloured* or *rosy-fingered*. A more recent study of Middle English colour terms (Burnley 1976) also runs counter to the Berlin-Kay hypothesis that there exists a distinction between "basic colour terms" and "secondary colour terms" since Middle English texts betray no such distinction. Even the "basic" terms could well be composite.[13]

But it is not necessary to revert to the literature of the distannt past to become convinced of the lexical complexity of colour. It seems likely, for instance, that even the colour vocabulary of everyday usage is scarcely ever free from stylization. In normal circumstances people do not use colours out of context or independently of need. Only in textbooks does one encounter statements of the kind *That is a red pullover*. A more probably real utterance such as *I like your red pullover* readily decomposes into implied comments such as "I like the pullover you are wearing. It's the tomato/plum/pillar-box/etc. shade of red that suits you" (or "It's the sort of red I like). The statement *He was wearing a red pullover* will normally occur as a recollection, when in many instances the predominant feature of the pullover (if indeed it was a pullover) recalled by the witness will be "bright and warm colour" and only seldom "redness" as such. Colour reference (as perhaps most other reference) is quite often metaphorical, with a strong "as if" implication, and many colour terms are themselves metaphorical. In an attempt to replicate Berlin and Kay's procedures it was found that informants who were speakers of an Oto-Manguean language (a North American language group) protested that the investigators' colour chart did not do justice to their own colour terminology. In the room in which the interviews were taking place the informants kept on asking for referents, complaining especially of the lack of brightness among the hues given on the colour chart.[14] The relative absence of the feature "brightness" was interfering with the anticipated replication.

Colour in language, as opposed to colour in optics, embraces an indefinite number of different qualities and even goes beyond being merely an intersection of various physical parameters, such as hue, saturation or luminosity. No extensive exploration is required to ascertain that colour words in English, for example, only incidentally relate to singular physical referents. The word *red*, as everyone knows, covers not only many varieties of "red" but also a wide range of different referents, from *red hair* ("orange-brown"}, *red deer* ("golden brownish"), *red metal, red admiral* (hardly any "red"), red-hot (very hot, and not necessarily glowing "red") to purely metaphorical "reds": *red herring, red-letter, seeing red, red-handed* and many others. In fact, the colour lexicon seems to be so extraordinarily complex that to try to unravel it would lead, in one direction, into a phenomenology and hermeneutics of colour and, in another, into cultural history, an enterprise that would dwarf any attempt of a more limited scope to establish "basic colour terms" for any particular language. Whenever a simple, yet slightly queer (in the Wittgensteinian sense) remark is made to the effect that "I am seeing a red object" I may honestly be formulating a scientific observation. But what I am really doing is invoking a linguistic-semiotic reality and an entire cultural history of the word *red*, traceable to its metaphorical origins, and doubtless reaching far back into prehistory, to a time when there existed a community (or communities) of human beings sharing a semiotic of verbal differentiation in a world that was not yet separate from Nature, where song, rhythm and *logos* were still in the crucible.

Colour words, **any** words, are things wrought from the contents of a *logos*-bearing consciousness, projected into an unformed world which achieves form only to the extent that it is differentiated, signified, through the scarcely known individual organism (yours or mine, for instance) that plots its own course. We all (even the colour-blind in many surprising respects) see "red", and share a range of praxis in which the word may be acceptably applied and its meanings interpreted. But that in no way implies that we see the same object or the same qualities in that object. That is perhaps the most important reason why we need to talk to one another. A lady is said to have complained to Whistler that she did not see the world he painted. The reply flashed back: "No, ma'am, but don't you wish you could?"

We are brought back, full circle, to Saussure's differential notion of the sign, and to a complexity of signification even Saussure himself may not have envisaged. Saussure was able to say little more than that meaning is not a "something" but a *function of difference* between signifieds – nothing is describable except in terms of other things. With characteristic precision Emile Benveniste has described what he believes was in Saussure's mind:

> When we say that a certain element of a language, long or short, has a meaning, we mean by this a certain property which this element possesses *qua* signifier: that of forming a unit which is distinctive, contrastive, delimited by other units, and identifiable for native speakers for whom this language is *language*. This "meaning" is implicit, inherent in the linguistic systems and its parts (1971, 108).

It was Merleau-Ponty though who, although he too emphasized that the sign itself has meaning only insofar as it is profiled against other signs, became aware of the sign's multi-dimensional complexity, as well as of the impossibility of separating out isolated sign occurrences from language as a whole (1964, 42). In language, Merleau-Ponty was saying, meaning is nothing other than the way in which signs behave towards one another and become distinguished from one another; meaning cannot be extracted from signs and conceived as an entity in itself. Language remains opaque, and nowhere does it leave a place for pure meaning:

> There are only differences of signification in a language. The reason why a language finally intends to say and does say something is not that each sign is the vehicle for a signification which allegedly belongs to it, but that all the signs together allude to a signification which is always in abeyance when they are considered singly. (Merleau-Ponty 1964, 88)

Merleau-Ponty seems to be saying that **words as lexicon** are confined to language, but that **words as signs** point to hidden realities, to a world beyond language. Whenever human beings speak or write, other than trivially or in a formula-driven manner, they penetrate through the medium of signs to what Merleau-Ponty called "the living landscape of words":

> At the moment language fills our minds up to the top without leaving the smallest place for thought not taken into its vibration, and exactly to the extent that we abandon ourselves to it, it passes beyond the "signs" towards their meaning. And nothing separates us from language any more. (Merleau-Ponty 1964, 43)

The sign, much more than the purely formal, differential device envisaged by Saussure, takes on an epiphanic character. When it is said that words lead a life within us, the reference is to their signifying essence, embedded in a depth of history and prehistory and in a tradition of use. Language, like our bodies, yields more than is put into it. Language precedes itself, teaches itself, and suggests its own deciphering (1964, 39).

In common with all other phenomena, symbols or signs are registered, and interpreted, in the shared intersubjective language mode. The individual's **response** (as distinct from interpretation), however, takes final shape in the differential organic mode. Response will range from satisfaction to ecstatic delight, from mild apprehension to dread, from misgiving to profound distrust – to take only three of the possible extremes. In many instances, unless the symbol or sign sheds high energy, it will go unnoticed. Only the genuine artist, with the doors of perception wide open, will discover symbols at every turn. In the telling lines of Baudelaire,

> La Nature est un temple où de vivants piliers
> Laissent parfois sortir de confuses paroles;
> L'homme y passe à travers des forêts de symboles
> Qui l'observent avec des regards familiers.[15]

Signs address persons, said Peirce. Signs have something to say to someone: their epiphanic "message orientation" cannot be neutralized, nor their potential discharged in any but oneself. Signs lead not to objects or happenings themselves, though these may appear as signs in their own right. They hold themselves poised, as it were, on the threshold of the intersubjective realm; they only cross the threshold and attain permanent "meaning" when the person who discharges the sign is an artist of some power. Shakespeare for example teems with symbols that can overwhelm. The work of a lesser poet, by contrast, will only affect those readers whose reactivity is ready to merge with that of the writer.

In the sign-symbol we are witnessing a world-unifying phenomenon: one that in different ways encompasses the whole of language in both its modes, but has its roots in world unknown. Take evil, for example. No one has any idea what evil is, and some even deny its existence. Those who believe in its reality, recognize it through signs. These signs will differ from culture to culture and from person to person. "Evil", the diabolical, is not something to be understood in the same way as truth or goodness, or even duplicity or villainy; it is beyond human reach, to such an extent that sceptics can easily dismiss evil as hypostasis. But the iconic signs,[1] not to mention the symbols of evil, are everywhere. Most commonly these signs have a contrived look, whether in the hocus-pocus of black magic, in the diminished seventh heralding the diabolical in Weber's *Der Freischütz*, or in the Nazi SS insignia. Or they can underpin a powerful work of art such as Conrad's *Heart of Darkness*, a work that seems intent on capturing once and for all the essence of evil within the human dimension. At other times, though, symbols can assume a cosmic stature. There is probably no objective difference between the mushroom cloud over Hiroshima and the same type of cloud over other large explosions – the familiar icon can be surpassed in awesomeness by many a volcanic eruption. But the Hiroshima spectacle "expresses" something of special significance for the particular human beings that we are in our time, the ones in whom the symbol is discharged. The coalescence of interpretation, horror, and responsiveness to the unknown is what guarantees the symbolic permanence of Hiroshima. With good reason no doubt, the contemporary Russian composer Alfred Schnittke has concluded that "the diabolical is unfathomable,".

6. Origins

In earlier chapters we touched upon that most unfathomable of
enigmas: on the one hand, the omnipresence of an unknown
impassable "out there", with its waves and particles, its mass and
energy, the unconscious with its symbol-originating powers and, on
the other hand, the familiar, patent world of intersubjective experience
– sunsets, rainbows, delight, distress, fun, fellow-feeling, books,
music, trifles and catastrophes. Even the most abstruse notional
models, the most resourceful if indirect procedures of physics, the
powerful tool of mathematics, however much they may seem to reveal
about the unreachable, belong squarely to the known and shared world
of the here and now. The vision of the poet or composer may reach
into the unknown beyond, but texts and scores, however prolific of
signs, form part of our familiar world. The world of everyday, the
shared life-world, seems reassuringly accessible, "child's play" by
comparison. Until, that is, we stop to think about it. There may be
nothing unfamiliar for example about an "apple". Yet, even after we
have exhausted all the possible sources of knowledge and experience
of apples, from encyclopaedic description to the collective wisdom of
biochemical and horticultural expertise, we are left with no more than
an operational understanding. We can cut up an apple, analyze it, even
reconstruct it synthetically, but we still never get to the essential apple.
We may turn to Cézanne's vision of an apple but, as we know all too
well, for all the more-real-than-real reality captured by the artist we
have before our eyes (as opposed to our "mind's eye") only paint on
canvas.

For our reality we depend on our incredible selves: our minds, our consciousness flooded with light, our dark creative will-driven organic being. What is more: the images shaped by us, triggered by an unknown source whether in our waking or dream consciousness, cannot have been **learned** from our surroundings or from other people. We must somehow either have "made" or spiritually inherited these images. Not too fanciful therefore Blake's figuration of this inner life-vision

> ....Thro' the Eye
> Which was Born in a Night, to perish in a Night
> When the Soul Slept in Beams of Light.[1]

With some notable exceptions, philosophy has been slow to pay full heed to the significance and nature of this bewildering divide between what might be occurring in the mysterious "out there" and what is being enacted in our life-world. Kant put us on to the right track, but Berkeley in his concern for a pragmatic solution overshot the mark, arriving at solipsism. Until quite recently, it was the poets (not least the poet-philosopher Coleridge[2]) who grasped the immensity of our debt to the potentialities of our inner selves, to the creative principle in each of us, to what Blake termed the "Poetic Genius".[3]

Armed with such preliminary observations, we may now be ready to proceed to the question of origins. But, first of all, let us make sure we understand what might be the implications of such a question.

It seems natural to want to inquire how and when this creative principle we recognize in ourselves entered the unconscious universe. But any attempt to do this would immediately lead us into serious error. It would be impossible to separate any view we might have of our human past or pre-human origins from the beings we actually are now, creatures both of *logos*[4] and of the unconscious element that our organisms have inherited from previous (known) organisms. As soon as we posit, however hypothetically, the moment of the emergence of conscious awareness and meaning, whether this be located in the "record" of *Homo sapiens* or, much earlier in calibrated time, in *Homo erectus*, or in some other presumed pre-human species, we are begging a large question, becoming committed to an evolutionary scheme. This is not, it must be emphasized, to deny Darwinian theory, which is perfectly respectable as a piece of science. It is only that this theory cannot (and perhaps its exponents would not always wish it to) underpin any view as to the emergence of the only kind of consciousness known to Man – human consciousness. There never was a "time" when human or pre-human beings "developed" consciousness, since (calibrated) time has never been other than a property of human consciousness, and before the latter came into existence (if indeed it ever did "come into existence") there was no such time. Now I am fully aware that an argument of this sort flies in the face of palaeontology, as well as of science as a whole. Palaeontology and evolutionary theory form an impressive segment of modern science. Evolutionism especially has become part of our shared awareness, along with the sub-atomic particles, DNA, and relativity, all of them part and parcel of our collective representations. But none of this alters the fact that measurable real time cannot be projected backwards beyond our own witnessing of it. History has admittedly been aided by a scientific approach in establishing the reliability of witnesses, but before the earliest written record there was no witness of a human kind. The one thing we can be confident of is that *logos* is antecedent to Man, which in turn also implies that language as a symbolic form somehow originated at the same time as Man.

Nevertheless, taking into account the fact that the palaeontological sequence happens to be a not negligible part of our shared outlook – a collective representation – we could do worse than review, albeit cursorily, certain aspects of the palaeontological record as well as the present-day scientific concern with the language-acquiring capacities of other species (but let us not forget, along the way, that all of this rests solely on observational hypothesis).

Estimates of the age of Man vary; but as the palaeontological record of tool-making hominids grows richer the advent of Early Man gets pushed back ever farther in (calibrated) time. The earliest known version of Man – *Homo erectus* – is now reckoned to have been in existence as long as two and a half million years ago. Of this vast stretch of reconstructed time Modern Man or *Homo sapiens* has occupied (depending on one's reckoning) a mere 100,000 years. The earliest segment of the past 30,000 to 40,000 years – the Upper Palaeolithic – has been especially remarkable. It was not only a period in which stone tool-making reached a high degree of refinement, but also one in which the great flowering of the cave reliefs and paintings took place. It has even been suspected that farming and domestication may have extended back into later phases of the Upper Palaeolithic.[5] The more that is known of *Homo sapiens,* the greater the conviction that these distant ancestors were not essentially different from ourselves.

There is widespread agreement that, phylogenetically speaking, language as a symbolic form antedates *Homo sapiens,* or Modern Man as such. A confusing fact is that several extant primate species possess the ability to use, and in cases of necessity even to fashion tools. What can easily be overlooked is the qualitative difference between the latter makeshift activity and tool-making as a culturally regulated, symbol-rich technique, passed on from one generation to the next, and changing only under particular circumstances. It is not a matter of intelligence or inventiveness (chimpanzees and gorillas are known to possess such capacities in a high degree) but of that specifically human ingredient – **culture** – and its evident adjunct – **language**. During by far the greater part of Early Man's hypothesized existence, tool-making in itself probably did not confer special advantages.

Extrapolating backwards in (calibrated) time it is possible to speculate that, as in the case of present-day precivilized peoples, *Homo sapiens* and very likely his immediate predecessors too, including Neanderthal Man (who appears to have been for tens of millennia contemporary with early *Homo sapiens*) "lived in communities each of which was distinct from its neighbours by its own distinct language, its own distinct social system, its own distinct value system."[6] There appears to be no genetic basis for the differences: only language, social system and values; nor is there scientific evidence of these differences being determined by geography or by economic conditions.

Observation and experimentation – from Köhler and von Frisch to the present-day – has established that animals of several different species can be taught to recognize names and other discrete messages, and this obviously calls for a fairly sophisticated semiotic capacity. Primates can distinguish between significant and non-significant names: between signal and noise therefore. They can also generalize to a surprising extent. More intimately domesticated animals, such as dogs and horses, can reliably detect changes of mood and intention in the rhythm and various other modulations of human speech. In recent years chimpanzees and gorillas have been shown to be capable of linguistic abstraction up to at least the level attained by human infants in their earliest "two-word sentence" phase of mother-tongue acquisition (Brown 1976, 53-74).

No primate, needless to say, has gone on to acquire fully-fledged language, despite the early promise[8] and an evident degree of mental capacity for so doing. In their study of a chimpanzee whimsically named Nim Chimpsky, the investigating team drew this negative conclusion:

> Our detailed investigation suggests that an ape's language learning is severely restricted. Apes can learn many isolated symbols (as dogs, horses, and other non-human species), but they show no unequivocal evidence of mastering the conversational, semantic, or syntactic organization of language (Terrace *et al.* 1979, 901).

This bears out the widely held conviction that language as we know it is specific to human beings. Apes, like other animals when motivated to "perform", quickly realize they can obtain an abundant supply of choice tit-bits by performing "linguistic" tricks for the benefit of their captors, and have even demonstrated their ability to pass on their skill to fellow primates. Nothing of the verbal attainment of these intelligent and highly adaptable creatures merits the label language as conceived by the present study. As sentient, canny, and mentally and physically agile creatures they are at least the equals of human beings, and in some respects clearly superior. In spite of their genetic vocal deficit, they seem to grasp very well the instrumental possibilities of speech; but speech is not something they need. The missing crucial ingredient appears to be the *logos* potentiality – reason, meaning, consciousness, the full reach of the Word – available to human beings.

Whenever we speak of "language" in other species, we are allowing ourselves to be deceived by a metaphor. The qualitative gap between the so-called languages of these species and human language appears to be unbridgeable. Anyone who doubts this has failed to grasp the categorical nature of language. Human language pervades the entirety of human life: words not only enable us to speak and communicate efficiently, but also to act, feel, imagine, and remember, always within the context of a particular culture. And culture is more than just a structured assortment of "things, people, behaviour, or emotions"; it is the totality of forms or the organization of such forms in the minds of persons.[9]

At some point in this discussion the reader may have been tempted more than once with the query: "But when did all this start? At what stage in human prehistory did language in this all-embracing sense originate? Was this event sudden or gradual?" We can never answer such questions since it was *logos* that brought about the possibility of such inquiry. It is rather like asking: "What was I before I was conceived?" The origins of *logos* are at the same time the origins of the world as **we** know it. In a radical sense we can never understand ("Big Bangs" or whatever) how the sun, moon and stars, and various forms of "life" existed before the advent of *logos,* since these "objects" were in a real and literal sense created by human beings – and not retrospectively either, since time as we understand it was of human origin – over long "ages" of created time and creative imagination, by means of what Owen Barfield called "figuration" (1957, 22ff.), and eventually by primitive empirical science. Merely to think about origins risks contradiction at every turn. Everything we can think of – the origin of the Universe, evolution, other worlds beyond space – hard as such a concept might be to swallow, is of our doing and making. We can only **reconstruct** pre-*logos* time, through either inductive reasoning or poetic imagination, the best avenue to the past being perhaps a combination of the two.

At one time it was thought that languages spoken by primitive peoples of today must *a priori* be less adequate and less developed than the languages of modern civilization. But, once corpuses of the former had been properly transcribed, analyzed and understood, they were found to be no less complex, no less supple and adaptable than "advanced" languages such as as our own. There is, it seems, no observable progression from crudely simple languages to ones that are conceptually complex. And no language spoken at the present time can be rated as more backward or less sophisticated than any other.

This does not in itself, it has to be said, constitute proof that the languages of Early Man were not qualitatively different from those spoken today. Languages possess uncanny ways of keeping abreast of each other, while retaining and refining their cultural distinctiveness, and every one of the speech communities now in existence, including the most backward technologically – the Pygmies of the Congo Basin, the Kalahari Bushmen, the Australian Aboriginals, the mountain tribes of Papua New Guinea, for example – have been in existence just as long as any in the more developed world.

Primitive communities tend towards conservatism, changing little. They are usually in a state of equilibrium, potential inner conflict being mitigated through immemorial institutional mechanisms, and in ritually discharged expressions of hostility towards other communities. The "drama of the individual life", never denied ample scope to unfold, remains all the while "sanctified by myth, revealed in ritual, and buttressed by tradition."[10] Individuals participate fully and directly in their cultural milieu, not as consumers, or even as competitors, but as actively engaged whole human beings. Society is organized not politically but on the basis of kinship: everyone is related to everyone else, either contemporaneously or through actual or mythical ancestry.

> Primitive people live in a personal, corporate world, a world that tends to be "thou" to the subjective "I", rather than an "it" impinging upon an objectively separate, and divided, self. [11]

Surprisingly, our civilized "urban" languages, whether in their instrumentality or in their shared intersubjective function, still retain more than a trace of the equipoise and spontaneity, largely lost to modern man, and of the subtle intricacy, delicacy and ingenuous humanity of our precivilized ancestors, "contemporary" as well as unimaginably ancient.

Language, it may be said, is no conglomerate of separable parts, no assemblage of pieces, but an all-or-nothing quantum. You either have language or you do not. Depleted language can be found in brain-impaired individuals, but there is no phylogenetically half-developed or inchoate language as such. There are those whose language performance may be disordered or otherwise defective, but the overall character of their disordered speech, however, is never random but derivable from a previously intact system. The "design features" of language appear to be universal, and there are good grounds for supposing that language could not have been constituted other than it is. The languages of today's precivilized peoples are characterized by the same immanent features as ours. The numeral system of the now extinct Tasmanians, arguably the most "primitive" people ever encountered by modern Man, may have been restricted to unity and duality, but even their languages contained those same awesome "shifters" (*I*, *you*, *they*, etc.) that perform such a fundamental ontological function in all known languages.

The languages of primitive peoples only **seem** unusual because they have inherited different presuppositions, different collective representations from our own. Even "civilized" languages – English for example – are by no means free from perceived oddities. Why, for instance, does English associate the colour term "red" with anger, "green" with jealousy or envy, or "blue" with low spirits? All the same, such quirks aside, it can still be confidently asserted that the languages of primitive peoples can differ, quite radically as we shall in due course see, from a language like English. These languages may be lacking in explicitness and grammatical orderliness, and their semantics may contrive some strange (for us) configurations. They will tend to be vague when precision seems called for. They may be poor in Russell's "definite descriptions"; weak in pronominal or adverbial deixis; defective as regards anaphora (reference by pronouns to their antecedents); confused about transitivity, and subject-object distinctions; lackadaisical when it comes to word classes, tenses, or abstract concepts – all this despite a high degree of formal and grammatical complexity of many a language spoken by primitive peoples. Although such a language will be well adapted to the environment and mode of life of its users it can be predicted that, for all its rhetorical exuberance and intra-tribal communicative efficiency, it will be less successful than English, for example, at conveying specific multi-stage instructions, or in compiling explicit messages, or in being precise and concise. All these latter functions are not necessarily "native" to English but have developed in tandem with linear writing, literacy and, above all, with the advent of printing.

If the faintest degree of possible exaggeration is allowed for, Malinowski may have been justified in his claim that the language of primitives is first and foremost "phatic communion" – that type of speech, familiar to everyone, which "serves to establish bonds of personal union between people brought together by the mere need of companionship," especially on occasions when collective action is called for:

> It is only in certain very special uses among a civilized community and only in its highest uses that language is employed to frame and express thoughts... Even in this function, however, it is not correct to regard language as a mere residuum of reflective thought. And the conception of speech as serving to translate the inner processes of the

speaker to the hearer is one-sided and gives us, even with regard to the most highly developed and specialized uses of speech, only a partial and certainly not the most relevant view. To restate the main position arrived at...we can say that language in its primitive function and original form has an essentially pragmatic character; that it is a mode of behaviour, an indispensable element of concerted human action.

None the less, although nothing of what has just been cited can be gainsaid, the likelihood remains that even in its earliest use language did possess a poetic-discursive dimension and generated a considerable oral literature. "Primitive" ritualistic graphic designs may impress us as little more than doodling, when in actuality they are keys to an entire religious culture, in dynamic relation with the perceived environment and with the entire span of real and mythical time

Explanations of the emergence of language as we know it abound, but none can account for the coming into being of shared human consciousness in language, in these pages ascribed to *logos*, an unknown but potent creative entity that has ways of its own, and acts in its own good time. For all that we know, *logos* may also have been at work in other species producing different modes of consciousness. Nor are we any the wiser about what has been called the organic mode of language; though it seems likely that other species possess many of the features and elements of this instrumental mode. There must be many different types of sensory code and "channel" by which discrete information can be processed and transmitted, ranging from the near limitless possibilities within the modulation of sound and the deplyment of the olfactory sense to the complex dance "rituals" of bees.[13]

Human beings are prone to cooperate socially and to experience events in common. But, over and above this, our own species has developed a capacity for what might be called (for want of a neater term) "active empathy". Somehow "you" and "I" are capable of "feeling" for one another, to the the extent that we know what the other is feeling even when we cannot experience directly the sensation itself. This frequently leads to selfless acts, not out of defiance of any instinctive urge for survival, but through an at least partly conscious awareness that "you" seem to be a version of "I", and *vice versa*. This reciprocity can be exemplified in various ways, but especially in the "natural" way in which "you" and "I" may exchange roles several times over during the course of an ordinary conversation. But it is at this juncture in the relations between self and other that the organic mode of language can actually get in the way, so to speak, of any expression of empathy. We often do not know what to say to people, even close friends, in deep distress, and our unpredictability makes it quite possible for us, albeit unwittingly, to be "unsympathetic", even cruel and wounding. (Some believe that dolphins, dogs and other creatures share this same active empathy, but their mode of communication, inasmuch as it is wordless, makes it impossible for them to inflict verbal non-physical pain.)

This brings our discussion to the nub of intersubjectivity, or suprapersonality (Bakhtin), in language. If "you" leave the community, in accordance, say, with the practice of exogamy, or for some more modern reason, that is one thing; but if the person I was talking to and sharing a laugh with last evening is now suddenly absent, not off on his travels, but for the reason "his body" is laid out awaiting burial, that is quite another thing. The phenomenon and pain of the death of someone to whom one is at all close highlights in a dramatic way the trauma that the "I" experiences in coping with the inexplicable removal of "you" from the life-world. It goes some way towards explaining why grief can be so deep (even fatal at times, so we are told) and mourning so necessary, and why, if grief and mourning are to retain their reality, they must not be allowed to remain personal: through the invocation of ritual, grief has to be discharged into the life of the community. "You" and "I" even when not part of the same group are as if Siamese twins. "Separated" we need support at all levels, from expressions of personal condolence to public funerary rites.

For our precivilized ancestors the question of survival after death would not be the problem it can be for the present-day isolated urban dweller. "Soul" would have a real existence. The community, still very small, would be virtually one extended family, so organized that mourning itself would be a social institution, a distinctly communal kind of mourning. The average modern funeral by comparison seems little more than a vestige. For the primitive there would be still other rituals. The Fox Indians of North America, it is reported, used to enact a game-like ritual in which the dead relative is substituted by an adopted living one, who was to be thought of exactly as the dead relative. For this community it was the only way of guaranteeing that the soul of the dead person would depart swiftly and safely. The adoption rites necessary for convincing the deceased finally to assume the role of protective spirit were usually accompanied by competitive sports in which the players are explicitly and repeatedly reminded that the living and the dead are playing against each other. It was as if the living were offering the dead the consolation of a last game before being rid of them, the odds being stacked overwhelmingly against the possibility that the deceased might win (Lévi-Strauss 1966, 31 and 199). Games, including competitive sports, depend absolutely on language function. All games have rules, and rules are made of language.

Reluctance at undergoing life-world severance on the part of both the living and the dead is reflected in the practice among certain Australian Aboriginal tribes of carrying around with them for considerable periods of time the remains of their deceased. Such mourners take an unusually long time to settle down again to a regular life. One tribal community, for example, stuffs the ears and nostrils of the corpse with soft paperbark to stop the dead person from hankering after his folks, and to encourage the spirit to depart (Berndt 1964, 410-11). The term for the newly deceased is "he (or she) who is far away". Mortuary rituals such as these, while assuming that death is not final, underline the need to take account of the changes brought about by a death, and to affirm that the living, despite their being coequals with the dead in existential and social terms, are nevertheless to be more highly valued than the dead.

*   *   *

The farther back in (real) time we might seek to go (if this were possible) language can be expected more and more to resemble poetry, and less and less a tool for manipulating the utilitarian artefacts unearthed by the palaeontologist and archaeologist. Meanings, it might not be too fanciful a projection, did not attain full consciousness in our early ancestors, but remained embedded in Nature: "Nature all alive in the thinking of man" (Barfield 1952, 93). Meanings could not become detached, but (like many meanings for many people still) could only be experienced and lived. Nor could the "poetry" of early man be said to have been created by individual "poets":

> Not man was creating, but the gods – or, in psychological jargon, his "unconscious". (Barfield 1952, 103)

Words would have inhabited a semantic-semiotic universe modern man can scarcely imagine. Today, words reflect predominantly the vast institutionally regulated assembly shop of modern civilization, in which everything is weighed, measured, apportioned, and circumscribed; a civilization in which poets find themselves alienated, cut adrift from a time when

> words flashed irridescent shapes like flames – ever-flickering vestiges of the slowly evolving consciousness beneath them. (Barfield 1952, 131)

In our own culture, words are outcomes, museum pieces, closer to fossils than living things. And as though showing approval of their new-found status (words are us, after all), words at times behave as if they possessed the same meanings for everyone more or less. To cast doubt on semantic universality is to be confronted by the dictionary, that formidable gate-keeper. What Russians used to call the Living Life is showing signs of retreating into poetry, art and religion, and that may well be where real life has always belonged.

Words and consciousness came into being together. The glimpses of nature. revealed at times through symbolism, or in the acoustic-semantic resonance of our words, are the living remnants of what has been rounded out over the ages like pebbles fashioned in the articulations of our minds, feelings and imagination. They embody the changing phases in our reactions to and reflections upon the world in which we find ourselves "thrown", and which we are left to shape into the successive images unfolding in time. An innocent word in our present-day vocabulary, even a completely "new" word, owes its form, sense and function to the many unrecorded phases of verbal activity in our human and pre-human ancestors. These words are the living witnesses to those ages of unrecorded time; sherds, stone implements and vestigial habitations speak only to science. Ordinary observations such as *Spring is here*, or *I love you*, or *Look, there's a rainbow!*

telescope not only aeons of human time but some of the unrecorded visions enshrined in early human poetry; not the poetry of isolated would-be writers, but of those who dreamt dreams, who only incidentally crafted tools and other utilitarian objects, but wrought, first and foremost, the objects of the shared life-world – concepts, feelings, sensations, images, the heavens, gardens, landscapes and wildernesses – through words.

7. Words, People and Things

Some four hundred years ago, there occurred one of those metamorphoses in human consciousness – possibly the most significant that has ever occurred – as though a blind had been raised on people's time-honoured way of seeing things. This occurrence coincided with the onset of the "Scientific Revolution" and also with the coming into being of modern philosophy.

Interestingly, there was one facet of this radical change that attracted the attention of one of the founders of modern science – Francis Bacon. Writing at the beginning of the seventeenth century Bacon sensed that "words" and the pursuit of knowledge were parting company. Words were actually getting in the way of the advancement of learning:

> For men imagine that their reason governs words, whilst in fact words re-act upon the understanding; and this has rendered philosophy and the sciences sophistical and inactive. Words are generally formed in a popular sense, and define things by those broad lines which are most obvious to the vulgar mind; but when a more acute understanding, or more diligent observation is anxious to vary those lines, and to adapt them more accurately to nature, words oppose it.[1]

This divergence had to do, Bacon thought, with a new kind of worship of idols or "false notions which have already preoccupied the human understanding, and are deeply rooted in it." These idols, especially the more troublesome "idols of the market", had seemingly "entrained themselves round the understanding from the associations of words and names."

What was really happening – and Bacon seems to have been on the verge of discerning this – was a divergence within the shared mode of language: the need for a new version of the shared language, one that was adequate to the canons of logic and at the same time capable of leading to a truer understanding of nature. Ironically, though the old idols were displaced (forgotten about rather than overthrown), new idols came into being. Barfield [2] noticed that, especially since the early seventeenth century, phenomena themselves – the objects, the shapes and colours we see, the sounds we hear, the surfaces we touch, not to mention the living creatures around us – had degenerated into a new and unforeseen set of idols. We moderns have grown accustomed to looking at things – a rock, say, or a tree or stream – in a particular way and to the assumption that that is **all** they are, namely, **objects**. Modern mankind lives in a world populated by idols: dead, inert things, to be used, manipulated, moved around, ignored, cultivated, more or less at will. But, again something of an irony, those in today's world who would overturn these idols are often leading figures of science or the philosophy of science. It is even becoming no small problem to identify prominent names in the physical sciences who have not at moments seemed downright anti-positivistic, and in a few cases even more than a shade "mystical".[3]

Only in recent times have growing numbers of individuals of every hue and inclination come to understand that things are not merely entities recognized and named by us. Their coming into being has been in large part our doing and making; through language, the medium through which consciousness is connected with living things and objects (Gadamer 1976, 76). We can and do, as Gadamer has said, "hear things in their own being" (1976, 71). In a real sense there were, for example, no trees – at any rate no trees we know as trees – until random sensations emanating through the mediation of signs from a world beyond, from configurations of energy, were "combined and constructed by the percipient mind into the recognizable and nameable objects we call 'things'."

An idolatrous frame of mind has had the effect, says Barfield, of inducing in us the belief that creatures and things – the world – have all along been essentially the same sort of perceptible entities they are for us today, the idolatrous assumption being that if there had been human beings around to observe the world as it was over a billion years ago it would have appeared more or less exactly as it does in today's reconstructions by geologists and palaeontologists. Geological era succeeding geological era, a changing panorama of plant life, of species adapting or following one another into extinction, capped most recently and most astoundingly by the emergence of Man – all this has become part of the modern mythological experience, comforting, or fraught with *Angst*, depending on one's disposition.

The prime hitch in all this cineramic retrospective is Man himself. The notion that ape-like ancestors emerged into the light of consciousness, looked around them and started using words to designate objects and creatures in their immediate surroundings is not only science fiction, it is bad science fiction. The false assumption has been that at some point in the dawning of human consciousness various human capacities emerged and that as a consequence language took shape. Instead, we now have to face up to the potentially unsettling realization that human consciousness, language, and the world as we know it, emerged in unison. To reach a particular state of awareness our remote ancestors had to be fully in possession of language and to achieve the latter they must have come by the requisite degree of creative awareness: a paradoxical circularity from which there appears to be no escape. Words and world came into being together. Barfield has put it like this:

> Man did not start on his career as a self-conscious being in the form of a mindless or thoughtless being, confronting a separate, intelligible world very much like our own, about which we then proceeded to invent all manner of myths. He was not an onlooker, learning to make a less and less hopelessly inaccurate mental copy. He has had to wrestle his subjectivity out of the world of his experience by polarizing that world gradually into a duality. And this is the duality of objectivity-subjectivity, or outer-inner, which now seems so fundamental because we have inherited it along with language. He did not **start** as an onlooker; the development of language enabled him to **become** one. (1977, 16-7) (Barfield's emphasis)

When they contemplate animals, people sometimes wonder if they see and experience things as human beings do. In one sense they must. They have eyes which in the case of some species of birds are undoubtedly more efficient than human eyes. The optical organs of animals and birds are receptive to a comparable range of physical stimuli and, in all honesty, we do not really know what goes on in their "minds". Other creatures must surely have varying degrees of awareness; the difficulty is only that of imagining it without indulging in anthropomorphism. What we do know is that the symbolic action of myth – a cultural and hence human activity – has played a very large part in the unfolding of Man's consciousness. Thus, to expect that my dog, despite an incredible sensitivity and acuity, and I "see" the "same" rose-tree or the "same" windfall apple will be unwarranted.

The world has undergone inconceivable change along with the human beings that participated in the shaping of it, in just how many or in what kinds of ways we know not. Konrad Lorenz although operating within the framework of evolutionism nevertheless supports the view that the ability of human beings to form conceptual images of the external world came into being over aeons of time "by means of adaptation to circumstances extant in a real external world." Lorenz agrees with Aristotle that animals have souls similar to ours but does not think that they possess minds (Lorenz 1987, 77-8). Human language must have changed in character (though not in essence) out of all recognition along with the world, and *vice versa*. But words are also records – though the very notion of record we should remind ourselves is a relatively recent innovation – of previous versions of the life-world; to the extent that, even over a short period of a few hundred years and on occasion in considerably less time than that, the verbal record (where we possess one) can reveal fundamental and startling changes in outlook.

Compare for example an ordinary medieval person and ourselves contemplating the night sky. Astronomy will confirm that the night sky has not changed significantly since, say, 1300. We must therefore be seeing the same night sky. Nevertheless we are forced to admit that we are not. For our not so distant medieval forebear the planets and the moon were "seen" as embedded each in their own separate revolving crystal spheres. In those times planets were not what they seem to us: more or less remote inanimate objects in orbits determined by gravitational forces with different masses and velocities and different surface conditions and climates. For medieval Man planets were more akin to spirits raying down their complex influences on earthly creatures and their destinies. Everything in "creation" was responsive to these influences. And, although it was not granted to mere mortals actually to hear it, an ethereal music was believed to be emanating from those transparent spheres. The planets themselves, and the moon especially, as well as the host of heavenly "bodies" were supposed to be linked by invisible threads to our own spiritual well-being and temperaments.[4]

This is intended to be neither poetry nor mysticism, even less, speculation. Like ourselves medieval people merely took their world for granted. They were just as convinced as we are that their world was the only valid world, whereas we are more likely to take the view that we have modern science on our side to shore up a conviction that we must be superior in important respects to these superstition-ridden medievals. Even though there are still people today who advocate astrology, it is "known" that influences from the planets and stars must be imaginary. Voyager II has sent back pictures ("Cameras cannot lie"!) of the outer planets, and we know that they are substantial (if somewhat uncanny). Are we right, and the medieval observer wrong? Could it be that in generations to come our own descendants, who can be expected to develop a world-view few today can even begin to imagine, will look back with amused condescension on us, as we now do on our own medieval predecessors? There are already in our midst harbingers of change, not least the work of Barfield. Science goes on leading the way but it seems to want to leave the idols intact.

So as not to stray too far beyond our scope however, let us return for the present to the starting point of this digression: the relationship between words and outlook.

We can make a start with the word *planet*. For us moderns *planet* is not the same word as it was for people in pre-Copernican times. Its **form** may have been the same but its **signification,** along with its semantic associations, have changed beyond recognition. The same applies to a wide range of other words whose meanings have been utterly changed by the advent of physical science. A small sample of these might include *star* (in medieval times a prick of light in a dark homogeneous vault or, alternatively, the souls of departed spirits), *space, mass, gravity, law* and *orbit* ("track" or "path" originally). Some of these words, like *mass* or *gravity*, have retained their pre-scientific meanings alongside their newer meanings. But many users of English may possess only a vague awareness of the earlier meaning of *gravity*, and may consider the older meaning a learned archaism; until perhaps they become acquainted, say, with Simone Weil's use of the word in *Gravity and Grace* in which the older and newer meanings are fused together. Even in an elementary physics class a teacher may initially experience some slight difficulty in separating the modern meaning of *mass* from its original "lump of matter" sense. Considering the spectacular success of so much applied science and technology we may be justified in dismissing outdated ways of thinking as wrongheaded or, as *The Oxford English Dictionary* sometimes coyly dubs them, "imaginary". More essential to our argument is the fact that within a relatively brief span of time the medieval "world", a fascinating if somewhat alien world that human beings made out of their raw sensations, has changed fundamentally. Within the longer time span we could no doubt identify changes between the time of the dawning of the civilizations of Asia Minor and the Mediterranean and the rise of Greece and Rome, but for the long millennia before that we possess no inkling. All we can be sure of is that changes must have taken place and that some of these changes may have been major enough to have had far-reaching consequences in the shaping of earlier versions of the life-world we know.

In their attempts to reach back to the "preliterate", "precivilized" eras of mankind anthropologists find themselves up against a host of problems inasmuch as both these attributes beg all sorts of questions. Was there ever a time, for instance, when *Homo sapiens* was "preliterate", lacking even an oral literature? We know that people living in the Dordogne, in Northern Spain, and elsewhere across the Eurasian continent during the period immediately before and during the last glaciation produced the most marvellously expressive and finely executed cave art, unrivalled by anything comparable since. And one authoritative interpretation of the arrangement and design of these murals and reliefs suggests that they represented a non-linear form of writing (we shall return to this point in a later chapter).[5] And "precivilized"? This very much depends on one's conception of "civilization". If present-day "primitive" cultures are anything to go by, they can at times be seen to be at least as highly developed as those cultures we are prepared to recognize as civilized. By the standards of the moral, institutional and purely human values acclaimed by civilization primitive cultures can surprisingly often be rated superior, at least in some respects, to their more "modern" urban-civilized counterparts (Montagu 1968, 2-3).

Not only that but, more seriously, there exists a readiness to lump together prehistoric Stone Age societies (the empirical artefacts of the archaeologist and palaeontologist) with contemporary hunter-gatherer communities (artefacts of the anthropologist and ethnologist).

> Primitive man has become almost a mythical figure in the literature of most European languages... He is a very useful peg on which to hang a variety of views, but this is variety only within a narrow range.[6]

The tendency may have become less marked than it once was but it remains difficult to locate a single term undisparaging enough to fit contemporary "primitive" peoples. There now exists general agreement though that the latter are not to be equated with archaic Stone Age Man. A primitive technology and a subsistence economy in no way imply an historical time lag, nor do they necessarily signify inferiority. The primitive peoples of today are, when all is said and done, our contemporaries, with their own particular wholesome, creative and natural relationships with the living environment. As a possible solution, it has been suggested that contemporary primitive peoples be regarded (paradoxically, no doubt) as "our contemporary precivilized ancestors".[7]

All questions of origin are bound to take us back to the imponderable hypothetical moment in time when our remote "pre-human" ancestors became "human". This event, although it must somehow have occurred, can never have reached the threshold of awareness. "You" and "I" must have become distinguishable entities aeons before there was conscious awareness of the occurrence. Even today most people would find this piece of phenomenology, embedded as it is in language, a superfluous item of knowledge rather than the wondrous breakthrough that it represents. Palaeontology can unearth signs such as, for instance, the discovery that on occasion even Neanderthal people buried their dead. But does such a discovery indicate self/other awareness of the kind so familiar to us? Or are there different ritual explanations we may never know of?

In their incipient consciousness the first human beings would not have found themselves already supplied with perceptions and concepts. Their dream worlds and some of their perceptions would have appeared to be shared and negotiable while other occurrences – physical pain and visions for instance – would not. For Early Man the boundaries between phenomena even in "survival" domains such as

food gathering and hunting would have seemed more fluid, less well
defined than the ones we moderns are accustomed to. Their inner
worlds and their shared worlds would not have been sharply
demarcated. There would nevertheless have been some striking
similarities between archaic and modern man. Like his modern
descendants Early Man would have emerged from childhood into adult
societies, each society different from the other, each structured from
particular sets of "collective representations" with its own canon of
beliefs, ritual, attitudes to the sacred, expectations, feelings and
responses that had been, so the tribal myths informed them, the same
for everyone and for all time. "Everyone", be it noted, referred not to
humankind as a whole – there was no such conception – in that other
human groups even if they were ever by chance encountered did not
automatically appear to be of the same "kind". Even in our own time
the word for "nation" in a language often means "the people" or "the
kin", exclusive of other peoples or tribes. The shared world of an early
community as expressed in its language and read through its
mythology was an order of things sufficient to itself, and each such
community would have been living at the point at which Nurture was
just beginning to prise itself free from Nature.

   We have to imagine time, aeons of time – not measurable in years
for the reason that calibrated time had still to be conceived – during
which our early predecessors unconsciously peopled their dawning,
their life-world as well as their Dreaming, with images, glimmerings
of concepts, sensations and feelings. Without knowing it they brought
to bear their "symbol-processing" capacity upon their raw sense
experience, instincts and intuitions. Their links with their fellow
beings (not necessarily always human, when even "human" itself was
not a clear-cut representation) began to grow in cohesiveness and
comprehensibility as they were able to mesh symbols expressed in
language and myth and in the world about them with the kinds of
textures of being that their organic mode of language was projecting,
like some beguiling play of shadows on their dim consciousness,
eventually making possible, in proportion as their utterances became
mutually aware (Bakhtin) a shared language progressively more viable
in terms of self and other intercourse. Even to try to reconstruct an
encounter with the people of these distant ages defies imagination, so
vastly different and incompatible would have been their world from
ours.[8] Their treatment of space and time would seem to us so utterly

preposterous, with objects and living things linguistically and existentially interrelated and brought together in irreconcilable forms, in irreconcilable places and times, in a locale that was no mere territory but a "magical" domain with an incredible story for a beginning and, in place of an ending, only mythological pathways radiating at once outwards and inwards into multiple realities, peopled by beings living utterly metaphorical existences in an entirely metaphorical world with an extreme of metonymy that would make the more outlandish modern poetry seem like rationality itself.

The world "out there" – beyond our ken but including our own bodies – has always formed part of a system of collective representations[9] and, in so doing, has taken on a certain kind of instrumentality. In early societies a human being had not yet become an independent organism but was as yet a vehicle of that strange energy sometimes conveniently referred to as *mana*,[10] that undifferentiated (but differentiating) presence that could possess both things and creatures. Man came about as an agent of signification and symbolic form.

Until quite recent times "civilised Man" made so bold as to hope to fathom the world of "primitive man" in terms of animism, fetishism, totemism, magic and the like. The world of primitive humanity had to be and could too easily be shown to be a bogus unscientific world of tedious and bizarre hocus-pocus in which the most improbable identifications were not only possible, but commonplace. In his fabled study[11] James Frazer had observed a close parallel between western science and primitive magic. Nevertheless, for all the systematicity and logicality of his thesis Frazer could not desist from dismissing primitive magic as "a spurious system of natural law as well as a fallacious guide to conduct... a false science and an abortive art" (1954, 11). In sharp contrast Frazer's contemporaries Emile Durkheim and Marcel Mauss (1963, 87) were interpreting the facts quite differently. Instead of pseudo-science they could see the history of scientific classification as the record of the stages by which social affectivity had become weakened, leaving greater scope for the reflective thinking of separate(d) individuals. It is not the case, they argued, that the more remote influences of the earliest phases of human thought have ceased to be felt by modern man.

Frazer's like-minded contemporaries on the other hand, not satisfied with dismissing primitive mentality as fallacious, persisted in imposing a modern outlook on a precivilized world and, in so doing, depicted a world that defied common sense. To take but one instance: in its more literal sense "totemism", nowadays for the most part consigned to the museum of foolish hypotheses, seemed to be proposing that primitive man identified himself in some inscrutable manner with animal species, with plants, and even with stones and various other inanimate objects.

Durkheim's discovery was that thought itself, all belief and all perception, constituted a web of social or "collective" representations. Long before individuals could even begin to reflect upon and analyze their own thinking they must have been participating intensively in a social reality, an essential antecedent of that which constitutes the private world of inner activity experienced by the individual:

> Collective representations are the result of an immense cooperation, which stretches out not only in space, but also in time as well; to make them, a multitude of minds have associated, united and combined their ideas and sentiments; for them, long generations have accumulated their experience and their knowledge (Durkheim 1961, 29).

Until such a time as a shared reality is imposed on it, not only the zone "out there" but even the things going on "inside one's head" remain unrepresented. "The world we accept as real is in fact a system of collective representations" (Barfield 1988, 20). Furthermore, the world is already shaped by the culture to which the individual happens to belong as well as by that individual's personal character. We do not merely see, hear or sense things, we bring to bear the entire gamut of cultural experience. As Barfield's simple but telling example shows,

> I may say loosely that "I hear a thrush singing." But in strict truth all that I ever merely "hear" – all that I ever hear simply by virtue of having ears – is sound. When "I hear a thrush singing," I am hearing not with my ears alone, but with all sorts of other things like mental habits, memory, imagination, feeling and (to the extent at least that the act of intention involves it) will. (1988, 20)

These are the shared representations and sensations in which the same subject has participated since his or her earliest years, as well as through countless generations of inherited cultural tradition.

It was Durkheim who first plainly understood that the collective representations out of which the whole of human experience and reality (as we know it) is woven are social in origin. In time the representations become autonomous realities (idols) that live a life of their own, in turn breeding new representations within a system of myths, cosmologies, social relationships, occult practices and religious beliefs. Durkheim drew attention to the manner in which such representations establish polarities, attracting and repelling each other, bringing about identity and difference; and to the fact that everything in social reality is related to everything else within an unique integrally articulated whole. It was Durkheim's view that even primitive classification had its origins in specific forms of social order – the clan and the religious practices of the tribe – and that classificatory systems

> merely express under different aspects the very societies within which they were elaborated... Cosmic space was primitively constructed on the model of social space, that is, on the territory occupied by society and as society conceives it... collective force and its power over men's minds served as prototypes for the notion of force and causality, etc.... If men did not agree upon these essential ideas at every moment, if they did not have the same conception of time, space, cause, number, etc., all contact between their minds would be impossible, and with that, all life together. (Durkheim 1961, 30)

Social life is something most of us take so much for granted that it becomes all too easy to fail to notice that even the most basic "biological" urges, the more powerful emotions, the *libido,* not to mention signs, are filtered *in toto* through the sensitive mesh of the world's many different cultures and social systems, and are shaped and channelled by the very "cast of mind" of the various social groups within which countless generations of human beings have been nurtured.

The "anthropologization" of primitive Man began at the time when Durkheim and Mauss were contrasting the world outlook of primitive peoples with that of our own specialized rationalized technology-driven civilization. Lucien Lévy-Bruhl, a disciple of Durkheim, went so far as to claim that precivilized human beings are not detached from their mental images and perceptions in the same way as their civilized counterparts.[12] They are still a part of the phenomena of the social and natural environment and "participate" in these phenomena in ways that people of today might find it difficult to conceive.

The world as we know it is peopled with objects, with creatures and beings that are named and frequently put to use by us. I am detached from them absolutely. A tree is a tree, a fish a fish, a lizard a lizard, and so on. Each genus and species has a name of its own and forms part of an order of things. With primitive peoples by contrast, identities have been forged between tribal individuals or groups and other creatures (and more rarely, objects or locations). These came to be known among anthropologists as totems; a totem being a process by which any natural object, any significant location, any creature, real or mythical, can become so closely identified with an individual or group that the same name is applied to both. This is no mere convention as it might be among us where, say, animal and other names can become appellatives, but is a clear indication that no dividing line can be drawn between the individual or clan and its totem in that each totem-pair possesses one body in common and is descended from a single common ancestor. In Central Australian Aboriginal societies this totemic bond is represented by what in certain languages is known as the *churinga* (or *tjurunga*), a symbol-object, a precious piece of carved or decorated wood or stone. The individual, insofar as any personal identity is perceived, feels that he (less likely, she) is the totem. That this is quite other than the equivalent of children's play-acting is apparent from the harsh sanctions that can be invoked in the event of ritual infringements, as also from the observed fact that damage to the totemic bond can lead to the sickness or death of the human member. Totemism has been described, if somewhat blandly, as:

> a view of nature and life, of the universe and man, which colours and influences the Aborigines' social groupings and mythologies, inspires their rituals and links them to the past. It unites them with nature's activities and species in a bond of mutual life-giving... a relationship between a person or group of persons and (for example) a natural object or species, as part of nature. (Elkin 1954, 133)

Man remains an integral part of nature, not sharply distinct from other species but sharing with them the same life essence (Berndt and Berndt 1964, 189). Yet another characterization of totemism is that it represents a "formal relation" between people and persistent elements in the physical environment.[13]

What the reader may or may not have noticed in all this "primitive mysticism" is that the species with which the totemic bond is formed cannot have come ready-made; the species themselves must have been "cultivated" through primitive but highly accurate scientific observation. The species may not always coincide with modern zoological or botanical classifications but, however these totemic species may be designated, they will be accurate down to the last detail. This meticulous concern for scientific exactitude has been observed among post-totemic but still tribal Mayan peoples in Guatemala. The Indian maize fields were noted as being more highly selected for type than those of their Latin-speaking neighbours. Such purity, given the tendency of maize to cross very easily, could have been maintained only by the most fanatical adherence to an ideal type. Each tribe was seen to possess several varieties that were sharply different one from another, yet within a single variety there were no observable differences from plant to plant.

Not surprisingly, the prime function of language in primitive communities is to sustain and reflect these often highly complex interlinked structures. Language in our own societies does this too but mostly in a vestigial manner. The salient difference is that, in our culture, to the point of idolatrous insistence on their separateness, we do not allow ourselves to become confused with the objects in the world around us. Yet we still sometimes do "magical" things with our words. Objects and creatures, to take a simple instance, can be counted. But when instead of objects we have "substances", still further verbal entities need to be created which will supply the discrete parcels of the substance that can be conveniently handled (*a lump of sugar, a shower of rain, a crowd of people* [Does three really make a crowd?], *a branch of an organization* or *business*, etc.). Our totemic scruples residually survive in "prides" of lions, "schools" of dolphins, "herds" of cattle, and so forth.

The totem, however much it may have been demystified, is no crude device but an integral part of an elaborate system by which classification, a fundamental aspect of all language, proceeds. Semantic and lexical classifications are inherent in totemic classifications which are as real and concrete to the primitive tribesman as our "better informed" classifications may be to us. As Lévi-Strauss has said:

the diversity of species furnishes man with the most intuitive picture at his disposal and constitutes the most direct manifestation he can perceive of the ultimate discontinuity of reality. (1966, 137)

The primitive's preoccupation with classification by species is an earnest one, reflecting as it does a high degree of observational accuracy on a level comparable to that of the modern botanist or zoologist: "a concern with differentiating features which pervades the practical as well as the theoretical activities of the people we call primitive" (Lévi-Strauss 1960, 153-4). Sometimes this concern can have the most alarming consequences for the outsider. Primitive peoples expend great care on the classification, in the most meticulous detail, of their flora and fauna. For the plant world alone classifications (*taxa*) running into several thousands are not uncommon, the upper threshold being limited only by the memory capacity and resourcefulness of the ethnobotanist. In Gabon for example an ethnobotanical listing of about eight thousand terms distributed among the languages or dialects of some dozen or so neighbouring hunter-gatherer tribes has been compiled. Lévi-Strauss relates what happened when a Westerner coming into contact with an African tribe attempted to learn the language (199, 5-6). At a very early stage her informants found it natural to collect a large number of botanical specimens which they promptly went on to name for her one by one. The problem for the learner quickly became not the language, but an inability to distinguish plant forms. For their part the native informants took an interest in plants for granted: even a small child would know the names of literally hundreds of plants. Her hosts failed to grasp that her dismay came not from the words themselves but from the sheer abundance of specimens that appeared to her to be identical.

Taxonomic structures among primitives, despite a high degree of delicacy, tend not to be rigid but, like the lexicon, adaptable through regular and recognizable formal transformations to the exigencies of the moment. Native institutions, because of their formal nature and their "hold" over a range of socio-semiotic content, can negotiate a safe passage between the pressure of the flux of events and the dictates of a highly structured system. Totemic structures also have the advantage of making it possible for the tribe to transcend a natural prejudice to regard people outside their tribal boundaries as alien or subhuman. On account of their universality, totemic classifications can counteract the "closing in" tendency and "promote an idea something like that of humanity without frontiers" (Lévi-Strauss 1966, 167). From tribe to tribe languages may differ markedly, but the universality of a potentially shared language stretches without limit in every direction until a natural boundary (an island-free sea or an impassable range of mountains or some such) is reached.

Take for example the Karam people of the New Guinea Highlands. The Karam are said to possess "an enormous, detailed and on the whole accurate knowledge of natural history."[14] As might be expected their *taxa* correspond only partially to those of scientific zoology. This may be especially so at the highest level "at which culture takes over and determines the selection of taxonomically significant characters." Just as modern science at various times evolved alternative methods of classifying species and sub-species, so it comes as no surprise to discover that Karam zoology follows a comparable if different order of classification; a difference albeit not too problematic for the modern outsider to accept. Problems arise only with what has been called a "special taxonomic status". Among the Karam, animals with this special status are the dog, the pig and, above all, the cassowary bird, a wingless ostrich-like creature. In the case of the cassowary bird there is no apparent reason for its special status; it is not domesticated and, though the scientific zoologist places it in the same *taxon* as birds, the Karam are adamant that the cassowary is no bird at all. Admittedly this curious-looking creature has hair instead of plumage and its head is virtually all bone. But the most important reason why the Karam do not consider the cassowary a bird – and most Karam are only vaguely aware of this – is that it is quasi-human and hence plays an integral part in Karam culture. Hunting the cassowary invokes sets of prohibitions and ritual precautions: in the event of one being killed the killing is done as if the bird were human.

To be sure, the cassowary – as the Karam know all too well – is only metaphorically human. But it is also metaphor that encompasses within the same bracket the focal ingredients in Karam cultural dynamics. In ways that neither the Karam nor the social anthropologist understands, the cassowary through metaphor and antithesis has come to feature in Karam life as a whole. It appears to be laid down by the rules of their particular culture that they must think of these strange creatures as "sisters and cross-cousins", treat them as such, and make significant and rule-derived modifications to their lineality, their lexicon and their behaviour towards them, and to lay down sanctions against their slaughter. In all this, language plays a key role in that the prescriptions written into the culture are maintained or modified through language.

It is perhaps only in urban civilization that language and social practice draws a clear line of demarcation between human and non-human. In the rural village, remote from the influences of civilization, the symbiosis of human and animal worlds reveals a complexity which expresses neither a sense of complete affinity with animals nor a clear-cut distinction and separation from them but rather a coexistence of both attitudes in varying degrees, in perpetual tension. For the rural Thai it has been said that "animals are effective vehicles for embodying highly emotionally charged ideas in respect to which intellectuality and affectivity cannot be rigidly separated as representing human and animal modes of conduct."[15] In their pre-urban state, people need animals – linguistically, socially, and emotionally – in order to forge a system of moral conduct as well as to resolve the problem of the place of the human community within nature. After all, it is not that long ago that Europe gave up bestiaries. And some sophisticates still find meaning in the Zodiac.

Language, we have gradually come to understand, is

> something more than a vehicle for exchanging ideas and information – more even than a tool for self-expression... or for getting people to do what we want. Every language is also a special way of looking at the world and interpreting experience. Concealed in the structure of each different language are a whole set of unconscious assumptions about the world and life in it. (Kluckhohn 1949, 45)

Incommensurability between languages in their different "worlds-apart" cultural settings can throw up the most intractable problems in fairly mundane situations. Take for instance the Australian Aborigines' claim to land ownership which in recent years in some Australian states has become a political issue. Liberal legislation has made it possible for land claims to be examined at judicial hearings. For the most part difficulties arise through the alarming disparity between the languages and cultures of the Aborigine population and English-speaking Australians. One such insuperable difficulty is that, although ownership is being claimed over a particular expanse of territory, the claimants have no conception of land ownership in any recognizably modern Western sense.[16] It is not that Aboriginal languages are conceptually undeveloped. Quite the contrary: they are in some respects richer than English in conceptual and terminological elaboration. In these languages the same word may mean "home, site, camp, country" (the latter frequently referring to hundreds of square miles of terrain). Maps can become legal fictions when place-names refer not even to the vaguest of locations but to songs and to goings-on in the Dreaming. Hardly surprising then that the courts, unable to cope, have decided to adopt the indigenous population's conceptualization rather than attempt to wrestle interminably with comparative metaphysics and epistemology, not to mention horrendous problems of translation.[17]

The Australian Aboriginal has been living in geographical isolation from the rest of the world for tens of millennia (except in recent centuries in the northern and northeasterly extremities of the Australian continent) no one can be sure exactly how many. Another very wide scatter of geographically and culturally separate peoples were the American Indians. The ancestors of the American Indians are thought to have crossed the Behring Straits from Asia in a series of widely separated migrations, before and during the last Ice Age, by an ice-free land bridge that once joined Siberia and Alaska. Not surprisingly therefore, the American Indian languages differ to an astonishing degree from those to which Europeans and non-Indian Americans are accustomed. It is not just that the structures and set of these languages depart from what Whorf termed "Standard Average European" but they differ extensively one (sub-family) from another. Furthermore, the world outlooks reflected in the different languages are incommensurate with anything a speaker of Standard Average European might expect, to the extent that the past four centuries of mutual distrust and misunderstanding between American Indians and Europeans therefore are hardly to be wondered at.

Culture-shock may come in large or small doses. The Hopi Indians build their dwellings in a highly characteristic manner. It is puzzling then to discover (Whorf 1956, 201ff.) that the Hopi language has no nouns for "room", "hall", "interior passage", "cellar" or the various other highly characteristic features of Hopi domestic architecture. For ceilings, walls and doors however the Hopi do have names. Thus a

Hopi can say "my ceiling" but not "my room". The buildings typical of a Hopi community have no separate names; not even the unusual and highly distinctive *kiva*, so-called (in Hopi, *kiva* means only "old house"), a sunken religious ceremonial building entered through a trap door by a ladder from a flat roof. Such terminological omissions when a particular architectural style is so typical of a culture seems incomprehensible to a Westerner. In Nootka, a language of the Wakashan group spoken on Vancouver Island, the shortest word would in English be a whole sentence. The single word-sentence *tl'imshya'isita'itima* is said to mean literally: "boiled (or cooked) food – -ed[result] – eat —-ers [agency] – go for – he does [manifestation]". This "translates" into English as "He invites people to a feast" (Whorf 1956, 242-3). In Navajo, an Athabascan language, speakers take for granted what is for them an ordinary verb form roughly translatable as "one animate object moves."[18] Here are some examples with literal translation equivalents and actual meanings:

Navajo (literal English translation)	*Meaning*
One moves continuously about with reference to	"is busy, preoccupied"
One moves into clothing	"one dresses"
A happening moves	"a ceremony begins"
One moves about here and there	"one lives"
One moves about	"is young"
Move happenings about here and there	"make plans"
Move words out of an enclosed space	"sing"

If abstractness (as opposed to concreteness) were to be taken as a measure of an advanced stage of language evolution then Navajo would rank at least highly abstract as English. In reality though, no language is more abstract than another. A language like Navajo, so remotely different from English, only **seems** more abstract, to the point of vagueness (but a vagueness that is at once poetic). All languages are immeasurably abstract; even the most concrete noun (unless qualified by adverbial deixis) embraces myriad possible referents. With the language(s) we speak with native fluency, we may feel secure until we really start to examine it (them). Many of the puzzles we encounter in so doing are distant reflections of a time in which everything was alive and human beings shared their world with other creatures and with the "spirits" of places and things. Sometimes, when we look beneath the familiar skin of words we may find ourselves in a world in which our distant forebears would have felt more at home than we ourselves. How can I be said to be "flying" when sitting tight in an airplane; and how can entities like time "fly"? How is it possible to "marry" someone at the same time as being "married" by a minister of the Church? I come across the name "Dick", but how is it that I know immediately that Dick is a male; or "Jane" a female? And why is a hunter "someone who hunts" and a player "someone who plays" but an angler not someone who "angles"? (A person with a language disorder may sometimes find real difficulty in reconciling the "leaves" he turns in an album with the "leaves" growing on a tree. He or she consequently has to be helped by a therapist to overcome such scruples). Most people understandably find conundrums of this sort rather silly or tedious; exactly in the same way as a speaker of Navajo who would find it ridiculous to express "living or being alive" in any other way than "one moves about here and there".

Among the first in his own time to be convinced that language is a self-contained organization which imposes formal constraints on the range of possible experience available to speakers of a particular language, Sapir had this to say:

> Inasmuch as languages differ very widely in their systematization of fundamental concepts, they tend to be only loosely equivalent to each other as symbolic devices and are, as a matter of fact, incommensurable in the sense in which two systems of points in a plane are, on the whole, incommensurable to each other if they are plotted out with reference to differing systems of coordinates. (1964, 128)

Just as culture is the artefact of language, so language is the repository of culture. The epistemic subtleties of the Hopi language can "make things strange" to a speaker of Standard Average European. The latter admiring a new-looking red shirt might say something along the lines of *I like that new red shirt* or *That new red shirt – I like it.* Whereas the Hopi would begin by drawing a distinction between recognition and inference, a distinction made evident in the use of two separate sentences: *I see that it is red* (recognition) and *I see that it is new* (inference). Through formal constraints the Hopi language compels its users to make the distinction. Whorf, who made this observation, put the question:

> Does the Hopi language show here a higher plane of thinking, a more rational analysis of situations? Of course it does. In this field and in various others, English compared to Hopi is like a bludgeon compared to a rapier. (1956, 84-5)

Whether or not such a claim can be ascribed to Whorfian over-enthusiasm does not in the end really matter. *Logos* remains its own master, not subject to logical or grammatical restraints. Language as symbolic form, as a vehicle of *logos*, may adopt whatever "incarnation" best suits the tendencies of a particular language and its associated culture. All actual languages are repositories of tens, perhaps hundreds, of thousands of years of unrecorded poetic (in the sense of *poesis*) endeavour that continually brings together the raw undifferentiated material of our world and the shared life-world built up in speech, and endows what was previously formless with form and signification.

> A fair realization of the incredible degree of diversity of linguistic system that ranges over the globe leaves one with an inescapable feeling that the human spirit is inconceivably old; that the few thousand years of history covered by our written records are no more than the thickness of a pencil mark on the scale that measures our past experience on this planet; that the events of these recent milleniums spell nothing in any evolutionary wise, that the [human] race has taken no sudden spurt... but has only played a little with a few of the linguistic formulations and views of nature bequeathed from an inexpressibly longer past. (Whorf 1956, 218-9)

PART TWO

WORDS AND MEANING

8. What is Meaning?

Meaning is one of the most widely used of words. It crops up in
areas of activity and no one can pretend to be unfamiliar with its
We all in fact know the "meaning" of meaning but, when ask
specify what meaning might be, we find ourselves unable to prov
satisfactory answer, or we get sidetracked among the word's mu
"meanings" such as the ones supplied, now over half a century ag
Ogden and Richards (1949, 186-7).[1] We tend to be more conf
perhaps in expressing opinions about what meaning is **not**.

Meaning, many feel certain, is not a "something", not a men
other separable "content" inherent in individual words, serie
words, or sentences. They would prefer to stay clear of any explan
that smacks of "ghost-in-the-machine" dualism, of the kind impli
attempts by linguists to establish a reciprocal dualist linkage bet
form and meaning.[2]   More appealing to the modern lay mind mig
the views of those who in the company of Ludwig Wittgen
consider "the meaning of a word" to be "its use in the langu
(1963, 20), or even more operationally still, a function of spea
interactions and the interactional context in which they use langu
A pragmatic line of approach such as the one adopted, say, by Ste
Tyler (1978) is almost bound to win favour. In keeping with pre
day trends Tyler argues that texts are not absolute, finished en
whose meanings are merely "the sum of their sentences"; any mo
than spoken discourse in which "words spoken in a contex
vacuum could inspire only fear, not meaning" (1978, 385). Mea
Tyler says, should be considered "a subjective interpretation giv
utterances...[taking] into account their role relative to other utterar

the speech act in which they participate, and the context in which the speech act occurs."

Words read and utterances heard are generally construed as intentionally meaningful. Scant attention for example is paid to someone talking to himself or herself, or mouthing empty or inanely random verbiage. If the intention of the speaker is misconstrued (by another native-speaker) it is usually because a conventional interpretation intrudes, or because conventional notions of the speaker's intentions have been applied. Unless they have deliberately placed themselves in an information-receiving mode (as they might in making a telephone enquiry or in consulting some agency or individual) people hear largely what they expect to hear. A now familiar indication of this, originating in an experiment, is to arrive late at a cocktail gathering with some outrageous excuse, of the kind: "Sorry I'm late. It took me rather longer than I anticipated to kill my aunt" only to receive a standard response from the the host or hostess: "Not to worry. Glad you could come..."

When meaning is contingent and interpretations are wont to be negotiated within a shared language and real-life contexts, successful conversation does not require every single element of the other's utterances to be identified. Utterances are interpreted holistically: it is the gist or drift, as well as the key words and indicative verbal gestures, that are listened out for. Holistic interpretations ("She was saying something about..."), not verbatim records of what was actually said, tend to be recalled. Objective "meaning" becomes impossible to determine, even when the distortions and misunderstandings that occur in everyday conversation can be discounted. Even facts – since to become "facts" they have to be recounted or described – may be "managed" to support a particular interpretation, with however no intent to deceive, not least in forensic contexts.

A parallel and different approach is that developed by J.R.Firth and subsequently more fully elaborated by Michael Halliday. Firth denied that meaning resides in "hidden mental processes" and affirmed that meaning consists of "situational relations in a context of situation and in that kind of language which disturbs the air and other people's ears, as modes of behaviour in relation to other elements in the context of situation" (1957, 19). Meaning according to Firth is "the whole complex of functions which a linguistic form may have" (1957, 33).

Semantics then is not just another formal, if intangible, division of language structure, alongside phonology, morphology, lexicology or syntax, but a "bigger integration" through a context in which human participants are not only talking but actually **doing** things. Meaning, Firth maintained, is present at all levels in language, not just in complete sentences and longer stretches of discourse. Even the quality of the voice, Firth insisted, is part of meaning in what he termed the "phonetic mode". Words themselves vary in meaning without limit, to the extent that "each word when used in a new context is a new word" (1957, 190). Very little of this has anything to do with the grammatical structure of language. A single word can in rare instances project a universe of meaning: *holocaust*, for example. Conversely however, not every sentence will be a bearer of full meaning: *Take it or leave it*, although grammatically a sentence, cannot become a meaningful sentence without the context from which one is able to infer what "it" might refer to.[3]

Widely accepted within linguistics proper is the view taken by Halliday, that the multiplicity of language functions is likely to be "reflected somewhere in the internal organization of language itself." A functional framework designed to take into account the internal semantic and syntactic patterns of language, Halliday believes, will reveal the "potential of the language system." Thus, a functional theory along such lines as these will, he says, at the same time be a theory about meanings, and not about the surface forms of language themselves, as if meaning could be embedded in the "grammar" of language. Only if language is regarded as the equivalent of grammar (and that is not the view taken by the present writer) can it be seen as being a "network of interrelated options which define the resources for what the speaker wants to say" or "a totality of what the speaker can do" (Halliday 1975, 5). In acquiring its mother tongue a child, instead of being initiated by stages through the instrumentality of the lexicon and grammar into a shared world of meaning or language proper, is supposed to learn how to mean, since the linguistic system as such is "semantic potential".[4] Culture itself, in Halliday's view, is a semiotic system: " a system of meanings or information that is encoded in the behaviour potential of the members [of society], including their verbal potential – that is, their linguistic system" (1975, 36).

Between grammar and semantics, says Halliday, there exists no sharp divide (1985, xix). Every distinction recognized in the grammar contributes to the form of the wording; and it is the wording that "realizes" the meaning and "in turn is 'realized by' sound or writing." Halliday concedes that the relation is a symbolic one, but that "it is not possible to point to each symbol as an isolate and ask what it means; the meaning is encoded in the wording as an integral whole" (1985, xx).

Halliday is not the only linguist to have grappled with the problem of meaning in language, and his particular approach has much to recommend it. The view taken by the present writer however is that the endlessly plastic features of grammar and discourse, the organized patterns of sound, the intricately arranged sequences of sound (morphemes and word-forms) are no more than a rich repertoire of **means** by which meanings (always potential, as Halliday also recognizes) are realized and expressed. Were it not for the grammatical "bits" and the multifold forms available in a language there could be no linguistic meanings. Meanings are not after all disembodied "ghosts", nor are they abstract entities ready to be clothed with flesh. In the first place, any "flesh" would be found to be just as opaquely abstract as any potential semantic content. Secondly, and even more to the point, the grammatical "bits" and forms interact with whatever it is I want to say or express (my utterances) and can undergo transformations as a result of this interaction, a process that can profoundly affect the outcome of messages and interpretations. Thirdly, we cannot for this reason maintain that the "bits" of grammar are **anything more than** mere "bits", even though they have their particular origin in my own brain (grammatically speaking, none of us speaks the same language). They are subject, indirectly, to an unimaginably complex network of socio-cultural controls: to such a degree that the very form of any messages, and not only what was intended by them, will be heavily determined by what other members of the speech community use as their linguistic instruments. Lastly – and this will occupy most of Part Four of this book – words appear to be the junctures at which the two modes of language, different as they are claimed to be, find themselves in direct and dynamic encounter.

It is an encounter that seems to me primal, and one that makes language distinctively human. All creatures, from primates to viruses, appear to have developed communicative means of transmitting and exploiting information and, in all probability, some of the more highly developed mammals possess some capacity, however narrowly circumscribed or inchoate, akin to human shared awareness. But no creature other than man appears to be endowed with the capacity to bring means and intention into a single system, a "dynamo" evidently guaranteed by that mysterious but energetically active entity – *logos.*

Meaning is holistic, inherent in language as symbolic form: as Husserl was aware, meaning is a descriptive ultimate which cannot further be defined. But the question remains: What place and disposition does meaning have in a life-world? Meaning surely cannot be assigned to some metalinguistic plane of description, when it is inseparably involved in people's lives, at every point.

Human beings are not merely steeped in meaning. Paradoxically though it might seem, human beings are, all of them, **creators** of meaning. This is not the same as insisting that, whenever a person speaks, something new is uttered. All speakers obviously make use of ready-made "language", but they tend to displace prepackaged expressions in sometimes interesting ways and, more often than might be supposed, actually do say things that, if not always completely original, match the uniqueness of their personalities and context. Such variability, nowadays identified as "style", implies that meanings are created virtually all the time. It has been maintained, by more than one authority, that every time a word or phrase is uttered its application is unique, if only because the aleatory quality of personality and the transience of context are unrepeatable. Even the repetition of what someone else has said (or written) will result in a slight, virtually imperceptible, semantic-stylistic shift. The most sincere and careful verbatim spoken repetition will itself guarantee stylistic distortion. No one, it seems, can copy anyone else, however hard one tries. Mimicked speech may have its uses, but unless the intention is parody, mockery or the like, it cannot be considered to have "said" or "done" anything. Stylistic-semantic shifts are unlikely to leave any trace on the language as a whole unless they are captured (the most significant of them, that is) and welded into what seem in retrospect to be "new" meanings. Shakespeare far outstrips all others in this respect.[5]

But there is no such thing as new meaning, only changed outlooks and new life-worlds. Shakespeare was less a creator of new meaning than a powerful agent in changing – and, most important of all, lending a particular impetus (an impetus that would seem to be still in the ascendant judging by his undiminished popularity) and potent charge to – our shared vision. The devices by which Shakespeare achieved this, as poet and dramatist, are apparent throughout his work. A speaker has no need of an "interpreter" intermediary, but depends absolutely on himself or herself for any sort of illocutionary (*i.e.* the force inherent in speech acts) outcome. Utterance gains or loses depending on skill and imagination in handling meaning. This is equally true if the utterance is written, though in this case the reader is heavily involved in the determination of meaning. Within the inner world of the self there appears to be no theoretical limit to what can be achieved through meaning. The constraints are twofold. In the first place, as Bakhtin has pointed out, language is far from being a neutral medium (1981, 349). It is populated – overpopulated – with the words and intentions of others. In forming an utterance I am borrowing words from other people's mouths. Bakhtin showed, persuasively, how in the language of Dostoevsky's characters "there is a profound and unresolved conflict with another's word" whether on the level of the lived experience, or in others' ethical standpoints in relation to oneself, or within the characters' own conflicting worldviews.[6] In the second place one is up against the unpredictable scope of the imagination as well as the problematics of **reference**, a topic that has vast implications for anyone preoccupied, even momentarily, with the nature of reality. The world "out there" impinges on meaning only to the extent that the shared language mode interfaces with the organic language mode; it remains subordinate, and even then only indirectly, to the physical and informational constraints affecting the latter mode.

Every speaker needs a listener (even if the listener happens to be oneself); every writer a reader. The speaker or writer creates, but the listener or reader **also** creates. A speaker says something that may never have been said before; the listener hears what is being said and winkles out of it a meaning that is also new. The difference between the two "meanings" – the speaker's and the hearer's – can be significant even though in all non-crucial instances, in everyday low-key interactions and negotiations that is, the difference can be discounted. Among close acquaintances when what the speaker "says" and the listener "hears" is **felt** to be identical, they are often said to be "on the same wavelength". As the "meaning gap" approaches zero, the participants in a real interaction will tend to subject their speech to various kinds of reduction: they will almost always abbreviate, leaving sentences unfinished or the ends of sentences inaudible, they will indulge in ellipsis, faulty cohesion, and so forth. But everything that is said and heard takes place within shared meanings and a shared life-world. Being human implies a spontaneous capacity, if not always to thrive, at least to hold one's own, however precariously; to orientate oneself in this world of meanings, never as a passive receiver but always in greater or lesser degree as an active creator of meaning. Meaning is perhaps neither linguistic, nor semiotic, but an inalienable part of human being.

Meaning is not divisible into parcels or measures; it is potential rather than actual. There appears to be no limit to the richness of meaning that can be engendered by the same utterance in different contexts. This is especially noticeable in written language. The same book or poem may be read time and time again by the same reader but each reading yields a new meaning in the perception and imagination of the reader. The same thing of course can happen with music and the other arts, but significant differences when they do occur usually stand out, and take one by surprise. With reading, disparity between interpretations is a routine occurrence, and usually passes unnoticed.

What ultimately then is the nature of the medium that allows speaker and listener, writer and reader, to create and re-create their meanings dependently, and yet at the the same time independently of each other, mostly without their being aware of any discrepancy? For an answer we return to Cassirer, who proposed that symbolic forms do not simply reflect what is empirically given, but **produce** it independently. Cassirer stresses that the symbolic forms are not different modalities in which an independent reality manifests itself but the different paths by which the human spirit proceeds towards its own objectivization or self-revelation (1953, I, 78). Meaning is the generated and generating symbolism underlying all language. This symbolism is present in all utterances whether profound or trivial. It permeates the intersubjective mode of language as well as every kind of verbal interaction, from the unremarkable "Sure!" "Gotcher!" "Well, you know..." to the oracular "Know thyself" or *Tat tvam asi.* This symbolic source is not to be conceived of as a kind of unlimited supply on tap, but as a special power present in human beings. Coleridge considered it a living power, a "repetition in the finite mind of the eternal act of creation in the infinite I AM" ([1817] 1962, 159), a reference to the unprecedented Hebraic conception of the Deity, which also played such a formative part in the development of Christian theology, and even in "Pagan" Renaissance humanist philosophies no less than in later secular ideologies. The reader may well feel that the foregoing discussion seems to have taken us too far from the practicalities of meaning in language. Why did we not start out from and on the whole keep to the kind of pragmatic, commonsense approach to meaning favoured, say, by Halliday or Tyler? There are probably many reasons why not, and all of them belong to an uncharted terrain hitherto largely unexplored by philosophy or linguistics. One aspect of language and meaning that has never been pursued specifically or systematically is one that finds no ready expression in our vocabulary. In psychology "affectivity" serves well, but the lay person might prefer the vaguer term "emotion". Freud gave it the name "libido". For all the lexical ambivalence, in English at least, it is doubtful whether language as a "symbolic form" would have come into being without a powerful driving force for which we have only vague, inadequate or purely technical designations. It is an *x*-factor, an unknown and unknowable force, that takes us inevitably into the Unconscious, into a domain that can only be "read", through the complex semiotic relationship between linguistic categories and functions on the one hand, and between the same linguistic categories and the unrepresented on the other. The link between the Unconscious and art, myth and religion has come very much to the fore since the time of Freud and Jung. But the Unconscious in language symbolism has been largely neglected, the writings Jacques Lacan being one significant exception.

Recent studies in empirical psychology have revealed that young infants, long before they are able to talk, are highly and complexly emotional. Their reactions to what goes on around them cannot be summed up in cold stimulus-response terms, but have to be qualified by sometimes intense internal states of feeling. These states are expressed in "subtly coded postures and attitudes, gestures, facial expressions and cries." It has been found that "infant and mother could enter into a mutual regulation of expressive moves as tightly organized as the performance of well-matched and highly practised dancers or musicians in duet."[7] Just as the newly born show awareness of the prosody and rhythmic regularity of human vocalization, so mothers, instinctively it appears, "make characteristic repeated cries with a falling intonation, greeting the child." These utterances, it is claimed, are "spaced to a regular beat" and "can lead the infant to move in sympathy, on the same beat." There is evidence also that even before birth the distinctive qualities of the mother's voice are learned. Interestingly, this faculty of mutuality has been termed Innate Intersubjectivity, an apparently inborn awareness of the subjective consciousness of the "other" as well as the "self". The success of the child's attempts at self-expression is said to depend on an "appropriate complementary expression of acts of meaning from the other," mother and child working in unison with a "dual representation of the 'self and other'." The whole of language, it is claimed, finds its earliest manifestations, though not necessarily its origins, in the "pleasure" sounds, the "coos" and vocal expressions of the young infant.[8]

Another facet of meaning, all but overlooked except perhaps by exponents of the New Criticism, has been brought sharply into relief in recent years by the French poet, critic, and anti-dualist Henri Meschonnic (1982). This has to do with what may be characterized, to risk a solecism, as the underlying linguistic form of the symbol.

Meschonnic's starting point is a brief but dazzling inquiry by Benveniste (1971, 281ff.) into the origins of the Greek concept *rhythmos*. After setting out his reasons for rejecting generally accepted etymological derivations of the word "rhythm" from the movement of waves or flowing water, Benveniste was able to show that *rhythmos* is more akin in meaning to form and more specifically to "distinctive form, proportionate arrangement, and disposition" (1971, 285). In early Greek the word *rhythmos*

> designates the form in the instant that it is assumed by what is moving, mobile and fluid, the form of that which does not have organic consistency; it fits the pattern of a fluid element, of a letter arbitrarily shaped, of a robe which one arranges at one's will, of a particular state of character or mood. It is the form as improvised, momentary, changeable. (1971, 285-6)

Meschonnic holds that rhythm and meaning are the same thing, but are present together only in discourse. The union of rhythm and meaning, Meschonnic maintains, is the outcome of a particular confluence of social and historical conditions, as well as the unique expression of particular individual beings: in short, a dialectic of the uniquely personal and the social.

In Meschonnic's view rhythm has little to do with metre or metrics.

Nor has rhythm anything in common with what is conventionallyunderstood by it. Rhythm is engendered not only by stress, pitch and metre but as well by syntax, collocation, metaphor and metonymy, by "intertextuality", by irony, even by logic; in sum, by what John Crowe Ransom termed "indeterminate meaning"[9] – the supra-logical supplement to any rational train of thought. Any or all of these factors may contribute to the unfolding of rhythm, or the sum-total of the meaning brought into being in the particular moment of discourse. In this way, form and sense appear not as a Saussurean duality, but as functions of a continuum which yields tone, mood and feeling, together with an objectively and logically patterned meaning and being.

Sense, according to Meschonnic, is created by the "rhythm" of a unit of discourse and is unique to that particular text. It cannot be reproduced without exactly replicating it in the time and place the particular meaning was produced, exactly as that actual unit of discourse or text in its entirety. This could not be perfectly achieved, even by a tape recording or video tape, in that the context is bound to be different. Nor could paraphrase succeed without creating a different sense. Sense begets rhythm, just as rhythm has always generated sense. Because of the inseparability of meaning and rhythm, a rhythmic configuration becomes at the same time a sense grouping (Meschonnic 1982, 215). Furthermore, rhythm cannot be anything fixed, inasmuch as a sense is something generated by a subject whose individual value is unique and unrepeatable. One striking illustration is Shakespeare's use of the everyday phrase "Give me your hand". First occurring in *Julius Caesar,* when Cassius says:

> *Do you confess so much? Give me your hand.*

and Brutus replies

> *And my heart too.*

the phrase occurs a second time in *The Merchant of Venice*, when the Duke receives the disguised Portia with the simple greeting:

> *Give me your hand. Came you from old Bellario?*

In these two apparently unremarkable uses the intonation, metre and pace are different. The second suggests a slight impulsion, with anticipation, while the first breathes compassion and a warmth of purpose that belies the ambivalence of Brutus' reply (Meschonnic 1982, 147). The seasoned actor will be an intuitive master of such variation, and might well concede that if one gets the rhythm right (both in the traditional and in the ontological sense proposed by Meschonnic) the meaning becomes transparent. Real discourse unfolds in accordance with its own "rhythm" within a particular time-shape, which resonates through the entire medium of an actual language, and even beyond.[10] Meaning thus becomes an activity of an utterance-bearing subject and, since rhythm is the organization of meaning in discourse, it is necessarily a configuration of the same subject within discourse.

Consequently, a theory of rhythm becomes a matter of ontology, to the extent that it is at the same time a theory of the subject in the act of speaking (Meschonnic 1982, 507ff.). Rhythm, in the new scope given it by Meschonnic, embodies and guarantees the creative and artistic essence of meaning as it manifests itself both in the speaking individual and in the shared mode of language. In the medium of meaning there are of course outstanding creators and performers, not to mention distinguished connoisseurs, but everyone in greater or lesser degree is a creator, performer and connoisseur rolled into one. The language of the streetcorner is no more exempt from artistic criteria and creative possibilities than the language of the poet: something few of our poets and writers have overlooked.

9. Meaning and Symbol

It will be recalled that in Chapter Five we took as our starting point the metaphysics of Cassirer and, in particular, his vision of language as a symbolic form and his emphasis on the primacy of language as the mediator between the individual, other human beings, and nature, as well as on the creative function of symbolism. Peirce's now well-known attempt, the most far-reaching and successful to date, to explicate the nature of signs was then touched upon (and elaborated in more detail in *Note 1* of Chapter Five). Lastly, attention was drawn to the unique insight of Saussure into the linguistic sign as a marker of difference when profiled against other signs. In the present chapter one of my foremost concerns will be to steer a steady course between, on the one hand, the dualism that inevitably arises through attempts to distinguish between linguistic form ("signifier") and semantic content ("signified") which few of those following in the wake of Saussure have managed to escape and, on the other hand, the kind of monism which assigns meaning limitlessly to the "whole of the linguistic system and its parts" (Benveniste 1971, 108).

The first point to be highlighted is that nothing exists that is already formed and simply awaiting an instance of signification. Leibniz, a forerunner of modern (as opposed to positivistic) scientific thinking, recognized (long before Peirce) that the sign serves as a means of discovery, offering not only a symbolic abbreviation for what is already known but also opening up new pathways into the unknown. If language were merely a copy, in a different medium, of pre-existent sensations and intuitions, it would long since have been found wanting and virtually given up. Why bother to expend, and allow one's children to expend, large amounts of time and effort in acquiring and mastering a complex signifying system – a language – if all it can do is notate, catalogue, repeat, translate, or classify what is already actual in perception, sensation, cognition or culture? Although we may not always be aware of it, language as a signifying entity has become the engine of our lives. Most crucially, language imposes form upon and makes sense of the "buzzing, blooming confusion" that would otherwise make not only an ordered social life, but even conscious life as such, impossible.[1] Nor are signs static ready-made entities. It can even said, with Cassirer, that the being of a sign consists entirely in its signification. Meaning is not even potential content (awaiting signification) but arises only in and through the sign itself.

Saussure was quite definite on this last point. He compared the linguistic sign to a sheet of paper whose opposite sides are two facets of one inseparable whole – signifier and signified – in such a way that neither side of the paper can be cut without cutting the other. For Saussure a signifier could not exist without a signified, and *vice versa*. Further, without the sign, there could be neither form nor meaning. But this in no way implies a biplanarity of the kind that preoccupied some of Saussure's successors. Saussure himself was at pains to emphasize that sign is not some hypostatized entity but an indicator of difference; not structure, but energy.

As against this, the opposite extreme will not do either. Although their overall approach to symbolism and signification could be confusing,[2] Ogden and Richards (1949) ingeniously argued that meaning is entirely a function of context. According to them it is this that lends individual words and verbal expressions their apparent multiplicity of signification (polysemy). They considered context to be

> a set of entities (things or events) related in a certain way; these entities have each a character such that other sets of entities occur having the same characters and related by the same relation; and these occur nearly uniformly. (1949, 58)

The meaning of a word, Ogden and Richards argued, is only fully comprehended when it has been contextualized. Meaning is a mere product of the components of context.[3] Although they were ready to concede that symbols and referents are complex, they were conscious also of the complexity of context in which the symbol is embedded. In their view the "component symbols", within the symbol taken as a whole, form a context of a "higher type" entailing a weaving together of contexts into still higher contexts (1949, 220). Ogden and Richards nevertheless remained seemingly committed to the axiom that "one symbol stands for one and only one referent" (1949, 88) regardless of the complexity of the symbol or its referent. This may have saved the appearances of logic but, as a consequence, signification becomes burdened with unnecessarily cumbersome specifications. Saussure's approach seems more elegant and suffers from no such one-to-one interdependence between signs and their referents which introduces an element of circularity and casts incidental doubt on a theory of context as the generator of meaning, a process which cannot even be satisfactorily described, let alone proved or disproved.

Signs can indeed provide, if only after the fashion of a shadow play, information about the world beyond language, whether this be the external physical world or the unconscious and semi-conscious contents of the hidden depths of the inner world, but they do not in any way furnish knowledge of the nature of those worlds. Signs, as Ogden and Richards were far from being the first to affirm, are never pictures of reality. Their familiar triangle[4] which introduces an intermediate and mediating stage between symbol and referent aligns them with those who would remove this "once universal theory of direct meaning relations between words and things," on the grounds that choice of symbolism is determined in part by the particular reference intended, and in part by "social and psychological factors", by which is meant the purpose behind reference, the proposed effect of the symbols on others and on one's own attitude.

At the centre of all this debate stands the sign, together with its function – signification. All the rest is peripheral: the means, the mechanisms, be they cognitive, affective, linguistic, social or cultural, which enable human beings – in the intersubjectivity of their life-world ultimately – to interpret what is being said. Whatever the limits to this interpretative process they are never purely cognitive, never purely dependent on linguistic forms or functions. Nor are they ever solely dependent on the abstract structure of social relations, nor even on cultural or aesthetic norms. As for language (as opposed to linguistic or grammatical processes) it manifests itself integrally in human terms, in all the undivided polysemantic richness of the word "meaning".

The complexity of the play of signification in human motivation shows in a comparison of the following group of statements:

(1) *A cat sat on the mat.*
(2) *A cat was sitting on the mat.*
(3) *A tiger was sitting on the mat.*

Sentence (1) is the proverbial textbook example, devoid of any semiotic or illocutionary dynamic, or of what we have so far been trying to identify as meaning. (Linguists might not always agree with what has just been said, in that the statement makes perfect "sense" and is thus semantically valid). Sentence (2) although it has undergone a simple grammatical transformation, into a different "tense", does possess limited semiotic motivation, the cat being somehow easier to visualize. But in sentence (3) it is no longer simply a question of one lexical item (*tiger*) replacing another (*cat*) – that is about all that happens according to descriptive linguistics – but of a qualitatively different world unfolding.

The traditional linguist's grammatical and lexical concerns have in no way touched reality. Ethnographically speaking, in English at least, "tiger" belongs to the taxonomic category of large felines or, alternatively, along with "bear", "elephant" and other large-sized creatures, to the childhood set of nursery-neutralized dangerous animals. In real terms the presence of "tiger" takes us into a sharply remote realm of experience and feeling, into the improbable, alarming and incongruous. A "tiger" can hardly be imagined as "sitting on a mat" in quite the same way as a domesticated feline. "Tiger" not only dominates the immediate context, but any subsequent stretch of discourse, right along to the point at which the range of semiotic can be neutralized. In this particular instance the neutralization may be considered automatic since an innocuous game of supplying language samples is being played. But when no neutralization is forthcoming as, say, in Blake's *The Tyger* the effect on readers will be directly proportional to their personal response to the unearthly diction of the poem and their capacity for distancing themselves from games played with "lexical substitution counters". In less sophisticated societies, of course, words are hedged around by sometimes deadly taboos: words can literally maim, or even kill. Even in modern urban settings they may not always be completely harmless.

Even the function of "empty" words like the definite and indefinite articles – as Ogden and Richards appear to deny in their suggestion that structural elements are the business of grammar (1949, 88) – can become symbols in their own right. Note what would happen if *A tiger* were changed to *The tiger* in sentence (3). "The" can be seen to have assumed an indexical (in the sense proposed by Peirce) character. Among the range of meanings released from the complex symbol ("the tiger") various new concerns are suddenly implied. The tiger could now be one that I have heard about or seen previously. It looks like being a partly tame tiger, especially as it has taken to sitting on mats (by comparison with "a tiger" when one wonders what it could be doing there. Could someone be mistaken?). To change *A cat...* to *The cat...* on the other hand entails no such symbolic motivation: both phrases verge on the semiotically neutral (though "the" is still indexical and a difference shows up even if at a purely "business of grammar" level). In actual fact it is the articles and other "unmotivated", so-called "empty" words that permit (at times epiphanic) glimpses into the functioning of language in relation to our unconscious selves.

*   *   *

Peirce thought that the meaning of a sign is some further sign or group of signs into which the original sign is transformed and more fully developed. Signification, while being in one sense a closed circuit, is in a more important sense boundless, reminiscent perhaps of a post-Einsteinian universe. Going further than Saussure is Benveniste's claim that in being universal or generic the sign has the advantage of standing outside the order of discourse. In the sign everything individual, everything contingent or circumstantial, is excluded. Signs have no reference to any external real world but only to other signs within the system:

> In the sign we have reached the intrinsic reality of language... and whereas the constitutive counterpart of the sign is the signified, which

is inherent to the sign, the sense of the sentence implies reference to the discourse situation and the speaker's attitude. (Ricoeur 1975, 74)

Any phenomenological equation between meaning and the shared mode of language must then be ruled out, even if meanings appear and are interpreted only within that mode. Meaning entails the whole of language, and therefore both language modes together; and especially the **interaction** between these modes. Language devoid of meaning in this full sense is a mere simulacrum. The source and origin of meaning is to be found in neither mode of language, but only in signs. True language cannot occur without signification (meaning in an active pragmatic sense). But signs themselves remain unpredictable. They can "erupt" unexpectedly in any region of the shared language mode. For signification to register it needs to be able to follow certain pathways and to reach certain junctures, at which a sign can be recognized as a sign of **something**. There would be no point in a signifying system in which signs were random and detectable only by chance. In my particular cultural environment for example a wave of the hand represents a gesture with the **potential** for becoming significant in any one or more of a range of possible ways. It may be a sign of recognition, a greeting, a beckoning, or a warning, to mention only the more salient possibilities. In order for the sign to be interpreted in an appropriate manner, it requires a framework of flexibly structured schemata of semiotic conventions that will make relevant interpretations possible. An at least partial knowledge of these schemata would thus constitute a person's command of the shared language mode. In modern parlance such a schema is known as a **code**.

Nowadays, code is a concept so widely adopted that few stop to consider what the term means. Only the more literally minded lay much insistence on the fact that code is a technical metaphor only; which along with other well-established technical metaphors has yet to prove its usefulness. And only sticklers for established lexical conventions would press the contention that only in strictly defined and "codified" inventories of signs – the Morse Code or the Highway Code for instance – can what Saussure called tthe "signified" be derived unambiguously from a "signifier"; or in the type of code precisely formulated by communication engineers ("an agreed transformation, usually one to one and reversible, by which messages may be converted from one set of signs to another") one that has been devised for some specific purpose and follows explicit rules (Cherry 1957, 187); or, finally, in those forms of code which are believed to be the outcome of biological evolution, as in genetics. If an **anti**metaphorical approach is to be even slightly adhered to, it would have to be insisted that "messages" can be "coded" in no other circumstances than when one set of signs can be algorithmically transformed into another set, in a manner already prescribed by a transmitter and a receiver, and can be read unambiguously. But we have seen that this is not how "messages" are "communicated" in language. Even the most liberal interpretation of this procedure would allow only that certain rather limitied functions of language can be described as code-like, as when discrete chunks of information can be said to be "coded" within a rigid scheme in which both transmitter and receiver know in advance what sort of message is to be "encoded" or "decoded", as for example in the following set of instructions: "Take a quantity p of x and add to it a quantity q of y. Then put the resulting mixture into an oven at $r \, ^{\circ} F$ and bake for n minutes." But, as most people would probably accept, this is language only in a highly restricted sense, mere coded instruction. It may be true that, since the time of Bacon, "instructional" language has become increasingly dominant in our lives. But, in its code-likeness, such usage can be relegated to a safely circumscribable domain of language, useful in its own way but lacking most of the essential features of language.

In recent times, and particularly in semiotics, the term "code" has come to be used in a perplexing variety of ways, having travelled quite far along its metaphorical trajectory, and taken on meanings capable of creating something of a problem. There seems to be no general agreement among the exponents of semiotics as to what a code in this transformed sense might be, and the concept itself calls for some careful examination. A consensus has yet to be reached as to what this new range of signification might be.[5]

Halliday's adaptation of Bernstein's definition of code – the principle by which semiotic organization can be said to govern the choice of meanings by a speaker and their interpretation by a hearer – may at first seem unexceptionable (Halliday 1978). Unnecessary problems arise, however, in separating code from language, and in placing it somehow "above" language and within the "symbolic orders of meaning generated by the social system"; when the concept of an intersubjective shared mode of language not only does not require such a separation but insists on the seamlessness of meaning – both within language in the strict sense and within the organization of social meaning in social institutions more generally. With this reservation declared I can however accept that "codes transmit or control the transmission of the underlying patterns of a culture or subculture." But it should be observed, in passing, that only in a shallow and more limited form can this transmission be achieved through "the socializing agencies of family, peer group and school" (Halliday 1978, 111). Codes of this nature, if we can assume their reality, must form an integral part of our life-world. Somehow we have had to learn them but, paradoxically, we already know them.

A "semiotic code", it has been said, does not in itself organize signs but furnishes only the rules which **generate** signs, themselves cultural units in the sense proposed by Quine.[6] An alternative way of approaching the problem would be to suggest that, although the relation between signifier and signified is always conventional, this relation may not be objectively demonstrable, but is more likely to be based on something "more intuitive, vague and subjective." There has to be a stage at which signification progressively dissolves into a system of hermeneutic interpretation. At this stage the sign would be only "more or less codified" (Guiraud 1975, 24). More rigorously, Umberto Eco attempts to define code in relation to signification (sign-function) both in itself as well as in its combinatorial possibilities within a particular context, the code thus becoming not only a "correlational rule" but also a "set of combinatorial rules." By such a means a "complex social type of competence" of the type manifested in language becomes interpretable not as a single unidimensional code but as a system of interconnected codes.[7]

In order to cope with the immense complexity of language, and with the mysteries of signification in particular, an originally simplistic notion of code has ramified into a concept embracing a system or network of codes and "subcodes". The latter are said to possess none of the definitive quality of codes as traditionally understood, but are supposed to be "transitory phenomena" impossible to establish or characterize as stable structures. To cap this, a "hypercode" has been proposed, under which would be gathered the various subcodes "some of which happen to be strong and stable, while others are weak and transient." All of which leaves one with the heady paradox that, although a message may be seen as a network of different messages depending on a repertoire of many different codes operating within different ranges of constraint, it does not appear to rely, despite its having to be capable nonetheless of being understood, on previously established codes. Caught in a "strange loop" the interpreter, working within a network of codes, is obliged to challenge these very same codes,

> to advance interpretive hypotheses that work as more comprehensive, tentative and prospective forms of codification. Faced with uncoded circumstances and complex contexts, the interpreter is obliged to recognize that the message does not rely on previous codes. (Eco 1976, 129)

The inevitable conclusion from all this must be that code-changing and code-production are built into any human semiotic.

Curiously, and as if surreptitiously, the current semiotic profile of "code" appears to be already written into the semantic of the word *code*.[8] Perhaps inevitably, code has grown into a concept implying negotiation, interface, exchange, elasticity, changeability, malleability. Seen from this angle a code resembles an organism which is highly responsive to the environment and the moment: in one direction tending towards the conventional, in the opposite direction towards the individual and unrepeatable. Correspondingly, the range of code stretches from the one extreme of the public-conventional to another extreme of the intimate and personal. Needless to say, code in this semiotic sense must be wholly confined to the shared mode of language; though this is not to rule out the possibility of different kinds of code operating in a more organic and completely unconsciously motivated mode.

Inasmuch as a (shared language mode) code is intersubjective it can make its appearance in almost any situation, even though its existence may be transient and unrepeatable. Relations between friends will be codified in less rigid, but more exclusive, forms than the ones these same friends, separately, might deploy in more public situations. Communicating with a professional colleague, say, is both easier and more difficult than communicating with a close friend. Depending on circumstances the former may call for a fair amount of socio-semiotic sophistication though a lesser degree of person-to-person sensitivity.

The latter by contrast demands a different order of semiotic prowess. In English for example, socially neutral locutions such as *Hello* or *How are you?* may be perfectly harmless when addressed to an everyday acquaintance, but can sound "cold" or "distant" to a close friend. In the latter instance much depends on the real-life context. If the close friendship happens to be an amorous one, the range of codes will again differ, depending heavily on the particularity of the relationship and the personalities of the lovers. Such codes can be exceptionally finely tuned, as exemplified by the intense and mutually destructive relationships that can, unforeseeably but dramatically, develop between lovers – between Vronsky and Anna Karenina, to take a supreme if fictional example.

Codes, if that is their appropriate designation, must lie at the very foundation of the shared language mode. Without them, sign or symbol would escape interpretation, and concepts would remain undifferentiated, or void even. Codes change constantly and without assignable limit. They share the prodigious adaptability of much of what else is known about human beings, and appear to be no less complex than neural-cerebral processes (insofar as these are at present understood). All the while, one has to keep reminding oneself that a code is something different from a cypher, which carries a high functional load. Empirical studies of the speech code for instance reveal that the actual physical signal is very poor.[7] And, although not in itself arbitrary, the speech code would appear so to "an intelligent but inarticulate cryptanalyst from Mars." Happily, human beings are not dependent on temporal cues when identifying acoustic events. The resultant efficiency of a speech code, with its huge difference in "cost" between signal transmission and auditory reception, further bears out the phenomenologists' claim that communication in the transmission-reception sense is an illusion. Messages, it may be recalled from an earlier discussion, are not "received" but reconstructed and interpreted. The physical signal therefore seems likely to be far less crucial in communication than an awareness of the multi-layered codes of very different sorts – whether in the shared mode (semantic, socio-semiotic and cultural functions) or in the instrumental mode of language (processing, distribution and channelling of information) – that underlie the greater part of our ability to lead normal, reasonably fruitful lives.

The life-world that is ours, whatever else it might be, resembles an endlessly ramified concatenation of a nevertheless seamless creative symbolism endowed with form and function by a bewilderingly intricate and versatile network of codes. At this point, and at the risk of complicating matters still further, I would like to introduce a working distinction between signs and symbols. Signs I will take to be those emanations of things, events and contexts which hold a certain value for oneself personally. In his exploration of signs Gilles Deleuze (1976,71) has suggested that learning (*apprentissage*) is accomplished not by the assimilation of content but through the intermediary of signs. Each stage of *apprentissage*, Deleuze reckons, has its own *ligne de temps*, which one is tempted to identify primarily as a "cognitive-aesthetic" code relating intimately to the life experience of the individual person, as opposed to a "socio-cultural" code that does not necessarily have any such relation. Both types of code have to be acquired through an *apprentissage* appropriate to the particular mode. This *apprentissage* will often be self-initiated and may unfold purely out of the signs themselves to which, over a period of time, the "apprentice" becomes attuned, especially in the case of a "skill" for which no mentor is to hand. Original thinkers, artists, poets, visionaries, prominent scientists must all have followed this path at some time in their lives.

The signs that prove most seminal will often "erupt" (Deleuze emphasizes the "violent effect of the sign") in ways unrelated to the immediate concerns of the "apprentice". Mozart at his billiard table or in the company of his pet starling come to mind, or Gogol's secret need to deck himself out after the manner of his characters when writing about them, or even more obviously Archimedes and his apocryphal bath. The codes guiding the interpretation of such signs are only in varying degrees personally idiosyncratic; they find their locus in a cultural nexus in which the novice may undergo overt "initiation". Incomparable though they may be – for the piano "Grade Eight", for university rowing a "Blue", for scholarship acceptance of learned papers, and so forth – signs may range from the meretricious, as with the demi-monde and fashion, to ones laden with longlasting significance as when people fall in love, undergo religious conversion, or die. The former sort gain what reality they momentarily come to possess solely from the codes, even though affectivity may express itself "significantly" in "nervous exaltation" (Deleuze 1976, 13). In a social gathering, where small-talk revolves around an axis of unladen signification, a particular guest in the course of a conversation with just such another guest may signal that he or she is about to say something funny, when the other detecting the sign will respond with laughter, even though what is being said may not be amusing by any objective measure.

Whatever the nature or quality of a particular sign, affectivity or motivation must be present. This applies even in the case of empty signs, as is obvious from the effervescence of sociable pleasure in all but the dullest cocktail parties; no less so, though at a very different intensity, than in the extraordinary case of romantic love, when the signs are copious and unfailingly imbued with fascination. When these erupt,

> the beloved takes on the appearance of a sign... [and] expresses a world of possibility unknown to us. The beloved implies, envelops, imprisons a world that has to be deciphered, that is to say, interpreted. Not a single world, but a plurality of worlds... To be in love is to try to explain, to develop these unknown worlds that lie wrapped within the beloved. (Deleuze 1976, 14) (English version mine)

Signs are indeed transient things. Their career depends not only on the objects and events from which they emanate but just as much and perhaps even more so on the emotive impulse and motivation of the interpreter. Symbols on the other hand appear to be more complex configurations, more permanent entities, akin to institutions. Yet, in other ways they do resemble signs writ large, both in their multivalency and in their self-revelatory structuring of difference. As will be seen, words can be either signs or symbols in this sense and sometimes, as indicated by the range of their semantics, both at once.

To illustrate the distinction I have selected a rather complex symbol from social anthropology, in particular from a study of the Ndembu community of Zambia, which has been richly documented in this respect (Turner 1967).

In the course of his analysis of Ndembu ritual symbolism Victor Turner found he was making little progress until he brought this symbolism in relation to other social events and phenomena:

> The ritual symbol becomes a factor in social action, a positive force in an activity field. The symbol becomes associated with human interests

purposes, ends and means... the structure and properties of a symbol become those of a dynamic entity, at least within its appropriate context of action. (1967, 20)

Turner takes as his model the latex-bearing tree known to the Ndembu community as the "milk tree". According to the Ndembu women the "milk tree" represents milk from human breasts as well as the breasts that supply it. The same tree also serves as a symbol of the social ties binding mother and child. It is a centre of ritual ceremonies: beneath it young men are circumcised. Even the abstract principle of matriliny, if only one aspect of it, is reflected in and has become "an element in the semantic structure of the milk tree":

Some of the meanings of the important symbols may themselves be symbols, each with its own system of meanings. At its highest level of abstraction, therefore, the milk tree stands for the unity and continuity of Ndembu society. (Turner 1967, 21)

What is more, the symbolism of the Ndembu milk tree serves to harmonize and promote social cohesiveness, in particular the aspect of dependence. The child depends on its mother for its nourishment so the men of the tribe "drink from the (metaphorical) breasts of tribal custom." In this way the milk tree equates nourishment and learning (Deleuze's *apprentissage*) in its context of meaning:

Symbols produce action, and dominant symbols tend to become focuses of interaction. Groups mobilize around them, worship before them, perform other symbolic activities near them, and add other symbolic objects to them, often to make composite shrines. (Turner 1967, 22)

In certain contexts the milk tree can also, at closer range so to speak, represent a female novice. Her particular tree, in that it is a sapling, symbolizes her new social personality as a mature woman. With characteristic ambiguity the milk tree in its "action context" at the same time gives expression to the conflict from now on existing between the girl-novice and the community of adult women she is about to enter. Here the tree takes on a more sinister aspect as "the place of death" or "place of suffering" since the would-be adults of both sexes experience duress beneath its cover. Over and above all this is the aspect of emotional release, a function always to be tied in with symbols. The ritual aspects are not relegated to the realm of the abstract but are brought into direct contact with powerful emotional stimuli: music, dancing, singing, rhythm, strong liquor, incense, bizarre apparel and so forth. In so operating, "the ritual symbol effects an interchange of qualities between its poles of meaning."

Finally, the cultural bias of the observer becomes itself a problem, for which reason an attempt has to be made to conceptualize the ritual symbol as "a force in a field of action." Only thus can its "critical properties of condensation, polarization, and unification of disparities become intelligible and explicable." The danger is one of "conceptualizing the symbol as if it were an object" and in looking for aspects of symbolism which can "logically and consistently be related to one another to form an abstract unitary system":

> the unity of a symbol or a symbolic configuration appears as the result of many tendencies converging towards one another from different areas of biophysical and social existence. The symbol is an independent force which is itself a product of many opposed forces. (Turner 1967, 45)

The dangers of cultural distortion which Turner believes apply particularly to tribal symbolism can also be seen to apply more universally to all symbolism. Symbols are undeniably "independent forces", endlessly absorbing ones at that, sufficiently so to engage human curiosity and ingenuity for an indefinitely long time to come. It is a tantalizing thought, but one not so easy to entertain, that symbols and signs, might be all that there is.

10. A Manner of Speaking

Meaning in language changes continually. The factors underlying language change are many and various, and are still undergoing fundamental review.[1] Perhaps the most important agent in changing or extending the sense of a word is metaphor. Metaphor has traditionally been regarded as a device of rhetoric, and little more than that. But in recent years presuppositions regarding the nature of metaphor have been undergoing radical change.

According to a tradition traceable as far back as Aristotle, metaphor has been said to be the application to one thing of a name belonging to another thing. An "idol of the market" by the time of Locke, figurative language, and rhetoric in general, had come to be considered a major obstacle in the way of "truth and knowledge".[2] It was generally believed that the literal (or standard) sense of a word, the real and only valid sense, was already in existence when its figurative or transferred sense developed. In the beginning for example it was supposed that there was only the "leaf" of a plant or tree and the "hands" at the extremities of the arms but through the corrosive effect of metaphor "leaf" also came to mean "a page of a book" and "hands" the "hands of a clock". Thus, when a metaphorical sense obtains – when for example an instruction reads: "Add several more loose leaves..." – the literal meaning is supposed to be temporarily suspended: that is, we are meant to believe that for the time being one no longer thinks of the leaves of a tree unless a deliberately poetic connotation is intended.

This was the classical view. According to this view, the metaphorical "leaf" was considered no more than an ornamental, and hence dispensable, way of saying "page of a book". But dissenting

voices have become more frequent.
Metaphorical extension of meaning, it is now argued, simply does
not happen. A metaphor, it now appears, does not achieve its effect by
taking on any special meaning. In the words of Donald Davidson:

> The central mistake... is the idea that metaphor has, in addition to its
> literal sense or meaning, another sense or meaning. The idea is
> common to many who have written about metaphor... The concept of
> metaphor as primarily a vehicle for conveying ideas, even if unusual
> ones, seems to me as wrong as the parent idea that a metaphor has a
> special meaning... I agree with the view that metaphors cannot be
> paraphrased, but I think this is not because metaphors say something
> too novel for literal expression, but because there is nothing there to
> paraphrase.[3]

Paul Ricoeur, though from a different standpoint, has pursued a
comparable line of inquiry. At the outset Ricoeur reveals the extent to
which philosophers and students of rhetoric alike have been misled by
the classical view. A metaphor, he claims, is not only a figure of
speech; it belongs integrally to the structure of propositions. Exactly in
the same manner as any predicate a "metaphor bears information
because it re-describes reality" (Ricoeur 1975, 22). Subscribing to the
even more radical view of Gadamer, Ricoeur argues that a
"metaphoric" is "at work, at the origin of logical thought, at the root of
all classification."[4] In a discussion of *mimesis*, which he believes to be
"at once a portrayal of human reality and an original creation,"
Ricoeur further maintains that metaphor

> takes part in the double tension that characterizes this imitation: the
> submission to reality and fabulous invention... This double tension
> constitutes the referential function of metaphor in poetry. Abstracted
> from this referential function, metaphor plays itself out in substitution
> and dissipates itself in ornamentation; allowed to run free, it loses
> itself in language games. (1975, 40)

Poetry does have the power to, and properly does, engage with reality.
Metaphor's deviations from normal discourse "belong to the great
enterprise of 'saying what is'." Put another way round, one could say
that metaphor's frivolous reputation arises from a post-Baconian mood
of "language enclosures", whereby any word or proposition lacking an

empirically verifiable referent was marked out for exclusion from reputable practice.

Echoing an earlier view (Beardsley 1962, 293ff.) Ricoeur considers the implications of the claim that, besides actual specific denotation, words command an unknown range of potential connotative meaning.[5] It is in this potential connotation that metaphor has its source. Metaphor can be seen to be a creation of language at a particular moment in time, and remains devoid of semantic status in the language until it becomes conventionalized and at the same time "dead".[6] Taking up Monroe Beardsley's discussion of Jeremy Taylor's metaphor – *Virginity is the life of angels, the enamel of the soul* – Ricoeur describes what he thinks is actually happening:

> Something develops in the language. There accrue to the language various properties of **enamel** that until then had never been clearly established as recognized connotations of the word. (Ricoeur 1975, 97) (My emphasis)

Metaphor does not merely thrust latent connotations into the foreground of meaning; it enriches the range of signification of a word (Beardsley 1962, 303). A good historical dictionary such as *The Oxford English Dictionary* will confirm the truth of this at least once on virtually every page.

What is ordinary reference anyway? Ricoeur asks. Whenever the assumption is made that there exists some such process as "ordinary" reference and, further, an attempt is made to distinguish between this kind and all other kinds of reference, including "poetic" reference, this becomes merely the "starting-point of an immense inquiry on the topic of reference" (Ricoeur 1975, 148). Right from the start the would-be inquirer is misled by the positivist prejudice that ordinary reference is unproblematic and can readily be accommodated within the language of scientific prose.

At this point the debate is joined by Quine, who insists that metaphor is crucial in the formulation of scientific theory: metaphor is "vital at the growing edges of science and philosophy." Electron microscopy, for instance, may have confirmed the existence of molecules, but the molecular theory of gases started out "as an ingenious metaphor":

Or consider light waves. There being no ether, there is no substance for them to be waves of. Talk of light waves is thus best understood as metaphorical, so long as 'wave' is read in the time-honoured way. Or we may liberalize 'wave' and kill the metaphor.[7]

All language, insofar as it is a symbolic entity, constantly "makes" and "remakes" the world. The alleged difference between metaphorical and literal statements can easily be shown to be factitious. Propositions have no exclusive claim to cognitive validity; feelings and emotions also function cognitively, in aesthetic experience.[8] Had this not been the case human beings would never have been able to convey specific subjectively experienced sensations: even the most basic sensations, such as sensations of pain, shades of colour, tastes, or likes and dislikes. We all know what "pain" is for example. Language gives the concept to us and no purpose is served by attempting to communicate it, **unless** I am experiencing an acute or unfamiliar pain at a particular moment and in a particular location, and feel the need to describe it to someone, especially a doctor. From this moment on, and until the pain recedes, I become heavily dependent on figurative language; and so too does the doctor's attempt to arrive at a proper diagnosis, unless that same doctor is hiding behind (metaphorically derived) medical jargon and mystique.

A no less radical approach to metaphor is the one proposed over half a century ago by Barfield. Starting out from Shelley's suggestion that a metaphor "marks the before unapprehended relations of things" perpetuating their "apprehension" until such a time as the words representing them become "signs for portions of classes of thought, instead of pictures of integral thoughts." If this were true all users of language would have to be regarded as fully-fledged poets (Barfield 1952, 67). If there had been an evolution of consciousness from simplicity and darkness to complexity and light, as Shelley implies, more pleasure would be taken in the diction of a modern writer who "wields these wonderful meanings" than is obviously the case. Barfield detects a wrong assumption in Shelley's argument that, because many examples of metaphor can be observed in the actual process of creation, all words must originally have designated familiar given objects. In reality, once an excursion backwards in time is made, a world of different givens is encountered: a world of concrete meanings that are not ours, but which over the ages have become split up into several discrete meanings. Not only do these older concrete meanings strike one as quaint but they also appear creatively original and "poetic".

Thus, at one time the Greek word *pneuma* signified "breath", "spirit" and "wind", all three meanings together. The separated-out material sense "wind" and the non-material meaning "the principle of life within a man or animal" are relatively late arrivals in human consciousness. It would hardly suit modern man to have a single word designating three such incompatible meanings:

> We must imagine a time in which 'spiritus' or *pneuma*, or older words from which these were descended, meant neither *breath*, nor *wind*, nor *spirit*, nor yet all three of these things, but when they simply had **their own old peculiar meaning**, which has since, in the course of the evolution of consciousness, crystallized into the three meanings specified. (Barfield 1952, 81) (His emphasis)

The "metaphorical" values, Barfield argues, had been present from the very beginning. Shelley's "before unapprehended" relation should be seen as the reverse: a "forgotten" relation. Though not yet apprehended, these values had once been grasped integrally. By the time that the distinct (metaphorical) meanings were "apprehended" they would already have become separate words. Metonymic displacement – in the form of myth or narrative, or in connections now perceived as metaphorical – must once have been intuited as undivided immediate realities. The modern poet, says Barfield, is striving by dint of his or her own devices to make others perceive such realities afresh. Poetry has undergone many changes over the ages – changes "intimately connected with the development of the rational principle (by which meaning is split up) at the expense of the poetic principle" and accompanied by a prolonged awakening from unconsciousness to consciousness:

> The same creative activity, once operative in meaning without man's knowledge or control, and only recognized long afterwards, when he awoke to contemplate, as it were, what he had written in his sleep, this is now to be found within his own consciousness. And it calls him to become the true creator, the maker of meaning itself. (Barfield 1952, 107)

In Barfield's view however poetry is much more than a recovery of an ancient wholeness of meaning; otherwise it would be of interest mainly to the archaeologist. Poetry is obviously a regeneration of meaning, and the creation of new meaning through the unremitting creative activity of metaphor.

Metaphor is neither solely a device of rhetoric, nor is it exclusively a device of poetry. Nor should metaphor be considered an ornament of language while the main body of (non-figurative) language is supposedly prosaic and literal.[9] In fact, all fresh uses of an existing word entail some degree of metaphorical extension, however slight: scarcely noticeable shifts in, or more rarely additions to, existing senses, of which many words already possess a good many. However widely extended the range of meanings of a particular word, they never exhaust its semantic potentiality. Each word carries within it a metaphorical spring, so to speak, and each time it is used the qualification "something like" is implied (Bolinger 1965, 567). Even if I make so categorical a remark as "This is a Ming vase" I am really saying "This is **something like** a Ming vase", even though the vase may be authentic enough and not a modern reproduction. Every time I use language to refer – which is extremely often – and say something unremarkable like "This must be an apple tree" or "There's a thunderstorm in the offing", then I am using language in the "as if" metaphorical sense. When I am trying to tell someone something, my openings may be made up of any number of more or less predictable "sociolinguistic" gestures but, as I approach the nub of my message, I will be caught in a mesh of metaphor; even though ostensibly I might still seem to be uttering the tritest of commonplaces.

In classical rhetoric there is that other useful and adaptable device: metonymy – the use of the name for the thing, and *vice versa*. Metonymy has been applied to good effect by Roman Jakobson, though well beyond the its more traditional bounds. In Jakobson's frame of reference metaphor and metonymy complement and at the same time contrast diametrically with each other.

The possible applications of metonymy in the study of language and meaning are probably richer and more numerous than is at present recognized. In its classical use metonymy may be characterized as a semantic shift which enables a word-form (or "name" in traditional rhetoric) to switch from being a signifier to a signified, from word-form to word sense. A simple example would be *cup*. Here we have a word-form (signifier) whose dominant sense (signified) is "a certain type of ceramic receptacle for drinking from". But among its secondary senses is "a quantity of liquid in such a receptacle", as in *I could do with a cup* (=quantity) *of tea* (or *coffee*). In the latter instance the locution *a cup of* is to be found already embedded in the secondary sense of the word *cup*. As a result, when the beverage is present and visible it is not even necessary to specify which liquid. *I'd like another cup if I may* would be sufficient.

In its extended use metonymy opens up a multi-faceted interface between words and world. Even such an innocent metonymy as "foot", in its secondary meaning "a unit of linear measurement equal in length to an adult (probably male) foot", has its quizzical side. What about, for example, *His foot is more than a foot long*? The sentence may well be condemned as a solecism, but it is not ambiguous. When words that are identical in form occur in the same sentence without any logical or semantic inconsistency, they are said to be different words, or "homonyms" (that is, different words having the same form).[10] But in this particular instance the double occurrence of "foot" in the same sentence produces not homonymy but different instances of the polysemy (different senses of the **same** word) of *foot*

If metonymy were confined to such curiosities it could safely be put aside as a quirk of the lexicon. But, as things stand, there lurks the suspicion that many (potential) word meanings and word configurations have their origin in a state of affairs that might more profitably be explored by poetics or hermeneutics than lexicology.

In its simplest form metonymy is "the substitution of an adjacent object for another." In its more uncanny aspect metonymy reveals itself as "the mutual penetration of objects" (metonymy in the real sense according to Jakobson).[11] This "mutual penetration" can be found in the most ordinary contexts, in successful advertising commercials (for example: "Singapore girl, you're a great way to fly – a metonymic reference to the alleged superiority of an international airline) as well as of course, regularly and all-pervasively, in modern poetry. In a couple of sentences, with an extraordinary metonymy speaking more than an entire volume of history, Pasternak captures in a poignant impression the tragedy of a lost generation of young people killed and (spiritually as well as physically) maimed in the First World War and the ensuing Civil War in Russia:

> Their childhood adolescence and their calling-up at coming of age
> were immediately fastened to an epoch of transition. The whole bulk
> of our time is threaded through with their nerves and is politely
> abandoned by them for the use of the aged and of children.[12]

The impressionistic bringing together of the imagery of the crucifixion
and the past and present of a casualty hospital within an historical
frame captures the meaningless profligacy in human lives during those
and all other times. In the words of another Russian poet Viktor
Khlebnikov, poetry "merges into history and collaboration with real
life".[13] Pasternak's poetry and prose abounds in metonymic and
metaphoric alchemy. Here is another example taken from *Poetry*:

> Offshoots of rainstorm muddily clump together
> And before dawn, for what a long, long time
> They scrawl from rooftops their acrostics
> And blow their bubbles into rhyme!
> (English version mine)

Here we have the texture of all, especially modern, poetry, with
metaphor interwoven into a larger metonymic frame. Anyone familiar
with classical Chinese poetry will know that the typical ode or lyric
poem consists of verbal images in metonymic contiguity, without overt
syntax to bind them together. The images spill into each other,
resisting the imposition of fixed meanings and readings. In European
poetry by contrast, metre, rhyme, assonance – even rhetorical figures –
are, as it were, spatial and temporal projections of this same
metonymy. One has to read not merely Pasternak's "words" and
"meanings" but especially their actual and stridently thrilling
polytonality:

> Compared with this even the sunrise took on the character of urban
> rumour still needing to be verified.

Images of the poet's world function as contiguous reflections,
metonymical incarnations of the poet's self or, as Pasternak himself
put it:

> Reality arises in a kind of new category. This category seems to us to
> be its own condition, and not ours... We try to name it. The result is
> art.[14]

But we need not confine ourselves to the more arcane reaches of modern poetry. Run-of-the-mill language, down to its simplest components, is forged out of time-buried metonymies. In English, people say "It is raining"; in Russian "Rain is coming/going"; in Chinese "Down falls rain"; and in Latin they said "Raineth". But even here the metonymies are not startlingly divergent. There must be many languages in which anything similar to these metonymies, even the familiar commodity "rain", is absent. In more than one North American Indian language for example the word "rain" cannot appear in lexical isolation, since these are types of language in which nouns and verbs have no separate existence. One may not therefore refer to "rain" as such, but only as part of a superordinate expression such as, for instance, "water sprinkling" (at the onset of a shower), or "(water) floats with me"(the equivalent of something like "It's raining cats and dogs").

"Words hurled at things" (Pasternak) have shaped our worlds over many millennia in ways we scarcely suspect. Speakers of "Standard Average European" languages move very much within a charmed circle of the familiar. Monolingual speakers of English may not appreciate that their language is packed with expressions that would puzzle, say, the non-English/Spanish speaking Navajo to the same extent as Navajo locutions (a tiny sample of which we looked at in an earlier chapter) would puzzle the native speaker of English. The former include for example the idiomatic so-called phrasal verbs which combine common verb forms with prepositional forms.

Take the average English phrasal verb *look up*, selected at random. The literal senses "look upwards" or "raise one's eyes" seem entirely unproblematic: we do not even notice that here we already have two quite distinct meanings. This distinction is carefully made in French, the language most closely related to English, by the use of two different expressions. It takes some little reflection on the part of the native speaker of English to see the difference between "looking upwards" (at the starry sky, an aircraft, etc.) and raising one's eyes – only a metaphor, surely! – ("looking up from", say, the page one happens to be reading). This is because the two quite different senses are merged into a single expression. Following that, our attention may then be drawn to the different figurative uses of "look up", as in the expressions "things are looking up", "looking someone up", "looking up a work of reference", and several others. If one can succeed in adopting a certain distance from expressions such as these, they can take on the strangeness of many a Navajo locution. But that is not the end of the problem (as far as the foreign learner of English is concerned). The symmetrical opposite of "look up" is of course "look down". The symmetry seems reassuring enough, until we begin to perceive that "things" even if they can "look up" can never "look down". One may "look up" (in the metaphorical sense) to someone, but we do not "look down" to anyone. One can "look down on someone", but again this is semantically not exactly the opposite of looking up to someone (the latter suggests "admire" rather than "not despise").

One might have chosen hundreds, perhaps thousands, of alternative examples, some of them bearing the hallmark of aeons of anonymous shaping of the language. English is not peculiar in this respect. Every language, including at times its separate dialects, constitutes a distinct "galaxy" of metaphoric-metonymic idiosyncrasy, reflecting the many disparate universes that human language has created and the different imprints it leaves on nature.

> We cut nature up, organize it into concepts, and ascribe significances as we do, largely because we are parties to an agreement to organize it in this way – an agreement that holds throughout our speech community and is codified in the patterns of our language. The agreement is, of course, an implicit and unstated one but its terms are absolutely obligatory; we cannot talk at all except by subscribing to the organization and classification of data which the agreement decrees. (Whorf 1962, 213-4)

11. Word, Meaning and Context

The quest for word meanings is futile, said Wittgenstein. The meaning of a word is none other than its use in the language (1963, 20). To discover the meaning of a word, only the ways in which the word is actually used should be considered; that is, in the variety of contexts in which it can actually occur. The oft-quoted comparison is that between a word and a piece in a game of chess. If someone wants to know what is a king or a pawn in chess it is not a knowledge of the shape, size or any other physical property of the pieces that is being sought but their **function** in the game. "This is a king" becomes an operative definition only if the chess initiate already knows what a piece in a game represents. In turn this knowledge depends on an understanding of the nature and purpose of a game, gained from prior experience of games in general: context of use always.

The only valid lexical definitions, Wittgenstein argued, are ostensive ones. Such definitions are produced by means of words, but only to the extent that there is no "last" definition, just as "there is no last house in this road; one can always build an additional one"(1963, 14). But ostensive definition, it must also be said, explains the use of a word – in its various senses – only in cases where the overall role of the word in the language is clear. If I am told by someone indicating a colour: "That is sepia", in response to a hint that I do not quite know what "sepia" is, then I am being given a helpful ostensive definition. But if someone were to ask: "What is a fairy?" or "What is a quark?" no ostensive definition could be supplied. In the former instance a picture of a stylized "fairy" could be produced or, alternatively, reference made to a particular essay by J.R.R.Tolkien. Likewise no one can be shown an actual quark, though an up-to-date encyclopaedia article on elementary particles in physics could provide ample coverage (and might possibly also mention that "quark" is borrowed from *Finnegan's Wake*).

Quark, along with words such as *fugue, gambit, liquidity* and thousands of others, happens to be a complex entity calling for specialized knowledge; unlike words such as *red* or *pain*, which belong to the common core of the language. Anyone claiming not to know the use of the words *red* and *pain* cannot be said to have mastered English. But this would not be so in the case of someone ignorant of "quarks" since it is inadequate knowledge of physics, and not the language, that is the problem here.

In Wittgenstein's view language is no more than a set of language-games and the experiencing of a word is just such another game.[1] The "physiognomy of a word, the feeling that it has taken up its meaning into itself" – in short, the "atmosphere" of a word – remains a private experience. I communicate in words my own experience of what I mean without knowing whether my interlocutor has had commensurate experience.[2] It is only when I lose sight of the ways in which the various types of games inherent in language are interlinked or, to use Wittgenstein's own expression, "when language goes on holiday" that things start to go wrong and philosophical problems of various kinds arise.

Meaning nevertheless should not be equated with use, in that the latter is only one of the several different functions of meaning. The same sentence for example can be put to a variety of contextual uses while remaining semantically constant. In the sentence *I find it uncomfortable* the context, including its use, may vary without limit but the meaning cannot be said to have changed. An expression of the kind *I am hot* may ostensibly command only a narrow range of meaning insofar as no two people can logically be said to have made the same **use** of the expression.[3] Meaningful expressions can be used in a variety of ways, including humbug, subterfuge, irony or fun, to mention but a few. Successful reference, one of the prime functions of use, on the other hand is never automatic or predictable in ordinary terms. The requirement for the correct application of an expression in its referring use is "something over and above any equivalent derived from such an ascriptive meaning as the expression may have." It is also a contextual requirement: *I am hot* can mean "I am following up significant clues" besides "I am feeling hot", depending on context.

Logic, it has been said, is not concerned with the different ways in which a sentence may be phrased, but only with "premiss-sentences" or "conclusion-sentences" neither of which has anything to do with the ways in which something may be expressed in a particular language. Furthermore, a distinction, it has been argued, must be maintained between linguistic problems that are philosophical problems and linguistic problems that belong to philology, grammar, rhetoric, and so forth, since only the former are problems about the logic of the **functioning** of expressions.[5] An approach of this latter sort is likely to prove unsatisfactory to philosophers of language who have found it hard to distinguish between certain classes of utterance and speech functions, or "speech acts" touched upon earlier. Austin, we may recall, was proposing that only sentences, not words, have meaning. To know the meaning of a word or expression, Austin insists, is to know the meanings of the sentences in which they can occur (1962, 56).

Words are not only aids, mere adjuncts, they are also names, "composites of sound with a meaning" as Aristotle described them. In being such composites, in the symmetry which obtains between form and sense, words immediately bring us up against a problem discussed at some length by Austin. but incapable of resolution simply by reference to the "syntactics of a word". The same word can, and most often does, "mean" a variety of different things, not all of which are in any obvious way related. Austin was evidently not unaware of this problem, urging that "a doctrine should be developed about the various kinds of good reasons for which 'we call different things by the same name' "(1962, 70). He emphasized the need to study **actual** languages, not ideal ones. In this respect Austin came close to Bakhtin's realization: that actual language consists not of sentences, but of utterances, incarnations of dialogic speech events, rather than composites of syntactic and lexical structures. The utterance takes us away from the stereotyped *A cat sat on the mat* to an opening up of possibilities: "There's something stretched out on the mat out there..." "What is it?.." "It looks like.." "No, it can't be..." "It's too large. Ah! Now I see! It's a..." The expansion of such an utterance could have proceeded in any number of ways. It takes no imagination to avoid a recapitulation, at the utterance level, of our stereotyped specimen. But consider the way in which Eugene Ionesco spun an entire play out of a textbook dialogue between an improbable Mr. and Mrs. Smith.

A very different approach to contextual meaning was the one adopted by I.A.Richards. Reacting against the taxonomies of classical rhetoric, founded on a "proper-name superstition" of figures of speech rather than on actual discourse, and in attempting to reestablish the "rights of discourse" at the expense of the "rights of the word", Richards denied that words possess any inherent sense of their own. Only discourse as a whole, says Richards, carries meaning. In any segment of discourse a particular word owes its meaning to what Richards calls "delegated efficacy" (1936, 32). Words acquire sense only in the abridgement of context.[6]   Words do not even "stand for" things or ideas, Richards argues, and the belief that they do is a hangover from an earlier magical theory of names (1936, 71). Nor are words constituted by any fixed association with configurations of data. All they do is refer back to the missing parts of the context, any constancy of meaning arising only from a corresponding constancy of contexts.   From an extreme nominalist position such as this, the most that words can achieve is to express the opposition between rival contexts and to bring about relations of opposition. A word can thus be compared to an algebraic function. In the English sentences *He could just about read by the light of the x* and *The x is made of green cheese* the only identifiable common value for "*x*" is "moon". *Reductio ad absurdum*!

In Richards' scheme the traditional relationship between word and sentence is thus entirely reversed. The meaning of a sentence is no longer the product of the senses of its component words. Sense of the latter sort, according to Richards, derives from the breaking down of the sentence into its lexical fractions, ascribable in the main to the effect of good authors who lend fixed values to words; even though, paradoxically, it is the literary use of words that restores "the interplay of the interpretative possibilities of the whole utterance" (1936, 55). This, Richards maintains, explains why the meaning of words has to be guessed from the context each time they are encountered.

Richards' "devil's advocacy" is matched only by that of another of his contemporaries – J.R.Firth. Firth set out to attain what many a modern linguist would eschew: a study of language as a feature of the total human environment where every piece of language forms an integral part of the "context of situation" in which it occurs. This "context of situation" harks back to Malinowski who had become convinced, mainly as a result of his experiences among the Trobriand

Islanders, that:

> the conception of context must burst the bonds of mere linguistics and be carried over into the analysis of the general conditions under which a language is spoken...utterance and situation are bound up inextricably with each other and the context of situation is indispensable for the understanding of the words. Exactly as in the reality of spoken or written languages, a word without linguistic context is a mere figment and stands for nothing by itself, so in the reality of a spoken living tongue, the utterance has no meaning except in the context of situation. (1949, 306-7)

Firth, a robustly independent thinker out of tune with much of contemporary linguistic opinion, was unimpressed by Saussure and dismissive of Bloomfield for (amongst other things) confusing the study of meaning with the study of grammar (1957, 15). It is easy to predict that he would have approved even less of those of Bloomfield's American successors, not least Chomsky, who would be seen by him as having reduced semantics to a mere algorithm of grammar.

What Firth desired above all was for every "language event" to be viewed as a living whole event. With this wholeness and vitality kept unswervingly before the mind's eye (and ear), it should be possible, thought Firth, to deal with a particular language at various levels simultaneously,

> sometimes in a descending order, beginning with social context and proceeding through syntax and vocabulary to phonology and even phonetics, and at other times in the opposite order (1957, 192)

The latter was described by Firth as a "serial contextualization" of our facts,

> context within context, each one being a function, an organ of the bigger context, and all contexts finding a place in what may be called the context of culture (1957, 32).

Such wholeness rules out the possibility of meaning being seen as a "hidden mental process." Meaning becomes inseparable from context of situation, from

> that kind of language which disturbs the air and other people's ears, as

modes of behaviour in relation to the other elements in the context of situation... I shall cease to respect the duality of mind and body, thought and word, and be satisfied with the whole man, thinking and acting as a whole, in association with his fellows. (1957, 19)

In Firth's view, context of situation is no inert setting in which "language events" take place; it is a nexus of real objects, effects brought about by verbal action and, especially, personalities.[7] The concepts of *person* and *personality* Firth reinterprets, via Dr. Johnson's dictionary, from Locke, who emphasized the extension of personality through consciousness, beyond the present and into the past. And language, like personality, is what Firth called "a binder of time", of the past and the future within the present:

On the one hand there is habit, custom, tradition, and on the other, innovation, creation. Every time you speak you create anew, and what you create is a function of your language and of your personality. From that activity you may make abstraction of the constituents of the context, and consider them in their mutual relations. In the process of speaking there is pattern and structure actively maintained by the body which is itself an organized structure maintaining the pattern of life. (Firth 1957, 142)

The fact that linguists are for the most part not even aware, Firth claimed, of the true nature of language and meaning is well demonstrated by the samples of language cited as illustrations in textbooks of grammar, theoretical as well as pedagogical.[8]

Once someone speaks to you, says Firth, you are in a relatively determined context and not free to say whatever you please. We may be born individuals but when we become social persons we also become a bundle of roles or *personae*. In any given context of situation there is both a positive force in anything that is said; there is also a negative force of elimination both as regards other events and circumstances in the situation as well as in the actual words used. It would have been interesting to know what Firth might have thought of recent ethnolinguistic studies and whether in his eyes these would have constituted "a different general philosophical attitude towards speech from that which has set our scale of values hitherto" (1957, 32).

Firth's writings, though relatively unvoluminous, abound in

documentation, exploring as they do the extraordinary range of behaviour of ordinary everyday words. Take the example of the word *sport*, one that is comparatively easy for the dictionary to handle. Here is a word that remains unexceptionable in its contextual behaviour until someone in a (by now somewhat quaint) British context comes up with the injunction *Oh, be a sport!* In this instance we are hearing not simply the plea of an individual, but the pressure and weight of social opinion. And what can one say about locutions such as *Say when?* as uttered in the context of offering someone a drink:

> Quite a number of readers will have lively recollections of the very practical use of these two words. Many Englishmen will at once place themselves in a pleasant situation with good glass, good drink, and good company. The two words fit into the situation. They have their "psychological" and practical moment in what is going on between two people, whose eyes, hands, and goodness knows what else, are sharing a common interest in a bit of life.[9] (1966, 110)

William Empson's studies of key words in the same culture have much in common with Firth's. From their very different angles, both writers had taken note of the poetic possibilities manifested in ordinary speech. In his exploration of *sense* and *sensibility* in Jane Austen's novel of the same name and elsewhere, Empson observes that "the complex structure of opposition" between these two words is not the novelist's doing alone, but is actually invented at least in part each time anyone attempts to use the words seriously (Empson 1951, 253). Whenever words are paired in this sort of way readers invoke sets of equations which assist them in coping with what would otherwise have been unmanageable swathes of history. The stock opposition, lightly parodied in the novel's title, has resulted in the words getting "worked down until they are a kind of bare stage for any future performance." Empson's commentary on "Sense and Sensibility" concludes with an intriguing remark:

> What the user needs, and feels he has, is an agreed foundation on which to build his own version; a simple basic difference between the words from which the whole opposition can be extracted. (1951, 269)

But what about the words themselves? Can words in isolation, as distinct from their occurrence in contexts of use or contexts of situation, have meaning? In their different ways Wittgenstein, Richards, Empson and Firth were all indeed right: words in themselves do not embody specific meaning. The "definitions" provided by dictionaries are not "meanings", but either glosses, or paraphrases, or a combination of the two. In Part Four of this book an attempt will be made to determine exactly what words are, how they come about, and what they do. It will be seen that, although words do not embody meaning with any degree of finality, they do embody **something**: they have the semblance of being particles of culture and feeling. They also possess certain wondrous properties which bring the two otherwise separate modes of language, discussed in earlier chapters, into dynamic relation with each other.

It is in the shared mode of language that meaning, expressed as it is in signs and symbols, is **registered**, "made known" and interpreted. The actual formal elements of language, generated as they are in the neurophysiology, the psychobiology, and in the creative poetic potentialities of the individual ("echoes from an unknown world beyond") have been shaped by the culture, and by the all-embracing life-world to which the individual as subject and object (the person) belongs, as much as by the system-like constraints imposed by what the grammar (linguistics) identifies as phonology, morphology and syntax. Meanings cannot come into being, cannot be made flesh, without form. Besides grammar, the forms in which meaning is "discovered" range over poetics, genre, styles (communicative, ontological, cognitive and cultural), social and semiotic structures, art, belief, ritual, to mention only the more salient categories of what constitutes being human. All this has given rise, understandably, to the ghost-in-the-machine presupposition that meaning must be a something "standing behind" the linguistic forms we actually perceive, just as it has, conversely, to the prejudice that because meaning cannot be registered directly by the senses it does not exist. Wittgenstein's proposal that "the meaning of a word is its use in the language"[10] we are now in a position to evaluate in its context. Salutary though such a claim might have been in its time; it does little more than defer the problem elsewhere.

Meaning cannot be observed, any more than, forms can be "observed". When I look at a page in a book, optically speaking I see only marks, and not word-forms; just as when I hear someone speak I register raw sounds with my auditory apparatus, which only by a long and complicated process acquire form, even if this process seems to the perceiver instantaneous. The forms I believe I see are all elaborate perceptualized outcomes of various informational, physical, biological, electrical and chemical events "out there". My capacity to "see" and "hear" these forms depends more on the context of my shared world and language than on the proper functioning of the physical organism.

Let us suppose that instead of a question of a standard kind – How do sequences of words express meanings? – we put a slightly different question: How do sequences of "grammatical" forms express meaning? A moment's reflection should reveal that the question is without value. It might perhaps have been put more successfully in this way: How is it that certain sequences of linguistic forms **coincide** with certain meanings? We would however soon become disenchanted with this "correspondence" approach to a solution since such sequences do not always, or even often, coincide. At one extreme lurks the bugbear of the ambiguous statement, in which one sequence coincides with two or more different meanings. Statements of the kind *They passed the port at midnight* or *Flying planes can be dangerous*, to choose two well-worn examples, are "disambiguated" not by matching form-sequence with meaning (since this is impossible) but, if one follows Chomsky, through some unexplained innate awareness of the difference in the deep structures (forms underlying surface sequences); or alternatively, if one subscribes to the approach of Firth, by placing the ambiguous statements in their proper contexts of situation. In either case one has to fall back, in the first instance on one's own subjectivity and, ultimately, intersubjectivity (How do you and I both know...?) and in the second instance on the delusory objectivity of a life-world which is equally intersubjective (Firth's solution has the further disadvantage that it assumes that the **fact** of ambiguity is already perceived.)

At another extreme, forms appear to be divorced from the meanings they call forth. As a word-form, the verb-noun *go* may be considered straightforward enough, and many of its meanings seem to lie within a manageable range (*This vehicle does not go* or *She has plenty of go* do not deviate too far from "standard" reference meaning "locomotion from one place to another"). But when phraseological configurations such as *go into* ("explore"), *go off* ("go bad, turn sour"), *have a go* ("make an attempt"), *go over* ("search") or the virtually unparaphraseable *Go to it!* or *Go on!* any serious attempt to link form with meaning would probably have to be abandoned.

A dualist, correspondence-theory approach to the relationships between "form" and "meaning", specifically at the level of word-forms and word sense, will evidently not do. This being so, there is little likelihood of finding ways of directly relating form sequences to specific meaning – an impasse, a "mysterious no-man's land which lies between words and their meanings" (Barfield 1933, 161). Yet, strange as it might seem, it is in this same no-man's land that language reveals itself as the creative "symbolic fusion" known as reality; a bonding that can, as Humboldt was well aware, "exert a power against Man himself", inasmuch as we ourselves, our personal beings, form part of that same reality. It is a no-man's land that bars us from more than a fragmentary understanding of how words can actually "mean":

> Concepts can be split up, words can be divided into components, to the extent that we are capable of so doing, and still we get no closer to an explanation of the mystery of how ideas are actually combined into words. (Humboldt [1836]1971, 131)

As it was for Humboldt, so it remains for us today.

Looked at in this light, words and their combinations have to be seen as something more than forms associated, however indirectly, with meanings. Linguistics, it seems, and the philosophy of language also, have been following false trails. A word is something more than a form linked to a meaning: it is an entity rooted in culture, a vehicle for signs emitted by objects and events "out there", whose essence somehow motivates linguistic forms and creates an "effect" which philosophers, linguists and lexicographers have called "meaning" or "sense". Words happen to be a rich, varied and apparently inexhaustible source and focus of signs and symbolism, whether from the distant past or from the present, along the dimension of the lived unit of time that we know as a culture. "Culture" is preferred to "language" at this juncture for the reason that it stands independently of the various lexical forms it may adopt, in place or time, from one (culturally related) language to the next. Furthermore, it is the word that serves as a link between hitherto unrelated cultures.

What kind of an entity then is a word? We shall concern ourselves at length with this question in Part Four. Suffice it for the present to suggest that the word resides partly in the Unconscious, interacting in sometimes peculiar ways (and not only in "Freudian" slips of the tongue) with our impulses, fancies, perceptions, motivations and feelings. Yet a word is also a particular link between our intersubjective selves. At the same time the word is public enough to find itself inscribed, albeit at several removes from its true nature, in the dictionary. In the hands of the poet, or indeed any timely practitioner of the verbal arts, the word can (to name just a few of its possibilities) inspire, disarm, play cat-and-mouse, undermine, mislead, shame, gladden, depress, and perform all manner of tomfoolery.

Possibly the greatest tomfoolery of all is that words not only represent or symbolize, but point towards, demonstrate, refer to what purport to be objects or events. "That is a wall over there" perhaps contains the further implication: "If you don't believe it, try giving it a kick." We mark out our world with what Peirce termed "index" signs, functions that depend absolutely on their object by virtue of standing in relation it. Indexical and deictic words have no semantic status except insofar as they represent some kind of object or event. Thus "you" stands in relation to the person being addressed and "it" to the object known as a "wall". Since the word "wall" could relate to any kind of wall, the whole sentence *That is a wall over there* is said to be a unique reference to a particular wall standing at some determinable distance from the speaker. This, in turn, gives rise to the preconception that a sentence of this type offers a particular account of the existence of **an actual thing** – a "wall" "over there" – and that the claim is at the same time **true** inasmuch as its veracity can easily be checked.

The semantic difference between a name, say, "wall" and a deictic sentence of the type "That is a wall over there" has attracted a fair amount of attention. The name "wall" can indicate any kind of wall, whereas the sentence is a particular and more complete kind of meaning whose truth value can be checked. This has promoted the belief that only complete sentences can "mean" in any precise way. Austin, as already noted, while he concedes that one can quite properly "look up the meaning of a word" in a dictionary, insists that the notion of a word "having a meaning" derives solely from the fact that it is only sentences in which the word occurs that actually "have a meaning". We may recall Austin's claim, that to know the meaning of a word is to know the meanings of sentences in which the word occurs, that the notion of "the meaning of a word" is a "dangerous nonsense-phrase" (1970, 60). But then the question immediately arises: How does one get from an assemblage of items that are said not to possess this full kind of meaning to a totality, a proposition that has meaning and can be deemed true or false? There is a problem in simply inferring that the meanings of sentences derive ultimately from the meanings of the component words, albeit in context, for the simple reason that the same words appear in a limitless range of other actual and possible grammatical sentences and in a variety, equally limitless, of contexts. If sentences were to depend for their meaning on their structural components, in accordance with the expectations of descriptive linguistics, or on contexts of situation (following the dictates of Firth) the meanings of every possible expression in the language would have to be supplied.[11]

In a short but much cited paper published at the end of the last century Gottlob Frege drew attention to what he saw to be an important distinction between two types of linguistic meaning: **sense** (*Sinn*) and **reference** (*Bedeutung*). Struck by the regularity of the connection between what he called a "sign" (what would now be called a "form"), its sense, and its reference, but also by a corresponding dissymmetry, Frege further noticed that

> to the sign there corresponds a definite sense and to that in turn a definite reference, while to a given reference there does not belong a single sign. The same sense has different expressions in different languages or even in the same language. (1974, 58)

For example the particular form (Frege's "sign") *violin* has a particular sense: "a bowed musical instrument of a certain type with four tuned strings." In turn this sense may correspond to a particular instrument, whether actually being played or lying around in my study. The latter (the "referent") by contrast can correspond to a variety of other senses, including "that marvellous-sounding instrument", "a thing that produces such an excruciating sound", "Sherlock Holmes's inseparable companion", and so forth.

Nor do natural languages, as Frege observed, always satisfy the condition that a word or expression stands in a one-to-one relationship to a particular sense: "one must be content if the same word has the same sense in the same context." *Violin* has one sense only, but *bow* has several, of which "violin bow" is only one. Furthermore, a sense does not always have a determinable reference. Frege's celebrated example *the celestial body most distant from the earth* has a definite sense, but he doubts whether it can be assigned even a potential referent.[12]

This brings us to the crux of Frege's thesis. The thought implicit in verbal expressions, Frege maintained, belongs not to reference but to sense. The **sense** of the sentence *The morning star is a body illuminated by the sun* differs from that of the sentence *The evening star is a body illuminated by the sun.* But anyone unaware of the fact that the morning star and the evening star **refer** to one and the same object could easily draw a wrong inference: that one of the statements must be false. In this fashion Frege made his point that the thought or sense cannot be the reference of either sentence since, no matter what one might think, the referents of the "morning star" and "evening star" are identical (1974, 62).

A further consequence is that the thought embodied in an expression as well as its truth value must also be different. The relation between a subject and its predicate in no way leads to a corresponding relation between a thought and what might be deemed true or false.[13] If Frege is right, then the position taken by Benveniste and others, that there occurs a qualitative semantic change once the level of the sentence is reached, must be wrong. The passage from non-reference to reference is not guaranteed by the subject-predicate structure of the sentence or by any other feature of language. Everything in language appears trapped within the domain of sense or meaning. We have been misled by the appearance that sentences may **seem** to refer while other features of language, lower in the alleged structural hierarchy, such as expressions or words, do not.

Bakhtin was probably familiar with Frege's position, but whether his perception of the distinction between sentence and utterance was prompted by it is hard to say. All we know for certain is that Bakhtin drew the sharpest possible distinction between sentences – mere sequences of grammatical forms and configurations of sense – and utterances, which embody the speaker's plan or "speech will" (1986, 77). A sentence, even when in a normal context, can of itself achieve nothing. It acquires its illocutionary efficacy only within the entirety of the whole utterance. Only the utterance is capable of reference, never the sentence.[14] Even the deixis (that function supplied by demonstrative pronouns, etc.) of grammar conceals Peirce's indexical signs, which derive their function from the dynamics of utterance.

According to Frege the step from non-reference to reference lies not in the verbal linkage of predicates with subjects, but in something else: namely, whether what is being said can be assigned to the categories "true" or "false", and whether truth and falsehood are the potential properties of particular utterances (or propositions). Thus, a proposition such as "This water is wet" would not qualify, since water cannot be "not wet" or "dry". More problematically, *A unicorn is a long-haired single-horned quadruped* has a perfectly valid subject and predicate. Furthermore, the proposition is comprehensible, and appears to have the potentiality for reference (Frege would undoubtedly have questioned whether such a proposition could ever find a reference). Even if its perpetrator were to insist on the validity of the potential unicorn reference (by producing, say, a picture, or by providing other testimony relating to the nature and habits of unicorns) he or she would at the same time be committed, in Frege's view, to an opinion about the truth (or falsehood) of the proposition, or at the very least open to the possibility of its denial. In reality no denial is possible because no specimen of a unicorn, or unicorn-like creature is presumably available for inspection. This particular statement about unicorns, then, must remain within the domain of sense. (The proposition *There is a unicorn in my outhouse* on the other hand is a different matter, since its truth or falsehood can immediately be checked. One could simply go and take a look.) Thoughts remain constant regardless of reference. A unicorn remains a unicorn independently of whether such a beast can be located; in just the same way as the morning and evening stars remain different in sense while sharing a common reference. It is not difficult to imagine what would have been Bakhtin's response to this sort of hypostatization. What remains constant in Frege's otherwise unfaultable scheme is not "thought" but the whole fabric of speech culture and its genres.

*   *   *

"Do you know I always thought Unicorns were fabulous monsters, too? I never saw one alive before!"

"Well, now that we **have** seen each other," said the Unicorn, "If you'll believe in me, I'll believe in you. Is that a bargain?"

"Yes, if you like," said Alice.

This exchange highlights the ontological uncertainties which arose in the aftermath of the Scientific Revolution. The Fregian distinction between sense and reference was created by empirical science and the accompanying scientific attitude that made people sceptical about the existence of things and creatures to which they had no access or which they could not take on (scientific) trust. But meaning or sense in language has always preceded reference, and it may even be doubted whether there would be any such concept as reference (at least in the form proposed by Frege) without any prior discontinuity in the realm of sense. It is not so much that the exigencies of verification breed a critique of sense (although this must have been very much in the mind of Bacon when he was writing about his "idols of the market" and the nuisance value of words) but that sense, once it has developed a particular level of conceptual and logical organization, enables users of language to become critical of statements and to take it into their heads to test them empirically. Reference has been said to be something firm, whereas meaning or sense is considered infirm, flabby (Quine 1969, 35).

The whole question of reference and its relevance to scientific truth has preoccupied modern philosophy. Was Copernicus right and Ptolemy wrong? The prompt answer would probably be: Ptolemy was obviously wrong since he believed the earth to be at the centre of the universe. But, although Copernicus' theory offers a far simpler means of "saving the appearances" than Ptolemy's, both theories account about equally well for the motions of the planets (in fact of course Copernicus went wrong in supposing planetary orbits to be circular, an error not corrected until the time of Kepler). Are we moderns wrong in continuing to talk about the rising and setting of the sun, when this is, scientifically speaking, nonsense? But how can this view be nonsense when we can measure and predict the rising and setting of the sun with great accuracy? How much more "flabby" is the sense of the statement "the sun is rising" than the corresponding scientific statement "the portion of the planet in which I am situated is now beginning to receive light directly from the star we call the sun"?[15] In a way, when we talk about the sun rising and the position of the earth in relation to the sun we are talking about different things; we are, so to speak, referring differently. H_2O is one thing, but the liquid I imbibe to quench my thirst is really another. They are different; yet, as we have all been taught, they are the same. There may have been the intention of referring to the molecular structure but, more likely, when the more familiar term "water" was used, the reference to that structure would have been unconscious (Rorty 1979, 267). In fact "water" and its molecular composition belong to different genres of utterance. They only get in each other's way when the genres are deliberately mixed, with mildly ludicrous results (as in *I'd love a glass of H₂O*).

As Gadamer points out, it is language which acting creatively reconciles all kinds of such paradoxical ways of relating to the world:

> By reconstructing another model, we can mentally liberate ourselves from the evidence of our senses, and because we can do this we can see things from the rational point of view of the Copernican theory. But we cannot try to supersede or refute natural appearances by viewing things through the "eyes" of scientific understanding. (1991, 449)

Science makes up only a part of our particular life-world, and it is language that opens up this world for us, a world that retains everyday appearances alongside the edifice of science. "In language the world presents itself" (Gadamer 1991, 450). Even though language and the world are related fundamentally this does not mean that "the world becomes the object of language." It is only that all attempts at knowledge and claims on behalf of the status of knowledge, including reference, are enclosed within "the horizon of language".[16] What is overlooked here is that language has never projected a once-and-for-all static horizon but has grown, and markedly so during the centuries, coincident with the emergence of science and the scientific outlook. "Reference", as Frege appears to have been aware, is but another creative transformation of language. What Gadamer calls the "factualness" and "distance" of language as it is constituted today has not just happened automatically. There exists in actuality a "positive connection between the factualness of language and man's capacity for science" (1991, 453). Bacon's lambasting of the prejudices of the naïve prescientific language of his time can, from a present-day point of view, be seen as an awakening to the new demands made on language by empirical science. The world "out there" remains as unknowable as ever it was, but language has rolled back its horizon to the extent that empirical science has increased its dominion over that world. At the same time there is a need to be constantly reminded that language cannot be transcended, or even comprehended, except insofar as it operates within the shared life-world, as a whole. Tampering with language, castigating it, "improving" it, yields in the final analysis only blurred reflections of the human condition.

A deeper question however remains unanswered. How is it, as Proust once remarked, that words can sustain a sense or meaning by virtue of their own arrangement? Sequences of words, sometimes single words, manifest sense just as soon as they are uttered or written down. Can this simply be because we, as *logos*-oriented beings, **expect** words to have meaning, or is there is there perhaps a broader and deeper explanation: that words have become woven together multidimensionally in an interpenetration of form and meaning in the patterns of a shared life-world?

The last of these concerns falls largely within the province of linguistics. For good or ill however, linguistics has predominantly adopted what seems to be a narrowed (as opposed to "narrow") semantic approach to meaning. Linguistics tends to be conscious of and preoccupied with relations between and within words more than with their linkage with the multi-faceted world that poetics, semiotics or philosophical hermeneutics have been in the process of exploring. One such reductive approach would limit sense to the internal workings of the language – a convenient and manageable project no doubt, but disappointingly self-defeating.[17]

Lexical forms, especially, are symptomatic of diverse, complex, synchronic and diachronic processes, largely covert and inaccessible to commonsense observation or expectation. Questions of semantic compatibility can only be settled ontologically, and never solely in grammatical or lexical terms. Despite its appearances language is nothing like a formal system, overlapping sets of algorithms which can be manipulated in the manner of some elaborate and fussy game.

Very little is known about the ways in which the lexicon engages with the world as a whole, what this lexicon is like, and how in fact it operates within the shared mode of language that constitutes a version of the life-world. The only thing known for sure is that it does. It is part of our common experience, from earliest childhood, that words relate to and open up for us the world, and that therefore they were worth learning. Children would otherwise either ignore them or, like chimpanzees and gorillas, toy with them for a while before giving them up, just as they will eventually stop playing the games learned in childhood. The naming of things and events is a part of the human ontology – not the same thing as merely using words, as John Stuart Mill supposed – and at the same time the name can be seen as an instance of something embedded in a world which has the property of evoking that name. Language is very far from being a mere set of devices, like some cloak enfolding and tracing the contours of thought. It has been appositely described as mould into which infant minds are poured.[18] The relationships between words, whether formal or semantic, do not exist apart from actuality, and are a consequence of the real properties of the shared world we inhabit.

PART THREE

WORDS AND TEXT

12. Speaking and Writing

Until not so long ago, linguists were wont to assume that speech is
central to language, and that writing is somehow subordinate to
speech. The most that would be admitted is that speech and writing
exist alongside each other, on parallel tracks, so to speak. Speech was
considered convertible into writing simply by word-to-word
transcription and, conversely, writing could be converted into speech
by reading aloud from a text.

It cannot be denied that much of present-day speech is heavily
influenced by writing. Yet, even today, the great natural divide
between the spoken and the written word though considerably
narrowed is still visible at every turn. Anyone who has had the task of
transcribing recorded natural speech and real dialogue (as opposed to
stereotyped film or TV soundtrack) from tape-recordings will have
experienced the frustration so familiar to inexperienced transcribers.
Instead of a sequence of neatly arranged sentences there issues a
cascade of improperly finished constructions, inaudible junctures,
sentences left hanging in the air, interspersed with awkward silences
and seemingly meaningless *huh*'s and *ha*'s. With dialogue, matters
can be even worse: the participants quite often do not allow each other
time to finish and seem too impatient to await their turn.

The reverse process can seem equally peculiar though quite
different. Readers who can read perfectly well are frequently unable to
capture the naturalness of speech, its rhythms, intonations, nuances
and so forth. With some celebrated exceptions even poets are known to
be notoriously unnatural when it comes to reciting their own work. A
large part of the reason for this is that writing takes almost no account
of varieties of pause length, stress patterns or vocal modulations of

various kinds. Broadcasters, even those with a natural flair, may require some preparatory training.

Only in the 1980s did views change, and speech was seen as divergent from writing in all kinds of ways, and hardly any of its characteristic rhythms and variability could easily be represented in writing.[1] The incompleteness of utterances is now accepted as a communicative device, with pitch contours supplying the necessary information in such instances. Modulations of volume and pitch, also silences, form an integral part of the continuum of speech:

> Such phenomena have both obvious and subtle effects on the meaning of what the storyteller says, but the possible **shades** of meaning are infinite, whereas the deciphering eye allows no shadings. (Tedlock 1983, 9) (His emphasis)

Writing has built its own independent domain, and takes us into dimensions of the word quite unrelated to those of speech. In today's world it is becoming increasingly difficult to locate speakers who have not been more or less profoundly influenced by writing. Our civilization, Derrida has reminded us, is a Civilization of the Book. Our entire culture, preoccupations, dilemmas, even our science, once hailed as the harbinger of a new and different non-literate culture, has been shaped, and in some cases triggered, by the written word. The essence of this Civilization of the Book was captured, well over a century ago, by one of Dostoevsky's characters:

> Leave us alone without any books, and we shall at once get confused, lose ourselves in a maze, we shall not know what to cling to, what to hold on to, what to love and what to hate, what to respect and what to despise. We [would] find it hard to be men, men of **real** flesh and blood, **our own** flesh and blood.[2] (Dostoevsky's emphasis)

Not only to his fictional character but to Dostoevsky also – himself one of the supreme exponents of the written word – did it seem that the printed book had been responsible for suppressing real life. The illiterate peasant, with his spontaneity and untrammelled command of the spoken word, was felt by many an educated Russian to be living worlds apart from people of the Book such as themselves. It is perhaps not by chance that the Reformation, the Spanish Inquisition, Statocracy and Bureaucracy, the Rape of the New World followed

Gutenberg's introduction in the West of the printed book.

The difficulty of locating and "actually hearing" true speech is greater than is sometimes realized; so great in fact that, here and there, writers have succeeded in substituting for it the **illusion** of real talk. Modern writers as different from each other as Faulkner, Joyce, and Pinter have continued an old and well-established tradition, traceable in English at least as far back as Chaucer. The Russian writer Gogol created an illusion so perfect that many a Russian must have sworn that Gogol's dialogue is indistinguishable from real speech – an illusion easily dispelled by a closer examination of the text. The language of writing, however true to living speech it might seem, is the only kind of language modern semi-urbanized people have access to. The language of true speech has become disturbingly remote from our experience.

Few now have any idea what speech uninfluenced by writing is really like. They may even be totally unaware of the distinctive nature and intrinsic value of true speech, with its own (largely unexplored) linguistics and rhetoric, its own aesthetics and poetics. Those who chance upon truly oral cultures can be taken by surprise by the degree of value and care that oral communities invest in their cultivation of the spoken word. Writing about a community of Pueblo Indians in the American South-west one author has this to say:

> I have often encountered people from various pueblos who distrust attempts to put their own languages in writing for fear of the mistakes and sacrifices [inherent] in the written word... Writing can record words, certainly, but cannot fully transmit an oral tradition. Voice, emphasis, tone, rhythm, facial expression, gesture, atmosphere, and many other things all convey meaning and nuance... Formulizing things in writing will introduce a new force into Pueblo life.[3]

The notion of preserving a spoken tradition is not one that would readily occur or recommend itself to the conventionally schooled modern. Furthermore, the latter would have little idea of the cultural and educational investment that can go into the maintenance of such a tradition. In some Australian Aboriginal communities training in the "reading" of "texts", not to mention the feats of memory that that entails, can amount to a life-long endeavour (Strehlow 1971).

One would naturally expect grammar to be an outgrowth of literacy and associated pedagogics. But grammar is more likely to have had its origins in attempts to regulate oral traditions. The earliest known systematic grammar, compiled in India probably in the fifth century B.C. by Pāṇini, who himself apparently drew on still earlier sources, was devised partly for ritual and partly for utilitarian purposes, the former to safeguard the oral textual integrity of the Hindu scriptures (at that time, and for many centuries to come, orally transmitted and unwritten), the latter mainly to facilitate memorization (Misra 1966, 15-16). The nearly obsessive Early Hindu preoccupation with phonetics and phoneticization betrays a broader intent: to ensure, as far as was humanly possible, that the oral tradition behind these texts would be preserved intact for future generations of Brahmins.

It will have been noted the term "oral tradition" has been used interchangeably with "speech". There may in fact never have been a time in which *Homo sapiens* was without an oral tradition of epic, ritual song and poetry. It could be a prior condition that, before the shared mode of language could develop in its most complete sense, some more or less highly developed oral tradition, transmitted from generation to generation and geared to a certain flexibility of improvisation but in accordance with strict rules, was already in existence. We possess vivid accounts[4] of how certain groups of Australian Aboriginals, only in modern times shaken rudely out of an archaic mould, learn sets of "songs", each of which is associated with a particular location along a "songline". The specific set of songs committed to memory depend on the ancestral totem of the particular individual (two individuals belonging to different ancestral totems, say, the Wallaby and Emu totems, would have different songlines). When members of the same totem chance to meet on their occasional wanderings they may "exchange songs" in accordance with precise rules which on pain of death may not be infringed. The Central Australian natives believe that these songs were composed not by human beings, but by the totemic ancestors themselves.[5]

A fluent speaker of Aranda, besides being a student of ancient Western languages and epic poetry, T.G.H.Strehlow writes with erudition and in scholarly detail of the prosodic complexity of these Central Australian songs, comparing them favourably with their ancient European parallels. Until recent times, it seems, Aranda men drew immensely rich polysyllabic vocabularies from their songs, making use of these vocabularies in everyday conversation, with the result that by the time they reached middle age their language had become quite different from that of women or uninitiated male children. A similar thing happened in Europe amongst those who had become steeped in the Roman and Greek classics, but what happened in Aboriginal communities seems even more remarkable:

> Generally speaking, the older the speaker and the higher his status in the community, the richer his vocabulary and the more elaborate his diction... It is this command over a difficult language, a language having a great range of vocabulary and capable of expressing an amazing variety of fine shades of meaning by means of suffixes and particles, that has always made me feel, whenever I have been conversing with the older Aranda men who had been trained in speech by means of the sacred myths and songs, that I was in the presence of men of education and culture: only a sound literary education could have produced that kind of command over a language which is possessed by the Central Australian native men. (Strehlow 1971, 247)

How and why, then, did the great oral traditions, first in one part of the world, later in others, and in modern times everywhere, go into decline? In Australia this cultural catastrophe was, we know, brought about by the damaging impact of officialdom, greedy mining prospectors and mostly well-intentioned planners and missionaries; of Western ways in general. But what was it that caused the oral traditions of ancient civilizations of the Mediterranean, South-eastern Europe and the Near East to give way to the written word and the book? Could it have been urban pedagogues and specialists, or was it pressures towards administrative and economic centralization?

The transition from an oral to a written culture can only have been gradual. Oral traditions continued to flourish alongside well-developed traditions of writing. One explanation for this relatively untroubled coexistence could be that, in its earlier stage, the use of writing was confined to calendars, records, inventories, ritual, and other utilitarian or specialized purposes. The earliest use of inventorial writing seems to be surprisingly ancient, dating back possibly to as early as the ninth millenium B.C. By then the practice of keeping stones and pieces of baked clay of different signifying shapes inside clay containers for itemizing commercial transactions or other kinds of record keeping was already established. The need to seal these containers and the inconvenience of having to open them to check the contents, must have prompted the practice and technique of impressing pictures of the enclosed tokens on the outsides of the containers while still wet and before being sealed. The impressed tokens have been found to be graphically identical with early Sumerian pictograms.[6] So came into being linear writing. Meanwhile the bardic domain and no doubt the vital parts of the culture remained oral, until such a time, centuries later, as the written word gained precedence in that domain also.

In the course of this complex and lengthy period of transition – from no writing to virtually all writing – the spoken word, the only mould in which language had evolved over hundreds of millennia, became itself profoundly influenced first by linear and later by maximally phonetic alphabetic writing. It has been said that Western-style grammar and with it its concomitant – logic – grew out of written language. In European languages even the shape of the word as we know it may be an outgrowth of writing.[7]

> Conditions arose in history – essentially those of settlement – where experience had to be recorded: we need to store knowledge, and put it on file. So we invent a filing system for language, reducing it to writing. The effect of this is to anchor language at a shallower level of consciousness. For the first time, language comes to be made of constituents – sentences – instead of dependency patterns – clause complexes – of the spoken mode. And with constituency comes a different form of interpretation of experience.[8]

The earliest linear form of writing is logographic writing (phonetic writing is a descendant of logographic writing), a system that becomes fully developed when a graphic sign acquires a phonetic value independent of what the icon itself might be said to represent, as in Ancient Egypt and Sumeria, or in present-day China.[9] The logogram – what Chinese call the "character" and the Egyptologist the hieroglyph – channelled speech into predetermined moulds.   Once you had logograms – specifically "transcribing" for example the "spoken words" sun and moon, day and night, now and then, field, tree and stream – certain logical restrictions were automatically placed on speakers, readers, and their language. The reader (or writer) of the logogram could not, for instance, be someone sitting here now – a magus sunk in rapt contemplation – and at the same time a hawk or an eagle soaring in the distant sky. The inner life of the "spirit" could not go on being the same thing as the "wind" blowing out there. People were obliged to concede that "the blowing of the inner spirit" had become frozen into a metaphor.

Such restrictions notwithstanding, a logographic system still allows some degree of individual latitude in speech. For instance, pronunciation can be allowed to vary considerably from one region to another without creating the need for a different representation in writing or different sets of glossaries. At the same time syntactic "entropy" of the kind evident, say, in English and other European languages is held in check. The classical Chinese canon, with its relative absence of prepositions, articles, conjunctions and the like, has remained relatively unaffected by the kinds of syntactic constraint that proliferate in alphabetic languages; with the result that, in principle, full scope remains to the reader as interpreter.

The progression from logography, through the syllabary, to alphabet writing has not been a sudden one. The complete synchronization of speaking with writing – the phonetic alphabet – could not have come about overnight; yet in retrospect it appears to have been inevitable. This process of synchronization first began in the Eastern Mediterranean in Ugarit and Byblos and went on throughout the second millennium B.C. The alphabet is especially associated with the Phoenicians, though it seems unlikely that it was they who evolved alphabetic writing. But, owing to their extensive maritime and commercial links within the Mediterranean and beyond, it seems more than likely that it was the Phoenicians who disseminated this new form of writing,[10] and especially the specifically alphabetized forms that developed first into the Greek alphabet, and subsequently into the Etruscan and Roman scripts, and much later into the Germanic runes and the Ogam and Cyrillic alphabets.

From the time of this synchronization onwards, the discourse of writing permeated the spoken medium. With the introduction of moveable-type printing in the fifteenth century, the language of letters became the property of all those with a modicum of education. In the Western world the concept of schooling itself became a by-product first of alphabetic writing and then of printing. Poets are the ones who have chafed most at its constraints, particularly those who in modern times have tried to break out of the straitjacket of alphabetic writing in a movement towards an "emancipation of the word".

When the claim is sometimes made that preliterate and literate

peoples are "brain different", it is not always racism. The fact that
urbanized consumerist Westerners speak more or less in the same way
as they write must affect the way in which the individual's brain has
formed and hence the way their brains work. Literate individuals, with
their greater left-brain dominance (and correspondingly undeveloped
right brains), are predictably more intelligent (in IQ terms) than
sharp-witted, more organized than resourceful, practical and single-
minded rather than spontaneously adaptable. The seeming riot and
chaos of real speech is something unfamiliar to highly literate people
whose "literacy" has become the only conceivable guide to what they
say and think. As soon as I stop to think about what I am saying I am
reaching for a written norm. Linguistics itself, while laying claim to
being a linguistics of speech, has all along been a linguistics of
writing; covertly however, and without its exponents being aware of
the real nature of writing.[11] It is now known that the sort of
grammatical analysis that the West inherited from Graeco-Roman
antiquity was in no small part a response to the need for an
educational programme which would wean children away from rote
learning, to prepare them for subsequent schooling in rhetoric (Harris
1980, 120-1). Grammar, it has been argued, is the brainchild of
grammarians, "a European cultural product. It is also one of Europe's
most successful cultural exports." Its imposition throughout the world
by missionaries and pedagogues has "constituted a disruptive intrusion
into the local linguistic ecology" (Harris 1987, 100).

The vestiges of spoken norms are those of the village, the outback,
the street market, the "speech fellowship"[12] of club or pub, shifting
however slightly from day to day, from place to place, from one knot
of folk to another. At this point therefore it might be as well to
distinguish between true speech and what is commonly termed a
vernacular. Although at its outset a vernacular is a spoken form of
language, its origin can usually be explained by the emergence of a
vacuum between writing and preliterate speech. A vernacular can be
seen as a regularization, a formalization of preliterate norms. It takes
root whenever speech based on the written norm has been perceived as
being too remote from ordinary speech and when there is a need for a
literate, if as yet unwritten, norm. Left to develop independently, and
without undue interference from the "higher" literary norm, a
vernacular will eventually yield its own crop of writers and poets.
This is what happened for example in the case of the

so-called "Romance"languages which in the early Middle Ages detached themselves from their "Roman", or spoken and written Latin, norm (Dante for example wrote in a Romance vernacular and, in so doing, created the basis of the modern Italian written norm). In some cultures, widely used and at one time "high status" vernaculars have nevertheless developed only very limited literary independence. The reasons for this are political or cultural rather than linguistic. For instance, over a considerable period of time, there have been separate and well developed vernaculars of Chinese, one of the most distinctive being Cantonese, spoken in southern China and Hong Kong. Cantonese is so different from standard (spoken) Chinese that many linguists count it a separate language altogether.[13] Yet, virtually all speakers of Cantonese consider their vernacular to be unquestionably Chinese. The prime reasons for this are cultural and historical but also, and especially, because they read and write the Chinese written norm. All this despite the fact that virtually all the words peculiar to Cantonese, and hence not occurring in Modern Standard Chinese, have "unofficial" written forms of their own (many of them of respectable pedigree) and in many informal situations – in everyday correspondence, for example – people make use of them.

Civilization as we know it has gone hand in hand with the development of the written word, whether this be in the West, in the Near East, in India, or in China. It could even be that writing is a precondition for the growth of what we call civilization. Halliday has put it like this:

> Writing brings language to consciousness... Writing puts language in chains; it freezes it, so that it becomes a **thing** to be reflected on. Hence it changes the ways that language is used for meaning with. Writing deprives language of the power to intuit, to make indefinitely many connections in different directions at once, to explore... contradictions, to represent experience as fluid and indeterminate. It is therefore destructive of one fundamental human potential: to think on your toes, as we put it.[14] (Halliday's emphasis)

At the same time, of course, writing has given human beings immense power and, along with it, the possibility of building their creative, pragmatic and communal lives. Without the Book there would be none of the world's great religions, no laws, no academia, no science or technology, none of the political power that nations can turn against each other, as well as against themselves. But, equally, it might be maintained, there would be no political ideology, no police state, no economic "slavery" either. Without the written word, it is even doubtful whether people would have come by their personal and private lives.

13. The Book

Speech is probably as old as Man, but there is evidence that writing too has a much longer prehistory than was formerly supposed. Leroi-Gourhan (1964, I, 269) has attempted to show that from very early times human vocal and graphic expression have been interrelated. Both have their roots in a common aptitude for extracting order and meaning from a world of chaos. Language itself could have been born of an intellectual and aesthetic coupling of sound and line.

The earliest known graphism is abstract and rhythmic, matching the equally abstract and rhythmic succession of phonic elements that go to make up speech. Only after a lapse of several millennia did graphic expression becoming vividly representational, attaining its Golden Age in the "Magdalenian" cave art – Lascaux and Altamira and, from reports as this book goes to press, even more gloriously at Combe d'Arc in the Ardèche – radiocarbon-dated between 18,000 and 10,000 B.C., which places them during the last glaciation.

Even at its most splendidly representational this mural art remains highly formalized, stereotyped almost. Its motifs, however marvellous their draughtsmanship, are repeated in similar sequences within the same location but also, and significantly, from one location to another. For this reason alone these Palaeolithic works of art have long been something of a puzzle to archaeologists and art historians alike. Comprehensive sense can be made of them, says Leroi-Gourhan, only if they are "read" as a **prelinear** form of writing: no transient, inchoate form of writing, be it noted, but a powerful and fully developed system within a long and secure tradition. Accordingly, if Leroi-Gourhan is correct, Early Man throughout the longest explorable segment of human prehistory was accustomed to incorporating forms of graphic representation in a non-linear writing system to which Modern Man has no key and little chance of finding one, hampered as he is by his linear speech-related writing (1964, I, 273). Those anonymous cave artists, not too remote in spirit and symbolic purpose from the equally anonymous sculptors, painters and wood-carvers of the medieval cathedrals, should be seen as the "writers" of non-linear "texts" in support of an entire mythology (myth in a truly Aristotelean sense), a whole literature of ritual narrative and epic.

The "mythograms" of Palaeolithic cave art, as Leroi-Gourhan styles them, would have been "read" just as surely as the present-day Australian Aboriginal "reads" his primitively inscribed and ostensibly meaningless *churinga*. The first truly linear writing, such as that found relatively recently, in Neolithic times in China, Egypt, Sumer, or the Indus Valley, as well as even more recently, among the Maya, is separated from the cave mythograms by a gulf of calibrated time: in most regions some seven to eight millennia. But during that long interval "mythographic" art survived, in some regions more explicitly than in others. During the same period writing was undergoing a process known as "semasiography" in which pictures were becoming specifically signifying icons, with the gradual accretion of more distinct meanings and, in due time, phoneticization; but as yet remaining far from linear, its "code" requiring a "key" that would likely elude the modern scholar. Perhaps the Mesolithic and stylized early Neolithic rock paintings of the Spanish Levant fall into this category, as undoubtedly do the stone carvings, possibly calendrical, for example at Newgrange in Eire. The view is gaining acceptance that, over a period of some 1,500 years, Mayan writing evolved from being semasiographic and even mythographic to a linear logographic system, with increasing phoneticization over time (Morley and Brainerd 1983, 532). In his translation of the Mayan *Popol Vuh* from a parallel text in post-conquest Spanish and alphabetic Quiché (a Mayan language) Tedlock suggests that

> the writing not only records words but sometimes has elements that picture or point to [meanings] without the necessity of a detour through words. As for the pictures, they not only depict what they mean but have elements that can be read as words... At times the writers of the alphabetic *Popol Vuh* seem to be describing pictures, especially when they begin new episodes in narratives. (1986, 30-31)

The title of this important Mayan text means "Council Book", a book of divination which in pre-Columbian times, in an earlier hieroglyphic version, is said to have been a priceless possession of the Highland Mayan rulers. Only specialists in divination would have known how to read it, each glyph being the key to a discrete narrative reading:

> When the ancient reader of the *Popol Vuh* took the role of a diviner and astronomer, seeking the proper date for a ceremony or a momentous political act, we may guess that he looked up a specific passage, pondered its meaning, and rendered an opinion. But... there were also occasions on which the reader offered "a long performance and account" whose subject was the emergence of the whole *cahuleu* or "sky-earth", which was the Quiché way of saying "world". (Tedlock 1983, 32)

A curious supplement to Leroi-Gourhan's theory of the origin of writing is to be found in Lévi-Strauss's study of the Nambikwara, a preliterate tribe of the Amazon. The graphic skill of the Nambikwara does not extend beyond the most rudimentary patterns of dots and zigzags. In his *Tristes Tropiques* Lévi-Strauss describes an intriguing incident (1973, 385ff.). The tribal leader, it appears, was a man of unusual acuity, enterprise and ingenuity. Although totally unacquainted with writing he had no difficulty however in grasping its role and purpose, not least the social superiority conferred by it. Requesting a note-pad he traced a wavy line or two on the paper, and gave it back to Lévi-Strauss, fully expecting the anthropologist to be able to read what he had written there:

> Each time he drew a line he examined it with great care, as if meaning must suddenly leap to the eye; and every time a look of disappointment came over his face.

It was as if there had been an unspoken agreement between the two of them that the chieftain's scribblings held a meaning that his European guest had to pretend to decipher. "His own verbal commentary was so prompt in coming that I had no need to ask him to explain what he had written" (1973, 388-9). It was at this point that something remarkable happened:

> No sooner was everyone assembled than [the leader] drew forth from

a basket a piece of paper covered with scribbled lines and pretended to read from it. With a show of hesitation he looked up and down his "list" for the objects to be given in exchange for his people's presents. To so and so a bow and arrow, a machete! and to another a string of beads! for him necklaces – and so on for two solid hours. (1973, 389)

At this juncture a detour into what is probably the most radical theory of writing to date may not be out of place. The thesis of Jacques Derrida (1974) is that writing – "archē-writing" as he calls it – is not only coeval with speech but actually comprehends within itself the totality of language phenomena, and much else besides. Linear, and especially phonetic writing, according to Derrida, is a perversion of true writing. This "perverted" kind of writing leads inevitably to the Civilization of the Book, an era which, Derrida thinks, is only now in the closing years of the twentieth century nearing its end.

Derrida has adopted an almost opposite position from that of Leroi-Gourhan. In Derrida's view speech and writing were once part and parcel of each other and only became differentiated with the phoneticization (and linearization) of writing. Not only that, but writing is claimed to be the origin of all things human (1974, 56); nothing like a linear proto-alphabetic writing, but truly a unity of natural voice and natural writing, originally related to voice and breath, not grammatical but of the spirit (pneumatological).

With "phonologism" came the text, and with the text came *epistemē*, science and social structures accompanied by all the mixed blessings of civilization that ensued. In sustaining discourse the phoneticized text, Derrida seems to be saying, has excluded genuine writing. On the other hand non-phoneticization, which is life, constitutes a menace to the substantiality and presence which "orders all objectivity of the object and all relation to knowledge," the "formation of form" itself.

Derrida's critique raises the question of origin and its possible interpretation. For the "deconstruction of presence" Derrida looks to the *trace* or "imprint" which, according to him, is the origin of meaning in texts, the "chains", the "systems of traces" that sustain the world. The "trace" itself is not the same thing as origin. It is anterior to intelligibility and sensibility, an "opaque" energy" that "no concept in metaphysics can describe". The term *trace* does not lend itself to easy translation or definition (definition in any case is not a game that Derrida seems to want to play). In one place Derrida equates *trace* with what he calls the "arché-phenomenon of memory" (1974, 70) and in another with "that which does not let itself be summed up in the simplicity of the present time" (1974, 66). Spoken language forms part of the *trace*, but in isolation cannot serve as the transmitter of culture. Even a community possessing nothing resembling any form of inscription would still have in its midst members in whose memories certain cultural arrangements – kinship relations, spatial dispositions, tribal lore and medicine – are inscribed. Preliterate peoples, says Derrida, understand the purpose of writing. All they lack is a certain **type** of writing: literate linear writing.

At the same time Derrida's polemic appears to be an attempt at deconstruction of the life-world as philosophers including Husserl and Gadamer have conceived it. Derrida implicitly poses such questions as: What inherent characteristic of the human species is it that has made the Word possible? What original form did the Word, or *logos* take? Derrida believes that all this had to do with an archaic activity in human beings, best described as writing. Writing, Derrida insists, is much more than just symbolic inscription. What he terms "primary writing" is the order within which mental images and all relationships are "pre-scribed", delineated, "drawn". As soon as the earliest human-like ancestor began to structure family and clan relationships, he (or more likely she) was delineating, inscribing concepts as well as ways of thinking and feeling into the "text" of the tribal memory.

Even unconscious knowledge must be differentially "inscribed" in the genetically adequate brain. Preliterate and literate alike are unconscious of the rule structure and generative mechanisms of language. Yet in a real sense the speaker somehow **already knows** what these are. Otherwise, the speaker would not be able to apply rules; a point first insisted on and reaffirmed more than once by Chomsky (1980). Furthermore, language in the shared mode has mapped the social behaviour and channelled the motivations of modern and primitive man alike. Social codes in turn have made it possible for human communities to distinguish between what is acceptable and proper to a particular situation, and what is "forbidden" or "unnatural".

Such rules and codes clearly display their essential nature in the domain of phenomenology. In any known language the pronouns "I" and "you" may exchange roles more than once in the course of an ordinary conversation. Whenever I refer to myself as "I" in such a conversation I am referring not to a physiologically ordered mass of molecules – in this instance my own body – or even to an ego, with a name and identity, but to a verbal role performed in the actual situation there and then. Roland Barthes stated the problem as follows:

> The "I" of discourse can no longer be a place where a previously stored up person is innocently restored.

In no linguistic interaction, Barthes pointed out, can the "I" be regarded as a single homogeneous entity. Every time I refer to "myself", I am making a **new** reference to a different referent. "The 'I' of the one who writes *I* is not the same as the 'I' which is being read by 'thou' "; a state of affairs that Barthes ascribed to a "fundamental dissymmetry" of language.[1] No matter who I am, Merleau-Ponty adds, whenever I speak it is never merely a question of a simple "I" experiencing the presence of others within the self. To the extent that what I have to say has meaning, or is said with intention – in short, as an act of speech – I become a different "other" for myself; and to the extent that I am able to comprehend what is being said I no longer know who is speaking and who is listening (Merleau-Ponty 1964, 97). In performing a speech act the "I" embedded in this act (e.g. *I promise...*, *Believe me...*) is no longer me, but a **projected** "I", an other, the agent of the *trace*, so to speak. Many languages, English included, formally accommodate this fact by permitting speakers to substitute *you* for *I* (e.g. *You could tell something was wrong*, meaning of course "I could tell...")

In traditional "representational" grammar a pronoun is defined as word standing in place of a noun. It can easily be seen however that a personal pronoun (*I* and *you* being the only true personal pronouns) is a totally different entity from a noun:

> Each instance of the use of a noun is referred to a fixed and "objective" notion, capable of remaining potential or being actualized in a particular object and always identical with the mental image it awakens,

whereas a personal pronoun cannot constitute a class of reference, in that there exists no such object, no such logical or real definable entity as "you" or "I" (Benveniste 1971, 218). Every occurrence of "I" refers uniquely. The shifter pronouns *I* and *you* do not refer in the same manner as noun subjects or predicates. The only reality to which personal pronouns refer is what Benveniste has called the "reality of discourse" and Derrida "primary writing". "I" signifies neither me nor anyone else, beyond "the person uttering the present instance of discourse containing the word *I*". The only way of identifying "I" therefore is by reference to the instance of discourse that contains it. "I" possesses no value even, outside the instance of discourse in which it is produced and conveys no "linguistic experience" outside the act of speaking in which it occurs. The words *I* and *you* announce the speaker as speaker and accordingly are fundamental to, "written into", the exercise of language as such. They "define the individual by the particular linguistic construction he makes use of while he announces himself as speaker" (Benveniste 1971, 220).

Primary writing must at the same time be "primary reading". As far as literate, and hence "articulate", cultures are concerned, reading has been inextricably linked to the written word. The difference between a Western sophisticate reading a sonnet or a philosophical treatise and the Nambikwara chieftain "reading" from arbitrary scribble looks so immense that any attempt at a comparison might seem ludicrous. And yet, if such a comparison is approached from a less familiar angle, some plausible degree of similarity might be detected.

"Primary reading" has its clearest beginnings in the work of I.A.Richards. It was Richards who first shifted the burden of literary criticism from the text itself to the reader by redefining a poem as

> a class of experiences which do not differ in any character more than a certain amount, varying for each character, from a standard experience... the relevant experience of the poet when contemplating the completed composition. (1926, 226-7)

The meaning of poem, Richards maintains, no longer resides in the text but in the (competent) reader interpreting it. Thus began the quest for the "standard reader", the "average reader", the "notional reader", and eventually the "super-reader"; and, following not too far behind that, the sort of absurd deduction that a poem may be non-existent until and unless it is experienced and recreated afresh in every new experience of that poem.[2] Luckily, dead-end quests of this sort subsequently gave way to a different and at the same time more productive approach, one that is epitomized by Barthes in his *Critique et Vérité*. A literary work, says Barthes, carries an array of different potential meanings upon which the "reading" of a particular reader, bringing to it his or her situation, is superimposed. In this way a work of literature is brought into actuality.

This turns out to be no simple act of recovery as would be, say, Northrop Frye's likening of a text to a mechanical device for bringing an entire artistic structure under the interpretative control of a single individual (1971, 248). Rather, it is something more in the nature of actual composition itself. In the Barthesian interpretation the reader is in an important sense writing the work he is reading. The literary work must be allowed an existence in its own right, but it cannot protest against the "meaning" the reader might choose to give it. No protest, at any rate, is possible once the reader has submitted to the constraints of the "symbolic code" that lies at its base; that is to say, after a reader has allowed a particular reading to become inscribed within what Barthes has called its "symbolic space". Even though the literary work might be independent of the different readers' "situations" bearing upon it, it always surrenders itself to exploration, thereby becoming the repository of an immense and ceaseless process of inquiry into what is actually being said (Barthes 1966, 55). The existence of a literary work no longer implies that it possesses an already prescribable interpretation or meaning. In a text it is no longer a question of "contents" but of the conditions under which content can come into being.

The relationship between reader and text according to Barthes is dialectical in nature. The minimal "unit of reading" (*lexie*) is not a unit of content but a stretch of text identifiable by the reader as having a specific effect or function, and distinguishable from what might appear in adjacent stretches. The key is dialectic and it is this that makes Barthes' *lexie* so different from Frye's *symbol* which also purports to be a unit of literary text (Barthes 1974, 13ff.). The level of *lexie* is said to represent the reader's primary **contact** with the text, and not the text as such...

*   *   *

We left Lévi-Strauss's Nambikwara chieftain reading from scribbles, and were about to consider what his improvised stunt might have in common with "literate" reading.

Whatever view one might take, reading is clearly much more than an algorithmic decoding of prearranged meanings inherent in the succession of words. Barthes was not alone in his conviction that there exists a complex and dynamic dialectical relationship between reader and written word. Proponents of the theory of "literary competence" argue that the reader possesses innate "readerly" capacities which with appropriate training within a literary tradition will enable that reader to read literary texts.[3] This is a view that becomes all the more plausible when we are dealing with texts with little or no syntax, with few of the "empty" words of language (articles, prepositions, etc.) which serve as discourse signposts. Readers of Classical Chinese poetry for instance will generally be faced with a choice: either to follow the existing commentaries (*i.e.* previous readers' readings) or to devise a reading of their own, in varying degrees *ab origine*. In a literature like that of Chinese the reader would be unlikely to develop a view of writing as a mere "supplement" of speech and would be less prone to the preconception that reading is simply a matter of appropriate decoding. It is only in Western languages where writing, intermittently, has been "transparent", where discourse sequences coincided tolerably well with the prescriptions of logic, that the reader could have been lulled into this frame of mind. Only now, in the latter part of the present century, can any text be "deconstructed" and read in a hermeneutic spirit, with meanings allowed to emerge freely, against a growing awareness of the dialectical ambivalence of temporal (cultural and historical) perspectives, through our own particular relation with the text and that text's relation to other texts ("intertextuality"). But, then, experienced and imaginative readers have probably always known this intuitively.

The literate, it seems, are not after all too dissimilar from the Nambikwara "reader" to the extent that in reading texts they must up to a point, but nevertheless in a very real sense, **write** them. Unlike the Nambikwara chieftain they would not of course be observed reading from their own gratuitously devised scribbles, but they are just as surely creating (rather than merely reconstituting) the meaning and content they discern among the graphic marks of the text. If they happen to be reading an ancient Chinese text or, alternatively, picking their way through *Finnegan's Wake* they will more easily become conscious of this. It is only when they are reading popular magazine articles, reports, or "pulp" novels that they notice nothing of this sort; what they encounter there amounts to little more than a predigested skein of meaning in its unimpeded transparency, and this requires virtually no "active reading". The author, as it were, has prepared the "reading" for a readership in advance. The resultant text is so like a mirror that it does not engage its readers as readers but abandons them to the mercy of none the less real controlling forces, of which they remain unconscious.

What then is a text? An answer to this question may lie anywhere between a linguist's standard description and the view, at the farthest extreme, that a text is no longer the property of an author but something to be realized within a reader's hermeneutic. Halliday for example characterizes a text – though by no means in any standard predictable manner – as "an operational unit of language", in the same way that a sentence is a syntactic unit. A text may be spoken or written, long or short, and includes "as a special instance" the literary text. In Halliday's frame of reference however, what he terms the "textual function" is not limited to the establishment of relations between sentences but is equally concerned with the meanings of sentences as messages both in themselves and in relation to the context.[4]

A sharply different and more persuasive approach is that taken by Stanley Fish. His view, a paradoxical one, is that texts exist in their own right but that they are dependent in every way on interpretation (1980, 272). Tantalizing though this view may seem, Fish has perhaps let his case rest too soon. He has desisted from explaining – perhaps because of the obviousness – that texts share the properties and characteristics of all other phenomena. A printed text, after all, is no more than a pattern of marks on a flat surface. What gives this pattern meaning as a text, what constitutes it epistemologically, the agents who supply the figuration, the interpreters, are you and me. Texts are of the same nature as rainbows, stories, tunes, sunsets, humour, looks, character, and the like. They exist but, because their context is unrepeatable, they are subject to interpretation. A text is never the same on different reading occasions, whether from reader to reader, or for the same reader. This implies that, try as I may, I can never "read" the same book twice. Or, from the more paradoxical slant of Fish:

> Because we are never not in a situation, we are never not in the act of interpreting. Because we are never not in the act of interpreting, there is no possibility of reaching a level of meaning beyond or below interpretation. But in every situation some or other meaning will appear to us to be uninterpreted because it is isomorphic with the interpretive structure the situation (and therefore our perception) already has. Therefore, there will always be a literal reading, but (1) it will not always be the same one and (2) it can change.(1980, 276-7).

None of this takes us to the roots of interpretation in that texts mediate, and are mediated through, a semiotic. A study of the phenomenology of mediation is needed, especially as we seem to be only at the beginning of our understanding of texts. What has so far been said applies also to spoken "texts" even though they are quite literally unrepeatable. Even when recorded or properly transcribed a spoken text has its context transposed every time it is replayed or reread.

The written word, it goes without saying, has many advantages over the spoken word. It occupies space as well as time and, not confined to the fleeting instant, is able to exploit without limit the power of the word to forge endless links of graphic form and sense with other words, well beyond the horizon of the immediate context. Because words are limitlessly related to each other the written word especially can conjure up new configurations of sense, lure symbols from the Unconscious, make the humdrum appear strange. In certain moods the written word can be tantalizing, outlandish, oracular; in others dazzling, mocking – what Vladimir Nabokov (in a reference to the wizardly diction of Pushkin) once called the "tomfooleries of language". Literary conceits are ancient enough, underpinning all writing even at its most "transparent". The language of literature is so different from ordinary language that it is best thought of as a second language (in a parasitical sense) (Barthes 1972, 267) or more positively as a language that is "not our own" (Preston, 1985).

This domain of the shared supra-personal mode of language that is not our own is endowed with a capacity comparable to our own for creating worlds, literary texts inhabited by people on the face of it similar to ourselves; the difference being that they are made out of words, and not out of flesh and blood. How does this "world of texts"

stand in relation to the life-world that is our own? Surely, a problem
for phenomenology to explore. In Derridan terms written language is a
kind of violence; not only through literary texts, which of themselves
are innocuous, but through the "text" of the shared world, peopled by
the self and others, all "woven" out of primal writing, but guaranteed
by a "metaphysics" that is "an exemplary system of defence against the
threat of writing" (Derrida 1974, 101), by a morality, and a reflection
"which denudes the native non-identity, classification as denaturation
of the proper [the reassuring seal of self-identity], and identity as the
abstract moment of the concept" (1974, 112). Supra-personality shows
up as the undoing of innocence.

*   *   *

Melville's *Moby Dick* opens with a simple invitation – "Call me
Ishmael". But **who** is Ishmael? Already, from the very first words of
the book, the reader is deep in story; the words are ringing with
vastness of the world that is about to unfold. Ishmael is a biblical
figure; so he cannot be easily dismissed as pure fiction. But, regardless
of any biblical allusion, Ishmael has from the outset taken on a larger-
than-life semblance of reality. He can refer to himself as "I", just as
plausibly as you or I. To insist that everything depends on the reader
with his inbred capacity for "reading" texts (that capacity is real
whereas Ishmael is other than real) does not remove the difficulty. As
was noted earlier the "I" of discourse has been said to be nothing more
than a verbal role performed in a unique context of situation. The
problem of stabilizing a constant "unshifted" referent for Ishmael is
exactly the same as for anyone else, "real" or "fictitious". Is the
Ishmael who bids the reader call him thus the **same** Ishmael who at
various points in the novel recedes into the background, and then
surfaces with his "Lectures on the anatomy of the Cetacea"? If he is
the same, then who is it in the hundred-and-first chapter that
addresses Ishmael? Are we to suppose that it is none other than
Ishmael himself?

From an ontological point of view, "fiction" has become much
more complex than it ever was, insofar as it has taken a new and
different role. Authors may be "pretending" to refer to people and

events, but at the same time they will establish with the reader a "set of understandings about how far the horizontal conventions of fiction break the vertical conventions of serious speech."[5] Coherence is crucial. Impossible as it may be to be hard and fast in one's opinions about what constitutes coherence, inasmuch as it will vary from genre to genre, coherence of whatever form is "in part a function of the contract between author and reader" in relation to the conventions. After making the point that a work of fiction need not consist entirely of fictional discourse, Searle raises an implication of overwhelming concern:

> Serious speech acts can be conveyed by fictional texts, even though the conveyed speech act is not represented in the text. Almost any important work of fiction conveys a "message" or "messages" which are conveyed **by** the text but are not **in** the text. Only in such children's stories as contain the concluding "and the moral of the story is..." or in tiresomely didactic authors such as Tolstoy do we get an explicit representation of the serious speech acts which it is the point... of the fictional text to convey. Literary critics have explained on an *ad hoc* and particularistic basis how the author conveys a serious speech act through the performance of the pretended speech act which constitutes the work of fiction, but there is as yet no general theory of the mechanisms by which such serious illocutionary intentions are conveyed by pretended illocutions."[6] (Searle's emphasis)

Searle proposes to consider the "conventions of fictional discourse" as a set of conventions which "suspend the normal requirements" established by rules. But, as Fish rightly points out, "an author is free to import whatever real world references he likes, and there will be no rules regarding the proportions."[7] In *Moby Dick* this proportion reaches, one might say, disproportion. The important thing about a novel of this order of literary magnitude is not whether its author is being truthful – we never doubt that he is – but the way fact is displaced and "made strange" in a literary fiction. But more about this in the next chapter.

Between actual utterance and literary fiction, between speech act and "literary act", there are interposed the constraints of time and space. In addition, a literary act is "issued" indirectly by an author who can up to a point control the universe of his fiction. (Up to a point only: we should not overlook the strange case of Dostoevsky who at times lost himself, literally, among the ins-and-outs of his characters). It would be a mistake to ascribe too great importance to this latter difference, for the reason that even as three-dimensional flesh-and-blood people we find ourselves no less "written" by and into the social and cultural life-world that is ours. Our field of possible action and (even more important) the "interpretation" of the things we do, the "story" of our actions, is dictated by the anonymous authorship of our immediate context and wider culture. Camus' anti-hero in *The Outsider*, we may recall, is condemned less for an alleged crime, from which he should objectively have been exculpated, than for being the sort of unadmirable character he is considered by public opinion to be. This absence of a clear line between reality and fiction in much modern literature is doing no more than reflecting the god-like supra-personality of the shared mode of language as against the always precarious condition of the life-world (*la condition humaine*) which everyone experiences, even if only at moments.

14. Language in Literature

The French poet Paul Valéry once wrote that "literature is and can be nothing else than a kind of extension and application of certain properties of language" (1956-75, XIII, 85). At one level this statement announces a rediscovery of the true nature of language, obscured as it had been by a long-established treatment of language as a scientific object and everyday commodity and, above all, by the subjection of language to relentless erosion by the rational principle.[1] Looked at from another angle however, Valéry's observation conceals an inescapable irony.

In our own century language has undoubtedly been thrown into sharper relief than at any time since the Renaissance by two opposite, yet collusive, departures: on the one hand linguistics, which until recently has played down the importance of language in literature, and on the other, the study of literature and its shunning of the prosaic mechanics of linguistic analysis – collusive, insofar as both linguistics and literary criticism, peering over each other's fences, so to speak, have been reacting against an earlier headlong momentum in the direction of an impasse in which language and literature would ultimately have been confined to hermetically sealed domains. Only in recent years have language and literature reversed this trend, and taken a fresh turn "in the process of finding each other again" (Barthes 1972, 134).

Language at its most natural, free, and real, it goes almost without saying, is poetry. "The best words in the best order" is how Coleridge put it. In poetry in this widest and not necessarily versified sense, language sheds the constraints imposed by the makeshift of everyday communication and by the straitjacket of social preconditions and norms. At the level of workaday exchange, language tends towards the approximate, the expedient, the inchoate and obtuse; it can be ugly, and designed to mislead. Under these conditions language holds itself in check (Bruns 1974, 2-3). Without this self-restraint, language could fail to supply that provisional sort of transactional communication which is our ordinary linguistic diet. Real language has to remain, as it were, in suspense. Meaning is seldom made flesh. More often, it is obscured by the demands of the moment. Because communication is a shared phenomenon, much of what is said remains incomplete and unuttered; listeners tend less towards interpretation than towards anticipation. In "scientific" and kindred styles of rational and algorithmic discourse, language keeps itself at several farther removes below its full reality, inasmuch as in such domains words are indeed used more – to adopt Firth's term – as "substitution counters" than as true vehicles of verbal meaning. In modern times real language outside literature has become uncommon, and some of the reasons for this have already been highlighted.

If "literature is made of language" it can perhaps equally be said that "language is made of literature". It is only that the rooted conceptions of language and literature in our day resist such an inversion. But now that poetry has once again come into its own, it can be considered, in the words of Wallace Stevens, "part of the *res* itself and not about it" (1964, 473). Without any longer sounding preposterous, writers can positively assert that poetic creation is the source of all language – the world itself speaking through poetry (Dufrenne 1963, 98).

One wonders therefore how long the opposing view, that the language of literature is somehow **deviant** language will go on being held. The prejudice could have been discounted or disregarded as a disappearing viewpoint, had it not been for its resurgence in modern criticism in a more scientific guise. One of the more extreme formulations had it that "poetic" language is altogether different from "standard" language despite there being a close connection between the two.[2] Poetic language, so it is claimed, should be considered a "distortion" of normal usage, a "systematic violation" of the norm. Poetry is made possible even, the argument goes, by a violation of this order:

The more the norm of the standard is stabilized in a given language, the more varied can be its violation and therefore the more possibilities for poetry in that language.[3]

For several critics in the Russian Formalist tradition the language of poetry was considered maximally **foregrounded** language. By this is meant that certain semantic or stylistic features of words or sequences of words are given unusual prominence. In its purest form, standard language was said to abhor foregrounding; although in certain kinds of writing, in newspaper headlines for example, foregrounding can be used to catch the potential reader's eye. Only in poetic language however was foregrounding supposed to surmount mere gimmickry, pushing the more immediate and pragmatic requirements of communication into the background, leaving only language, pure and unadulterated, in all its expressivity. The norm, according to this species of argument, is something poets cannot dispense with for the reason that their work is projected against this norm as background. Only as a consequence of the existence of such a background is the poet's language perceived as a distortion of the norm.

At first sight, the subsequent shifting of the burden of stylistic analysis from the "linguistic" to the "contextual" norm might seem to offer a more adequate alternative to the undiluted sort of deviationist theory. Following Riffaterre (1959, 171) one can too easily be persuaded that a "stylistic context" is one in which "a linguistic pattern [is] suddenly broken by an element which was unpredictable," the contrast itself being the result of of this type of interference in the "stylistic stimulus"; while the context itself is envisaged as being "a linear segment oriented in the direction of the eye's progress in reading a line." The more clearly delineated the pattern the more pronounced and striking would be the contrast. The appearance-saving value of this approach becomes apparent when it is realized that it enables the notion of an "intrinsically stylistic device" to be discarded. To take a single example: hyperbole has been said to function as a stylistic device only in contexts in which it is **norm**ally absent. By specious reasoning such as this it can of course be shown that hyperbole is in no way an intrinsic stylistic device. Such devices furthermore are said to appear in clusters: the "accumulation at a given point of several independent stylistic devices", each device contributing to the expressivity of the other (Riffaterre 1959, 172). The presence of such convergence, says Riffaterre, proves its own stylistic reality, convergence allegedly being the only stylistic device that can safely be represented as conscious. Once "stylistic facts" have been detected, the linguist can go to work on them.

The circularity of such reasoning becomes all the more apparent in what is claimed to be the nature of "style" itself – with style being reduced to little more than an emphatic augmentation of information already conveyed by linguistic means: "language expresses, style stresses". In reducing style in a literary work to "a written individual form of literary intent" stylistics becomes a watered-down linguistics, just another metalinguistic ghost-in-the-machine, capable of handling only hypothetical "stylistic devices", decipherable by some notional "average reader" or "super-reader", and in some unexplained manner inseparable from the text itself. If that is all stylistics is, we can do without it.

Stylistics must surely find its justification in the study of the styles of individual writers and particular texts, or in the style of a period or even a literary movement. Language in poetry, it can nowadays be insisted, does not "deviate" from any "norm" and only becomes abnormal through becoming artificial or affected. This is not to deny that the language of poetry or prose can make strenuous demands on the reader. A particular poem or book may take several readings, sometimes over a considerable period of time, as its meaning and hermeneutic develop and undergo repeated transformation in the consciousness and inner life of the reader. Even the initiated may take a longer time to read, say, Conrad's *Heart of Darkness* than a much longer novel by Dickens or Balzac.

It is in the mysteriously shared and individually shaped language of the personality that style leaves off and a very different human factor takes over – I hesitate to invoke that awkward and neglected word "soul" (a word which earlier generations had no difficulty with but which remains such an obstacle for people today.[4]) To face the consequences of becoming one's true self – an act keenly dramatized in Joyce's *Portrait of the Artist as a Young Man* – through cultivating an artistic medium or calling, to incarnate in words the sense, passion and path of one's inner life, more for oneself at times than for the benefit of others, must rank among the primary tasks of the modern writer.

Language, we no longer need reminding, is far from being a static thing. It is perpetually at work in the world, transforming the state of things in which utterances occur. Once words are uttered they become transfused with purpose, with *energeia*, swept up into a living context. If literature is indeed made of language, and language is in perpetual activity, then literature must be an at least commensurate activity. The logical consequence of this (and writers under a variety of political régimes need no convincing) is that the literary text can no longer be regarded as a passive thing waiting only to be read.

Modern poetics has had much to say about the role of the author in the production of a literary text. Even when the text is not "spoken" by an invented narrator, or by a "lyrical I", a "persona", or a set of fictional characters, the incautious novice is forewarned against falling into the trap of identifying what is actually written with the "voice" of the author. This is not because the author is being exempted from responsibility, but because real live communication is not of course taking place. The text does not have the author communicating with a reader. In a text there is never any direct encounter. When "speech acts" do occur in a text – which is frequently enough – they are recognized as being of a different character from speech acts in non-fictional discourse. In literature, one might say, there is no facticity of impact of the writer on the reader even though the author may create an effective illusion of this through the use of stylistic and poetic devices. In any literary text, what language **does** or **achieves** takes place **in** and **through** the reader. The "out there" never impinges, except insofar as the text consists of printed or inscribed marks. Nor, obviously, do readers approach the text the same way as they would react to utterances emanating from someone present, either actually or in the surrogate expedient of writing. Simultaneously, readers enter into a dialogue with the text, and with themselves. This is no game of solipsism but the coming into play of a different modality within the domain of shared language. In the words of Ricoeur, the understanding of a text is not an end in itself, or even for itself:

> It mediates the relation to himself of a subject who, in the short circuit of immediate reflection, would not find the meaning in his own life".[5]

Even so, the reading of a piece of literature proliferates with events for which there are available no obvious explanatory categories: nothing actual is happening to the reader, who yet may be repeatedly aroused, maddened by excitement or rage, reduced to tears or laughter, changed even. There is something operating, akin to the Austin-Searle "illocutionary force" inherent in speech acts, yet quite different. In reading, state of mind predominates over force (there is no possibility of changing anything directly), verisimilitude over factuality, authenticity over verifiability, play over competition, multiple layering of meaning over explicitness. Continually, readers have to keep reminding themselves that the activity of language in literature is not, after all, a world apart from language activity taken as a whole. *Homo ludens* remains *homo ludens*; it is only the rules that are somehow not quite the same.

How many readers, one wonders, when reading a literary text actually read it exclusively as "fiction"; if, that is, by identifying a text as fiction the implication would always be registered that it falls outside the limits of the verifiable, in that it does not consist of facts? (Culler 1975, 128). Even though fiction, once it is recognized as such, has the added disadvantage of reducing the reading of literature to a set of conventions, it is doubtful whether too many readers maintain an awareness of the distinction between fiction and non-fiction when actually engaged in reading. Also, prohibitions forbid the author's arbitrary crossing of the fiction/non-fiction boundary, and sanctions can be harsh; as when an account of events presented as "true", implicitly or explicitly, subsequently proves to have been an invention. Certainly the most important, and possibly the only, difference between a claim made about the suicide of a "real person" and Anna Karenina's throwing herself between the wheels of a moving train is that the former can (presumably) be checked and verified, whereas Tolstoy's account of what became of Anna cannot, and would never have been intended to be. There may even be a suggestion of an implication that no one in his right mind would think of trying to verify Tolstoy's account since it is so obviously fictional. Yet, when the difference is examined further, it soon becomes apparent that real persons' claims are not always routinely, let alone systematically, verified; and this despite the range of verificatory means available. Even in forensic contexts a real person may, as Austin puts it, have "abstracted from the dimension of correspondence with facts" (1976, 145) or diverted an interlocutor's attention. The interlocutor has willy-nilly turned into a witness and, through this fact and the potential testimony of others present, the real person's statement has become, so to speak, inscribed in the social memory and record; to the extent that if there is a subsequent change of mind or alteration of the testimony, the same person may be held to account.

But nothing of this forensic sort happens in every instance in which speech events occur. An advertising agency for example would not be held accountable for extravagant claims made on behalf of a client's products; nor would a teacher or preacher for unverifiable claims. What could easily escape notice however is that the moral force of Anna Karenina's pronouncements, witnessed by no one but the reader, commits her just as surely as any "real life" act; even though, owing to her fictional nature, nothing undertaken by her could become actionable.

The novel in general has one *prima facie* advantage over real life: the reader has direct access to a person's innermost thoughts, feelings or intentions, whereas in real life such access is by and large denied. The objection that this could not be the case, on the grounds that a fictional person's thoughts, etc. are put there by an author, will not wash, if only because a real-life individual in order to render account of his or her thoughts, feelings or intentions is obliged to select an "utterance genre" (Bakhtin) for this purpose. In such a case the thoughts, etc. will have been "put there", inscribed by an "author" who is that same a flesh-and-blood individual. There must, readers will object, be a flaw in this argument somewhere; but it is a flaw by no means easy to find. An acquaintance may, in all good faith, have attempted to tell someone what has been taking place in the intimacy of his or her awareness. But, as soon as this is under way, the account may become impossible to distinguish from fiction. An account is always a story and can only become fact in a forensic setting. It is this accountability within the limits of public sanction that makes the real-life person different from Tolstoy's fictitious character. In everyday life, claims, intentions and so forth must be actually uttered and witnessed to become factual; even when no sanction will necessarily be applied, as in the case of a small child in suburbia who informs his mother of the tiger living in a nearby copse. Lying is not a matter of faulty reference or non-correspondence with truth; nor for that matter is fact or fiction a matter of reference or correspondence. There can be just as much fact in literature (*Moby Dick*, we may recall) as in real life; and life contains fiction in plenty. Verisimilitude, whether in literature or in ordinary life, rests on conventions that have nothing to do directly either with language or with genre. Also they are conventions that can change, sometimes abruptly, with time and place. Long after the end of the Middle Ages, people could be condemned to horrible deaths at the stake for reporting events that would seem to us utterly implausible.

In ordinary life verisimilitude can prevail over truth. Conversely, in literature, truth can displace verisimilitude. Our real lives are lived as narrative, whose constraints are not linguistic but social. Our "stories" must dovetail with everyone else's; otherwise there are penalties to be paid. This being so, verisimilitude cannot be coextensive with truth. Facts and shared events become woven, not always by any preconceived plan, into a shared plausibility. The larger and more complex the society the greater the burden borne by verisimilitude. In literature, narrative may be built largely on invented facts and events, but that does not necessarily allow verisimilitude free rein. In a major work of prose a delicate tension can be observed between the conventions of genre, the devices of language, and the play of verisimilitude. *Moby Dick* contains so much fact that the novel becomes in large part documentary, through having drawn much of its content from Melville's own whaling experience and the vast amount of whaling lore collected by him. But all the fact in *Moby Dick* is offset by the outlandish, couched throughout in symbolism and strangeness of style. By contrast, Kafka's *Metamorphosis* stands at a weirdly opposite pole to verisimilitude. Yet the narrative and setting is vividly life-like, to the point of absurdity. In literature, fantasy and fact, strangeness and matter-of-fact – in counterpoint, so to speak – have the effect of counterbalancing, even nullifying, each other; thus managing to preserve the requisite level of verisimilitude while opening up the possibility of truth.

In the language of literature, praxis is encountered at a higher pitch than in ordinary life. The verbal praxis – what we achieve through language in our day-to-day interactions – may already seem complex enough; certainly it is not easy to master or manage, and is easily seen as being diffuse and messy. In literature by comparison, praxis takes on a form and a meaning that is difficult to attain in real life. Our own lives get woven into form-giving narratives not through any desire to turn life into fantasy, but through a constant striving to engender cohesion and sense. In his early piece *La Nausée* Jean-Paul Sartre appears to be saying that our lives are lived as novels, within the conventions that the novel provides. No doubt the fascination of TV soap operas, for all their narrative simple-mindedness and inconsequentiality, can be ascribed to this need to keep on "writing" our lives. Philippe Sollers has described the predicament well:

> The novel is the manner in which this society of ours expresses itself, the way in which the individual must conduct his life in order to be accepted. For this reason it is essential that the "novelistic" point of view should be omnipresent, plain for all to see, and untouchable. Furthermore, things go on as if these books had been written in advance; as if they were part and parcel of that anonymous and all-powerful language and thinking, which hold sway, in our inner lives as well as outside, all the way from the most public sort of information to the most silent inwardness; exaggeratedly visible and for that reason invisible. Our identity depends on it, as well as on what people think of us, and what ideas we form of ourselves – the manner in which our lives are imperceptibly structured. Who am I taken to be, but a character in a novel? (1968, 228) (Translation mine)

For all we know, depressions and other disorders, even physical ones, result from a failure to maintain this narrative. What cannot be denied is that language works in the same way in real life as it does in literature. The genres may not always be the same, with those of literature being more clear-cut, but they are always recognizable none the less. Furthermore, from the point of view of verbal praxis no two works of literature are the same. The self-contained, if not entirely homogeneous or straightforward, praxis of daily life is too easily outstripped by that of literature with its almost endless multiplicity of possible worlds, sometimes finding their embodiment even within the same work. In everyday living the appearances are too easily saved by verisimilitude, temporality, causality, myth, and much else; in the novel, a semblance of truth (as opposed to verisimilitude, which the novel is good at), and ultimately truth itself, has to be created **in spite of** the conventions, which save, but also obstruct.

There remains the unanswered question, fleetingly touch upon previously: What can the words of a literary text possibly be **doing**? And in what possible manner can words in general amount to the doing of anything, except in the restricted class of performative instances singled out for discussion by Austin? Words are but words:

tokens, signs, forms − bits of feeling and culture, at best. Flesh-and-blood deeds and actions − "sticks and stones" − on the other hand can have a decided impact on the situations in which they occur.

One of the foremost exponents of verbal praxis in literature, Stanley Fish, has claimed that an "utterance" in a literary text is not an object, not a thing-in-itself, but an **event,** and that this event is at the same time the **meaning** of the utterance (1972, 386). In other words, what an utterance in a literary text **does** is what it **means.** Literature, Fish agrees with the New Critics, has little to do with rational explanation. This last sets out to fulfil a need that most literature deliberately frustrates (1972, 410). The difficulty however with such an argument begins at the point at which the objective reality of the text gives way before the "active and activating consciousness of the reader." When it becomes a question of reader *vs.* artefact the objective reality of the text is dismissed as a "dangerous illusion" (1972, 384).

Not that one should reject Fish's notion of the reader as an "actively mediating presence", but, to place the entire burden of meaning on the experience of the reader, requires more of a case than Fish appears to offer.[6] It is a pity that the evidence is presented in the form of isolated lines or chunks of prose denuded of their contextual setting. On the other hand, the addition of a more extended context would almost certainly have weakened the argument that what a text actually does involves "an analysis of the developing responses of the reader in relation to the words as they succeed one another in time" (1972, 387-8) or that "the reader's response to the fifth word in a line or sentence is to a large extent the product of his response to words one, two, three and four." Veteran readers of literature would in many cases insist that this is exactly what does **not** happen. Readers take in whole sentences, even whole paragraphs, sometimes at a glance, and do not (as they might with speech, which is instantaneous and temporally sequential) "decode" words and phrases in printed sequence. In general it is untrue that "in an utterance of any length, there is a point at which the reader has taken in only the first [word], and then the second, and then the third, and so on" or that "the report of what happens to a reader is always a report of what has happened **up to that point**" (1972, 388) (Fish's emphasis). This is especially doubtful in the case of readers already familiar with a text. Only when a sentence has been deprived of its setting can it be true that "there is a direct relationship between the meaning of a sentence and what its words mean," or, at another extreme, that the meaning of a sentence depends on the way a reader experiences it.[7]

The reader cannot be discounted, as writers from Richards to Culler, Barthes and Fish have cogently argued; but the reader is by no means all, and his or her role as an interpreter of texts has to be kept in just perspective. We might do worse then to return to a question that was raised in the previous chapter and left unanswered: What is a text, and in particular, a written text?

As might be expected, texts can be as varied in nature as in occurrence. In considering them as a series of types, distributed along a notional spectrum, the fundamental qualitative differences among them can perhaps more easily be perceived.

At the nearest remove are the more homogeneous variety of text, ones that ostensibly describe operations or processes (*e.g.* sets of instructions), or represent states of affairs (*e.g.* factual reports, conditions, specifications), or present cases or arguments. Such texts are not necessarily easy to assemble and, quite often, their adequacy depends critically on the expository skill and technical familiarity of the drafter. But, once an adequate text is to hand, a standard reading becomes possible. Interpretation becomes necessary only when communicational "short-circuiting" is occurring, when writers have their better eye on the expert or professional.

Close to these are a second category of text. I am referring to the kind of text in which almost every overt statement might be said to be prefaced by the covert: "This is my/the consensus view, or reaction, or advice." "Don't you find it fair comment/witty/true/perceptive?" Texts of this variety include much of journalism and kindred writing as well as popular books, whether fiction or non-fiction. With such texts as these, hermeneutics becomes a luxury almost, a "pleasure", the playground of the critic bent on probing the hidden socio-semiotic underlying such texts – as did Barthes so brilliantly in some of his most entertaining essays.

At a somewhat farther remove are the many different texts which on first reading may easily be confused with the category of texts just discussed. The difference is that these are the texts that evidently brim with sufficient semiotic and symbolism to cause them to undergo a sea change in their passage from one generation to another, or within the same readerly experience of the same individual. They are texts that having become outmoded subsequently undergo a revival. They depend much on the interpreter. They are the books and poems that "grow on one", acquiring fresh layers of meaning, years after earlier readings have lost some of their immediacy or, not infrequently, quite faded from conscious memory. Whether the reader has become a "better" reader in the interim is beside the point. The important thing is that the relationship between the reader and the text has undergone a shift. These texts probably constitute a multiple category, in that they are so different one from another. There is one group for example, which includes novels such as *Wuthering Heights* or *Great Expectations* or *Sons and Lovers* which change primarily within the consciousness and life-experience of the individual reader. But there is another that includes books which have shone from age to age, and can be read now (if the reader is so inclined) as contemporary "deconstructions": *Don Quixote* for example or *Gargantua and Pantagruel*.

Much farther along and approaching the furthest remove are those texts that do not to depend in any way on the vagaries of the reader but seem to stand bathed in their own radiance, "works of art" that are endlessly approachable and yet impenetrable to readings of any finality. Tantalizingly they beckon hermeneutical interpretation with every passing phrase or line, generating over time whole libraries of commentary and exegesis. Such texts may even seem to be the creation of no one single person, even in cases where single authorship is beyond doubt. It appears to matter scarcely at all, for example, that *The Iliad* could be a composite epic, or that Shakespeare's authorship remains shrouded in uncertainty. It might even seem indecent to suggest that such texts depend for their actuality on the varying interpretations of the reader. Indeed, works of art of this order are only "texts" when considered superficially. They are more like complex symbols that draw their power and meaning from the well of the Unconscious, through a protean activity that sustains our lives.

Which brings us at last to the category of "text" which lies at, some would say beyond, the farthest human limit; texts so remarkable as to seem outside the possibility of human origin. From this category the oldest "book" in the Confucian canon, the *I Ching* or "Book of Changes" has been selected. It has been said that this book lies at the root of all Chinese philosophy: Lao Tse, as well as Mencius and Confucius. The *I Ching* is unlikely to have been a work of single authorship, assuming its present form and integrity as late as the early Chou Dynasty, in the early part of the first millennium B.C. But like The Bible, which contains pre-Hebraic elements, the *I Ching* appears to have antedated its own integration by centuries, even millennia. The book shows clear affinities with oracular inscriptions found by modern archaeologists on bone or tortoiseshell fragments from much earlier periods. But the logography of these inscriptions is so well developed that an even earlier period of unknown duration has to be assumed.[8]

The *Book of Changes* can be read as great poetry, though not without the aid of commentaries, as the original language is so obscurely archaic. But, with the help of various commentaries, the effect on those who come to it with an appropriate hermeneutic has been variously described as extraordinary, perplexing, overwhelming. The *I Ching* is first and foremost an oracle book; that is, it supplies answers to questions, when these are not frivolous; answers that can be particularly clear when they are concerned with personal dilemmas and self-knowledge. Because these answers are determined by seemingly chance throws of coins or divisions of yarrow stalks, some unknown element of now-ness has to be assumed to be implicit in the text itself – what C.J.Jung, unperturbed by his growing reputation as a crank, termed "synchronicity": "the coincidence of events in time and space as meaning something more than mere chance". In common with every other text, the *I Ching* is capable of responding in the only real time the life-world knows: the present. The Book however is no slave to the chronological instant, as it can easily be shown that questions can be stored, sometimes for significant periods of time. until the interpreter has access to the text or is in the right frame of mind. What synchronicity means is the whole experience and knowledge of the self as this has developed out of previous – and different – states of experience or knowledge in relation to the life-world context – the objectively as well as the intersubjectively real context – that constitutes the present: Heidegger's "authentic present", characterized by him as "a waiting towards, the moment of vision [that] permits us to encounter for the first time what can be 'in a time' as... present-at-hand" (1962, 388). What the *I Ching* offers is a moral topology of the authentic present, from which readers-interpreters divulge to themselves, whether out of the often surprisingly direct imagery of the text or from its sometimes more arcane indications, the shape and direction of a way out of an impasse.

The *I Ching* is unlikely to have been a work of single authorship, assuming its present form and integrity as early as the first millennium A literary text, indeed any text, potentially at least, brings together potent entities and energies, which are the source of our seeing, feeling and understanding. These same entities and energies have their roots in nature, in the unknown "out there", and are bonded together into the dynamically kaleidoscopic mosaic of our life-world. The entities are called, at the risk of debasing them, words. The poet is constantly renewing words and transforming the mosaic, even changing it utterly so that as a result of what a poet of uncommon stature has wrought (and in our world "poets" include men of science), the universe is no longer the same. Real language is the "exceptional" language of the poet; normal language merely a conventionalization, a stylization, a fossil, serving purely social or practical ends. The poet could well be the *persona* through whom Nature makes sense to herself:

> Until the used-to earth and sky, and the tree
> And cloud, the used-to tree and used-to cloud,
> Lose the old uses that they made of them.
> And they: these men, and earth and sky, inform
> Each other by sharp informations, sharp,
> Free knowledges, secreted until then,
> Breaches of that which held them fast. It is
> as if the central poem became the world.[9]

Literature is where real words, "said words", congregate: "Together, said words of the world are the life of the world."[10]

Not only literature (Valéry) but we too (Stevens) are made of words. Stevens's "central poem" represents the inviolate order of things, which is also the order of words (Frye), subject only to its own poetic laws. It is the "essential poem at the centre of things".

> We do not prove the existence of a poem.
> It is something seen and known in lesser poems.
> It is the huge, high harmony that sounds
> A little and a little, suddenly,
> By means of a separate sense. It is and it
> Is not and, therefore, is. In the instant of speech,
> The breadth of an accelerando moves,
> Captives the being, widens – and was there.
>
> *(A Primitive Like an Orb)*

15. Style and Being

Stylistics – as distinct from style, an age-old concern – has been described as "an attempt to put [literary] criticism on a scientific basis" (Fish 1980, 70). It owes its origins, first to the Russian Formalists (Shklovsky, Eikhenbaum, Tynyanov and others) and later to writers associated with the Prague School,[1] most notably Mukařovský. Bridging these two successive phases, and extending some decades beyond them, is Roman Jakobson, linguist, poet, philologist and literary theorist. Jakobson is probably most renowned outside linguistics for the article he published jointly with Lévi-Strauss, offering a stylistic analysis of Baudelaire's poem *Les Chats*.[2] Fish's dismissal of this piece of stylistic analysis as a "monumental aridity" (1980, 94) comes as something of a surprise, given the article's virtuosity. In its own right, and as a paragon exemplar of the application of linguistic criteria to a literary text, the analysis cannot be denied validity and "relevance".[3] The main snag though with Jakobson's method is that when it is applied to a notoriously bad poem the results can be, stylistically speaking, just as interesting and as striking;[4] leading one to suspect that stylistic analysis, fascinating though it might be for the applied linguist or "stylistician", does not touch the essence of a poem or help discriminate between the worthwhile and the worthless.

In the nineteen-seventies stylistics appeared to take an auspicious turn with the publication of several studies, among the more sensitive, careful and searching of which is an essay by Halliday on William Golding's novel *The Inheritors*.[5] Very briefly, in this essay Halliday is concerned with a single feature of stylistic difference, between the language of the "new people" and that of the older "Neanderthal" people, who occupy the greater part of the novel, referring to themselves only as "the people". The latter are a tiny band of survivors who eventually, during the time span of the novel, become extinct. Halliday singles out transitivity[6] as the main linguistic feature distinguishing the two groups of people. The argument he sets forth is cogent enough. We may recall that Halliday's theory of language, along with linguistic theory in general, attempts to blend meaning with grammatical structure; something that, if the approach adopted in the present book is anywhere near correct, is not possible. Fish, who maintains a distinction between meaning and grammar, is critical of Halliday's method and conclusions. I have to agree with Fish that syntax, a function of the instrumental mode of language, cannot "express" meaning (Fish 1980, 83). Meaning in language may depend in all kinds of ways on the instrumental mode for its realization, its "flesh", but this does not imply that meaning is **generated** by such instrumentality.[7] The difference in viewpoint between Halliday and Fish verges on the ideological. For Halliday language is a single phenomenon, but Fish distinguishes between formal grammar and the reader's interpretation and meaning. Halliday maintains that a linguistic theory must be, first and foremost, a "theory about meanings" and not merely about forms and constructions; that language is a "potential" rather than a set of facts and no less significant a phenomenon than the unimaginable sum total of what speakers (and writers) can do with it. Such a view cannot be gainsaid but, in its present shape, linguistic theory is unlikely to be able to reveal anything reliable or of value about meaning.

Voices sceptical about a linguistics-derived stylistics grew in number and volume, culminating in a series of essays by Fish himself (1980). These voices have left "applied linguistic" stylistics in disarray. Fish has shown up the circularity and drawn attention to the triviality of a stylistics of this sort. Generative Grammar, in its successive phases, Fish claims, has provided the "perfect vehicle" in that "since its formalisms operate independently of semantic and psychological processes (are neutral between production and reception) they can be assigned any semantic value one may wish them to carry" (1980, 77). He is particularly incensed by stylisticians' attempts to make out that present anomalies and contradictions in interpretation will be satisfactorily resolved once data become available in sufficient statistical quantities to render their conclusions incontrovertible. This can happen, says Fish, "only if the ability of human beings to confer meaning is finite and circumscribable within a statistical formula":

> Statistics will never catch up with the phenomenon they seek to circumscribe. But one can avoid this realization simply by forever advancing the date when the availability of more data will make everything all right.[8]

There are, says Fish, only two varieties of stylistics. The one (exemplified by the Jakobson-Lévi-Strauss analysis) "falls apart in the middle" for the reason that, in its attempts to contrive an analysis based on alleged formal components of language and in making specious claims about meaning or value, it is bound to fail. The second variety, recognizing no divide between grammar and meaning (the approach of Halliday, for example) is interpretive from first to last. This is what linguistic stylistics is supposed **not** to be, inasmuch as "formal patterns are themselves the product of interpretation."

> The lesson to be drawn from the plight of stylistics is a hard one, especially for those who still dream of a criticism, or even of a linguistics, that begins with free-standing and independent formal facts and builds up from those facts to the larger world of discourse: the dream, in short, of an analysis that moves in a principled way from the objective description of a text to its interpretation.(Fish 1980, 266)

In any concrete utterance grammar, interpretation and meaning converge. It is this phenomenon, running together as it does the separate modes of language, which has bedevilled attempts to build an analytical stylistics.

On the other hand, without determinate and determinable criteria, the hermeneutical activity that Fish variously characterizes as "constituting a text" or "interpretation" appears likely to remain hopelessly subjective or, at best, vacuous. Nor need hermeneutics assume the aspect of a received epistemological or socially institutionalized framework (of the kind for example that Derrida might revile). There must be ways of identifying potential meanings, messages, devices of implication, nuances of tone, intentions inherent in a text, as well as of reducing the ultimate difficulty, verging on impossibility, of stabilizing the interactions among the dynamic features found in many, even non-literary, texts – what Meschonnic has marked out as the *rhythmos* of the text (1982, 215). The potential of a text is already embodied in that text. It cannot be supplied as such by the reader, but is something that can be brought to different forms of actuality only by a receptive reading. The receptive reader may detect different voices or different signifying roles, invoking fresh symbolism from a text which to another may seem flat, but he has not "supplied" anything. At moments, especially when there is speech movement, as in dialogue or interwoven direct and indirect speech – the ceaseless counterpoint of dialogic dynamics – the reader may participate not merely in the conventional cut-and-thrust, but also serve as midwife in the generation of a "world". Even when such movement may be absent the same reader can remain alive to a text's stylistic potential for change.

Fish provides an amusing example (1980, 274-5). Taken from its context, loosened from its setting at the entrance to a club, the sign PRIVATE MEMBERS ONLY immediately takes on the funful meanings: "Only the genitalia of members may enter"; "You may bring in your own genitalia"; or the Gogolesque "Only genitalia may enter". But it is not always necessary to remove a text from its setting for verbal high jinks to occur. A Russian "funk" poet of pre-Stalinist days discovered in the revered lines of Pushkin many scores of examples of puns and neologisms, some of them bizarre, others funny in an absurdist way, occasionally obscenely so. They are said to be "displacements",[9] and are produced by a quirk of the Russian language, whose word boundaries are not marked by pauses but suggested by stress patterns and lexical morphology. When the language is made regularly metrical, as in verse, different phonological and morphological sequences from those suggested by the printed text may be "heard", especially when a poem is read aloud. Displacements give free play to the Unconscious, and it is likely that Pushkin, who must have been sensitive to them, avoided taking evasive action in part deliberately, and may even have cultivated them. Semantic content (*i.e.* the "meaning" of a word or expression) is, after all, not what determines the meaning of text, but only of form and, hence, of the unconscious motivations (signs) behind the deployment of these forms.

As Bakhtin was well aware, however closely and in however detailed a manner the language of a poet is analyzed, this will never amount to a definitive stylistic analysis of the poet's work, inasmuch as the analysis will relate to generalized language patterns and norms, and not to the work itself, which will remain untouched by it. The principles governing the creation of a literary text have nothing in common with principles operating within linguistic systems (Bakhtin 1981, 264). The unity of style may derive in part from the latter in that the author is aiming at communicative precision besides art. But style in itself is determined by the poet's own personality, working within the living context of shared supra-personal language.

Yet style is nothing amorphous. The problem with any "mapping" of style is that it is mercurial. Style reflects the open-endedness of the writer's (or speaker's) communicative intention which is always hedged about by the "word" of the other. It is in addition a reflection – "refraction" might be more apt – of the multifaceted being of the reader. In Bakhtin's view speech genre and style are two aspects of a single phenomenon: "Where there is style there is genre" (1986, 66). The transfer of style from one speech genre to another not only alters the way a textual style reads or sounds but also violates and at times renews the genre. W.H.Auden for example well understood this device when in his Christmas Oratorio *For the Time Being* he had a radio voice make the following announcement: "All male persons who shall have attained the age of twenty-one years must proceed immediately to..." concluding with the conventional broadcast ending: "You have been listening to the voice of Caesar".

Speech genres are the stuff of style, and it is these that permit entry, successful or abortive, into everyday intercourse, whether this be the relaxed ambience of the club room or the tension generated by a fractious board meeting. But in the domain of the literary text – and it is this that makes it possible to distinguish between the literary and non-literary – speech genres become detached from their social nexus. This does not imply that the genres become thereby any less real, or discountable; only that they react one with another, at times mirroring each other, suggesting possible paradigms of interpretation of what may be happening, unnoticed and unawares, in the non-fictional world. Most crucial of all: whether fictional or non-fictional, text develops on the boundary between two different consciousnesses (Bakhtin 1986, 106).

These "consciousnesses" need not necessarily be identifiable as separate individuals. Take, for instance, someone writing the sort of book you are now reading. There is a single author. But, on the one hand, there is the reflection, sifting, comparison, evaluation, encounters with the ideas of the other, that weave themselves together as the "text" of a single "consciousness". On the other hand, within the same individual (also the author) there is a second "text" that is being created, at times defensively, even irritably, too rarely generously, by another "consciousness". As anyone who has settled into such an undertaking will know, very little of it is simple or straightforward. There are moods of frustration – leading in some cases to depression – moments of delight and surprise, temptations of every kind for the second consciousness to make play with the contents of the first. It is not hard to grasp Bakhtin's meaning when he says that whenever one expresses oneself, whenever there is act (in an intentional rather than purely physical sense), a text is being created (1986, 107). What is expressed, or done, can only be understood in the dialogic context of its time and place, whether as a reaction against something or someone, as a response, as a stance, or as a set of motives, conscious or unconscious.

Style, and stylistics (the study and analysis of style), have almost no relation to the debate touched on in the earlier paragraphs of the present chapter. On the contrary, stylistics should have to do with "texts" generated by our actions and inclinations, by the dialogic counterpoint running between one consciousness and another, whether this happens to be two (or more) actual individuals (of which one is the self), or geminated consciousness within the same actual individual, or whether this takes place within a fictional text or in real life. Stylistic movement, or being, originates in dialogic interplay.

The works of Dostoevsky, to take a single example, offer an unending series of particularly acute and intense interactions between the language of the self and the other. This dialogic conflict, Bakhtin points out, takes two forms. In the first place there are the unresolved conflicts at the level of lived experience (another's word concerning the self), in ethical activity and attitude (another's judgment, recognition or non-recognition by the other), and in world views ("two ideas in Dostoevsky means two people (1973, 23-4)"). Dostoevsky probably remains unsurpassed in his exploitation of unresolved, and unresolvable, interaction. Dostoevsky's characters do not communicate (no one does, for that matter); they reflect (?refract) and counter-reflect each other's discourse – a "typography of Dasein", so to speak

– and in turn the self-and-other-imposed limits of their own personalities.[10] But the second mode of conflict can seem even more absorbing, taking the reader into the problems not only of Dostoevsky's writings, but of novelistic creation in general and, not too remotely, into real-life speech interaction. This second type of conflict consists in the author himself becoming embroiled with the characters he has projected on the canvas of his novel. At moments the author hovers on the verge of becoming yet another character in the novel – different again from the fictional narrator – in which his very own identity is at risk.

*   *   *

"Hell is other people", was the realization of Garcin in Sartre's *Huis Clos*. Dostoevsky's connoisseurship of the infernal potentialities of dialogue does not always, insofar as the fictional outcomes are concerned, exceed the experience of real people. The notorious difficulty speakers experience in predicting the reactions of others to their words, and the sometimes resulting pain of an actual encounter, as well as the difficulty of matching one's own projected "scenario" with that provoked in the other, Dostoevsky exploits to the full.

One of Dostoevsky's most extraordinary encounters is that between Stavrogin, a complex and cynical man of spurious power, and Tikhon, a "holy man". The encounter takes place in an episode which for reasons not definitely known was excluded from his novel *The Devils*, but was published posthumously as *Stavrogin's Confession*.[11] Stavrogin is meant to be a Superman, a charismatic revolutionist, disdainful of the ordinary norms of good and evil. But despite the cynicism of his outlook he is none the less tormented by an awareness of having "transgressed". He has been in search of some one individual spiritually up to the task of hearing the confession of an exceptional person such as he believes himself to be, and at the same time capable of absolving him. Stavrogin learns of Tikhon, a former bishop now living the solitary life of a monk, said to be a saintly man and reputed to possess unusual spiritual powers. Stavrogin's diabolical scheme is that he will confront this revered and kindly ascetic with a printed confession in all its grisly detail of a crime committed by himself and at the same time conduct an experiment in cynicism: he wanted to observe the reactions of the old man as the dastardly events unfold, in a deliberate gamble with his own and the holy man's ontological composure. But, from the outset, reality and projected scenario fail to coincide. Even Tikhon's cell, which Stavrogin had imagined as being sparse and severe, turns out to be tastefully if simply furnished, with "secular and classical" engravings displayed alongside religious icons. Even his library contains more than a sprinkling of modern, even dubious, fiction. Stavrogin is taken aback. He had not reckoned on anything other than a stereotype; nor with the possibility that Tikhon might be as complex a human being as himself. Stavrogin's first impulse is to back out. But, before he could do so, Tikhon "suddenly raising his eyes, fixed such a steady and thoughtful gaze on him; the look on his face became so queer and unexpected, that Stavrogin could barely avoid a shudder." The visitor is overcome by an uncanny sense that Tikhon already knows his purpose in coming.

Tikhon finds himself able to win protection through the gaps that inevitably open up in Stavrogin's prepared "text". And Tikhon is skilful and practised enough in dialogic encounter to exploit these gaps, for his own safety. After an exchange of some length, in which Tikhon is evidently getting the better of him, Stavrogin blatantly turns the discussion to the question of religious belief, a favourite trick of his. He has "rehearsed" his "lines" to perfection, but the wily old recluse is ready for him:

> "I suppose you do believe in God?" Stavrogin blurted out suddenly.
> "I do."
> "It is said that if you have faith and command a mountain to move, it will move... That's a load of rubbish though. Even so I'm rather curious to know whether you could move a mountain."
> "If God wills it, then I shall," Tikhon murmured very quietly as if to himself, lowering his eyes.
> "I'm not interested in whether God himself could move one. Could **you**? It's you I am asking. If you can do it, I'll reward you by believing in God. So there, how about that?"
> "Perhaps I could move one."
> " 'Perhaps' is a neat way of putting it. Why the uncertainty?"
> "My faith is not quite perfect."
> "What! You mean to say that even **your** faith isn't perfect."

"Yes...perhaps that's it: I believe, but my faith is not perfect."

"Well, at any rate you do believe that with God's help you would be able to do it, and that, after all, is something... You are a Christian, I take it?" Stavrogin was mocking.

"Let me not be ashamed, Lord, of Thy Cross," Tikhon replied, almost in a whisper, with a note of impassioned agitation in his voice, bowing his head still lower... [11]

Although the encounter between Stavrogin and Tikhon is a product of Dostoevsky's imagination, the sureness of touch stems from the novelist's insight into the dialogic conflict so often inherent in real-life interactions, ordinary and extraordinary. There is never any question of a puppet show, with the author manipulating the strings. On the contrary, Dostoevsky is an observer in an experiment conducted between two people engaged in mortal ontological combat.

In this struggle Tikhon's advantage is not religion or spirituality, but aesthetics. It is through the **form** of his words, through his verbal **style**, that he is able to counteract the corrosive force confronting him. Everything about Stavrogin by contrast, even his mask-like looks and irresistible personal magnetism, is devoid of form, "ugly". The "confession" itself is crudely written, Dostoevsky having gone to some length to strip the text of every vestige of Rousseauesque literariness, turning it into a naked self-revelation, a blatant admission of bestiality. Its form is that of an *aide-mémoire*, sprinkled with officialese and cliché, bristling with grammatical inaccuracies and stylistic malformations. As one Russian critic has described it: "The impression is of a damp rag of reality, drawn from the very dregs of human existence and thrown on to the pages of a novel in all its raw untrimmed state and repulsive unsightliness" (Grossman 1965, 162).

The entire interview is skilfully stage-managed by Tikhon. When Stavrogin eventually seeks his forgiveness, the only appropriate response is: "Provided you forgive me too". Stavrogin's uncontrollable sneer at such apparently fake humility is of no avail. At every juncture the tables are turned on him. What he cannot bear is to hear from the old man's lips that instead of being outraged when they read his "confession" people would only... laugh.

Stavrogin turned red in the face; his expression was one of alarm. "I foresaw this. I must have seemed to you ludicrous... Don't look so disconcerted. I was expecting this.

But Tikhon does not spare him the unpalatable prospect: "The horror will be universal, but so too will be the laughter."

"Tell me then, where exactly in this document do I make myself look ridiculous? I know perfectly well already of course but I'd like you to put your finger on it. Go on, say it, with as much cynicism as you can muster... Tell me with as much frankness as you are capable of..."
"In the very form of this great penance of yours there is something ridiculous..."
"So it's the form you find ridiculous?" seethed Stavrogin.
"The substance also. Ugliness kills."
"Ugliness? What ugliness?"
"The ugliness of the crime."

Suddenly ethic and aesthetic are fused. Tikhon has cunningly manipulated the dialectic, to the extent that Stavrogin is trapped, caught completely off balance. What Stavrogin had begun to think was some kind of stylistic talk, a diversion, became just then the old man's first line of defence against a sophisticated and intelligent monster whose crime was past all horror. In this posthumously published work of Dostoevsky's are to be found new means of exploring, through the dynamics of human dialogue, the nature of human reality and being.

In Dostoevsky's novels, dialogue contains, latently, the wide extent of good and evil. Dmitri Karamazov, we may recall, finds Man too broad, and would have him narrower. The wide spectrum of the human heart is reflected in dialogic interaction. It may be no exaggerated claim that in Dostoevsky's later work there is not a single thought, idea, opinion, intention or sentiment which is not embedded in dialogue. Dialogue can be compared to the relationship in music between keys, harmonies and rhythms. The same thought in two different harmonic-rhythmic settings becomes two (or more) different thoughts. The mode of expression and utterance – the style – are what counts. Even moral truth depends not on what is said, but on who says it, how its said, and in what circumstances. In the words of Dietrich Bonhoeffer, himself a victim of Nazi moral and intellectual degeneracy:

Telling the truth means something different according to the particular situation in which one stands... The truthful word is not in itself constant; it is as much alive as life itself... If "the truth is told" without taking into account to whom it is addressed, then this truth has only the appearance of truth, but lacks its essential character... Each word must have its own place and keep it. (1955, 327-8)

As participants in a shared world of discourse we belong, whether we like it or not, to other people's words and worlds, and find ourselves enmeshed in different layers of reality and objective truth at the same time. Again, Bonhoeffer:

In our endeavour to express the the real we, we do not encounter this as a consistent whole, but in a condition of disruption and inner contradiction which has need of reconciliation and healing. We find ourselves simultaneously embedded in several different orders of the real, and our words, which strive towards the reconciliation and healing of the real, are nevertheless repeatedly drawn into the prevalent disunion and conflict (1955, 332)

The word "prevalent" in the previous quotation is by now probably redundant. "Disunion and conflict" has become the dominant complexion in all societies, no longer ruled by time-honoured socio-cultural convention, by received code and ritual, by a mostly eudemonized and predictable symbolism. The shared domain of language, through which and in which the self and others are projected, has become the stylistic mode *par excellence*. We make our own codes and rituals, playing everything by ear, as it were. The latent living symbols that could illuminate our sensibilities and dilemmas cry out for expression. In our time they enter our individual experience and consciousness, surreptitiously, as epiphanies. Stylistics has become a word that helps us to delineate, to differentiate, a hermeneutic of discourse. Not a strictly scientific concept, perhaps, but one that may help us find our way through the "prevalent disunion and conflict" and stave off another Holocaust. But stylistics is not independent of the organic mode of language; nor can it be. The sounds we utter and the marks we inscribe on paper (or enter into computers) are the delicate instrumentation used by us to guide, in a constant feedback somewhere between Kierkegaardian dread and coffee-table complacency, each others' interpretations of what is (if anything) that is being said. And it is at this point that we should return to the word and, in particular, to words as such.

PART FOUR

WORDS AS SUCH

16. The Word as Artefact

A word, as we have already seen, is something quite other than a discrete form linked to an discrete meaning; it is a something rooted in human culture and feeling, but also in an embodiment of extra- or supra-human symbolism and energy. In a manner as yet unknown, and combined into a single interworking, these fundamental constituents generate language, and make possible meaning as we know it through its manifestation in language.

It should not then be at all surprising that the word as such is notoriously hard to come to grips with. As we have already seen, opinion is widespread that attempts to isolate the word as an object of scientific inquiry are bound to be fruitless, and that other features of language – grammar, morphology, syntax, discourse, propositional logic, and so forth – offer more promise.

Bakhtin took a boldly original view: that, in common with the vast domain of meaning for which it serves, so to speak, as an evanescent but epiphanic *persona*, the word remains aloof from any notional language structure, and shows itself only in the hermeneutics of utterance, as a piece of reality. Unfortunately such a view as this runs counter to the layperson's intuition – or should one say, preconception – that words are concrete and readily identifiable, a fact attested by no less an authority than the dictionary. This lay preconception overlooks the fact that the dictionary has been in existence for only a short time (Shakespeare had no access to any decent dictionary of English[1]) and that since the eighteenth century the lexicographer through the medium of the dictionary has exerted a radical influence on opinion regarding the nature of words. It also disregards the aeons of time during which *homo loquens* was able to rely for his words only on his own experience and the received wisdom of the tribe, a seeming eternity of time during which words were being fashioned in the crucible of shared perception and creation. So many of our words still radiate the "sheer presence of the past" (Gadamer 1991, 163).

Every.one knows what a word is, especially a word in one's own language. But, whenever an attempt is made to hold on to it for the purpose of inspecting or analyzing it, the word proves elusive. We can savour a word on the palate of our sensibility. There it is – *river*, to me personally an English river, with its soft resistant flow, its fitful eddies, the inky reflections of watery moods. And then *friend*: transparent firm bonds, without fuss, considerate, for good; different somehow from *ami*, with its frankness, warm but discreet intimacy, badinage. Whatever the choice of word (unless a strictly technical term) no gloss will ever contain it. Everyone will gloss it differently, in however slight a degree, and there will always lie open the possibility of it being "stretched" to accommodate some unforeseen sense.

Having worked for many years with American Indian informants, Edward Sapir became convinced of the **aesthetic** nature of the word. By an unusual and roundabout route therefore, Sapir found himself aligned with those who have lived most intimately with words: the poets. Words, says one French writer have "a weight, a light, a taste of their own":

> Before writing down a word I taste it as a cook tastes the ingredient which he is going to put in his sauce; I examine it against the light as an interior decorator examines a Chinese vase which he wants to set against a suitable background... I only use those words whose intimate flavour and whose power of evocation and resonance are known to me."[2]

Words are are not just art objects though. They are **living** artefacts, as if possessed of a consciousness of their own, unpredictable, insidious things: Shelley's "winged snakes" for example. After a lifetime's "intolerable wrestle with words and meanings", "learning to get the better of words," T.S.Eliot came to regard them as antagonists. Rimbaud was struck by their propensity for metamorphosis. He was convinced that once words are brought into contact with one another they can actually be observed undergoing molecular alchemy. Longinus by contrast felt that "words offer resistance to one another, taking their stand in a firmly based grandeur."[3]

No one needs to be told that words consist of series of letters or sounds arranged in a specific order. But everyone knows also that words are far more than that. They are enigmatic and elusive entities. Frustration derives from our inability to get to grips with words in such a manner that they present themselves, lie open blandly before us. But others, including perhaps the majority of poets and writers, would take the view that this is not what we should expect. Derrida in his radical undermining of any "metaphysics of presence" may – perhaps without knowing it and, ironically, despite his radical opposition to *logos* – have the word on his side.

Lexicographers must share some portion of the blame for the tendency to handle words as if they were mere commodities. "The words in a dictionary," one of their critics has complained, "are all seemingly equal, which conveys the misleading notion that the vocabulary of a language is just a list of otherwise unrelated words" (Tyler 1978, 184). But, then, lexicographers only need remind us they are kept busy enough, without concerning themselves with a task that looks either like someone else's or (more likely) downright nugatory.

In marked contrast the poet has remained on the most intimate terms with words, so much so that these elusive entities can be thought of as running in the poet's veins, beyond any analytical reach. Students of literature on the other hand seldom fare so fortunately. They may talk a good deal about language and about words but, true to form, words slip through their fingers without their even being aware of it. Linguists, who might be expected to be particularly adept at handling words, have for the most part proved inept or ill-equipped, at times shirking the task altogether. They have worked almost exclusively with lexical **form**, to the point that even lexical sense tends to be equated with form. As noted earlier, form is not only a remote abstraction; it is an epistemologically complex as well as poorly understood abstraction.

Take for example that epitome of form: the **morpheme**, the smallest morphological unit. In English, "forms" such as *try, limit, common, -ing, -ness, -ly,* along with thousands of other such specimens, are described as morphemes; when in fact all we have before us, as far as the graphics are concerned, are iconic representations (how such elements might be represented acoustically defies ingenuity, unless one resorts to the abstruse schemata of physics). The written "morpheme" *limit*, for instance, contains five "letters" each of which may be said to be more recondite than the most complicated (*e.g.* Chinese) logogram. Logograms do at least consist mainly of stylized pictures or iconic representations of concepts linked to rhyming or alliteration. But what could the five "letters" of *limit* possibly represent? The short (linguistic) answer, of course, is that in speech they represent "phonemes" (sounds), and in writing "graphemes" (graphic marks).

In linguistics, the word (usually "lexical unit" or "lexical item" is preferred) is often relegated to the status of a "free" morpheme: a morpheme that can occur in isolation, independently of other (subordinate or "bound" – *e.g.* -*ing*, -*ness*) morphemes. Morphemes, phonemes and graphemes, separately or in combination, may well have important roles to play in the instrumental language mode, in the parcelling and distribution of information, in differentiating at the abstract level of signification, in ensuring that communicational exchanges are optimally effective; but they tell us nothing of intrinsic interest about words.

The word as a lexical unit is said to lie between "word boundaries". The word-boundary approach however can easily be shown to be circular, in that the words in a particular language are felt to exhibit the "boundaries" they have only because that is how they seem to a speaker of that language. Note my deliberate use of "felt" rather than "perceive" or "conceive". The combination of the separate morphemes *black* and *bird*, when it stands for a species of bird for example, is felt by speakers of English to be a single word whereas, when the combination denotes any "black" "bird" – a raven or crow, for instance – it seems to be really two words, not one. As if to confirm this feeling, in the latter instance a space is inserted between *black* and *bird*. In speech there is additionally a significant shift of stress: *black* '*bird* (any bird that is black) becomes '*blackbird* (the species). This feeling varies subtly from one lexical unit to another. In general, speakers of English would have *red wine* as two items, whether a generic type of wine is being denoted or a wine of red colour (in contrast to "white" or "rosé"). Perversely, by comparison, *hotbed* is felt (and spelt) as a single word, regardless of whether "a bed of earth heated by manure" or "a place that favours the rapid spread of some condition, such as vice or corruption" is meant. And though the boundaries remain constant there is no shift in stress in either case. In languages such as French or Russian there is no symmetry between the written and spoken language. Their graphology clearly indicates word boundaries when the spoken language recognizes none.

Nor is the word easily accommodated within the categories and frames of reference espoused by linguistics. This can be seen most clearly in the various attempts to identify "word" in the hierarchy of levels proposed by structural linguists. Even though a hierarchical scheme serves well for grammatical structures, all the way from phonological distinctive features[4] to the fully articulated sentence – no doubt reflecting the information schemata of the differential-organic language mode – it seems ill-suited to the word. This has not however deterred linguists from locating the word somewhere between the (hierarchical) levels of the morpheme and the phrase, and in some instances devising a new term for it.[5] For a start, the dividing line, assuming there to be such, between morpheme and (lexical) word is awkwardly untidy. *Forth* can function as a "free" or "bound" depending on whether or not it forms part of a single word (e.g *They went forth* as against *forthrightness* or *henceforth*). In most word-forms final *-er* (*e.g. runner, sitter*) is a bound morpheme, but in some commonly occurring word-forms (*e.g. letter, otter, butler, better*) it is not. The latter are considered to be unanalyzable word-forms until, that is, someone comes along and changes the rules, as in *He outbuttled the butler*. (Although "burglars" have been around for centuries, no one can strictly be said to have "burgled" until the middle of the last century, when the word *burgle* was derived as a "back-formation" from *burglar*).

The possibility of establishing a stable differentiation of levels for morpheme and word must remain in doubt, especially when the former bears such scant resemblance to the latter. The morpheme has its basis in the flow of information, between the processing capacity of the brain and incoming and outgoing signals. The word, if only because it owes its origin separately to both the shared and organic modes of language, cannot be assigned to the same hierarchical series as phonemes, morphemes, or syntactic features. Word-form as such – the phonotactic or graphological shape of a word – can be regarded as morphemic, but the semantic value and characteristic stamp of a particular word, using the morpheme and grapheme only as the means towards semiotic and expressive ends, is situated at the remarkable signification-generating interface between the separate and otherwise unrelated modes of language; comparable to some unseen tectonic collision from which energy and, with it, symbolism and meaning well up into the otherwise empty shell of language form and hence into our life-world.

Inasmuch as the word is "recognized", **interpreted** in the shared intersubjective mode of language and, hence also, in the veins of shared culture, it is natural that the "feelings" we have about words are motivated less by our individual feelings, inclinations and drives than by the shared consciousness and sensibility of those using a language in a particular place and time. In a naturally bilingual community – one in which speakers use one language for one set of purposes and in one set of domains, and another for different purposes and in different domains – speakers and writers unconsciously retain separate "feelings" about words as they move from one language to the other. Wallace Lambert (1972, 54) in one of his many empirical studies showed that French Canadian bilingual speakers feel quite differently about *église* and its English counterpart *church*. The former was found to be associated with gothic cathedrals while the latter suggests rather a tallish wooden building used on Sundays for communal worship.

Even the "morphosemantic" status of words can vary between languages. Literate speakers of Chinese, for example, count every syllable as a separate word, reflected by or reflecting the fact that each syllable has its own written character. In Chinese the syllable is thus a lexical unit. English words such as *cowslip* or *cauliflower* which are, as far as the speaker of English is concerned, entirely unanalyzable single lexical units would be taken by the speaker of Chinese to comprise several such units: the word *cowslip*, if it were borrowed phonetically and reconstituted in Chinese, would be reckoned to contain at least three syllables or "words", and *cauliflower* as many as five. When words are adapted directly from English into Chinese, their (perceived) syllables, written each with a separate character, are usually "relexified" with each syllable (word) projecting a preferably benign potential sense.[6] Anomalous as it might seem to a speaker of Chinese, the same speaker of English who resists the notion that *cowslip* and *cauliflower* could be anything but single words has no difficulty in conceding that *sunshine*, *daybreak* or *taxicab* are lexical compounds. How one draws the line depends on the lexical conventions operating within the language of the particular speech community.

Our feelings about words are guided by what we perceive to be their integrity. Words are expected to conform to recognized specifications, and these are aesthetic and historico-cultural more than morphological. No speaker of Chinese for example (even though he or she, if bilingual, might experience no physical or psychological difficulty with the pronunciation) would tolerate the English word *bus* being rendered phonetically in Chinese as *b-u-s* or *b-a-s*, partly because there are no words in that language ending in the consonant *s*, partly because *s* in terminal isolation is not a complete syllable, but mainly because it does not "feel" right. Instead, *bus* would have to become a two-syllable word, as it does in Hong Kong Cantonese *ba-si*. In English, to take a different example, words are required to be alphabetically locatable in the dictionary. One so thoroughly habituated therefore might experience frustration at not being able to find many Welsh word-forms, *fasged* to take one example, in a dictionary of Welsh. This is because Welsh, along with other extant Celtic languages, transforms initial sounds in accordance with certain rules. One would need to be familiar with these rules before the fundamental form – the form cited in the dictionary is *basged* "basket" – could be deduced. Likewise, to find the meaning of *ngheffyl* it would be necessary to be able to work out the form *ceffyl* "horse".

The farther one strays from English the more expectations can go awry. The following is a "word" cited by Sapir from Paiute, an Uto-Aztecan language: *wii-to-kuchum-punku-rügani-yugwi-va-ntü-m(ü)* – roughly: "knife...black...buffalo...pet...cut up...sit...(plural)...(future) (participle)...(animate plural). An entire complex sentence would be needed to translate this Paiute word into idiomatic English: "They who are going to sit and cut up with a knife a black bull or cow." What the speaker recognizes intuitively as words may vary considerably from one speech community to another. So much so that Sapir, impressed by the ability of preliterate American Indian informants to divide the flow of speech readily into "words", concluded:

> The best we can do is to say that the word is one of the smallest **completely satisfying** bits of "meaning" into which the sentence resolves itself. (1921, 34) (My emphasis)

Sapir's approach to words as "miniature bits of art" stands poles apart from the more positivistic claim that in the case of the word there is nothing to be proved or demonstrated, for the reason that in every language "the word asserts itself in an indisputable way" (Rossetti 1947, 18). There may be nothing to be proved or demonstrated, but there is a great deal to be explained and accounted for.

In Australian Aboriginal languages there may never have been anything resembling a lexicon in the generally accepted sense. In these languages it appears that a word may be coined afresh, from a set of particular morphosemantic specifications whenever it is brought into use (Jones 1978, 278). Speakers of Aranda for instance are able to recast words into fresh lexical forms, not arbitrarily, but in accordance with received principles (Strehlow 1971, 57). This is said to happen for example whenever prose forms are transformed into metrical verse. It is a transformation that goes well beyond superficial changes in accentuation, in normal accordance with the requirements of rhythmic measure; and it is one that leads to a radical restructuring of the words themselves, even to the point of additional syllables being inserted. Over and above this, and surpassing anything in the alliterative and rhyming practices found in ancient Germanic and Scandinavian literatures, is the reluctance of the poet to begin a line with any of the initial syllables of the words making up that line. Sometimes, for example, each line in a couplet begins with the final syllable of the previous line in such a way that the prose sequence:

> Kauauala tulbanama
> Tnatantjala tulbanama

becomes in verse:

> Makawawe
> Latualbino
> Matnatantji
> Latualbino

It may be noted that the first syllables in the second and fourth verse lines have been carried over from the last syllable of the word in the previous line: the final *-la* of *kauauala* in the first prose line has been transposed to (*la*)*tualbino* in the second verse line, and the final *-ma* of (the first occurrence of) *tulbanama* has shifted to (*ma*)*tnatanji* in the third verse line (accompanied by regular mutations: *ja* becomes *ji*, and *ua* becomes *we*).

Little wonder that early European observers concluded that songs such as those of the Aranda were merely strung-together nonsense sequences. In their ignorance they took it for granted that these (for them) crude savages had not risen to the level of articulate or intelligent speech (Strehlow 1971, 65) whereas, in truth, these Central Australian songs are manifestations of a prosody more complex than anything known to the European, ancient or modern. Whether this phenomenon of lexical re-formation is an isolated occurrence, or whether it reflects archaic features of oral literary cultures everywhere, that have vanished with the appearance of linear writing and urban civilization, it is impossible to say. But the phenomenon itself should not seem an anomaly, inasmuch as the lexical word does not belong to any system of grammar but to a world of sounds and symbols and intersubjectively shared understandings and feelings. The form or forms that the word assumes are merely *personae*. The word is free to override the word-forms in which it is "personified", and often does.

Presuppositions about words are conditioned by sets of conventions applying in the languages one happens to speak or write. The bearer of these conventions is above everything else the lexicon, and the framework in which these conventions are set is a culture. If the cultures of two or more language communities are the same or similar, as in the case of "common European", the conventions will operate with a high degree of similarity. Chance might be expected to play a significant part in transferability of these conventions between different cultures and speech communities, but closer investigation will usually disconfirm such an expectation. The cultures of China and Japan, for example, show asymmetrical mutual influence. Whereas China has borrowed almost nothing from Japan (while however acknowledging its superior achievements in Chinese scholarship), Japan has incorporated earlier strata of Chinese culture into its own highly distinctive culture, to the extent that it would be no exaggeration to claim that a Sino-Japanese linguo-cultural world came into existence as a result (Lord and T'sou 1976, 51-3). This cultural transfer was effected in large part through extensive borrowing from the Chinese lexicon and from the writing system intimately associated with it.

To understand is to interpret. Many a Chinese might feel that the Japanese, in borrowing things Chinese, have distorted them. But distortion, at times verging on the grotesque, is bound to occur:

borrowing means to adapt, and to adapt means to change.

Speakers (or writers) of a language do not need to grasp the essence of what it is they are talking (or writing) about. Words not only make such nescience possible but even depend on it for their efficacy. The ordinary user of language would readily admit that this happens in the case of words which have been taken from specialist contexts: words such as *laser*, *cosmic radiation* or *microwave*, for example. It is not that the physicist alone is in a privileged position to supply a detailed "reference" for the sense "laser" or "microwave" or hundreds of other specialist terms, but that, more practically, within the shared mode of language words perform a wide array of functions, only one of which is to supply accurate, technically adequate descriptions. This can be more easily seen if we take another look at our humdrum example *apple*, a word that raises just as many problems as the most abstruse concepts in physics. Most people – unless they happen to be biochemists, fruit connoisseurs, expert apple-growers, or a Cézanne – treat "apple" as if there were nothing remarkable about it. But in using a word like *apple* one is rarely saying anything essential about an "apple". Language makes it all too easy to regard a word such as *apple* as a mere token, even when one's concern may be to influence others or to modify their own situation in some way. Only when someone becomes a craftsman in words (poet, writer, or other practitioner) does he or she manage to draw from the well of a word some degree of reality – what Gadamer has recognized as the "ideality of meaning" present in the word itself (1991, 417) – and in rare instances to propagate it.

A further and most important point about the lexicon, frequently overlooked, is that it does not automatically absorb the ever-growing accumulation of technical and specialized terminology. Terminological items are strictly lexicographical, useful in their own spheres, but not to be considered an integral part of the lexicon – **until**, that is, they establish **live links** with it. When this does happen, a term that was originally technical undergoes semantic adaptation and extension. Examples that spring to mind include: *paranoid*, *inflation*, *transistor*, *catalyst*, *magnetism*, *natural selection*, *gene*, among hundreds of others. Items of this kind mostly continue in use as specialized terms. But once they enter the lexicon proper all kinds of unpredictable and surprising things can happen to them.

The lexicon, consisting as it does only of living words as opposed to inert terminology, resembles the complex tribal symbol discussed earlier. None too fancifully, the lexicon can be compared to the Ndembu Milk Tree (see Chapter 9, above), with its various functions analogous to morphosemantic "fields", as well as to Empson's "complex words". By virtue of its living, breathing character the lexical word resembles a leaf on a tree sustained by unseen energy; with its life "blood" and its symbolic nourishment concealed in some unseen realm, that sustains everyone and everything. Little imagination is required to conceive what life might be like if words were to have their organic bonds with other words in the vocabulary dissolved. Only then might we discover, from a dearth of it, the "meaning" of meaning. Firth was right: meaning is the whole of a language.

A word, thus, is nothing like a series of letters written down, nor is it the series of letters I once read in a book for the first time, nor the re-creation in my brain provoked by acoustic events "out there". These are, as Merleau-Ponty insisted, "mere reproductions of the word, in which I recognize it but which do not exhaust it" (1962, 402). In truth, the word has never been "inspected, analyzed, known and constituted." Nor can it be. The word becomes real only in the moment of being caught up by "a motor power given to me along with the first experience I have of my body and its perceptual and practical fields." This is the word's "behavioural style" (Merleau-Ponty, 1962, 403). The meaning of a word lies not in any simplistic dualistic coalescence of form and content, nor is it a product of context, nor has it any ultimate dependence on sense and reference, nor is it a sign as such, nor is its meaning merely its "use". On the contrary, the meaning of a word is the image (in the imagination more than in vision) assumed by things, ideas and events in shared experience and feeling, as these are presented to us through the symbolic form which (according to Cassirer) is language. And insofar as they are mediated by a particular culture, as "pieces of the world's behaviour", they become in some inscrutable way also living particles of our intersubjective selves.

*   *   *

As long as words represent particles of ourselves, the claim can legitimately be made that words are living artefacts. But, whether living or dead, artefact always implies "something made". In the presence of an artefact it has to be assumed that someone, somewhere, and at some time, actually created it. Some words are indisputably the work of known artists: *chortle* and *galumphing* never existed before Lewis Carroll coined them, nor did *brainwash* before George Orwell wrote his terrifying last novel. Shakespeare appears to have been the source of many new words which made their first appearance – with a surprisingly modern flavour – in his writings: *dwindle, sanctimonious, pedant, obscene, critic* as well as *critical, amazement* and *generous* are only some. More numerous by far though are the new and often uncannily modern senses Shakespeare wrought from existing words. In some instances these new senses so completely eclipsed the earlier meanings that they may be considered virtually new words. Among the many examples are: *magic, creed, charm, apology, fashion* and *fashionable.* Before Shakespeare shaped their modern meanings, *magic* and *charm,* for example, had been terms of witchcraft:

> The fact that the first examples quoted in the *Oxford Dictionary* are taken from Shakespeare cannot, of course, be taken as absolute proof that he introduced them. But there are so many of them, and the *Dictionary* is so thorough, that there can be no doubt of his being the first in most cases and among the first in every case. (Barfield 1933, 139)

Admittedly, the authors of new words and senses are in most instances anonymous. Sometimes we may know the approximate date of a word's origin: *brunch,* for example, began its ungainly life among university students during the last decade of the nineteenth century; while the debonair *twirl* – a blend of *whirl, twist* and *trill* – originated, one can almost tell by its flavour, in Elizabethan times. But the origin of the vast majority of words, in no matter which language, is lost in the vastness of time and, along with them, most of the changes in sense and feeling which make them peculiarly English, or Russian, or Chinese, or Navajo.

Although that body of opinion, which has its point of origin in Humboldt and holds that language is to be seen as a totality of speech utterance, with words having no existence outside connected speech, is not easy to fault, the "crystallizing" of the flow of connected speech into separate "words" has nevertheless to be viewed as a semiotic moulding of reflective perception and feeling: an aesthetic and also a deliberate act. If evidence from the languages of our "contemporary precivilized ancestors – Aranda, for example – is to be trusted, it would appear that, for ages past, individual words have been the conscious creations of the people using them.

The next question is more difficult to answer: Out of what "material" were the words of preliterate cultures made? A convenient answer would be that words, as Saussure and those of like mind have supposed, are "marriage unions" (to borrow Jespersen's metaphor) of sound and sense. This solution is dualist as well as simplistic. The "material" – if that is not too misleading a term – out of which words are fashioned must be the same as that out of which language as a symbolic form has come about. This material must therefore have been compounded of our entire organic behaviour and our intersubjective life-world. Words have their origins in world energy and its symbolism. The creation of words is threefold: firstly, creators of words are giving unique expression to physical being; secondly, they are enhancing a life-world through the shared mode of language; and finally, they are enriching the world as such from the realm of symbols, in both its subjective and objective aspects.

The bi-modal approach to language adopted in these pages makes it possible to argue that the word acquires its life through the convergence of phenomena projected by symbolism (see especially Chapters 5 and 9, above), by motivated impulsions and gestures within the differential-organic mode of language, and by crystallizations of feelings, imaginings and insights, "traces" at work within the shared mode of language that is at the same time our intersubjectivity and culture: our life-world. This goes some way towards explaining why innovating word-artists do not need to propagate their own creations: either these creations propagate themselves, or they do not. In the same way as any other artist working in a different medium, all the true word-artist needs do is "exhibit" for others what has been created.

In his *Poetics* Aristotle claimed that all art, and especially poetic art, is *mimesis*, a term that translates pallidly into English as "imitation". This translation can be misleading, in that it implies the independent existence of objects to be copied. Artists need no reminding of the impossibility of making an exact replica of a work of art. Talented forgers owe their success not to any superior skill at meticulously accurate reproduction but to their ability to re-create versions of the originals which the spectator, and more particularly the "innocent" spectator, finds most convincing. "There is no essential difference between the artist who paints a landscape and another who copies a picture" (Gombrich 1977, 259). Matching implies creation. Also, "seeing" means guessing at, and re-creating in one's own consciousness what has reached the senses by way of the "out there". Even photographs depend for their reproductive fidelity on the features and organization of visual impressions and the visual "field" to which the average viewer is attuned. Experienced developers are aware of the different outcomes in photographic prints that can be obtained from the same negative.[7] Visual sensation contributes only in part to perception. Knowledge, expectation, attitude. imagination are just as important, possibly even more so:

> Imitation and representation are not merely a repetition, but knowledge of the essence. Because they are not merely repetition, but a "bringing forth", they imply a spectator as well. They contain in themselves an essential relation to everyone for whom the representation exists. (Gadamer 1991, 114-5)

Those engaged in *mimesis* resemble children at play, affirming their own being in what they are doing. They allow what they know to exist, and to exist in the only way that they know. The notional unbiased observer does not exist. Virtually every aspect of experience enters into and is made to form part of our view of things: "The visual field is the product of the chronic habit of civilized men seeing the world as a picture."[8] In an earlier discussion, the point was made that phenomena – "appearances" – are not just givens; they are something we have to work actively to achieve. Roger Fry's "gradual discovery of appearances"[9] applies not exclusively to the history of art, nor is it merely passive, as he seems to imply. All appearances are actively developed and brought into being, historically and biographically, by human subjects in accordance with the cultural determinants and dynamics of their life-world.

So, we may now be in a position to attempt a sketch in profile of what happens when a word comes into being. But, first, we have to keep clearly in view the fact that a word never makes its appearance gratuitously: the ground for its appearance must already have been prepared for it. This is a hermeneutical more than cultural or sociological question: the calling forth is enacted both in the potential creator and in the immediate intersubjective life-world.

It has to be kept in mind that there is no object or event waiting to be named. Discrete objects and events have no actual existence as such until language endows them with it. Without language an event would not yet have entered the world of appearances, and an object supposedly awaiting denotation would previously either not yet have been in existence or would already have entered into some different cultural nexus. Words for objects are, and must always have been, type-words, words representing whole classes of token-objects. It was never a question of Archaic Man looking at, say, a tree and naming it: "that is an oak tree", or "a cypress tree", or whatever other kind of tree. Archaic Man would have experienced a greater chaos of sensations than those we experience. Out of this chaos, through the agency of the word, various groups of recurrent phenomena would in time have become stabilized, *e.g.* types of trees. The particular taxonomic divisions that were stabilized would (to us) have seemed arbitrary, lumping together incompatible species which we moderns with our scientific methodology and knowledge could not have accepted. Early Man would have been guided in his "cutting up of nature" by ritual and aesthetic as well as by utilitarian considerations. The particular words that were thus brought into being would have meshed (in the shared mode of language) with other words for different schemata of tree consciousness, and would ultimately have yielded those vast abstractions *tree, forest, grove* or *heath.* Subsequently, these abstractions would at the same time have become determinants of perceptions and sensations: we only "see" "trees" because we have words denoting an infinite possible range of trees.

This impetus towards the creation of a new word would have originated in some individual. In a **potential** sense speakers of English have always "chortled", but they never **actually** did so until Lewis Carroll invented the word. As they now know, "chortling" is a different kind of activity from "chuckling" or "giggling" or "guffawing". Evidently a sign, in the Saussurean sense, is emitted which delineates or differentiates a particular set of (previously unattainable) characteristics within a particular range of vocal expression. In some instances, a new word may not itself be freshly coined, but may appear as a novelty in the vocabulary of the speaking (or writing) individual, who then becomes aware that a new word is being acquired. There are many examples in the dictionary, and they must often be the means by which new senses are borrowed from other speech communities. Such is the case with *punch* (the beverage) which has no historical connection with "kick" or "vigour" but originally only with the Hindi word *panch* "five" (the number of ingredients in a beverage). And, to take just one more example: a *godown* is sometimes thought of (especially by people unfamiliar with "godowns") as a place into which one descends by, say, a ramp, whereas the word is derived (possibly *via* Portuguese) from a Malay term for an ordinary street-level store or warehouse. There are many less exotic examples which we may never become aware of, unless we have reason to explore the dictionary. The speaker or writer has managed so far without the new word or sense, but from now on the shared mode of language has undergone a kaleidoscopic displacement, every possibly related word or sense in the individual's vocabulary having undergone a readjustment, however minuscule. However, the exact "position" in the vocabulary "occupied" by this new word will only rarely coincide with any dictionary-based plan (even if one deliberately sets out to make it so). Furthermore, it is a common experience that, after "registering" a new item, the individual will be struck by its recurrence within a short time after its acquisition. The shared mode of language permits a certain margin of individual variation, but maintains a commonality sufficient to support effective interaction.

Yet, an operational metaphor such as this is really an illusion. The shared mode of language is no objective realm awaiting scientific description: our very lives, phenomenology and hermeneutics would insist, are projected in and by it. Acquiring words is one thing, but actively producing words in speech or writing is quite another.

So far in these pages no account has been provided of what takes place in the concretion of a word (though a detailed consideration of this is given in a later chapter). Suffice it for the present to suggest that something like a "sign-emitting turbulence" occurs, following which something "registers" within the shared intersubjective awareness (which must be organized in a similar manner for all who share a particular culture). The "eddies" generated by these sign emissions must be structured in rather complicated patterns. Convergences can be said to take place between, on the one hand, loosely structured ranges of feeling, activity, iconic representation qualities, perceptions – word meanings, in short – and, on the other, sequences of sounds (or graphic marks). In case any two or more of the latter sequences become too much alike they become prone to mutual semantic contagion. For example, a speaker (rather than a writer who has the advantage of being able to correct "errors") who already "knows" the word *vigorous* acquires, say, the word *rigorous*. There is now the danger of confusing the two word-forms and meanings; of using *vigorous* when the sense "rigorous" is intended – an "error" of frequent actual occurrence. If enough speakers (and especially writers) begin to tolerate the convergence, semantic and lexical change will be said to have occurred. The traditional meaning of *disinterested* ("unbiased by personal interest") is still widely understood but in the opinion of one of the more progressive dictionaries: "If you are *disinterested* in something, you are not interested in it. Some users of English believe that it is not correct to use *disinterested* with this meaning."[10] This suggests that *disinterested* is not only ousting *uninterested* – which from an aesthetic and cultural (unconscious) point of view may have outlived its usefulness – but may already have done so. (At the same time the language becomes poorer by one culturally irreplaceable concept.)[11]

With new words, as with new senses, *mimesis* is achieved by the same process of convergence (of the two modes of language). Man's first words no doubt shared a similar origin, though with much greater latitude on the instrumental-informational side of the convergence where, as in some Australian languages even today, words are shaped as the urge to shape them arises. It is sometimes assumed that Archaic Man imitated Nature; but it seems just as likely that, in this origination of origins, Nature reproduced herself as language (and as human consciousness as a whole) in the very act of *mimesis* (Primary Imagination). Surviving onomatopoeic words in English may even lend support to this suggestion. Words such as *cuckoo, hullabaloo, swish, rasp, gush*, along with scores of others, do not "imitate" anything, if only for the very good reason that there is nothing "there" to imitate. An animate object "out there" becomes a "cuckoo" only as the result of some "figuration" (Barfield) on the part of an anonymous individual or individuals, some original mimetic act. From that moment onwards the word *cuckoo* became a piece of verbal art, convincing speakers of English at least that the word is derived by onomatopoeia directly from the "cuckoo sound" the bird is supposedly "heard" to make. As Bakhtin observed:

> the word is, after all, not a dead material object in the hands of an artist equipped with it; it is a **living** word and is therefore in all things true to **itself**; it may be anachronous and comic, it may reveal its narrowness and one-sidedness, but its meaning – once realized – can never be completely extinguished. And under changed conditions this meaning may emit bright new rays, burning away the reifying crust that had grown up around it. (1981, 419) (Bakhtin's emphases)

Bakhtin was of course aware that a word is not exactly the same thing as a work of art. Though the latter can be subject to the change Bakhtin mentions, the work of (visual or plastic) art is never an actual living object. Whereas, that is exactly what a word is: a living entity, and not in any metaphorical sense. Like any living being, a word carries around with it the "taste" of a particular "genre", *rhythmos*, a particular class or profession, an ideological trend, a group ethos, particular people, generations, and even a moment of time:

> Each word tastes of the context and contexts in which it has lived its socially charged life; all words...are populated by intentions. (Bakhtin 1981, 293)

The word exists not in dictionaries but in people's hearts, minds and imaginations. It is from other people's contexts and intentions that the word has to be taken and made one's own (1981, 294).

The use of words in live communication is "always individual and contextual in nature." Bakhtin understood that the word exists for the speaker or writer under three aspects. Firstly, as a neutral word, it belongs to nobody. Secondly, as the **other's** word, it belongs to another person and is "filled with the echoes of the other's utterance" (Bakhtin 1986, 88). Lastly, as my own word, with its particular speech tendency and strategy, it becomes imbued with my own personal style, and I am helpless to do anything about it. It is this "dialogic orientation" of one word among other words that creates new and significant possibilities in discourse. In literature, it creates the potential for distinctive prose, reaching its fullest and deepest expression, Bakhtin thought, in the novel (1981, 275).

For these and many other reasons, there can never be a one-to-one relationship between a word and its object; nor is the encounter between word and object an unimpeded or even a unique one:

> Between the word and its object, there exists an elastic environment of other, alien words about the same object... and this is an environment that is difficult to penetrate. It is precisely in the process of living interaction with this specific environment that the word may be individualized and given stylistic shape. (Bakhtin 1981, 276)

In directing itself towards its object the word enters "a dialogically agitated and tension-filled environment of alien words, value judgments and accents." In Bakhtin's terms, the word in its transit undergoes a "spectral dispersion" in an atmosphere filled with alien words, through which passes the "ray-word". It is the "social atmosphere" of the word, and the atmosphere that surrounds the object, that causes the facets of the resultant image to sparkle. In this manner, the word "conceptualizes" its object.

17. Words in Relation

The lexicon, it has been argued, is that domain of language in which, through the agency of words, the organic and the intersubjective modes of language interface. The word's particularity in this respect results in the strangest of phenomena, many of which on account of their everyday familiarity are for most of the time taken for granted. These phenomena are at their most evident and idiosyncratic in the relations that are established, temporarily or permanently, between individual words.

Sound and graphic sequences, only some of which achieve the status of words are produced in the opaque regions of the organic mode of language at the same time as within the bright but not always less inscrutable portals of the intersubjective mode. These sequences may be anything from a single syllable, or even a sub-division of a syllable, to units several syllables in length. The main difficulty arises from the fact that the morphological and phonotactic shape of these sequences are determined by both language modes at once, each according to its separate designs and guiding principles. In the case of the organic-differential mode, the term "principle" is used figuratively. This mode is neutral as regards regulation, form, style or expressivity. Its concern is with the efficient transmission and reception of data from which messages can be interpreted (not the direct concern of this mode either) and acted upon effectively. These "principles", which are apt to take on the appearance of "rules" (formulated and sustained however in the metalinguistic operations of the intersubjective mode), are more or less complex processes occurring below the level of our conscious awareness. They have to do in the main with information distribution and exchange, system equilibrium maintenance, all of them functions of the brain as well as of events within the immediate physical environment, in which the efficiency of communication coding, control of inputs in relation to outputs, signal-to-noise ratios, channel capacities, redundancy and error, transmission and reception rates, and no doubt much else, is finely tuned and controlled.

It is the shared intersubjective mode that categorizes and regulates, thereby creating a plethora of rule exceptions, which bedevil the most commonly used words and expressions especially. The shared mode, as far as English for example is concerned, treats *vary* and *invariably* equally as "words". Linguistics on the other hand maintains that *vary* is a single (free) morpheme, while *invariably* consists of no less than four morphemes, with the morpheme *vary* having undergone a graphemic (but not a phonemic) modification (to *vari-*). The "principle" that the adverbial form in this instance is *invariably* and not *invariablely,* with the morpheme *-ly* simply added to the adjectival form (in accordance with the more general rule: *homely, finally, boldly,* etc.) is one that has its etiology in the organic mode, but its socio-cultural "etiquette" in the shared mode of language. The organic mode takes no prescriptive view of either *vary* or *invariably* or indeed any other lexical form in the language. But if anyone were to try (in English) to insist on the word-form *pstrum,* it would be "disallowed" by the phonotactics of the language (though not by the graphemics) and the perpetrator would either be "compelled" to suppress the *p*-sound (as he or she does, uncomplainingly for the most part, in *psyche, psalm,* or *pseudo*) or give it up. The disallowances and compulsions in this and comparable instances are partly the work of the organic mode, for reasons having to do with information management, and partly of the shared language mode which behaves as a kind of censor. (The potential element of fun inherent in coinages such as P.G.Wodehouse's *Psmith,* however, is apparently the sole property of the shared mode). It probably goes without saying that the regulatory behaviour of the organic mode differs from one speech community to another: German and Russian for example do not suppress the initial *p*-sounds in the forms just given being pronounced – yet another example of convergence or collusion, recurrently, between the two different modes of language.

The sense or meaning that such sequences achieve can be equally puzzling. A few minutes spent with an historical dictionary, say, *The Shorter Oxford English Dictionary,* should be sufficient to convince one that word meanings are seldom simple or straightforward. A word such as *crocodile*, for example, might seem to be as elementary an instance as one could find. Yet the dictionary draws our attention to two additional (and not rare) "meanings": "a person who weeps hypocritically, etc." and "a girl's school walking two and two in a long file". Meaning pervades every recess of the shared mode of language, but also of course extends well beyond language, into art, music, understanding, ritual, and most other human domains. Word meanings are different however: they participate to the full in meaning in the general sense but, besides this, words have to cope with the demands of the intersubjective life-world, with brain-determined differentiation and, above all, with their own symbolic, and hence supra-human, origin. All of this together makes the seemingly innocuous word-meaning or sense so mercurial, so apposite, so reassuring, and yet potentially so revelatory and potent. It is not difficult therefore to appreciate why, in common with all other complex processes, words and word-meanings function as a **system,** a system that in this instance relies on a continuously renewable and renewed, and hence live, convergence between the separate language modes.

The particular fusion generated between these two altogether different modes of language, whose energy casts up "words" that in large part seem so recognizable, takes place below the threshold of conscious awareness. A perpetually active and dynamic, as well as evanescent, concurrence maintains and at the same time allows for the requisite degree of fluidity, thanks to a flexibly managed and constant matching of sound sequences with potential senses. It is this process that allows for the emergence into consciousness of the words we want, and thus makes it possible for us to speak and write.

The fusion of sound sequence and potential meaning in no way resembles the mixing of metals to obtain an alloy, or of ingredients in cookery. Differentiality and semantic potentiality, though radically unlike each other in essence, are alive to each other, if in obscure ways. Their relations appear to be not once and for all, but provisional and open-ended; more like, perhaps, the unimaginably complex but impermanent synaptic contacts between axons and neurons in the human brain. That is why convergence, or concurrence, the matching of sound sequences with semantic categories, operating below the familiar surface forms of words, has to be as variable and unfixed as it is. We may never fully know what it is that motivates our use of one word or set of words in preference to another. In creative contexts, utterance occurs only at the exact moment when the speaker, or more usually the writer, "feels" that the words about to be used are the "right" ones, and "in the right order". And, as writers especially need no reminding, even this sense of "rightness" may often succumb to doubt as a particular piece of work proceeds. Owing to the illusion of permanence engendered by the dictionary – a cultural institution – few appreciate the fine equilibrium existing in the lexicon with which they operate or the symbolic source of words themselves, which supplies the *energeia* for the covert interchange between the mysteries of brain-controlled and brain-driven activity on the one hand and the marvellously versatile nexus of socio-cultural codes of an intersubjectively perceived and experienced life-world on the other.

*   *   *

Saussure was among the first to recognize that any sample of speech or discourse has two, as it were rectilinear, dimensions. The first of these dimensions, which has to do with the linear, sequential linkage of morphemes and (lexical) words, Saussure called **syntagmatic**.[1] The second, but more elusive, dimension simultaneously subsumes all the potential sequences that could have occurred in place of any part or the whole of a particular sample of discourse, and is termed **paradigmatic**.[2]

In the sample *They took a poor view of his brusqueness of manner* for example all the lexical items form part of that remarkable but all too familiar syntagmatic relationship known as the sentence. It will be noticed though that some items of the sequence appear to be more intimately related than others. The phrase *took a poor view of* looks like an idiom or set phrase, and the items in *his brusqueness of manner* strike one as having a more immediate connection with each other than any of them separately has with other items in the sentence. The pronoun *they* refers either anaphorically to persons mentioned in some previous sentence or deictically to a context of situation (*e.g.* onlookers, acquaintances). How we know these things, one cannot say for certain. Among the various hypotheses and models, the most convincing is probably the theory developed and several times revised since the nineteen-sixties by Chomsky. But the latter provides no plausible rationale for rejecting in the given context (or perhaps in any context) a seemingly unremarkable alteration *poor* (in *they took a poor view of...*) to *rich* (*They took a rich view of* is ruled out). To most speakers of English however the latter alternative would seem to be a mistake, poor style or, most likely, downright odd. Yet an equally odd substitution – of *ulterior* for *interior* in the phrase *ulterior decorator* – becomes a source of lasting amusement, in that it so aptly captures the busily ambitious individual very deliberately on his or her way up the career ladder. Those querying the validity of the expression could be pacified on learning that the perpetrator was the poet Dylan Thomas. Equally amusing, albeit for very different reasons, are the types of transposition (of initial sounds between successive words – *caught a bar* for *bought a car* – a dysphasic phenomenon) routinely made, tradition has it, by the eponymous Rev. Spooner, and at times by most of us.

The paradigmatic dimension, by contrast, subsumes all the possible word-forms, phrases, or sentences that could fit harmoniously into a particular "slot" within a speech sequence or text, long or short. The number of possible alternatives is limited by the context, by stylistic factors, and by the lexicon itself. In the sample sentence briefly discussed in the last paragraph, *unfavourable* or *critical* could have replaced *poor* in the phrase *take a poor view of*, and *brusqueness* could have been replaced by *aggressiveness* (the Thesaurus supplies a range of other possible substitutions). Style and context work together to limit the range of substitution and to guide selection. For example in the last sentence of the previous paragraph, my earlier draft had *from time to time* instead of *occasionally*. To my mind (other writers may take different view) *occasionally* is a slightly heavy word for the context, but it does have the advantage of being formally congruent with *routinely*; but what clinched the substitution was the sense that the repetition of *time* might attract interference from *tradition* – a markedly temporal word – which could make the sentence even more difficult to read than it already is. It will be surprising if the reader even approximately endorses my prognosis, inasmuch as individuals notoriously differ, less in their own right than under the impact of "the words of others": rhetorical models, educational influences, and so forth. At this point readers are invited to ponder the incredible degree of complexity inherent in bridging the differential activity going on within the organic dimension and the shaping and shifting of the socio-cultural and aesthetic codes taking place in the shared language mode.

Saussure emphasized that the syntagmatic and paradigmatic dimensions are interdependent and condition one another: the reader may have noticed that it is difficult to consider the one without reference to the other. This is not however to deny the usefulness of the paradigmatic-syntagmatic antithesis. Jakobson's development of Saussure's schema as sequence/simultaneity and his application of it to language pathology has been influential, rationalizing the clinical categories once proliferating in the study of aphasia. Though falling short perhaps of the degree of congruence with theory that he might have been seeking, Jakobson's model demonstrates that the discrete brain functions can in some degree be aligned with the Saussurean dimensions.[3]   In aphasic disorders of the "sequential" type patients find difficulty in handling sentence connectives and functional elements (conjunctions, prepositions, pronouns, etc), the "empty" words, semantically speaking, of the lexicon. So they tend to speak with a terseness approaching telegraphese. Conversely, someone whose language is disordered along the simultaneous dimension will experience problems for example with synonyms, and may not be able to recognize their semantic equivalence. In serious cases semantic classes may break down altogether, with the normal hold on critical distinctions between "wife", "daughter", "parent" and so forth becoming precarious.

Saussure's not trivial point about mutual conditioning can be illustrated by combining the following sentences which, until they are combined, remain syntagmatically neutral with respect to each other:

   (1a) *Richard is a friend of mine.*
   (1b) *Richard lives in the Lake District.*

When combined, sentence (1b) will "naturally" follow sentence (1a):

   (1c) *Richard is a friend of mine and lives in the Lake District.*

To reverse the order (*Richard lives in the Lake District and is a friend of mine*) would be to "foreground" my relationship with Richard in some way or lead to the expectation of a suitable context. The synonyms *dwell* and *inhabit* stand in direct paradigmatic relationship to *live*, and induce the following set of alternative possibilities:

(2a) *Richard lives in the Lake District.*
(2b) *Richard dwells in the Lake District.*
(2c) *Richard inhabits the Lake District.*

Sentences (2b) and (2c) are possible, but unlikely; not so much because they violate grammatical rules, but because they are collocationally and stylistically anomalous. However, *He dwells in the heart of the Lake District* or *The Lake District is inhabited mainly by Cumbrians* are unexceptionable. Word order – that facet of language so closely aligned with the syntagmatic dimension – is a function of constraints operating within the organic language mode, whereas style is regulated by socio-semiotic codes and aesthetics. In any possible conflict the shared mode can override the organic mode of language and correspondingly, in this instance, style overrides grammar. This appears to be confirmed by the acceptability of the following examples in which collocational (syntagmatic) incompatibility has been, so to speak, ironed out:

(3a) *Richard lives in a different dimension.*
(3b) *Richard inhabits a different dimension.*
(3c) *Richard dwells in a different dimension.*

It has to be noted however that these particular sentences are more or less "queer" in the Wittgensteinian sense; and semantic equivalence among them is difficult to determine in that their references are so vague. Also, none of them naturally (*i.e.* within existing socio-semiotic codes) replaces the second half of sentence (1c), above. At the present time there is no really satisfactory explanation for such quirks of the lexicon. Covert relations have nevertheless been found to connect a modifier (*e.g.* an attributive adjective) with its noun.[4] The phrase *stony path* for example is not equivalent to the paraphrase "a path having stones in it"; rather it is a path having so many stones in it that it would be more aptly paraphrased as "uneven because of the many stones breaking its surface". Similarly, an *industrial country* is not merely one in which there are industries.

The syntagmatic dimension of word compounding, in particular, is a highly complex one, and far from well understood. Ostensibly harmless, socio-culturally acceptable word compounds, such as *fuddy-duddy*, *disc jockey* or *hitch-hike*, can raise innumerable problems. In the first example neither *fuddy* nor *duddy* are "allowed" a separate existence as words (free morphemes) in their own right. This is an instance therefore of two lexical non-entities (according to the dictionary at any rate) combining to produce an acceptable and useful colloquial compound. The argument that *fuddy-duddy* should therefore be counted as a simple (as opposed to compound) word may be all right in theory, but it will lack credibility, since *duddy*, as a diminutive form, draws attention to the possibility that it might in some paradigmatic manner be related to *dud*, which it is not. *Disc* and *jockey* by contrast bear no (morphological or semantic) relation to each other until they coalesce into a lexical compound having a third completely unrelated sense. The most complex of the three examples though is likely to be *hitch-hike*. Over time the verb *hitch* has developed a number of different senses including "to jerk", "to hobble a horse", "to catch or hook on to something", and the noun form has the meaning "a temporary stoppage". It must be more than idle speculation to suggest that all these different senses combine to produce the modern semantically complex sense of *hitch,* found only in the compound *hitch-hike* (The back-formation *hitch* as in *to hitch a lift* raises a different set of problems taking us into fresh complexities which would lead to a lengthy digression).

The sequencing of words is not always mere syntactic convenience. Sequencing can evidently also form an integral part of style and code function in language. Although predominantly a symptom of information management and exchange taking place within the organic language mode, word order can undergo creative transformation within the individual's style. Syntagmatic units and phrases develop a conventional set of relations (collocations) with paradigmatic sets, but these conventions can easily be and often are broken. No immediate syntagmatic link suggests itself for the series: *truck...polar bear...last night...see...* But, if someone were to combine them with any degree of insistence into the expression: "Last night I really did see a polar bear driving a truck", the person listening, completely unaware of the uniqueness of what is being said, might simply reply: "You must have been seeing things!" If idiosyncratic vocal inflection and semantic emphasis are added to even the most commonplace of expressions, one might have to agree with Chomsky that all utterances – not least, ones that are trivial, facetious, or nonsensical – are probably unique.

Sensitivity towards stylistic variation and speech genre (knowing for instance when to say *He was given a reprimand* and when *I told him off*) depends to some extent on cultural or social sophistication; but sometimes not. It is well known and well documented that even unsophisticated speakers regularly resort to "code-switching"[5] – switching, that is, from one language, dialect, or discourse style, to another – in order to convey differences of attitude, intention, illocutionary force, or even their relationships with others. Code-switching as a socio-semiotic device belongs to the shared mode of language, though the means and the (unconscious) strategies it relies on are lodged in the instrumental language mode.

Lexical "institutionalization" by comparison appears to remain unaffected by stylistic or code variation. In common with many other lexical compounds, *country house* retains the normal pauses between its constituent items and undergoes no shift in stress, regardless of whether it indicates "a house in the country" (non-institutionalized) or "a residence of the gentry" (institutionalized, though only in British English). Thus a sentence of the kind *He doesn't like country houses* remains ambiguous until a suitable context neutralizes the ambiguity. This kind of phenomenon takes one outside the lexicon into anthropology and sociology. Asymmetry between expressions such as *country house* and *public house*, or between *country house* and *country walk*, can probably be explicated in formal linguistic terms but they find their true rationale only in the context of the particular culture in which they have become institutionalized; in the ethnography of speaking, that is. In American English, for instance, neither *country house* nor *public house* (but excluding *pub*) assume the institutionalized denotations they have in British English. Institutionalization leads to petrification, with syntagmatically sequenced units becoming fixed expressions:

> As soon as any regularly constructed expression is employed on some particular occasion of utterance, it is available for use again by the same person or by others as a ready-made unit which can be incorporated in further utterances; and the more frequently it is used,

the more likely it is to solidify as a fixed expression, which native
speakers will presumably store in memory, rather than construct
afresh on each occasion. (Lyons 1977, 536)

An institutionalized syntagmatic sequence that is greater in length
than a word compound may take the form of an aphorism, a proverb, a
cliché or other ready-made phrase, a fused expression or idiom. For
brevity's sake, only the last of these will be discussed.

Longer integral syntagmatic wholes are generally idioms or fused
expressions. The idiom has been carefully defined as "an expression
whose meaning cannot be accounted for as a compositional function of
the meanings its parts have when they are not parts of idioms" (Chafe
1968, 109ff.). The idiom is peculiar in a number of ways. It is opaque:
that is, unless its meaning is already known or a very explicit context
is provided, it is unlikely that its meaning can be deduced. In virtually
every instance an idiom can be replaced by a single word or verbal
phrase; whereas real compounds (*disc jockey* for example) require a
lengthy paraphrase and, as hermeneutical philosophers and translation
theorists have been maintaining, a paraphrase inevitably yields a
different meaning from its original. The syntagmatically complex
idioms *let the cat out of the bag* and *have a bee in one's bonnet*, for
example, can be replaced without serious distortion or loss of meaning
by *divulge* (*a secret*) and (*be*) *obsessed*, respectively. There is perhaps
nothing crucial in this distinction between idioms and lexical
compounds, except that it furnishes yet one further illustration of the
asymmetry one should expect to find between the shared domain of
(interpreted) meanings and the information-oriented world of
morpheme sequences.

Asymmetry is particularly marked in so-called "fused" verb
phrases. In *take a fancy to*, for example, the item *fancy* can be
replaced by the synonym *liking* (*take a liking to*). The negative of *take
a liking to* however is not *take a disliking to* but *take a dislike to* or
conceive a dislike for. To contend that the lexical form *disliking* is
unacceptable is not a perfect explanation since the problem could have
been turned around and the point made that *like*, the symmetrical
opposite of the noun *dislike*, is in current use (as in the phrase *likes
and dislikes*). To rationalize that *take a liking to* should really have
developed historically as the unacceptable *take a like to* leads only into
a syntagmatic void.[6]

In fused expressions of this sort, the syntagmatic and paradigmatic dimensions interweave to produce some curious and not always predictable dissymmetries. If for example one wanted to substitute *bias* or *grudge* for *dislike* in the phrase *take a dislike to* it would be necessary also to find a substitute for the verb *take (e.g..develop a bias against)*. Whenever the constraints are known they are rarely syntactic but, more often than not, the institutional peculiarities of the language practice of the speech community. The phrase *in the long run* can just about be matched by *in the short run*, but *in the longest run* or *in the quick run* are disallowed, not for lexical or syntactic, but for institutional reasons. Speakers of British English talk of *lost property* but speakers of some other languages, more logically perhaps, prefer to speak of "found property" or "lost and found". But speakers become so inured to fixed collocations or fused expressions that they accept them without question, and tend to resist alternatives.

Defined differently, an idiom may be said to be a string of word-forms having both a unitary "metaphorical" meaning – without there being any necessary connection between the metaphor and the component lexical items – and a "literal" meaning, conveyed by the same sequence. Thus *kick the bucket* may mean either "die" or "strike a pail with the foot". If the expression is used out of context it will usually be assumed that the metaphorical meaning ("die") is operative. Idioms however are subject to curious institutional restrictions; that is, they cannot undergo the same range of syntactic transformations as their literal counterparts. If the phrase refers to an actual "kick" and a non-metaphorical "bucket", the transformations *The bucket was kicked very hard* or *Did anyone kick the bucket?* are possible and acceptable, given an appropriate context. But if the intended meaning is "die" these particular transformations would sound funny or distasteful. Generally, modifiers cannot be inserted into idioms without producing some extrinsic effect. It is as if the entire idiom were haunted by some paradigmatic ghost of "die", limiting the transformational possibilities. Practically the only modifier that can be inserted into *kick the bucket* (when "die" is meant) would be the word *proverbial* (*He kicked the proverbial bucket*) and this of course does no more than emphasize the metaphorical sense. With an idiom such as the latter, owing to the risk of indelicacy, the restriction is understandable but it is hard to see what might be the socio-cultural objections to tinkering with, say, an idiom like *let the cat out of the bag*. Surely, *He divulged a secret and could not conceal the fact* is stuffy by comparison with

He let the cat out of the bag but could not get it back in again... Or is it? An innocent query of this sort opens up the still larger question of socio-cultural and aesthetic norms of acceptability and, in turn, entails hermeneutics. Whichever way one looks at it, the extended idiom in this instance sounds deviant, facetious, too silly for ordinary use.

"Haunting" is not a concept encountered in linguistics but, as already hinted, it can sometimes appear as if one word, simple or complex, were haunted by the presence of other words that could have occurred (paradigmatically) in their place. With an ordinary word such as *friend* (to take a single example at random) there would seem to be a host of other synonym candidates waiting in the wings. It is not difficult to envisage a monologue such as the following: "*I have a* **friend**... *well, not really a friend*... *more an* **acquaintance**... *actually a* **colleague**, *you could say a* **team-mate**... *No, not a* **crony**, *for heaven's sake...A* **partner**, *an* **associate**, *so to speak. You know what I mean...*" We have here a set of synonyms, any one of which could be appropriate, depending on the nuance intended. These are stylistic nuances, governed by aesthetic norms of taste, discrimination, and delicacy of socio-semiotic perception.

Inasmuch as the human brain is aesthetically and stylistically neutral any word (within a particular word class[7]) could potentially become the synonym of any other, given the nigh boundless network of associative pathways within the cortical memory. As it happens however, synonym paradigm membership is always subject to referential, stylistic, contextual, and informational constraints. In the first place, synonyms must be similar or virtually identical in (potential) meaning. Recognition of difference and similarity is a function of the differential-organic mode of language. In the second place, synonyms must share the same range of collocation – a socio-cultural matter.[8] In the sentence *Socrates died by self-administered poison* nothing is amiss, but *The skyscraper died* is ruled out since constructions of concrete and steel cannot "die". *The old house died of neglect* is possible if a metaphor is intended, but *The old house committed suicide* is ruled out on the grounds that suicide is a wilful, and hence human, act. There is also the not-so-residual problem raised by knowledge criteria in relation to truth-conditions. An historical claim for example to the effect that "So-and-so died of old age" might need amending in the light of advances in medical knowledge. Even the claim that "Héloïse died of a broken heart" might at some future time be deemed pure metaphor and rephrased along the lines: "Héloïse died of an undiagnosed physical condition exacerbated by stress"(!)

Collocational restriction, unproblematic though it might appear, hides a tangle of unknowns in the patterning of the lexicon. For instance, although all organisms are known to die, only human beings can "kick the bucket", a fact which highlights not only the idiosyncratic nature of collocation but its grammatical indeterminacy also. Young children for example cannot "kick the bucket" but clearly it would be a waste of time trying to establish at what age or under what conditions anyone can appropriately be said to have "kicked the bucket". Even if there existed the prescription that the idiom should be used only in the case of an older person who has been doggedly holding on to life and is at the same time not too well loved, whether by his immediate fellows or by the public at large, a reliable rule of usage would still not have been provided.[9]

Because synonyms range from complete parity of sense at the one extreme through a cline of increasing semantic dissimilarity to an opposite extreme of rather vague resemblance, it is not easy to arrive at a usefully definitive typology. At one extremity are located what have been termed "absolute" synonyms.[10] These are found, it appears, only if their contexts are without exception identical. The main drawback with this category of synonym is that a language has evidently no use for it. Even if identical synonyms were to come into existence they would be so unstable that the impulsion towards semantic differentiation would be overwhelming. In the early Middle Ages for example the words *shirt* and *skirt* existed separately in different English regional dialects and were identical in meaning ("a knee-length garment") and context. But when the same words fell together in the *koine* of Middle English, they acquired the gender-separate references and senses they have today. (Interestingly though, now that "shirts" as items of clothing are interchangeable between the sexes, we might notice that in more recent times the word *skirt* has already acquired a derogatory connotation in certain of its uses.) In contemporary English the unresolved identical-synonym alternations are those operating between the different national speech communities, especially American and British (*elevator/lift*, *apartment/flat*, *truck/lorry*,etc.).

A second and useful class of synonym is known as the "cognitive" synonym. With this type of synonym the context need not be identical;

only the truth-conditions. Examples of cognitive synonyms might include *somnambulism* and *sleepwalking*: their meaning is the same, even though their contexts are different (*somnambulism* would be inappropriate in a context where *sleepwalking* would do, while the latter might appear somewhat out of place in a professional context). The contextual discrepancy will not in every case be measurable, and will be heavily governed by what British linguists have termed "register". In British English, for example, *clever*, *brainy* and *bright* share the same sense but tend to occur in different contexts. *Brainy* tends to be used most often by people of inferior education (to refer to those of superior education) whereas *clever* is neutral in this respect. *Bright* can easily sound condescending.

By far the largest class of synonyms is that consisting of semantically related pairs subtending different truth-conditions. With such pairs it is usually possible to assert an attribution of one member of the pair while at the same time denying an attribution of the other. Examples of this include: *He is not very* **intelligent**, *just* **shrewd**; *She is not so much* **beautiful** *as* **handsome**; *His behaviour was* **eccentric** *rather than* **pathological**. The band of the "synonym spectrum" occupied by this third type of synonym is wide indeed: all the way from close synonyms to the extreme at which synonymy disappears altogether...only to reappear, paradoxically as the converse phenomenon – **antonymy**.

Antonymy presents a complex issue. It is not exclusively a semantic phenomenon, but in part a reflection of the activity of the differential mode of language. Antonymy is supposed to cover all oppositions in lexical meaning but, in reality, not many antonyms are demonstrable "opposites". A distinction is generally made between two very different types of antonym: "gradable" and "ungradable". *Hot* and *cold* are examples of the former: the opposition is a relative one. Moreover, *hot* is relative not only to *cold* but also to *warm* and a variety of other temperature gradations. In addition, *hot* can become *hotter* and *hottest*. With other items – words such as *female* for example – gradations are absent. Either a human being (or animal) is or is not "female"; semantically it would be impossible for someone to be "more female", and "less female" does not necessarily lead in the direction of the hermaphrodite. But speakers cannot be over-pernickety: they would understand perfectly well the meaning of the question: "Which is the more female of these two women?" even though they might feel – or even reason – that "feminine" (which is gradable) should have been the adjective used. As long as interaction is proceeding satisfactorily the differential language mode pays scant attention to the niceties of the shared mode.

In many languages the most commonly used antonyms are morphologically unrelated (*good-bad, better-worse, happy-sad*, etc.) When this is not the case the antonym is formed by negative derivation: *friendly-unfriendly, trustworthy-untrustworthy*, etc. These are all examples of related opposites. The positive term in an antonym pair tends to take precedence over the negative term. *How good is she?* is the normal way of ascertaining the relative degree of skill or ability of someone; but to ask how "bad" someone is would be unusual, marked behaviour, implying a definite degree of "badness". Yet another class of antonyms has to do with direction: *up-down, left-right*, etc. are examples of directional oppositions. Antonymy is so puzzling that a phenomenological solution seems called for:

> It may well be that our understanding, not only of directional opposition, but of opposition in general, is based upon some kind of analogical extension of distinctions which we first learn to apply with respect to our own orientation and the location or locomotion of other objects in the external world. (Lyons 1977, 281)

Such an ordinary, yet perplexing, concept as the antonym takes us into areas of ourselves and our life-world we know little about. Freud, no less, drew our attention to the antithetical sense of primal roots, a *coincidentia oppositorum* already built into our vocabulary.

Just as synonyms may (paradigmatically) fulfil a definite syntagmatic role (*e.g.* a *black heart*, but a *dark horse*) so, conversely, word-forms may often be aligned with more than one sense. Potential ambiguity is avoided through the expedient of having only one of these senses operative in any particular context. This underlines the importance of context in the regulation of sense. Thus, in *They headed for the bank* the immediate linguistic context does not make clear which of two possible senses of *bank* applies: "an establishment for the custody of money, etc." or "the margin of a river". In real life such ambiguities seldom arise since the context of situation will nearly always disambiguate. In cases where disambiguation presents problems, there exist standard devices for taking care of such an eventuality: an example from English would be the response: "Funny ha-ha, or funny peculiar?"

Sometimes – as in the case of *bank* – the different senses are perceived to be sufficiently distinct to warrant separate dictionary entries, especially when it is known that their etymologies are different (*bank* meaning "river margin" is of English origin whereas the monetary *bank* derives from the Italian *banca*). But, whether senses are judged "sufficiently distinct" however, depends less on etymology and just as little on the schemes adopted by the lexicographer; though quite heavily on the perceptions of the speech community. One indicator is the pun. Where a pun is possible, then most probably the two distinct senses can be considered an indication of the words being separate (homonyms): not a very useful indication however, inasmuch as puns appear to be more difficult to perpetrate than they might seem, and their occurrence is most often unintentional. Ambiguity is not a reliable criterion either, since both homonymy (more than one sense, more than one word) and polysemy (more than one sense, but a single word) can result in it. In real-life contexts, the homonymous *They passed the port at midnight* is just as likely, or unlikely, to result in ambiguity as the polysemous *They went to see the head* (head of a body, or head of a department?). The relationship between the two senses of "head" in the last example is said to be a metaphorical one but, as we saw earlier, metaphor has become a vexed question. If during a visit to an Italian church a companion were to ask me: "Did you spot the hand of Giotto in that last mural we were looking at?" my response would most unlikely be "Do you mean Giotto's actual hand, or the intervention of the painter?" since I assume the speaker's meaning to be the same as mine: the metaphorical one primarily, but containing more than a little of the literal meaning of "hand" also. Metaphorical extension then is not a useful criterion for deciding whether we are dealing with one word or more than one word. Whether the distinction between homonymy and polysemy has any basis in reality is hard to say.

In examining the polysemy of a particular word, one might be forgiven for concluding that the number of different senses a word possesses is arbitrary, especially as the type and fineness of mesh employed by different dictionaries varies. Should one conclude that the polysemy of particular words is infinitely divisible? Or, alternatively, should one (in the company of the dictionary-makers) look for semantic quanta, or take the view that any polysemantic sub-division is a matter of individual interpretation?

The answer to these last questions is the exasperating: "Yes and no". "Yes" because, as was noted earlier, every time a word is used a speaker or writer engages in what might be called "implicit polysemy", to the extent that without knowing it an imperceptible change of sense is introduced. "No" for the reason that, if messages are to be viable, there must somehow be morphosemantic quanta that make interpretation possible. The most likely answer however remains "yes and no", in the sense that, in using a word, one is not usually conscious of polysemantic sub-division, particularly in live speech: the polysemy of a word is holistic, to the extent that on consulting a dictionary it is found that in one's own speech different senses have been conflated; and yet, by and large, the interlocutor manages to "select" the meaning (*i.e.* the polysemantic sub-division) that seems most appropriate. On the one hand, philosophers find themselves, it has been claimed, constantly up against the problem of determining whether words of key importance to them (*know, believe, aware, good, ought,* and so forth) do have more than one sense. On the other hand, the "sense-spectra" approach lends support to the view that polysemy might be infinitely divisible:

> There are cases where variant readings of a single lexical form would seem to be more appropriately visualised as points on a continuum – a seamless fabric of meaning with no clear boundaries. (Cruse 1986, 71)

In the next chapter I hope to show that semantic variation is real and operates within a "morphosemantic" framework and system.

Real-life context (context of situation) is one thing, but linguistic or "textual" context is quite another. Neither is an inert given, merely an active force in its own right. In exerting contextual control the text draws upon the combined associative potential – whether this be paradigmatic or, in the wider Firth-Halliday sense, collocational – of every single word in a unit of discourse. But contexts are not as straightforward as might be supposed. For a start, sensitivity to context, as Ricoeur acutely observed, is a function of polysemy:

> The use of contexts involves... an activity of discernment which is exercised in the concrete exchange of messages between interlocutors, and which is modelled on the interplay of question and answer. The activity of discernment is properly called interpretation; it consists in

recognizing which relatively univocal message the speaker has constructed on the polysemantic basis of the common lexicon. To produce a relatively univocal discourse with polysemic words, and to identify this intention of univocity in the reception of messages; such is the first and most elementary work of interpretation.[12]

Yet in spite of all this, each particular word, as Saussure first noted, resembles "the centre of a constellation" (1960, 126). "A word", Saussure observed, "can always evoke everything that can be associated with it in one way or another." The speaker or writer addresses a particular instant in which a word or sequence of words is being produced, but the words in the context (including both those already revealed and those as yet unrevealed) are, potentially at least, themselves undergoing hermeneutical appraisal also in that same instant. The illusion of the written text spread out in two-dimensional space conceals this dynamic interplay of act and potency, while the transience and instantaneity of the spoken utterance serve as its very image. A recent striking observation has pointed up the difference between the "passive" action of context, where "it serves as a kind of filter", and "productive contextual selection" in which "the context acts rather as a stimulus for a productive process" (Cruse 1986, 68-9). This "productive process" is engendered not solely by the constellatory foci of lexical units, or even by their having contracted collocational relations beyond the confines of the linearity of text and speech but, above all, by the exigencies of the life-world and the complex semiotic that finds its mirror image in language, and in the lexicon especially. *Truth* and *beauty* were (and still are as far the dictionary is concerned) unrelated, but when Keats wrote *Beauty is truth, truth beauty* he was indulging in no mere poetic fancy, but bringing two words into a new metonymic relation by this same productive process, and changing our world as a result.

The reader may already be at the point of suspecting that synonymy and polysemy-homonymy are really two reciprocal aspects of the same phenomenon: perceived semantic difference. A synonym appears quite often to be one member of some polysemous cluster of different senses. For example, *colour* is a synonym of *hue*, *pigment* and a number other lexical items. But this particular sense of *colour* is also one of several other senses grouped, as may be seen from the dictionary, under the entry COLOUR. These latter include "a flag, or standard", "racial difference". The reverse is also true. Under the different lemmata for

HEAD a fair number of different senses are given. One of these is the "anatomical head", which is at the same time a synonym of *skull*, *cranium*, etc. Another sense – "a person to whom others are subordinate" – makes it a synonym of *chief, leader, boss, director* and several other items. This "asymmetric dualism" was first described by Sergei Karcevskij (1929, 33ff.), a prominent member of the Prague School. In the line of Saussure, Karcevskij proposed that a word is an intersection of synonymy and polysemy. The semantic value of a word therefore is not something stable, but capable of being decided only in the concrete situation of actual use. The main drawback with such a model is that it leaves the question of the nature of synonymy and polysemy-homonymy unresolved. It is a model that could be turned inside out, making polysemy-homonymy and synonymy projections of the (linguistically and phenomenologically) mysterious word. Brought to its final reduction, all that we, along with Saussure, are left with is **difference**. Shortly, I hope to show that the word is rooted in the shared-intersubjective mode of language as well as in the differential-organic mode and, in so being, performs a remarkable, unique, even miraculous, function.

Meanwhile a question naturally suggests itself: How is it the lexicon does not collapse into chaos? It is in answer to this question that the importance of "morphosemantic concurrence" as part of the total picture comes into its own.[13] As will be seen in the next chapter, morphosemantic concurrence results from a provisional and temporary interface of sound (or graphic) sequence and sense. The resultant integration may be envisaged as a "particle", so to speak, of the real world in which, through the agency of language, we live. It is precisely also this same confluence of form and sense which keeps the system of the lexicon in working equilibrium. Take, for example, the word DASH. Like many other unexceptionable word-forms it can take on any one of a number of different potential senses. These senses include (though the listing is by no means exhaustive): (i)"disconcert" (ii) "violent collision" (iii) "haphazard" (iv) "ostentation" (v) "patch of colour or light", and (vi) "impetuous, hasty". Each one of these six potential senses can be found to be synonymous (or antonymous) with a fairly large number of other lexical items. Interestingly, the specific linkage is with sets of word-forms that share the same final segment -ASH and, more specifically still, with a set of semantic categories that exactly match these six discrete senses of DASH:

ASH$_1$ "disconcert" – *dash, abash*
ASH$_2$ "violent collision" – *dash, clash, smash, crash*
ASH$_3$ "haphazard" – *dash, slapdash, trash, hash*; (antonym) *cache*
ASH$_4$ "ostentation" – *dash, flash, splash, panache*
ASH$_5$ "patch of colour or light" – *dash, plash, splash*
ASH$_6$ "impetuous, hasty" – *dash*(ing), *rash, brash*

From this single example – but one of many – it can be seen that word-forms and word senses are intermeshed along the twin axes of synonymy-antonymy (similarity/opposition of sense) and polysemy (likeness of word-form), and that a displacement along one axis will produce a corresponding displacement along the other. Of particular interest is *panache*, a relatively recent importation from French, directly from Rostand's play *Cyrano de Bergerac*. Cyrano's French meaning does not fit exactly any of the six categories, but has been aligned in English with the "ostentation" set, with its "show-off" connotations. Potentially, *panache* could also have become a synonym member of the "impetuous, hasty" set. Had this happened, slight readjustments of the senses of other members of the sets would be detectable.

The phenomenon just mentioned looks odder than it should, mainly because the dictionary is a Procrustean entity which artificially moulds senses in relation to word-forms. The dictionary has bred the notion that word meanings exist as discrete phenomena in their own right, when words never acquire more than potential meanings and, even then, only as the end result of a prodigious degree of morphological and semantic (*i.e.* morphosemantic) interplay: a unique interplay between the two modes of language, producing language, integrally and familiarly. Word senses or meanings are not, so to speak, souls awaiting reincarnation, but those features of words available in the intimacy and lucidity of the shared mode of language, though only in the wake of an untold amount of semiotic and differential activity originating in the organic language mode. Changes in word-formation, graphic or auditory, predispose one to **feel** that they are accompanied by discrete quantum-like changes in meaning. This prejudice has endowed the lexicographer with considerable power, directly to influence the character of meaning, and to discourage "its users from seeing a language as consisting in a form of continuous activity." Words have become "units having their own static and separate existence from the ongoing course of human affairs," to the extent that "the columns of the dictionary provide a physical location for this separate existence" (Harris 1980, 133).

Once dictionaries can be seen in their proper perspective and a more realistic picture begins to emerge of the nature of the lexicon, an entire undiscovered dimension of language – the lexicon – opens up, with fresh hermeneutical undertakings suggesting themselves. It may eventually become possible to delineate in sensitive and productive detail the three-way collaboration among: firstly, the human brain within the context of the entire registration of the organic mode of language;[14] secondly, socio-cultural code-facilitated intersubjectivity; and thirdly, the potent underlying symbolism. It is through this triple collaboration that an equilibrium has been maintained – an equilibrium that is so vital to our situation and purpose as human beings, both in maintaining a version of reality (a life-world) and in drawing upon and directing the particular linguistic *energeia* that is the salient property of humankind. No doubt also, new ways will thus be opened up of achieving a fuller, truer understanding of what it is to be human.

Once lexicographical convention gives way to more adequate ways of approaching the lexicon, we shall be able to see more clearly than hitherto that words are more than mere lexical units, fusions of word-forms and senses, listable in a dictionary. We shall more easily appreciate that dictionary items are other than what they seem, putting forth, dendrite-like, all manner of external and internal relations with each other. Predictably, such relations will be found to be no less complex than the human beings and the human preoccupations they reflect and embody, not to mention the complexity of their brains.

In certain directions this loosening up of lexicographical convention has already begun. In various earlier studies of the lexicon, the phenomenon of "collocation" was understood in a restricted sense only: nothing more than the tendency on the part of some words to co-occur with greater frequency in certain contexts than in others. It had been proving difficult to give any precise meaning to "collocational restriction" without taking into account the entire constellation of lexical items with which they are connected, whether within actual texts or in spoken discourse, or within the language as a whole. Halliday, following J.R.Firth, neatly untied the knot by extending the concept of collocation to embrace all lexical relations, by redefining collocation as "the relationship between one lexical item and another with which it is associated"[15] thus opening up the possibility of recognizing relations between words separated in space and time. Although Halliday's procedures for tackling this breathtaking possibility are modest (though innovative) they have alerted scholars to the reality of "potentials of collocability". It was an associate of his, Angus McIntosh, who concluded that there are possible sentences in English which are rejected not because they violate any grammatical rule, nor because they lack a situation in which they might find a pragmatic use, but because they depart from what he called "tolerated ranges of collocability".[16] When for example the following sentences are compared:

> (1) *The molten postage feather scored a weather*
> (2) *The flaming waste-paper basket snored violently*

sentence (2) is found to be more acceptable than sentence (1), though neither sentence of course finds ready acceptance. Both sentences are grammatical insofar as neither breaks any rules of English syntax. Neither sentence is ever likely to find a use, though this would not in itself cause them to be written off as unacceptable. Sentence (1) is rejected nevertheless. There appears to be a range, says McIntosh, "however laborious it may be to define or describe, which is represented by the fairly strictly limited inventory of nouns which may (for example) without question be qualified by the word *molten*."[17] This set of available alternative possibilities of which this inventory consists is just as much a part of the shared language as it is of the organic-instrumental language mode, and a full account of this set would go a long way towards constituting the morphosemantics (in Firth's terminology "meaning") of a word such as *molten*.

For all its breadth of possibilities collocation is concerned only with the "external" relations between words. To date, linguistics has had nothing of signifance to say about the "internal" relations, about what might be going on within a particular word when a particular sense, nuance or implication is called forth, not so much by the context as by a writer's intention or by the fancy of a particular era. Since apparently linguistics has lacked the will, and perhaps also the imagination, to extricate itself from a preoccupation with formal aspects of the word, it is not surprising that the inner sanctum of the word has been explored not by a linguist but a poet and literary critic. Uneasy about straddling "the borderland between linguistics and literary criticism" William Empson (1951) set about doing linguistics, with the aim of diverting lexicology, if only briefly, away from the "Rational" and towards the "Aesthetic": to a facet of language reaching back to our preconscious origins but still virtually unexplored.

By the time Richards embarked upon his classic study of meaning, the "emotive" side of language was becoming recognized as different from, as well as subsidiary to, the main "symbolic" function of language which, according to Richards, is the production of statements (1936, 149). What had been identified as the "Theory of the Great Divide" encouraged generations of professional analysts of all kinds to seek out, wherever it might lurk, that lexical scapegoat – the emotive use of words. This not to deny the immeasurable value of bringing about a public awareness of the artfully devious and consciously bogus use of words that was especially rampant in the inter-war years and after, rightly condemned by such writers as Orwell and diagnosed by him as a major contributor to the rise of totalitarianism. But on the negative side (though this was surely not Richards' intention) all manifestations of word meaning, expression and feeling that do not fall clearly within the category of logically formulable propositions tend to be set aside as unworthy of serious attention. Empson is not opposed to the separation of feelings from word meanings. He is simply unable to conceive that feelings can be so separated. Part of the problem is that people react to verbal emotion in set ways, and the emotive use of a word does not necessarily reveal anything of significance about their inner feelings at that particular moment.[17]

Rather than follow the lexicographer's or the linguist's subdivision of a word into its different polysemous meanings, Empson can be seen exploring the living symbols underlying word configurations: each "micro" symbol, as it were, a single foliole of the all-encompassing "symbol tree" of the lexicon. From the outset he draws a crucial distinction between "head meaning"[18] and "the meaning which the user feels to be the first one in play at the moment" (he calls this the "chief" meaning). The different senses of a word are not dormant, lying around somewhere (safely stored in dictionaries) waiting to be galvanized into activity by a context. Intrinsically (rather than potentially) all the meanings are present in every use. That is why they can vary markedly from one individual style to another and, under the pen of certain authors, can actually **grow**, both in the work of the author and in the mind of the reader:

> The meaning of the key words will grow in your mind, but once you have got the full meaning, it is the fully unified one. The complexity of the word is simply that of the topic, and the linguist cannot pretend to tidy it up. (Empson 1951, 40)

One of the examples Empson cites is meaning of the word "God" in the work of Aquinas. To come fully by this meaning, he suggests, the reader would need to have "read very deeply" into this philosopher-divine's writings; otherwise only an inadequate notion could be gained of what Aquinas meant by the existence of God.

"Complex words" are quite unlike simple words, in which dominant and subsidiary meanings are readily identifiable. Empson examines the use of the word *sense* in Elizabethan times. The Elizabethans, he says, appear to have been so interested in the problems of sensuality that "the idea often pokes itself forward" even when the immediate context calls for something quite different. But, because the Elizabethans were also so fond of jokes about sensuality, this meaning also tends towards the jocular. "Intrusive" seems more appropriate in such instances than "dominant" meaning, insofar as it appears to be an unwanted meaning that keeps getting in the way. Empson goes on to suggest that, if the Elizabethans had been subjected to an experiment to determine the dominant meaning of *sense*,

> their first reaction... might well [have been] "This word is the material for a joke, and how can I use it to make a joke about the experiment?" (1951, 48)

Empson's theme is handled with such careful elaboration that it is hard to isolate particular examples. A clear illustration though is provided by a complex pun. In an aside, Angelo (in *Measure for Measure*) speaks of his fascination for Isabella:

> *She speaks and 'tis*
> *Such sense, that my Sense breeds with it. Fare you well.* (ii. 2. 143)

The meaning of the first occurrence of *sense* in this passage is the one most familiar to the twentieth century reader – "wise and reasonable" – but even here the connotation of "sensuality" asserts itself. Though at first "sensuality" looks as if it is to the fore in the second (capitalized) occurrence, Empson thinks that the use of the word *breeds* suggests that the sensuality is somehow growing inside the meanings in Angelo's mind. If Empson's interpretation (*via* mine) is correct, then we are dealing with much more than a simple pun. Only the more accomplished actor could supply the necessary emphasis and let the complexity of the pun play freelyon the audience (1951, 274).

All this stands in stark contrast to Richards' view (in Empson's interpretation) that the sense of a word, however "elaborate", is single and that anything in addition to this sense has to be explained in terms of feelings. Empson takes the more discriminating view that "much of what appears to us as a 'feeling' (as is obvious in the case of a complex metaphor) will in fact be quite an elaborate structure of related meanings" (1951, 57). The relations between words are not fixed: a writer can actually alter any given set of internal lexical relations by imposing a new dominant sense. This is because a word carrying a wide range of meaning has no dominant sense:

> Two meanings may exist in a word for a long time, it seems to me, without anyone seeing any point in connecting them. The decision to take the connection seriously... is a fairly serious step on the part of a *Zeitgeist* or an individual. (1951, 83)

An example of this, taken at random, is the word *gay*. For a long time the sense "dissipation" existed alongside the "dominant" sense: "disposed to joy, light-hearted," etc. Only in recent times has the "dissipation" sense been allowed to fade, now supplanted by the more positive overtones of the more dominant sense, to produce a meaning that brackets both the notion of sexual deviance and the contemporary moral and social approval of homosexuality, with the merest hint of some of the other independent senses of *gay*: "showily dressed", "airy", and "attractive". The "*Zeitgeist*" achieved all this almost unnoticed.

Not surprisingly, Empson is critical of existing dictionaries, devoting an entire chapter to lexicographical criticism. Polysemous compartmentalization, it may be conceded, has been a well-established practice ever since Dr. Johnson's day. What Empson wanted to see is a dictionary in which the **interactions** of the different senses of a word are included. He cites some illustrations of how this could be achieved without enlarging the dictionary beyond its present size. The difficulty with such an approach however is well illustrated by his proposed dictionary entry for *wit*, which has the serious drawback of being restricted to Empson's own inevitably idiosyncratic view. But, now that the dictionary is available as computer software of hitherto unimaginable capacity, its size and complexity could be vastly increased, in selective and hierarchically arranged "nesting", so that different types and degrees of interaction over time and in different locations could be displayed and observed. Even an interactive element would not lie beyond the bounds of possibility. It would certainly remedy the present situation in which "the dictionary is a collection of senses presumed to be separate, because no dictionary admits that words are used in two senses [or more] at once" (1951, 40). This interaction between different senses of words is at work in the language – any living language – right now. Take the use of the word *style* as it occurs in *There is something about that person's style*. In *The Shorter Oxford Dictionary*, subheading (III) under the noun entry STYLE gives several possible senses that might be operative in this particular context. They are: (I) "manner of executing a task or performing an action or operation", (ii) "a mode or fashion of life" (life-style), (iii) "fashionable appearance, deportment", and (iv) "a person's characteristic bearing or appearance, as conducing to striking appearance". What Empson would have identified as the word's "chief" sense in this particular instance is tucked away beneath a later sense [4b]: "the 'sort' that (a person or set of persons) would choose or approve", a meaning that entered the language only in the time of Jane Austen.

This randomly chosen illustration shows how the most ordinary instance of speech communication triggers a play of meaning infinitely rich in implication, feeling and mood. More boldly than anyone until now, Empson has attempted to explore few of the ways in which words can rainbow their multiple meaning, or as he himself puts it: "the ways in which a word can carry a doctrine." An entire play of Shakespeare, Empson has attempted to show, may be built on the complex punning of a single word: Iago may not be a "personality" in his own right but "he is better than these; he is the product of a more actual interest in a word" (1951, 231).

18. The Lexicon

Words themselves are such complex entities, each so different in scope, currency, form, flavour and function that it would be natural to expect notional models of the lexicon to be at least equal in sophistication to the complexity of their nature and role in our lives. But not so. Although signs of change are no longer rare, there exists at the present time nothing approaching a comprehensive or adequate model of the lexicon. Saussure, along with a number of his European successors, opened up tantalizing prospects, a few of which have been pursued with imagination and determination. But an overall grasp of how the lexicon works is still wanting. In North America, beginning with Bloomfield, most linguists have relegated the lexicon to the status of an appendage to language structure, a list of unexciting irregularities, mere leftovers. This tradition has persisted, with the lexicon characterized by one authority as "an unordered set of morphemes,"[1] a view echoed by Chomsky whose approach to language has in most other respects been so radically innovative.[2] The description "unordered", needless to say, implies that the lexicon is no more than a curiosity shop. As one of the less dismissive authorities has put it:

> It is almost a dogma among us that vocabulary is the least significant part of language (save for a group among us who even doubt that vocabulary is really a part of language after all).[3]

Lexicography has done no better. With the lexicographer's productions having enjoyed such a degree of cultural, educational and (not least) commercial success it might seem surprising that this would be so. But lexicography continues, despite the advent of the micro-chip to offer an ill-assorted congeries of methods, none of which has been property elaborated, validated or consistently applied. Without exaggeration it can be said that:

> the indifference which lexicography displays towards its own methodology is astonishing. Perhaps lexicographers are complacent because their product 'works'. But it is legitimate to ask in what way it works, except that dictionaries sell.[4]

The dictionary has played such a pervasive role in our lives (Webster compared Johnson's dictionary to Newton's discoveries in physics) that modern civilization would probably have taken on a different shape without it. The "notable increase in frustration, confusion and unhappiness" that its absence would have created can readily be imagined. But, if the dictionary has become essential to our well-being, it has also proved a severe impediment, the vindication of a tendency to regard dictionary entries as facts, beyond dispute and (despite sporadic revisions) as if settled for all time. Dictionary words have become idols indeed.

Owing to its institutional prominence and prestige the dictionary has held too powerful a sway over people's thinking about the lexicon, not to mention, language itself. The assumption has grown up that the lexicon, covertly the most potent and active organ of our language, bears a marked resemblance to the printed dictionary. It scarcely matters whether we have in mind an alphabetical historical dictionary of the kind exemplified by successive editions of the *Oxford English Dictionary*, or the encyclopaedic dictionary epitomized by Larousse, or Roget's *Thesaurus of English Words and Phrases*, the "stroke-order" non-alphabetic dictionaries of China and Japan, or the corpus-derived computer-generated dictionaries of today; none of them presents anywhere near a true analogy of the living lexicon. Even in the differential-organic mode of language, in which the brain plays such a dominant role, it is difficult to believe that lexical 'entries', the *differentia* of words, are stored in a dictionary-like manner. And as far as the shared mode of language is concerned there cannot be any determinable structural "map" that would make it possible for "word meanings" to be kept in separable, let alone watertight, compartments after the manner of the dictionary.

It seems therefore to be the right moment to examine the range of "mechanisms" stemming from the interplay between intersubjective and the differential-organic modes of language, as it is these that allow the effective blending of socio-cultural perceptions with informational schemata, a process all the while sustained by the symbolic *energeia* welling up from the unconscious which, taken together, make the production of words possible. Knowing the extraordinary feats that words perform many times each second, we should not expect these to be other than complex. Nevertheless, as this task has not been undertaken in any holistic sense previously, it should not be expected that any model proposed, here or elsewhere, should be anything more than provisional or incomplete.

In most cases people consulting dictionaries believe that they are looking up the "meanings" of words. In fact what the dictionary provides are glosses: paraphrases drawing upon series of other words. This is not to deny the usefulness of dictionaries. They do for instance supply a range of possible uses for their separate entries even when these are unnecessary. In the case of "apple" the dictionary informs one that it is generically a fruit and that it has been used in a range of figurative senses, to the extent that it can be known in advance when "apple" would be an appropriate choice in a particular context. In general only people who have an urgent, usually professional, need make anything like a habit of consulting the dictionary. Most of the time people get along perfectly well without the help of a dictionary. Everyone for example knows that an "apple" is a kind of fruit: "the round fleshy fruit of a Rosaceous tree...found..widely.. in Europe... and cultivated in innumerable varieties all over the two Temperate Zones."[5] Or do they? More to the point, do they need to? People need to know almost nothing about "apples" before they can use the word *apple*. Conversely, they do not need to be aware of any dictionary prescription before they can talk plausibly about apples. Real words and dictionary entries are so incompatible that it is safe to assume that words do not have "dictionary definitions".[6] The dictionary is more a reflection of an obsessive need for orderliness and rationality than the outcome of any compulsive desire to have in our possession an inventory, for reference purposes, of word "meanings". The most the dictionary can do is to "supply hints and associations that will relate the unknown to something known" (Bolinger 1981, 312ff.).

This, it may be noted, is not the same thing as asserting that all the dictionary can do is suggest certain aids to the understanding of sentences in which particular words occur; or as maintaining, with Austin or Quine, that meaning resides not in the word but in the sentence.[7] Nouns especially can sometimes be interpreted as (paradigmatically) condensed sentence-periphrasis. For example, the "dictionary definition" of *apple* partially cited above can be considered a potential periphrastic substitution for that lexical item in most contexts in which it occurs. But this, to my mind, is better envisaged as only one of the many devices employed by the differential-organic language mode to have "words" inserted, as paradigmatic lexical items, into linguistic contexts, part (but only a part) of the process of getting them to "work". The sentence *Apples are not the same things as oranges* has little to offer except to someone concerned with logical issues, in that everyone recognizes the truism.

Dictionaries can be invaluable guides but they tell us very little about how the lexicon actually works. We do not carry around in our heads the analogue of a dictionary in which we look up the words we need. The reader may on occasion have been struck by the degree of reliability with which people produce and use words. Of course some people are more articulate, some more precise, and some more eloquent than others. And the potential "size" of their vocabularies will vary depending on their social and educational background, breadth of experience, social occupation, and many other factors. But the observation that speakers and writers on the whole know how to use the words available to them can be amply borne out.

Yet, when we examine our own verbal performance, we may only seldom be able to recall consciously learning the words we use (other than technical or specialized items which, as I have already argued, are not necessarily always words). Most of us can perhaps recollect more or less numerous occasions on which we consulted a dictionary, but how many "meanings" can we actually recall from having looked them up? The poorly considered view that "a vocabulary which is within the competence of the ordinary speaker is in the form in which the dictionary presents it"[8] does not stand up to the mildest of tests. The "ordinary speaker" is notoriously incapable of reproducing such specifications. And even "sophisticated" speakers are often taken aback on discovering how inaccurate their recollection of dictionary specifications can be (Lord 1974, 240).

To return to our original question: if the lexicon really is so complex and phenomenologically unique, bestriding the two complementary but so extraordinarily different modes of language (yet itself something different again from either) can anything worthwhile be revealed about it, beyond its astounding articulation, its self-regulatory mechanisms, its multi-dimensional mode of operation? Can anything useful be said about it as the midwife of "reality", the dominant mediator of meaning in our lives, of you and me? The honest (rather than modest) answer should be: something perhaps, but by no means the whole of it.

The first point I would like to make (provisionally, I hardly need add) is that the word and its "organ", the lexicon, appear to exploit separately, in every imaginable way, and to the full, the possibilities inherent separately in the shared and differential modes of language and serve as vehicles for the release, uniquely, of signification. I shall begin with the differential-organic mode of language, not because it is more manageable or less complex than the rest, but because its symptoms look more clear-cut.

Most words in English consist of two or more syllables. In addition many of these words consist of more than one morpheme, and hence are morphologically more or less complex. The word *uncomplainingly* for example consists of four morphemes: *un–complain–ing–ly*. Of these only *complain* is a "free" morpheme; the rest are "bound". Morphology plays an undeniably important part in the *modus operandi* of the lexicon, making it possible for instance for words to undergo word-class transposition *(e.g. read, reading, reader, readerly, readable*, etc.). I am not proposing however to say anything further about morphology at this stage, partly as very exhaustive and useful studies have already been made and partly because morphology plays only a peripheral role in the model I have been working towards.[9] What has seldom been recognized however is that words perceived as simple ("free") morphemes can at the same time be morphosemantically complex.

Take for instance the trio of English words *tunnel, runnel* and *funnel* which are all considered morphologically simple (and therefore of no further interest either to the grammarian or the lexicographer). These three words not only bear a formal resemblance to one another – all three terminate in the rhyming segment -UNNEL – but they are semantically related as well. The iconic common denominator among these words can be characterized as "a hollow cylindrical or semi-cylindrical section". Their interwoven histories are intriguing, and worth a short digression.

Tunnel and *funnel* entered English, from French, towards the end of the Middle Ages. Originally *tunnel* had three different senses, all of which suggested a cylindrical pipe or shaft: (1) the shaft or flue of a chimney, (2) a pipe or tube in general (a slightly later sense), (3) a net for catching partridges consisting of a pipe-like passage with a wide opening. As separate senses all three eventually died out, except in dialect, but senses (1) and (2) went on to combine, perpetuating themselves in the modern and dominant meaning "tunnel" which dates from the canal-building era of the late eighteenth century. Typically, these early canal tunnels were cylindrical passages and, when the canal was supplied with a normal depth of water, the tunnels even looked like half-cylinders. The word *funnel* had a very different origin, having been borrowed from the French wine trade. A "funnel" was an inverted cone-shaped vessel with a small tube projecting from the apex, through which liquid or powder could be poured. By the end of the seventeenth century however, three additional senses of *funnel* had become established: (1) a tube or shaft for lighting or ventilation purposes (during the subsequent Industrial Revolution *funnel* came to denote the metal chimney of an engine or steamship), (2) the flue of a chimney, (3) a cylindrical metal band fitted to the head of a mast. All three senses of *funnel* are suggestive of semantic contagion (technically "paronymic attraction") from *tunnel*. This "contagion" or "attraction" must have been so strong that for a period *funnel* and *tunnel* became identical synonyms. The third item *runnel* appears to have been native in origin but did not become established in Standard English until Elizabethan times. Its original sense was "a small stream of water". But by the end of the seventeenth century the word had acquired a further sense which has since become the dominant one: "a small watercourse or channel; a gutter". A typical English eaves-gutter is of course a long horizontal half-cylindrical section.

This unconventional lexical comparison highlights a "sound-icon" element common to three words: namely the final sound sequence, or segment: -UNNEL. This segment lies at the point of convergence, semantically and instrumentally, between all three of these word-forms and their polysemy. It thus constitutes, even if it cannot be assigned a morphemic role, a knot of potential "meanings". This sort of segmental rhyming linkage between words and their different (potential) senses can be shown to pervade the entire language, though not in every instance with such dramatic clarity (though there exist very many examples which show the same degree of markedness. Earlier, mention was made of *vigorous-rigorous*. Other examples include *glitter-flitter, glow-flow, glare-flare, stutter-sputter-utter, mother-smother, demonstrate-remonstrate*, and so forth). In fact most English words can be shown to fall into rhyming sets, with corresponding semantic linkage. On p.243, above, I gave the (shortened) scheme for -ASH; in the *Appendix* (*Figure 2*, pp. 294-5) a more complete scheme for -AM is given. This is but one example among many, but sufficient perhaps to suggest that the lexicon is at one level a vast web of such rhyming sets.

Just as rhyming segments serve differentially, so also do initial (*i.e.* alliterative) segments, though less sharply and less actively, in Modern English at least (though this may have presented a very different scene when the older English tradition of alliterative verse held sway). Furthermore, rhyming (or alliterative) segments can overlap. For example *channel* is linked to *runnel* through the segment -NEL (but not to *panel* or *flannel*, which have established separate links).

In case the reader may suspect that this quirk of the lexicon applies only to English, it has to be said that this principle of rhyming and alliterative set formation is clearly observable even in the monosyllabic "words" of Chinese; so much so that over the centuries Chinese scholars attempted to formulate an adequate theory to explain the phenomenon. They did not succeed, partly for the reason that their investigations were confined to the written language. Regular patterns of concurrence had been observed between word meanings and the sound values of the "phonetic" radicals incorporated in the great majority of Chinese characters.[10]

The next major class of form differentiation appears to be a crucial one. It is so deceptively similar to (yet so very different from) the rhyming-alliteration scheme of differentiation just described that, for a some time, its distinctiveness and difference in function escaped notice. Only gradually did the difference come to light, through anomalies which emerged in the course of an analysis of a sizeable corpus of Chinese, in its Cantonese dialectal variety. Eventually, in the course of a subsequent analysis of a sizeable English lexical corpus, the discrepancy became obvious. What emerged was so unexpected that it became necessary to review the already provisionally complete analysis of the Chinese corpus. The English schemata proved not only to accommodate the Chinese data remarkably well but, more significantly, pointed to more satisfactory results than had been obtained for that language in the previous analysis.[11] It is a phenomenon that pervades the entire lexicon; in a manner comparable to, but differently from, the -UNNEL, or -AM rhyming sets outlined above, which are independently patterned (though very possibly interfaced in productive and interesting ways with the system about to be described). Very briefly, what happens is that sets (or rather, "subsets") of phonologically related initial sequences or final sequences of phonemes occurring in potential word-forms build up associations within a hierarchy of semantic categories. To take a simplified example: the final sequences or segments of *lot* and *plot* not only rhyme and are (potentially) related in sense but are aligned with the semantic category "tract of land", within a complex semantic hierarchy, permeating the entire language. The determinants of set membership however are not the rhymes or alliterations as such (although these supply the framework for the sets, so to speak) but the **primary stressed vowels** in the word-forms and their characteristic configuration in alignment with a specific **semantic category**. Since an explanation of this requires some degree of acquaintance with phonology, the phenomenon is fleshed out in greater detail in the *Appendix* (part 2, pp 296-7.)

It is to the shared-intersubjective language mode that we look for the **realization** of meaning in the lexicon, even though the source of meaning resides in the symbolic depths of our being. It is necessary as a preliminary to present a brief sketch of various matters, with a view to providing a context against which the approach described below can at least be comprehended (even if not positively evaluated).

The search for discrete parcels of sense is not new, and the assumption that semantic features and components in language must exist is by now well-established, probably reaching its high point with several studies published in the 1950s and 60s.[12]   One difficulty with this "componential analysis" and the search for "semantic distinctive features" (stimulated by Jakobson and Trubetskoy's earlier formulation of distinctive features in phonology) is that it is impossible to be sure what a semantic distinctive feature could actually be. The element of indeterminacy seems too great. Only if the scope of an investigation were narrowed down to artificial dimensions or particularities of minute scope, would it make any sense to formulate neat componential analyses. This is not because, as far as meaning is concerned, words are obtuse; but because, at the intersubjective level, they are mirrors of their users: ourselves and the multi-faceted cultures we have created. Language will play the componential analysis game, but only up to a certain point. Words can also be wanton for the reason that they partake of some of the same nature as ourselves.

A formidable critic of componentialism is Anna Wierzbicka.[13] In her critique of a celebrated analysis of the verb *kill* (McCawley 1974) which, it was claimed, conceals no less than four semantic features: CAUSE, BECOME, NOT and ALIVE, combined hierarchically as follows: (CAUSE (BECOME (NOT (ALIVE)))), Wierzbicka argues that "dead" for instance cannot be resolved into the components "not alive" since "alive" is semantically more complex than "dead". A claim to the effect that "Bill is alive" would only be used to correct the view that "Bill is dead", and not *vice versa*. Furthermore "causing to become" is not causality in the abstract but the setting in motion of an entire network of relations: causal, spatial, temporal, and volitional. And to relate "die" to "kill" rests on a superficial semantic perception of the distinctiveness of these two concepts: one can for instance say "He didn't die, but was killed". Real semantic deep structures, Wierzbicka concludes, are

> incomparably more complex than simple neat formulas... This may be discouraging. But there has never been any good reason to believe that the underlying structure of human thought is particularly simple. (Wierzbicka 1980, 182)[14]

A contrasting approach to meaning in the lexicon is the one associated with the concept of "semantic field". The notion that words and their senses occupy a kind of semantic space originated between the wars in an attempt to understand how words undergo changes of meaning in relation to each other, disposed as they were supposed to be within "fields", a continuum without gaps.[15] Semantic field studies, as they have emerged however, have more to with what Lévi-Strauss (but in relation to mythical thought among primitive communities) characterized as "intellectual *bricolage*" (1966, 17). Words as they appear in notional semantic space can be precisely described in the same language Lévi-Strauss adopted for myth.[16] It is in historical semantics that this "bricolage" – making use of "odds and ends" already available and "moving existing pieces around" – aspect of the lexicon is most clearly visible: a continual readjustment in morphosemantic relations undergoing displacement within semantic fields.

Any reality that the semantic field might possess must be a **semiotic** reality. The field itself is an illusion generated by *differentia* guaranteed only by the symbolic energy registered and interpreted by way of intersubjective socio-semiotic codes. *Bricolage* itself seen from this perspective looks like yet another form of abhorrence of an ontological void. Words and their meanings, held in suspension by the signifying energy out of which they ultimately emerge, like so many holograms, fill up our world leaving no empty "space". A leading exponent of semantic field theory, Adrienne Lehrer (1974), has frankly declared her lack of interest in any epistemological or psychological reality of semantic fields as such, and uses the field model as an investigative tool only: semantic ecology, so to speak.[17]

In the course of an analysis of a substantial Chinese (Cantonese) lexical corpus it soon became apparent that the (potential) senses of words align themselves, in accordance with the "hidden protocols" of the shared-intersubjective language mode, into semantic categories which "crystallize" out of the continuum of the life-world and arrange themselves in hierarchies (though they are not coincident with the types of hierarchies hitherto proposed) (a small sample of an hierarchy for Chinese (Cantonese) is given in *Figure* 1, below). These categories differ from the semantic features of componential analysis; nor do they appear to fit any semantic field model (though there seems to be a possibility of phonological tensions developing over time which could result in semantic displacements). The prime characteristic of the semantic category arising from this investigation is that it directly impinges on, reflects, and is affected by, reality as we know it. This is the main reason why semantic categories have to be regarded as impermanent, though prone to institutionalization. A semantic category can be thought of as the semantic common denominator among a set of synonymous (and antonymous) lexical items which share either an initial (alliterative) or a final (rhyming) word-form segment .

One of the more startling discoveries has been that the English and

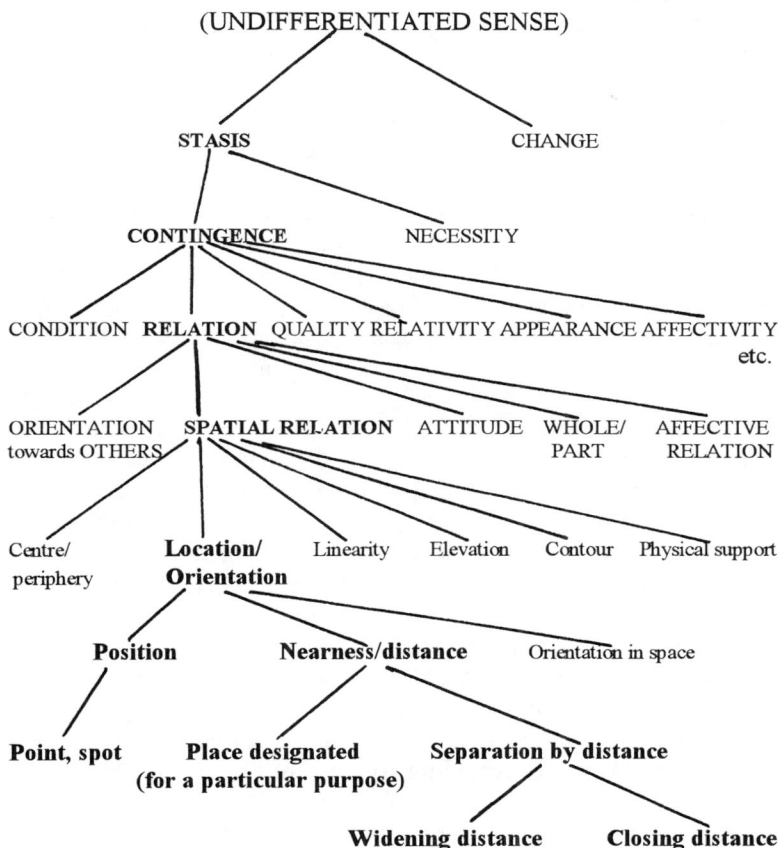

Figure 1: Section of a hierarchy of semantic categorization in Chinese (Cantonese).

Chinese categorizations are not all that different; and that their hierarchies of semantic categories appear to be the same or very similar. The few salient differences can be accounted for mainly by cultural factors: for example, English has "seafaring" categories while Chinese does not. The "finer mesh" obtained in English for the most subordinate hierarchical levels can undoubtedly be accounted for by the richer and more highly differentiated lexicographical material available for English. *Figure 1*, above, represents only a minute section of a suggested hierarchy of Chinese semantic categories. One can be reasonably certain only of the four lowest levels (in this instance) in that the higher and more abstract levels are not empirically supported by data (but they are inferential rather than conjectural). This same sample can be found in English, the only modifications (the addition of *locus* and *scene of action* under *position*) being most likely the result of the richer amount of lexicographical information available for English. Since English and Chinese are such different languages – typologically and historically unconnected – this may point to universality as far as semantic categories in (post-)civilized languages are concerned: a similarity from one language to the next of the ways in which the (intersubjective) world is "cut up". What hierarchies emerge, and whether there exists any universal residuum once morphosemantic analyses of further languages, including American Indian and various "aboriginal" languages, have been carried out, remains to be seen.

At this point in my exposition it is essential to keep firmly in mind that word-forms are no more than syntagmatic sequences of sounds and morphemes; they are, as it were, moulds into which real words are poured. It is only at this stage that we are able to describe that most remarkable event not only in language but in the whole of human life: the coming into being of a word. Descriptions can rarely be other than clinical, and for that reason the success of the description which follows will depend to a considerable extent on the reader's indulgence. Admittedly, there must be still other dimensions, whether of phenomenological or purely technical interest (others may be better able to discern "the wood from the trees").

It is at this juncture that two separate modes of language coalesce. On the one hand, there are the separate sets of **initial** and **final sound segments** of (potential) word-forms (differential-organic mode); and on the other, the **semantic categories** arranged in hierarchies (shared-intersubjective mode). These initial and final sets now interface with semantic categories. This results in the formation of morphosemantic subsets (*i.e.* one subset of either initial or final sound segments interfacing with a semantic sub-category). It is a phenomenon that has been labelled **morphosemantic concurrence (MSC)**, and the

MSCs for the initial and final sound segments in English are currently being identified and classified.

The term "concurrence" was preferred in view of the transience of the morphosemantic concurrence (MSC), a transience that may be short- (a few decades) or long-lived (a few centuries or more). These MSCs are reinforced and further provided, as it were, with iconic (line, sound, shape, texture, movement, etc.) anchorage by the particular rhyming sets of one syllable or longer that were discussed earlier (see pp. 256ff., above).

The next and even more remarkable stage of morphosemantic concurrence consists of one (and sometimes more than one) of the initial segments in an initial MSC coalescing with a corresponding final segment (or segments) in a final MSC to **form a specific word sense linked to a particular word-form.** This is not only a linking up of particular items subtended by different MSCs, but – and not less important – the bringing into mutual relation of entire swathes of the lexicon which otherwise remain separate. (This does not amount to a claim that neural codings for complete word-forms exist somewhere in the brain's memory. At this stage in the investigation, and without further experimentation, it is impossible to say. But if, prior to this coalescence, complete word-forms do exist, they do not appear to play any part in the process just described). Each time this interface occurs a minor tremor, so to speak, passes through the lexicon, with pathways being opened up, others closed, and still others renewed; in such a manner that every such occurrence becomes a kind of lexical renewal. In Part 3 of the *Appendix* (pp.297-299) an attempt has been made to show, in diagram form, how three MSCs representing a single semantic category coalesce in the generation of four candidate words (though not yet **actual** words, please note).

Finally, and most extraordinary of all, the potential or candidate word opens itself to the utterance dynamics of the human context at the same time as to the epiphanic *energeia* of sign (according to Peirce) and symbol. Words only become meaning-bearing, sense becomes meaning, only when words are **used** and when indeterminable but extensive areas of the lexicon are activated. And we should not overlook the extraordinary paradox that we respond to words aesthetically, culturally, cognitively, imaginately, but never lexically. By a double paradox, it is the lexicon nevertheless, or my particular version of it, that enables me to be me.

If my brain or nervous system and, in turn, my personalized lexicon develops faults I may become, amongst other possibilities, dyslexic, agraphic, amnesic, mildly or severely aphasic or, at the very least, (tiresomely or perhaps lovably) eccentric.

Probably only a small proportion of potential words become actual words, but the speaker or writer has little control over transformations when they do occur. Communication of an everyday sort can occur without the use of "actual" words. Also, the **degree** of actuality will vary considerably from utterance to utterance. Words can kill, but more often than not they impinge on the awareness of the other with a culturally controlled impact. The words of a Shakespeare become endowed with a more universal power than any I might invoke in a letter to a friend or lover.

The events just outlined happen of course, to all intents and purposes, instantaneously. The brain guides and is guided by the totality of features (in the shared mode) "tagged" for information-differentiality – coded perceptions, cultural predispositions, socio-semiotic codes, hermeneutical interpretation, and whatever else might be inherent in the shared mode of language. It would appear that incoming acoustic sense impressions are interpreted and broken down into possible series of phonemes. These are matched with potential senses, and semantic categories traced. Feedback circuits operate in both directions: candidate word-forms (not as yet candidate "words") reflecting the operations of the instrumental-differential language mode as well as the semantic potentialities of the shared language mode seem to be particularly crucial. Here is the point of interface between the two separate modes of language: the differential information-gathering and processing within the organic mode on the one hand, and the semantic interpretations and the socio-semiotic codes of the shared intersubjective mode on the other, enabling the symbolism of language to generate actual living words and real utterances. If by mischance I interpret what impinges on my ear, say, as "I'm bringing my filing next time", when I know the person addressing me primarily as a musician, my brain (organic mode) and my shared language context enable me to adjust my interpretation to "I'm bringing my violin next time". Checks for correctness of interpretation depend not on the lexical forms used or on any semantic categories applied *per se*, but on whether there exists a potentially appropriate message. And appropriateness in such cases depends on ranges of tolerance among speakers and listeners as well as on various social and ethnographic parameters.

By now it must be apparent that the word is very far from being the miscellaneous inert token that some linguists have taken it to be. On the contrary, the word looks as though it is situated at the very heart of language: an occurrence, semiotic in nature, at the live interface between two incommensurable modes of language. The word is the culmination of a complex and virtually instantaneous sequence of operations, the outcome being that the word produced or the word interpreted is able to resonate through the whole of a person's language and throughout the life-world that person shares with others and, ultimately, the whole of mankind. The word is a work of art, a symbolic expression potentially valid for all, but having its "micro-semiotic" origins in an actual living being and personality, and in the latter's engagement with the words of others. It is a paradox that even though the symbolism, the unique feeling projected through my words, has its origins in myself, meaning and resonance are found only in a world shared by others. My words take on a unique non-illusory value for me only when they find their response in others.

19. Words in Time

In a comprehensive historical dictionary such as *The Oxford English Dictionary* one can see at a glance that in many cases a word has acquired a bundle of several, sometimes many, (potential) senses spread out over time. The exceptions are either items of recent provenance, or ones that denote singular objects, like *hippopotamus* or *helicopter*, or terminology designating technical or other specialized processes or entities. Some words, though relatively few, have dropped out of use; others, especially those rich in polysemy, often have senses that have become obsolete. But, on the whole, word-forms and word senses appear to be remarkably durable.

Innumerable studies have been made of lexical and semantic change. Word-form transformation can be explained. The processes of change in word sense have been categorized and are fairly well understood. I would like to pose a different sort of question which, if it were posed outside the context of the rest of this book, might seem "metaphysical" or, worse, nugatory. My question is: What is it in a word that endures – for a longer or shorter time – and, in time, lapses into obsolescence? Related to this is a more veiled, and even more dubious, question: Can there be anything in a word that survives change in word-form or a series of changes in meaning? No definitive answers can be provided to either of these questions at the present time, but there is enough substance to furnish a worthwhile beginning.

We can do worse than start with Owen Barfield's seminal and dazzling "poetic archaeology" of the English word *ruin* (1952, 120ff.). *Ruin* is derived from the Latin verb *ruo*, which embodied the notion of "swift disastrous movement". The English word, Barfield suggests, points to and encapsulates an even earlier integral sense: "rush-fall-collapse". The original unity of sense evidently broke up into three different senses, each carried by a separate word. By the time the Latin noun *ruina* came into existence, the older fuller pre-Roman meaning had become reduced to "a thing fallen". Nevertheless, Barfield maintains, in the course of time at least part of the earlier meaning was recovered, and enriched even, in the work of individual poets. Not until Shakespeare however was the "exact, whole significance" of the word *ruin* restored. In Spenser's line

> *The late ruin of proud Marinell*

for instance, "fall" or "disaster" can be substituted for "ruin"; but in Shakespeare's *King John,* when Salisbury, confronted with Arthur's corpse lying in a heap after a fatal fall from the ramparts, finds himself

> *Kneeling before this ruin of sweet life*

a new word is introduced into the language, *ruin* in this instance being impossible to paraphrase.

Shakespeare was of course more than merely a successful poetic archaeologist. In restoring the word *ruin* to its new meaning Shakespeare must intuitively have been drawing upon the latent possibility of using the word as a transitive verb, and on new customs of usage associated with comparable nouns, when he tapped yet another vein of potential meaning in the same word, this time in *Antony and Cleopatra:*

> *The noble ruin of her magic, Antony.*

There must, says Barfield, have been a strangeness for his contemporaries in such an unfamiliar, though integral, use:

> The word *ruin*, then, has grown with Shakespeare's help into a warm and living thing, a rich piece of imaginative material ready at hand for anyone who has the skill to evoke its power.

Ever since Shakespeare gave the word its old-new clothes, *ruin* has gone on growing in poetry, from Milton to Tennyson, and has thus become "a piece of many minds", with nothing more being necessary than to surround it with the right words.

Barfield attributes "soul" to words, but my anti-dualism resists. It is not difficult to "see what he means", but I would prefer to think of this quality as an aura − perhaps Barfield intended no more than this − a bloom, revived uniquely each time a word of a certain order draws from its symbolic depths a power released autonomously, and at least in part through its textual proximity with other words. Once a word is extracted from its poetic setting, that aura vanishes. Objectively, what we are then left with is a sequence of sounds, a string of letters, a timbre perhaps, at most an associative recollection, a reverberation. There is nothing in *The noble ruin of her magic, Antony* that will foil the instruments of the linguist, particularly a Firth or a Halliday. *Noble* and *magic* are neither of them outlandish words; nor is the context in any way odd. But no amount of analysis will get even as far as the threshold of the incomparable blend of the words that make up Shakespeare's line. Even the placing of *Antony*, which looks like a simple apposition, a mere proper name after all, seems irreplaceable.

The dictionary already mentioned reveals that the pre-Shakespearean senses of *ruin* are still in existence and nowhere near obsolescent. But in its earlier sense of "the remains of a decayed and fallen building or town" *ruin* has been infected by the Shakespearean "downfall" and "devastation". In English, "ruin" is not a suitable epithet, except facetiously, for a modern building that has simply fallen into decay; nor is it easily used of edifices that have not suffered some disaster, at the very least from the ravages of time. The most secular-minded tourist who sheds a momentary tear over the ruins of an abbey or other ancient pile is being affected by what Barfield calls "the dangerous beauty" of the word, as much as by the scene itself.

A word at this point about memory. Probably no concept in psychology has undergone so many modifications as memory. Every generation has brought with it a revised model. We seem now to have entered a phase − one that should have become obvious long since − in which memory can be seen to be no longer purely individual but also communal. The whole notion of purely individual memory can now be dismissed as illusory. It is no chance therefore that, as far as language is concerned, words and memory are so closely interlinked.

Correspondingly, it should be expected that, just as words bring together the separate modes of language, so too does memory. Chomsky, who has shed so much light on what I have been calling the organic mode of language, the way it works systemically in relation to the brain and its innate schemata, brought to our awareness something that must have mystified many of those who have given the matter any thought. I am referring to his realization that the speaker must in some cases be aware of the history of word-forms and phonological change. Chomsky's point is illustrated by the the example of *right-righteous*: that, unless the speaker were already somehow aware that the underlying abstract form of *right* cannot be its modern pronunciation /rait/ but must be its Middle English forerunner /rixt/. Otherwise the form *righteous* in its derivation from *right* would, on the model of *expedite-expeditious*, *ignite-ignition*, have been /raiʃəs/ (?*righsious*) and not, as it is now pronounced, /raitʃəs/.[1]

At this juncture we return to the question of institutionalization mentioned in an earlier chapter. We can now, I think, see that, in the lexicon, institutionalization is an inter-modal function promoting the persistence of word-forms and the stabilization of word senses once these have crystallized into morphosemantic concurrences (MSCs). It is easy, I also think, to predict the entropic increase in chaos that would have prevailed if the formation and dissolution of MSCs had been left to morphosemantic processes alone. Lexical institutionalization is therefore to be envisaged, so to speak, as a compact struck between the shared and organic modes of language to regulate lexical change. "Compact" is of course a figure of speech: more concretely the relation between the two modes should be seen as the product of memory, both corporate and individual. This memory, if Barfield is right, must in some cases at least be extremely long-term, and passed on chromosome-like from generation to generation (except of course that in this instance the "chromosomes" are socio-cultural and not biological).

Take the word *mountain* (from O. Fr. *montagne, mountaigne*). This word, along with its synonym *mount* (from *munt*), came into English from Old French some time after the Norman Conquest. Although *munt* was the more common word for "mountain" in Old French, in English it must very early have become institutionalized in proper names for mountains or other prominences, probably because English already possessed *hill*, a more or less exact synonym, and *barrow* (from OE. *beorg*). Originally the accent on *mountain* would have fallen regularly on the second syllable, as it still did in Chaucer's rhyming schemes (though not always so when not at the end of a line).[2] This meant that *moun'tain* would have rhymed with words such as *cer'tain* (the earlier pronunciation), *attain, maintain* and would therefore already have acquired a firm prosodic footing. In addition *mountain* became associated through a final MSC again with *certain, attain* and *maintain,* but also with *down, beacon* ("a conspicuous hill"), the Celtic British *tan* (as in *tan-hill* "fire-hill" or "beacon") and probably also *-don* (appearing in proper names such *Hambledon, Bredon*). *Hill* remained an exact synonym of *mountain* (in its "prominence" sense), until ultimately the difference was firmly institutionalized (in Britain) by fixing the minimum height of a mountain at 2,000 ft. – any summit lower than that remaining a "hill". In Old French, the sense "a heap, pile" formed part of the polysemy of *munt*, and not part of *montagne* (as it eventually was to do in English *mountain*). The situation may never have been so clear-cut in Anglo-Norman but, whatever the reality, the "heap, pile" sense became associated with a newer form *mound* (no doubt through the long obsolete "military earthwork" sense of *mount*). *Mound, mountain* and *mount* of course make a strong alliterative triad, as well as being related through an initial MSC with other words such as *moat, mote, motte, munition* (in its older sense: "serving as a defence"), *mole* ("breakwater") and doubtless others.[3]

Morphosemantic institutionalization only becomes possible when word-forms or word senses become too similar and are picked up as being such by the differential-organic mode: they need to be be kept distinct in order not to become confused. As long as they remain distinct (*skirt* and *shirt*, for instance) the organic mode can underwrite, as it were, institutional convenience in the shared-intersubjective mode. But once words have already become identical in form (homonyms) the differential mode can no longer cope, except with the positive intervention of the shared mode, through morphosemantic concurrence (MSC) interface. This is what can be assumed to have occurred in the case of the three coalesced "bank" forms: (1) "a river margin", (2) "a financial institution" [from Ital. *banca*], (3) "a bench occupied by rowers" [from Fr.*banc*]. These three different "banks" have become affiliated to different MSCs, because of their difference in sense, so that it is easy for the shared language mode to institutionalize them as homonyms if it so wishes. All that the differential-organic mode could facilitate was a metonymic displacement from the "rowers' bench" to a "bank of oars"; and this was presumably only possible on account of the rhyming feature *-ank* common to *rank* and *bank*.

A morphosemantic approach to the lexicon is never simple. How much more convenient the dualist rationale by which the morphology and the semantics of words are treated separately and in parallel. Word-forms can then be regarded as phonological and morphological derivatives from earlier forms, both known or hypothetically reconstructed. This is essentially what the "comparative grammarian" of the last century was doing when he reconstructed – sometimes ingeniously and mostly rigorously, it must be admitted, – improbable parent forms allegedly present in some hypothetical Proto-Indo-European language.[4] As for word senses these could have been treated by some other parallel method: by reconstructing for example semantic fields for portions of the vocabulary used in various earlier periods of the language. This would have been a kind of *bricolage* in reverse, in which semantic field relationships of the present day could be contrasted with reconstructed field relationships of some earlier period. In English this could conceivably be done, given the relative wealth of written records dating from late Anglo-Saxon times, and related historical and archaeological studies. But, if a purely semantic approach had been adopted, the morphosemantic interplay of words that Pierre Guiraud managed to ferret out of the history of the French lexicon might have gone unnoticed.

Unhappy with an etymology based purely on comparatist derivation, Guiraud's approach sought to take account of popular usage, the play of synonymy and polysemy-homonymy, puns, and various other not entirely "respectable" kinds of verbal play.[5] The concept of morphosemantic field developed by Guiraud can be seen as an exploration of covert as well as manifest lexical relations, whether these happen to be semantic or morphological. It is thus quite different from the notion of semantic field in the Trier tradition, especially inasmuch as it brings together ideas that would not otherwise be viewed as related (Gordon 1982, 154-5). But, adopting an approach to semantic fields not dissimilar to that of Lehrer, Guiraud envisages the morphosemantic field as being a dynamic ambience in which each term occurring in the field acquires motivation by being situated in it. The relations between items in a field may be purely linguistic in character – synonymic identity, homonymic clash, paronymic attraction, word borrowing, dialect usage, and the like – or they may be external to the system of language as such, and brought about by virtue of their occurrence in real-life contexts (Guiraud 1956, 287-8).

Guiraud was able to show that pairs or larger groupings of words which appear to be homonyms (words that are identical in form but semantically unrelated) on closer inspection reveal that they were at one time semantically related, having occupied the same morpho-semantic field in some regional dialect. His procedure was to assemble as many lexical items as possible, both standard and dialect, in former as well as in present-day usage, relating to some particular creature, object or activity. By eliminating all those items found to have no historical linkage, he was able to construct a core "field". For example his initial corpus for the candidate field "cat" contained as many as 2,000 terms (Guiraud 1966). These were finally reduced to some three hundred. In this way Guiraud was able to clear up various etymological puzzles. How was it possible for instance that the Modern French word *maroufle* came to have three unrelated meanings: "boor", "paste", and "tom cat"? At one time, Guiraud discovered, these three senses rubbed shoulders within a common morphosemantic field. Particularly striking was the clue linking "paste" and "tom cat": a defunct word *chas* meaning "a starch paste". This word *chas* had, as it would still have in present-day French, the same pronunciation as *chat*. Guiraud was thus able to show that the modern homonymic identity between *maroufle*₁ ("tom cat") and *maroufle*₂ ("paste used as a fixative") is traceable to an earlier and no longer extant morphosemantic linkage (*i.e. maroufle* acquired its later "paste" meaning from an earlier parallel association between *chas* and *chat*).

Morphosemantic interplay, as must already be apparent, forms an essential part of the shared mode of language in its pluridimensional interface with the organic mode. It is this same interplay that makes poetry, as distinct from discursive prose, the idiosyncratic activity that it is. It is also what gives a language, any language, its character, its distinctive physiognomy. Without this two-way interaction the world's cognate languages would long since have fallen together, with words becoming mere interchangeable tokens and all semantic associations "homogenized". We would long since have become indistinguishable from sci-fi robotic humanoids, and language as we now know it would have become extinct. The twenty-odd meanings of "meaning", unearthed by Ogden and Richards, do make life that much less comfortable. To find no congener for "home" in any related (European) language causes only marginal inconvenience. But to have four different meanings for the single word *love* can be awkward enough to present a problem; sufficiently intriguing at any rate to provoke C.S.Lewis to write a whole book on the subject.[6] There happened to be a separate term for one of these four meanings in Latin *caritas* – feebly rendered into English (some might suggest "pidgin Latin") as *charity*.

But fortunately "borrowing" does not always seem to be such a hazardous business. In respect of word borrowing, some languages appear to be more conservative than others. English (along with Japanese) is one of the least conservative languages in this particular respect. A perusal of *The Shorter Oxford English Dictionary* will soon reveal that entire pages can go by without a single word entry of English origin. The reason why English has so many words of foreign origin is not known. Even the words *foreign, alien,* and *stranger* are non-English in origin.[8] This is perhaps surprising when one considers that Old English made use largely of its own lexical resources whenever a new word was needed. Since the time of the Scandinavian incursions of the ninth and tenth centuries however, word borrowing has been the principal means in English of acquiring new words and concepts. For this to occur there must have been extensive bilingualism.

Bilingual communities only rarely share the characteristics of United Nations interpreters, switching in a conscious and controlled manner from one language to another. Nearly always, as was seen earlier in a French- Canadian context, bilinguals use one language in one context or domain, and their other language in another. This must have been the case among Anglo-French speaking classes in post-Conquest England when *pig, bullock, calf* and *deer* were confined to the farmyard or heath, and only *pork, beef, veal* and *venison* allowed past the butcher's knife to the table. Even today in England (and in other countries still applying English Law) *estop* (*estoppage*) has a a precise legal meaning that the ordinary (English pedigree, and cognate) *stop* will not cover.

By the time of Chaucer, bilingualism would have become completely unconscious (those who affected a command of French would, like Chaucer's Prioress, risk ridicule). The present-day speaker of English will often be unaware that many of our everyday words (words as common as *flower*, *alley*, *lieutenant*, *chair*, *chapel*, *channel* or *marriage*, even the adverb *very*) are French; and all but the sophisticated speaker may fail to recognize that more recently borrowed items which still retain (except in regional dialect) something of their original pronunciation, such as *café*, *bouquet*, *chef*, or *reservoir*, are likewise from French. The Anglo-French bilingualism in England and other parts of the British Isles during the Middle Ages produced a "macro"-culture, so to speak, with a common fund of potential meanings, in which only the word-forms in the bilingual's languages are different.[9] This was reinforced during the Renaissance and later by extensive borrowings and proliferations of synonyms from Latin and Greek. The fund of common meanings did not however imply semantic homogeneity, as it might have done elsewhere.[10] Words of English and Scandinavian origin still retain a certain weight and flavour of their own.[11] The seams are still visible. A striking illustration is to be found among the various synonyms for "courage". The English words *daring*, *manliness* or *pluck* sound less like cultivated attributes than their more prestigious French-derived equivalents *courage*, *valour* or *gallantry*. The English words seem to ring with greater spontaneity, like the inherent virtue of sturdily real things, old stone, a rough wooden bench, but they are not qualities one gets medals for. The word *fortitude* (from Latin *via* French) sounds like an idealization when compared with a word of Anglo-Saxon origin like *steadfastness*; the latter also seems more human, if tougher, less "packaged" somehow than that other Latinism *intrepid*.

Not only linguists and lexicographers have wondered why certain words have been borrowed and others not. Part of the reason is of course culture and cultural attitudes:[12] most languages have at various times borrowed terms for new technologies or imported occupations, but the only systematic explanation available at the present time for selectivity in borrowing is to be found in morphosemantics, and in the interface between the separate modes of language.

Take for example the word *umbrella*, a loan-word from Italian, borrowed early in the seventeenth century. In its passage from Italian to English, the Italian form *ombrella* underwent two kinds of change. Firstly, an eventuality it shares with loan-words in general, *ombrella* ("sun-shade") took on an English pronunciation. In so doing, its initial vowel became phonologically aligned with /ʌ/ (as in *up, other, under*, etc.), and its final vowel with the frequent and productive morphological (and morphosemantic) termination *-er*. Secondly, because there was no morphosemantic concurrence (MSC), initial or final, to accommodate the **sense** of "sun-shade", it became aligned with an already existing final MSC that reflected its shape and function. The foundations for this MSC were the earlier borrowings *cambrel, tumbrel, timbrel* and *whimbrel* (all comparatively rare in usage but, as will shortly be seen, critical in this instance) but also the numerous word-forms in *-el* (more commonly occurring orthographically as *-le*). The final vowel /ə/ of *umbrella* /ʌmbrelə/ is treated by the morphosemantic system as a morpheme (or "quasi-morpheme"), and is overridden (compare items in the *Appendix*, p.300: *hollyhock, phlox*, etc.). Thus, *umbrella* forms a set with *angular, perpendicular* (in my analysis VERTICAL/OBLIQUE) and with *bowler, titfer, topper, tiara, coiffure*, etc. (HEADGEAR.); with *cupola*, but also with *mantle* (in general "cover" but more particularly "a shade employed in various mechanical devices") as well as with *parasol* (a later borrowing than *umbrella*, and possibly facilitated by MSCs including *mantel, cupola*, and *umbrella*).

Crucial in the borrowing of *umbrella* nevertheless are the rhyming set: *cambrel, tumbrel*, etc. *Cambrel* began its obsolescence in the seventeenth century, but its use in the last century as "a bent piece of wood or iron used by butchers to hang carcasses" is on record. More significantly, a variant of cambrel survives in American English usage in a variant form *gambrel*: a "gambrel roof" is described as "a curved or hipped roof" and must be familiar to those who have lived in or visited New England. The cross-sectional elevation of a gambrel roof looks distinctly like the cross section of the canopy of an unfurled umbrella. A *tumbrel* was "a cart so constructed that the body tilts backwards so as to empty out the load": a tilting motion is employed to shake excess water off the surface of an umbrella. *Timbrel* was also in use as "a tambourine or the like that could be held up in the hand".

The etymology of *whimbrel* may well be uncertain, but a picture of the bird reveals a slender downward-curving beak with a noticeable angular dip ("hipped") a third of the distance from the extremity. The iconic amalgam of these different senses matches many of the specifications of an umbrella.

Another interesting case is *cello* (the official abbreviation of *violoncello* is *'cello*). The abbreviated form, nearly always spelt without the apostrophe, would have found an immediate (morphosemantic) home in English, for the reason that there already existed in the lexicon words such as: (1) *fallow*, "pale brownish or reddish yellow", an exact description of the colour range of the instrument's varnish; (2) *mellow*, a fair description of the sound, particularly in its middle registers, and (3) *felloe*, the now obsolete term for "the curved pieces of wood which joined together formed the rim (of a wheel)", an apt way of looking at the wide curved rim of the instrument. For good measure, one could add (4) *billow*, in the sense of the swell of a wave (the contours of the front and back surfaces of the instrument when viewed sidelong); (5) *swallow*, in its specialized sense: the concave space forming the sheave of a pulley wheel (for those unfamiliar with the instrument, the concave grooves on the scroll at the top of a cello resemble a pulley's concave grooves); and (6) *hollow*, which a cello essentially is. Senses (1) to (6) represent an inventory, surprisingly complete, of the main features of a "cello".

Loan-word studies, though a long established and highly productive sphere of research, are still probably in their infancy. On the one hand, taking in a word from another language is analogous to throwing a handful of small stones on to the surface of a pond, its repercussions for the host language being unpredictable. On the other hand, without the requisite morphosemantic templates, it is unlikely that a word will be successfully borrowed or given the stamp of lexicographical approval. *Malaise* for example has been in use in English since the eighteenth century and is by no means a rarely used word. Yet it is still considered by the *OED* to be "not naturalized, alien".

How far morphosemantic considerations are reflected in socio-cultural attitudes, or *vice versa*, it may be too early to say. It does appear however that, morphosemantic factors being more or less equal, some lexical borrowings experience a more difficult passage than others, no doubt owing to the blocking effect of sensitivities and attitudes built into a culture's intersubjectivity (and hence taking effect in the shared mode of language) – ultimately institutionalization in a different guise. The French word *gentil* "high-born" entered the English lexicon as *gentle*. (Anglo-Saxon had its own words for "noble" and "nobility" but these dropped out of use no doubt as socially inappropriate once Anglo-French bilingualism came to prevail amongst the English upper classes). Although *gentle* in its original (borrowed) sense has not survived, except in fixed locutions such as *gentlefolk* or *gentle birth*, the word itself has become an intimate part of the English lexicon, albeit with the different and now indispensable sense "gentle in manner". This happened in the sixteenth century when, as a result, English found itself once again with a lexical gap, despite the existence of *noble* (another Middle English borrowing) and the nominal form *noblesse* (virtually unused since the seventeenth century except in the expression *noblesse oblige*, pronounced in the French manner, a factor that does nothing towards the word's "naturalization"). So, in Shakespeare's time, the word *gentil* was borrowed a second time, with the accent this time on the second syllable (*genteel*), as in French. Nevertheless, before too many years had passed, *genteel* came to be used mainly in an ironic sense, no doubt reflecting the mood of the age. During the Restoration a third attempt was made to import the same French word, now pronounced in the Modern French way, and rendered into English as *jaunty* (but with accent back on the first syllable again). It took probably less than ten years for *jaunty* to take on its present meaning "sprightly in manner", no doubt as a way of lampooning the seigneurial style slavishly copied from Versailles. In France itself *gentil* had to await the relatively more secure aftermath of the French Revolution before it could relax into the sense "nice, or pleasing".

Invisible lexical imports, known as "loan translations", are a different matter altogether. In these instances only the sense is borrowed, not the form. For the sense to become lodged in the host language, it might look as if lexical reconstitution ("relexification") takes place. But this cannot be the case: institutionalized meaning finds its place in the intersubjective mode of language and can only occur within the consciousness of one or more bilingual (and at least partially bicultural) speakers or writers. For this reason "translexification" might seem a more apt description.

The most straightforward kind of transference (if anything in language can be said to be straightforward) can be observed when a technical innovation or scientific concept is borrowed. In such instances either the foreign word is directly borrowed (with or without phonological, graphological, or morphological modification), or is lexically reconstituted. Thus the American invention "telephone", itself a lexical reconstruction on a Greek model, becomes *téléphone* in French, *telefono* in Italian, but *Fernsprecher* ("remote speaker") in German, a word reconstituted independently, using German morphemes, from the same (imaginary) Greek model. In Cantonese it becomes "electric speaking" (*dinwa*). In another instance *skyscraper* (again an American innovation), the original coinage is too complex, phonologically or morphologically, for direct borrowing, though metaphoric resilience has contributed to lexical reconstitution: French *gratte-ciel*, German *Wolkenkratzer*, and Russian *neboskryob*, all embodying a metaphor of sky- or cloud-scratching. A different case however is *peninsula*. Although the English word was borrowed from Medieval Latin, the word has a longer history, traceable to Classical Latin (*paeninsula*). Many languages have adopted the meaning, but relexified this sense differently. English and Italian retain the notion "almost an island", while the relexification "half an island" appears in German (*Halbinsel*), Russian (*poluostrov*), Chinese (*bun-dou*), and other languages.

Languages which form part of single "linguistic area" may have different lexical forms but a common semantic. Romanian for example, which is located in a linguistic area in which there exist several Slavic languages and dialects (Serbo-Croat, Bulgarian, Ruthenian, etc.), has directly inherited some of its core words from the Latin *koine* of the Roman Empire. One such word is *lume* (Latin *lumin(em)* "light"). Through contact with neighbouring Slavic dialects, in which "light" and "world" coexist in a single form, Romanian too inherited this double meaning. In actuality there may be no such thing as semantic change; perhaps there is only potential word sense actively distributed through a wide range and hierarchy of categories. Recent studies appear to confirm this:[13] between languages senses are borrowed; in the same language they are transferred (as I have hoped to show through morphosemantic concurrence). It is these transfers that are registered, over time, by the linguistic historian as semantic change.

Highly instructive is the not particularly rare situation in which words are borrowed and subsequently "returned" to their language of origin. Such an instance is *realize*, in its sense "to make real, to carry out", taken over from French in the early seventeenth century. It was only in later times that the English word developed a quite different and dominant sense, as in *They didn't realize that...* or *When we realized what was happening...* Earlier this century, this English sense was borrowed by French and added to the polysemy of *réaliser*. Postwar "Franglais" – that bugbear of the purist – saw not only the importation of English meanings, but sometimes the accretion of new senses to familiar words. In French, for example, *suite* signified "continuation", "series" and especially a "guard of honour", but now the word came to mean also "apartment, hotel suite". Ever since Roman times *vice* had meant only the opposite of "virtue", but from now on the word would take on the American English sense "debauchery, prostitution, drug racketeering". A complex case of reborrowing is *typhoon*. The word appears to derive in the main from Cantonese *daifung* "strong wind", with an admixture probably from Hindi *tufan* "hurricane" and from the Greek god *Typhon*, the stirrer up of tempests. *Typhoon* was reborrowed by Cantonese as *toifung*. Speakers of Cantonese do not necessarily connect *daifung* and *toifung*, mainly because, despite their spoken similarity, they are written with different characters.

Languages and cultures then do not need to be close for borrowings to occur. All that is necessary is the existence of a certain degree of bilingualism in the host language (which may not even be active bilingualism but as in the case of some Franglais expressions the result of the impact of American films) which at the same time implies a selective attitude of acceptance on the part of host-language speakers. The Greek language and culture was vastly different from that of Hebrew, from which nevertheless the Greeks with some degree of success absorbed many Mosaic and Christian, but otherwise alien, concepts. Hebraic concepts such as *sin*, *righteous*, *angel*, *ungodly*, *idol*, *Paradise*, along with scores of others, were effectively transmitted by way of vernacular Greek to the entire Roman and Western world. Sometimes these concepts found suitable lexical vehicles in Greek, and sometimes not. "Idol" itself, of Hebraic origin, came to be associated (morphosemantically) with Greek *eidolon*, a word dating back at least to Democritus, having more to do with "image" and "imagination" than with idols proper. Yet the marriage of a Hebrew meaning with a Greek lexical form and sense led to a morphosemantic blend which has stood the Western world in good stead (when Bacon was writing of idols he was using the word in this blended sense). Over the centuries many words develop integral meanings built up of strands from more than one cultural tradition. *Brain* is a relatively simple word (even though the organ may be unimaginably complex) but *mind* is much more complex lexically. *Mind* is an English word originally, but its sense became oriented in the direction of "memory" (*That puts me in mind of...*etc.). But because of the importance until relatively recently of Latin in intellectual discourse and, in turn, because of the impact of Greece on Rome in earlier times, *mind* contains more than trace of Latin *mens* and Greek *nóos* ("mind"). Speakers of English do not even try to coin words such as *mindly* but are content with *mental*, a latinism (from *mens*). Even though a particular word is identified as being and is felt to be characteristically English, it will in many instances prove to be, like our genes, an amalgam.

The historical career of meaning in language is one with, and just as variegated as, the societies and cultures in which a particular language or languages have flourished. The student of historical semantics can trace the morphosemantic warp and woof of words and their senses just so far as the inscribed record permits, and even that, especially in its earlier phases, requires imaginative, open-minded, as well as careful, interpretation.

But then a word cannot be quite the same thing as a historical fact. For a historian, for example, a star is and always has been a star. A star is not a problem of the same order, say, as outcome of an armed conflict or the onset of a revolution. But (as we may recall from earlier discussion) a star, along with all other phenomena, is always a potential, and sometimes an actual problem for the historian of meaning in language. The potentiality of sense, the semantic historian needs to keep at the forefront of his or her mind, may on occasion have created the phenomenon itself. What was "electricity" for example before the concept and related terminology were devised? The term *electron,* from which *electric* is derived, meant simply "amber", a substance with static electrical properties now used mainly for making beads. Before the early beginnings of particle theory (the electron being the first) electricity was as mysterious as demons. Even today, and even for those with a goodish grounding in quantum theory, electrons remain among the most abstruse of our concepts. Any semantic categories that accommodate "electric" or "electricity" (there may be none for *electron*) will relate more to the technical and economic aspects of electricity than to any theory. Any answer to the question "What was electricity before the advent of modern physics?", beyond that of being "a property of amber and some other substances", is bound to have profound metaphysical implications.

A word meaning, we may need reminding, does not resemble in any way the gloss given in the dictionary. A word sense is more akin to a "feeling about" an object or event, a metaphorical flavour and gesture. Looking at a rising land mass, I may call it a "hill" or a "mountain", or a "rise", "slope" or "climb", or even an "escarpment". I can think of it as a geological formation, or I may be reminded of a painting or a piece of music, or it could be any one of an indefinite number of possibilities. The word or expression that forms in my consciousness will depend on my purpose, intention or motivation. If I am a cartographer I will probably not think in terms of "hills" or "mountains" except in so far these words appear in the toponymy. Instead I will give precise measurements of altitude above sea-level, and will use appropriate terminology in my reports. If on the other hand I am a poet I may be equally precise, but in a language that is in greater or lesser part my own devising.

When he made the claim that the meaning of a word is none other than its use in the language, Wittgenstein was at least partly right. He only neglected to take into account the social semiotic that endows "use" with the possibility of "meaning", and the morphosemantic moulds in which words are made ready for signification. Also, Wittgenstein overlooked the human motivation (*energeia*) which breeds significance among words that in everyday use may lack any. The chess-game analogy (like all analogies) goes only so far, in that it does not reckon with the fact that, in using words, human beings are prone to change the rules, even to invent or abolish the games themselves.

AFTERWORD

20. On Being Human

Our prolonged excursion, first into the realm of the word writ large, and later among words as such, has been undertaken with the aim of attaining a clearer and at the same time a renewed understanding of the nature of language and words. On the way, an unexpectedly novel view of ourselves, as human beings, has begun to come into focus. Throughout the ages philosophy has puzzled over the relationship between the visible, tactile body and the life principle that animates it, reducible in our own time to the "mind-body problem", and has, over time, proposed solutions consonant with the outlook of a particular era.[1] Although in the preceding pages no attempt has been made at anything like a systematic philosophy, or even at philosophical criticism of any rigour, I have argued that as yet there exists no theory that is **specifically** consistent with even a small part of what language has to tell us about human nature. There has been no lack of interest among philosophers – from Plato through the Neoplatonists, Cusanus, Locke and many since – in language as such; and contemporary and not so contemporary exponents of phenomenology and philosophical hermeneutics have taken a view of language as language with a view to bringing to light what language might have to tell us about ourselves as human beings. But so far there has been no comprehensive **linguistic** model of language which can be admitted into fundamental discussions of what it means to be human.

My aim has been to find such a model – though I am aware that the one I have put forward is far from being definitive – and at the same time to show that language phenomena, when properly assessed and harnessed, can provide us with a unique understanding of our own nature, one that is intended to complement the invaluable insights of contemporary hermeneutical philosophy. Language gives us a tantalizing glimpse of ourselves, as creatures woven seamlessly into two inconceivably disparate worlds; worlds that are linked only by language. The first of these worlds is the world of cognition and imagination, perception and intuition, discourse and dialectic – what the Greeks recognized as the domain of *logos*. The second stands in sharp contrast, endlessly fascinating too, and no less mysterious: the strange phenomenon of the human organism and its place in the world. It is by courtesy of this mostly opaque entity – a live physical body in a zone of organized matter, DNA, genes, energy, multi-level exchange of information, biological interaction and reaction; an unconscious psyche, tuned in to realms unknown; all of this an inseparable part of *Dasein* – that I reside among realia which only physical science, genetics, and ethology have access to, and even then only remotely and circularly, by applying procedures (artefacts of that selfsame *logos*): observation, hypothesis, measurement, and inference.

Paradoxically, though this second aspect of ourselves can appear alien and unfamiliar, yet it is also the familiar wellspring of my individuality, our idiosyncratic likes and dislikes, our deeper moods and quirks of temperament. It is where I have my toothaches but not their pain, where I have hunches but not the bright ideas, the physical attraction I have for another but not the emotion. I do not always feel that I really inhabit this alien world. The world I feel to be my own is a luminous world, a world of familiar objects and knowable beings, a world in which human beings somehow share all the things, feelings and thoughts they consider human, intersubjectively, even supra-personally. Most of the time we behave as if all this were independent of us, as if it were everything there is – minus oneself. This is accompanied by a lurking suspicion that, when all that is perceived and understood is objectivized, the only thing remaining is a poor emaciated ego, endowed with a physical body and salvaged from materialist annihilation only, say, by Freud and his successors, or the purveyors of cult mysticism.

I do not, in theory, need a body. Yet, without a body, I could never have become myself and would never have become available to others. It is not that I have a physical body with a subtle spiritual body tucked away somewhere inside – a view exploded as long ago as Aristotle.[2] It is simply that I am and, to exist, I must have a body, and an adequately functioning body at that. Aristotle's actual reason for the union of soul and body can today be discounted, though we can concur in his "community of nature". Most important of all, it is my body that enables me to act: no body, no action.

The renewed perspective on existence that a true understanding of words engenders encourages one to attempt to grasp how creatures other than human beings can have their own life-worlds, with their own quasi-social and perceptual horizons; the same perspective also provides some inkling into the nature of these alternative worlds which, for all we know, may be quite as complex ontologically as our own, if in vastly different ways. The astounding navigational and location-finding powers displayed by migratory birds, for example, could imply an alignment with time and space that has no affinity whatsoever with the time and space "inhabited" by human beings, an unimaginable "state of unconsciousness" bringing two distant points in time and space together, without any intervening interval, and capable of overcoming the limitations of biology and (classical) physics, except when an (unconscious) power of will forsakes them. Only then will they perish. For higher creatures one may posit, in addition to a range of "instinct" of the kind just noted, an inchoate power of *logos*. *Logos* is unlikely to have had its origins in *Homo sapiens*. It is only that *logos* seems to have realized itself completely in Man (if there are beings with *logos* to a higher power than Man we are simply unable to conceive what they might be like, unless we subscribe to a belief in angels or sci-fi super-humans). The "illumination", whether of *Homo sapiens* or of some earlier Proto-*Homo sapiens* (Neanderthal Man, for instance) was made possible by words, by meaning and symbolism in the same, or at the very least some similar, configuration to that outlined in the preceding chapters of this book.

It would probably be best to avoid applying the description "language" to the undoubted cognitive and communicative capacity observed in primates, dolphins and other species. "Language" would be misleading, and would do little credit to them. Despite our language-like encounters with Washoe, Sarah, Koko, and other primates, the only "words" we can teach them are the ones we have already lodged in a dead repository of institutionalized lexical tokens. We could never teach them any **real** language, any more than we can teach our fellow human beings. Their innate potentialities exclude real words, as well as the cultural semiotic based on words. Nor could they "teach" **us** their awareness or culture, whatever inner form these might assume. The irony behind all this is that we are showing signs of turning ourselves into idol-ridden functional models of artificial beings, particularly in our rationalist consumerist urban environments, when we token-ize even among ourselves for much of the time. A subtly idiosyncratic use of language is becoming rare and unwanted; a trend that has become a distinct convenience in a world in which people are as if seeking to make it difficult, even impossible, for themselves to communicate in any **true** sense.

Domesticated animals, dogs and horses in particular, are a different case. These creatures, especially dogs, have lived in symbiotic relation with Man since earliest times, and can thus be said to share in real ways aspects of human culture and semiotic. What they evidently lack is the capacity which allows the interfacing of the two modes of human language which only human beings appear to possess. Whether this capacity has to do with brain size and complexity, or whether it is a peculiarity of human ontology one can only speculate, according to one's inclinations. There is perhaps something in dog-lovers' cliché claim that their canine companions can achieve anything in the way of communication except talk. If on the other hand we had over the millennia lived in close proximity with primates, they might (with their more developed brain capacities) have come to share not only our culture but even, to a limited degree, our language. They might have become so indistinguishable from us that we would only think of them as apes in momentary lapses of "specie-al" prejudice. To horses and dogs, human beings must appear to be the most extraordinary of creatures. On the one hand, human beings must in certain respects be completely transparent to these perceptive and sensitive but speechless creatures; yet, on the other hand, these same beings seem to them to be perpetually directing the most extraordinarily modulated bursts of sound (or, to them, non-transparent paralinguistic gestures) towards other human beings and, in so doing, establishing what must evidently, unmistakably amount to some special kind of rapport.

It was the (now influential) Russian psychologist Lev Vygotsky, writing in the Stalinist Russia of the 1930s, who first observed that human beings represent a coalescence of two distinct and unrelated phylogenetic strands which at some point in the prehistory of mankind merged, to produce language. A comparable phenomenon, Vygotsky claimed, is also observable in ontogenesis, in the early development of the human infant.[3] The first of these strands Vygotsky identified as thought – the Rational Principle, so neatly captured in the word *logos*. The second strand – speech – has its remote phylogenetic origins in the primeval wilderness of hominid prehistory. Phonation, with its subtle and endlessly varied patterns of intonation, intensity, pause and rhythm, became speech, the purely vocal, expressive and kinetic side of language, linked to our sometimes savage propensities towards song, incantation and dance. (Vygotsky's coalescence lacks only the morphosemantic interface of words themselves.)

The phylogenetic-ontogenetic merging of the two separate strands of language is so complete that nowadays linguistic philosophers hesitate to distinguish between thought and word. Nelson Goodman asks:

> What sort of thing is a mind that words can be in? And how can words be in it?... Thinking is not only like but may actually **be** speaking, [and] silent thought [may actually be] in the words we speak to ourselves. Such a proposal has the virtue of not needing a mind for words to be in. Rather, thinking like speaking is performance.(1982, 212)

The fact that words have one foot in grammatical order and regulation is obvious, indeed tautologous, from their compliance with logic and syntactic order. But their resistance against complete subservience to logic and grammar finds its reflection in their quirkiness, unpredictability and the (continually shrinking) domains in which the protean alogical principle still holds sway. In early times the balance had been different but, with the rapid advent of civilization, linear writing and, much more recently, printing, rationality has almost completely reined in the spontaneous and ambivalent in human speech. In the last few centuries this reining in has become so much of a straitjacket that modern poets have been goaded into resistance.

Modern linguistics has in many respects furthered and perpetuated this rationalist encroachment. The inordinate quest for systematization and general theory has infected not only the Chomskys but even the humble data-gatherer who willy-nilly has to espouse one theoretical framework or another. One writer, after conceding that "no currently available formal theory is capable of encompassing all the facts concerning word-meaning," immediately adds: "linguistics has certainly developed beyond the stage where a collection of pretty and curious specimens, however attractively arranged and aptly and minutely described, would be an acceptable offering," the ultimate aim being to pursue "an exploration disciplined by a consistent method of approach, and by a predilection for systematic, recurrent and generalizable facts rather than for peculiarity and idiosyncrasy" (Cruse 1986, xiii). Apart from its revealing slant (not the first such revelation by any means) on the insecurity of linguistic theory, this commitment highlights the persistence of the straitjacket that linguists, with few exceptions, have sought to impose on what must be the most fundamental, yet at the same time vulnerable, principle in our lives – the word.

When they are at their most telling, words can be highly particular and idiosyncratic. They can be regimented and disciplined, like tamed animals, into ways that may not be entirely natural to them or, by extension, to ourselves. The more we behave as if language were becoming the fully rational entity Francis Bacon hoped for, the more this tendency is reinforced. We may be the shapers, the schematizers of language, but it is also we who are shaped and schematized by language: our destinies cannot be separated. This is not to decry the appropriate use of scientific method or even to deny its applicability to the phenomena of language; but merely to affirm the need to remain infinitely sensitive to our "specimens", which cannot be compared with the inert data of the physical world. The "bits of machinery" devised by us to assist in our analysis of language, as Empson suggested, "need to be kept sharply separate from the delicacy and warmth of the actual cases they are to be used on" (1951, 19). Words divulge their own worlds, in ways peculiar to themselves. Their interplay invokes signs and symbols that beckon towards a hermeneutic for which a special preparation is required; what Deleuze lightly identified as an *apprentissage des signes*. We may think we can learn to control words, but ultimately they will have the upper hand.

The taming of the word brings with it its own hazards. The word has the capacity to lure us by stages into versions of ourselves that we might come to disclaim as being human. Orwell's warning that words will do our thinking for us if we let them is another way of saying that words enter into relations with one another without our active assistance. The problem seems to be not that we know too little about the behaviour of words (even less than we know about our own biochemistry) but that our analytical approaches can barely touch them: an awareness that sharpens at moments when we – and especially those beings of rare insight, craft and imagination we call poets – are able to find expression for things miraculously beyond what they, in their humdrum moments, would consider themselves capable of.

Appendix

Part 1: The Morphosemantic Function of Rhyming (and Alliteration)

In *Figure* 2, below, it will be noted that, except for the items at the lower end of the table, every sense has more than one corresponding form; and, conversely, every form is linked to more than one sense. This use of the rhyme ending (as well as the initial alliteration) is one of the important ways in which words maintain their differential character.

The items in square brackets indicate antonyms. This particular set exhibits a rather low proportion of antonyms for English sets as a whole. But, in general, Chinese sets have a rather higher overall proportion of antonyms, both as regards its rhyming and alliterative sets and its MSCs. The reason for this cannot at present even be guessed at. This rhyming-alliterative process in morphosemantics is unconscious, and a function of the organic mode. However, at the point at which rhyming or alliteration assume an aesthetic (stylistic) role, they cross over into the shared-intersubjective mode, becoming an at least partly conscious cultural role.

	bam	cam	clam	cram	dam	damn	dia-phragm	dram	exam	flim-flam
crowd				+						
woman					+					
sheep										
foodstuff			+	+						
meat										
beverage								+		
eating				+						
framework					+			+		
partition					+		+			
mound		+			+					
machinery	+									
clamp, vice			+							
projection	+			+						
body part			+				+			
measure								+		
signal										+
symbol										
vehicle										
weaving				+						
game					+					
fanciful										+
plan of action										
broadcast										
theatrical										
study				+						
examination				+					+	
noise (clang)			+							
prevent			+							
block, stop up			+	+	+					
thrust (into)				+						
condemn						+				
deceive	+			+						+
secretive			+							
beat, thrash										

Figure 2: Morphosemantic matrix for final (rhyming) segment -AM /æm/ in British English.

gam	gram	ham	jam	jamb	lam	lamb	mam	pram	pro-gram	ram	sham	slam	tram	yam
+			+			+								
							+							
						+				+				
	+	+	+			+								+
		+				+								
										(+)	+			
			+										+	
				+										
			+							+				
			+											
				+										
		+	+											
	+									+				
		+	[+]											
	+													
									+				+	
					+								+	
												+		
			[+]							+				
		+	[+]							+				
		+									+			
										+				
			+											
			+											
			+							+				
												+		
											+			
[+]														
			+		+					+		+		

Notes: [ ] indicates antonymous sense.

gram (foodstuffs) = "chick-peas, food for horses" .   *dram* (framwork)= "section of a raft of staves" .   *ham* (broadcast) = "amateur radio operator" .   *lamb* (crowd)="body of ruffians".
gam (1)(crowd)="school of whales"; (2) (secretive) ="whalers' ship meeting with another ship to gossip".   *tam-tam* (gong) also rhymes with *clam* (noise: clang) = "clash of bells". The author recalls as a child *Ram-tam* as a proprietary brand of porter.   *ram-jam* ="cram full".   *jam* (plan of action) = "tough situation".   *gram* (symbol) (ana-, crypto-, hexa-).

Part 2: Primary Stress and its Role in Morphosemantic Concurrence

The first point to be made is that English syllables contain stressed and/or unstressed syllables. A single-syllable word will normally carry a (primary) stress (but very common monosyllables such as *the, a, in*, etc. usually will not).

There are different degrees of stress: primary and secondary. Words of two syllables will have one of its syllables carrying primary stress, whereas words of three or more syllables will carry both primary and secondary stress.

A second point: vowels and diphthongs (in any language) are classified according to the position of the mid-point of the tongue: whether raised ("high"), lowered ("low"), or forward ("front"). In Chomsky and Halle's scheme (1968) vowels (and diphthongs) may be any of the following: +high, -high; +low, -low; +front, -front. In the morphosemantic analysis of both the Chinese (Cantonese) and English lexical corpora, +back (as oppsed to Chomsky and Halle's -front) also plays an important role.

It appears that not all primary stressed vowels or diphthongs contribute to morphosemantic concurrence: The ones (in R.P. English) that are marked are the following:

+high, +front: /i:/, /ɪ/, /aɪ/, and /ɔɪ/. (N.B. Although the diphthongs are of the "falling" type, with a heavier stress on the first vowel, only the second vowel in the diphthong appears to play a morphosemantic role.)

+high, +back: /u:/, /ʊ/ and /aʊ/.

+low, +front: /æ/.

+low, +back: /ɑ:/ and /ɒ /.

Henceforth these marked vowels and diphthongs are referred to as **key vowels.**

Thus, MSCs are classified as:

> H (MSCs containing only primary stressed +high vowels or diphthongs)

HF (+high, +front)	F (+front vowels only)
HB (+high, +back)	LF (+low, +front)
L (+low only)	LB (+low, +back)
B (+back only)	

Over and above this, there is what might aptly be termed a "ding-dong" factor. What happens is that HF, HB, LF, or LB type MSCs may, and quite often do, attract their opposites (HF may attract LB key vowels, for example, and *vice versa*). Provided these "opposites" are in a minority the classification is modified to HF(OPP), HB(OPP), LF(OPP) or LB(OPP).

Initial and final phonological segments of (potential) word-forms, in English and in Chinese, group themselves into sets according to:

(i) either their **initial** or **final** segments of (potential) word-forms (these are alliterative or rhyming segments **except** that morphosemantic concurrence appears to (a) discount the difference between voiceless and voiced in consonants, (b) run /θ/ and /ð/ together with /t/ and /d/, and (c) treat vocalic endings (including /ə(ɹ)/) as a single category, regardless of their phonology. I say "appears" because a definitive picture will not emerge until more of the corpus has been analyzed).

(ii) the syllable of a (potential) word-form that carries the **primary stress,**

(iii) whether the primary-stressed syllable contains a **key** vowel (if there is no key vowel, it appears not to influence the classification of the set).

To return to our simplified example – *lot* and *plot* – these present no problem inasmuch as they both carry the major stress and both contain the key vowel /ɒ/. But the word-form *site* /saɪt/ also finds itself aligned, as a "ding-dong" opposite, with the *plot*, *lot*, etc.set, through the diphthong /aɪ/.[12]

Part 3: MSCs and the generation of candidate words and actual word senses

MSCs – at least one initial MSC and one final MSC – coalesce within the framework of a semantic category to generate candidate words and actual word senses

In *Figure* 3 it may be seen that three MSCs (one initial and two

final MSCs) subtended by the semantic category EQUILIBRIUM,
BALANCE coalesce in the production of four candidate words: *trim*,
teeter, trebuchet and *top-heavy.*
It should also be noticed that the potential word-form alignments for
the initial and final MSCs are different. This difference (in the

Semantic Category	**Initial MSC**		**Final MSC**	
EQUILIBRIUM, BALANCE	T108	H(OPP)	M.92	HF
	/trɪ/ [*trim*]		/ɪm/ [*trim*]	
			/iːm/ [*beam*]	
	/tʌ/ [*tongue*]		/iːm/ [*redeem*]	
			/ɪbrɪəm/ [*equilibrium*]	
	/tɔː/[*turn*]			
			TV.438	F
	/tiː/ [*teeter*]		/tə(ɹ)/ [*teeter*]	
	/tre/ [*trebuchet*]		/ʃə/ [*trebuchet*]	
	/tɒ/ [*top*-heavy]		/vɪ/ [*top-heavy*]	
			/tə(ɹ) [*centre*]	
			/sə(ɹ)/ [*balancer*]	
			/ɛə(ɹ)/ [*square*]	
			/eɪ/ [*weigh*] /rə/ [*libra*]	
			/ɪ/ [*stability*]	
			/ɪ/ [*neutrality*]	
			/ʌ/ [*recover*]	

Notes: [H(OPP)] includes the high -front vowels and (in this instance) one low-back vowel.
The "central" vowels in *tongue* and *turn* are neutral. [F] includes all (stressed) front vowels.
[TV] includes final segments consisting of any vowel (or diphthong)(in British English and
some American dialects -*er* ending is pronounced as a central vowel without *r*-colouration).
The serial numbers are for reference only.
Trim = "to adjust a balance so as to equalize it"; *tongue* = "a small delicately poised
balance"; *turn* = "beam of a balance"; *teeter* = "see-saw, to balance onself unsteadily";
trebuchet = "a small delicately poised balance"; *redeem* = "counterbalance, compensate
for"; *square* = "to balance".

Figure 3: Sample coalescence of initial and final Morphosemantic
          Concurrences (MSCs) subtended by the semantic category
          EQUILIBRIUM, BALANCE

Saussurean sense) is important in that it enhances considerably the power of the system. Through their initial and final segments, separately, word-forms can and do generate a range of senses (polysemy and homonymy) which enable the lexicon to retain its flexibility and counteract lexical "entropy".

At this point and, in passing, a comment about lexical frequency will not be out of place. It must be obvious that some word-forms included in the MSCs cited in *Figure* 3 would appear in "word-frequency counts" much more frequently occurring than others, and others would simply not appear. This is not a matter that can be passed over lightly, but at this point in the current investigations the importance of this variable of frequency, either for word-forms or polysemantic variance, is not known. None the less, it is important to keep in mind that a word that is of rare occurrence for one person may be fairly common for another. For me, *trebuchet* is a rare word, but for someone engaged in assaying precious metals the term might not seem at all rare. The same applies to the many hundreds of technical words which play an integrated role, however marginal, in the lexicon (*trebuchet* happens to be such a word in that it has had more than one discrete sense)

Interface between the initial and final MSCs (in *Figure* 3) is indicated by dotted underlining and linkage. For *trim* alone, the *Shorter Oxford English Dictionary* itemizes more than twenty different senses (many of them not so rare) for the two entries taken together. Every one of these different senses is likely to occur in a separate semantic category. Thus, if anyone were to attempt to conceptualize interface of such complexity, a network of considerable size would need to be projected, bringing together as it would a large number of MSCs. Yet the human brain seems to be able to cope with tasks of this magnitude, especially in circumstances in which we may run together in our lexical productions several different senses, placing the burden of discrimination on context.

Part 4. MSCs and Sub-morphemes

MSCs, it has to be said, do not behave like morphemes; nor are they "sub-morphemes" (as characterized by McCune (1985) in his study of Indonesian). That they are not sub-morphemes can be demonstrated from peculiarities of the English lexicon. In English the terminal phonological segment *-er* in some instances is a (bound) morpheme and sometimes not. When it is a morpheme this common ending can be paraphrased as "one who/that which..."; *e.g.* a *reader* is "one who reads" and a *runner* "one who/that which runs". But in many lexical items *-er* (*e.g.* *corner*, *pullover*, *trigger*) is morphologically inseparable and, more to the point, cannot be substituted by any other bound morpheme (as would be the case with *reader*, *reading*, *readable*, etc.). Nevertheless it can be seen that *pullover*, for example, along with *trouser(s)*, *slipper*, *garter*, *drawer(s)*, *muffler*, *sweater*, *sneaker*, etc., are subtended by an MSC icluding items with the final segment *-er* and aligned with the meaning "garment, accessory". In some instances the same item can be both morphologically single and composite: when the former, *sweater* aligns itself with the set [*pullover*, etc.] but when the latter, it means simply "one who sweats". The reader may have noticed that what has been identified as MSC "garment, accessory" subtends a few items which normally occur in the plural. It can be shown that MSCs override morphological considerations such as plurality. Not only that, but MSCs appear in certain instances to treat the morphological alternation plus-*s*/minus-*s* (plural/singular) as allophonic variants (*i.e.* allomorphic variants of the same final consonant in this instance). This is particularly obvious in words ending in *-k* or *-x* /-ks/, as the following sample indicates (for further discussion see Lord (1970, 32)):

Pivotal indicator: *cock*, *clock*, *weathercock*, *box* (as in "box a compass").

Enclosure: *dock*, *paddock*, *lock*, *parrock*, *box* (as in "witness box").

Wedge: *chock*, *forelock*, *lock*, *fox* ("wedge driven into split end of a bolt").   **Flowering plant**: *hollyhock*, *candock*, *stock*, *phlox*.

Pump: *penstock*, *box* ("piston of a pump").

Entangled strands: *lock*, *hassock*, *tussock*, *fox* ("twisted rope yarns").

Bovine quadruped: *bullock*, *ox*..   **Veneral disease**: *lock*, *pox*.

Undesirable person: *brock*, *shylock*, *warlock*, *lock*, *fox*..

Receptacle: *crock*, *box*.   **Conventionality**: *stock*, *orthodox*.

Leading position: *cock*, *cox*, *box* ("driver's seat on coach")

Decrepitude: *crock*, *ox* ("misfortune, old age")

Bore, drill: *stock*, *box* ("to make a cavity in a tree for collecting sap").

Notes

1. Language and Being: An Introduction

1. Edmund Husserl (1859-1938) in his *Logical Investigations* brought to bear "the phenomenological method on the problems of the constitution and understanding of meaning, problems which clearly transcend the realms of pure mathematics or logic. In a very important sense, *Logical Investigations* must be read also as a theory of hermeneutics, or more accurately, as the establishment of the ground and possibility of hermeneutics" Mueller-Vollmer 1990, 166).

2. Husserl, at one point in his extended treatment of this and related concerns, characterizes the life-world as "in principle an intuitively given world, given, of course, only in the flowing and fluctuating of its streaming horizon,... the life-world has the universal structure of of a finite, subjective-relative world with indeterminately open horizons" (Husserl 1970, 103ff.).

3. Even the contemporary English word *language*, if we follow *The Oxford English Dictionary*, has no separately identifiable sense that equates with the concept of "language" we are presently concerned with. Ferdinand de Saussure, it may be recalled, had to forge his own conceptual terminology from the available French lexicon.

4. See also Gadamer (1976, 59-60).

5. The editor of Gadamer's *Philosophical Hermeneutics* (1976, xi) writes: "The task of philosophical hermeneutics is ontological rather than methodological. It seeks to throw light on the fundamental conditions that underlie the phenomenon of understanding in all its modes, scientific and nonscientific alike, and that constitute understanding as an event over which the interpreting subject does not ultimately preside." In the Foreword to the Second Edition of his *Truth and Method* (1991, xxviii) Gadamer himself explains that "my real concern was and is philosophic: not what we do or what we ought to do, but what happens to us over and above our wanting and doing. Elsewhere (1976, 94) Gadamer claims that "hermeneutical reflection ...exercises a self-criticism of thinking consciousness, a criticism that translates all its own abstractions and also the knowledge of the sciences back into the whole of human experience of the world. Above all, philosophy ... is the actualization of such hermeneutics, which blends the total structures worked out in semantic analysis into the continuum of translating and comprehending within which we live and pass away."

6. Selected for particular mention are: Ferdinand de Saussure's *Cours de Linguistique Générale* (1913), translated into English as *A Course in General Linguistics* (1960); Otto Jespersen's *The Philosophy of Grammar* (1929); and Edward Sapir's *Language* (1921) (See also Mandelbaum (1949)). Mention should also be made of the important work of Jan Baudouin de Courtenay, William Dwight Whitney, Leonard Bloomfield, Karl Buehler, J.R. Firth and Antoine Meillet.

7. An actual experience related to me by my very good friend Shirley Barham.

8. Thomas S. Kuhn is best known for his *Structure of Scientific Revolutions*. The notion that, historically, science has proceeded through a series of "paradigms", succeeding one another in time has been influential. A paradigm is described as "universally recognized scientific achievements that for a time provide model problems and solutions to a community of practitioners" (1970, viii).

9. In his *Idiota* Nicholas da Cusa asserts that Man creates the objects around him and also determines or "legislates" their meaning and value. In his *De Coniecturis* he also characterizes Man as the "human god" creating and perpetuating his own microcosmic world – the world of culture and history. Mankind does not bring about anything new but "discovers that everything that it creates through its unfolding already existed within itself." In *De Ludo Globi* the same writer presents man as engaged in a cosmic play, the inventor of games in which God and the universe are contained. See Watts (1986, 20-22).

10. Heidegger (1962, 209). The nearest one comes to a definition of *Dasein* might be the following (1962, 32): "*Dasein* is an entity which does not just occur among other entities. Rather it is ontically distinguished by the fact that, in its very Being, that Being is an **issue** for it... this implies that *Dasein*, in its Being, has a relationship towards that Being – a relationship which itself is one of Being. And this means further that there is some way in which *Dasein* understands itself in its Being, and that to some degree it does so explicitly. It is peculiar to this entity that with and through its Being, this Being is disclosed to it. **Understanding of Being is itself a definite characteristic of *Dasein's* Being.**"

2. The Shared Word

1. The Neogrammarians, or *Junggrammatiker*, flourished in the latter half of the nineteenth century. One of their central preoccupations was with language change, and with speaking individuals "who have learnt their

mother-tongue in the ordinary way, and who now employ it in their daily intercourse with other men and women without in each case knowing what they owe to others and what they have to create on the spur of the moment" (Jespersen [1922] 1954, 95).

2. This is close to the view expressed by Robert Le Page in Kelly (1969, 144).

3. Cited in *From Notes Made in 1970-71*, in Bakhtin (1986, 137).

4. "It is only from the side of the transcendental ego and its constitutive accomplishments that the problem of intersubjectivity can be resolved, that the 'like ego', the intentionality of the so-called transcendental empathy, can be understood. It is curious enough that a mere object of perception, a corporeal thing, is only able to become an *alter ego* by means of a form of idealizing apprehension" (Gadamer 1977, 187).

5. To my knowledge, the first to draw attention to the drawbacks of Saussure's and others' schematic representations of the speaker-hearer communication circuit was Bakhtin (1986) in *The Problem of Speech Genres*. Bakhtin dismisses such diagrammatic representations as science fiction.

6. This is Merleau-Ponty's interpretation, and nowhere in the *Investigations* does Husserl make such a claim. Husserl appears to be arguing for a universal grammar ("in the widest of senses") along the lines of the *Grammaire Générale et Raisonnée*, emphasizing the validity of both *a priori* and empirical bases of grammar (Husserl [1913]1970, 493ff.).

7. "When I speak or understand, I experience the presence of others in myself or of myself in others... and I finally understand what is meant by Husserl's enigmatic statement, 'Transcendental subjectivity is intersubjectivity.' To the extent that what I say has meaning, I am a different 'other' for myself when I am speaking; and to the extent that I understand, I no longer know who is speaking and who is listening" (Merleau-Ponty 1964, 97).

8. Cited in Habermas (1978, 168).

9. So far as I am aware, Bakhtin was the first to use the term "shared language". See his *Discourse in the Novel* in Bakhtin (1981, 281).

3. *Logos* and *Poesis*

1. I have decided upon the term **mode** as the most effective way of designating these aspects of language. I have followed the "philosophy" usage cited in *The Oxford English Dictionary*: "A manner or state of being of a thing; a thing considered as possessing certain attributes that do not belong to its essence, and may be changed without destroying its identity."

2. This ethological aspect of language is well represented in Harvey

Sarles (1977). Sarles advocates an ethology of human behaviour with language and communication as its focus. In one place he writes: "Observation of language should include what happens on the faces and in the bodies of the interactors. It is intriguing to note that bodily relations also shift when conversational topics shift from, say, the 'here and now' to a narrative" (211). This is no distance from the position of J.R.Firth, but Sarles goes further. We literally "read" each others' faces and bodies: "Interaction involves shared rhythms,... the heart or pulse rate is also susceptible of being shared, and... eye contact is sufficient to set up shared rhythmicity" (234).

3. First described in Benjamin Lee Whorf's paper "Grammatical Categories" in Whorf (1956, 87-101).

4. See Louis Hjelmslev (1953). Hjelmslev proposed a structure of language in which "expression" (or form) and "content" (sense, meaning) can be regarded as parallel planes, the modifications in one plane being reflected in the other, such that they could be accounted for and described systematically.

4. Communicating and Relating

1. J.R.Firth elaborates on this in his "Personality and Language in Society" (1957) and elsewhere.

2. Especially in (1962) *q.v.*

3. See the counter-argument raised by Roy Harris (1987, 148-52). Harris also discusses the scheme proposed in Searle (1969, 63).

4. See his articles published in *Glyph* (1977), reprinted in Derrida (1988).

5. A lucid interpretation of Derrida's *Glyph* articles can be found in Christopher Norris's "Deconstruction and 'Ordinary Language'," published in Birch (1985, 107-24).

6. See, for example, Berry (1969) which contains a readable, and probably not too dated, review of these processes.

7. This for example is Liberman's claim in Neisser (1967, 192).

8. The work of Eric Lenneberg, cited in Neisser (1967, 192).

9. Saville-Troike (1982, 40) goes on to explain how this was borne out by an investigation carried out through the Bureau of Indian Affairs, when parents were asked what sort of language they would teach their children. "Without exception, every parent responded that most important would be to ask and respond to questions about clan membership, since many children would encounter people from outside the family unit for the first time on school entry, and there could be serious social and religious consequences if they did not know how to behave properly" (p. 41).

10. See Emanuel Schegloff "Sequencing in Conversational Dialogue", in Gumperz and Hymes (1972, 372-3).

11. "To behave as a 'speaker' or 'hearer' when the other is not observably available is to subject oneself to a review of one's competence and 'normality'. Speakers without hearers can be seen to be 'talking to themselves'. Hearers without speakers 'hear voices'... Summons-answer sequences establish and align the roles of speaker and hearer, providing a summoner with evidence of the availability or unavailability of a hearer, and a prospective hearer with notice of a prospective speaker." Schegloff in Gumperz and Hymes (1972, 379).

12. See Charles Frake "How to Ask for a Drink in Subanun", in Giglioli (1972, 87ff.) "The strategy of drinking talk is to manipulate the assignment of role relations among participants so that, within the limits of one's external status attributes, one can maximize his share of encounter resources (drink and talk), thereby having an opportunity to assume an esteem-attracting and authority-wielding role... The Subanun drinking encounter thus provides a structured setting within which one's social relationships beyond his everyday associates can be extended, defined, and manipulated through the use of speech. The cultural patterning of drinking talk lays out an ordered scheme of role play, through terms of address, through discussion and argument, and through display of verbal art... In instructing our stranger to Subanun society to ask for a drink, we have at the same time instructed him how to get ahead socially" (*ibid.*, 91-93).

13. Ethel Albert: "Cultural Patterning of Speech in Burundi", in Gumperz and Hymes (1972, 74).

14. *Ibid.* (pp. 75 and 77).

15. Dell Hymes: "Ways of Speaking", in Bauman and Sherzer (1974, 442).

16. Roger Brown and Albert Gilman: "The Pronouns of Power and Solidarity", in Sebeok (1960, 262; 264-7).

17. "The apparent decline of expressive shifts between T and V is... difficult to interpret. Perhaps it because Europeans have seen that excluded persons or races or groups can become the target of extreme aggression from groups that are benevolent within themselves. Perhaps Europeans would like to convince themselves that the solidarity ethic once extended will not be withdrawn, that there is security in the mutual T "(*ibid.* p. 280).

18. See Paul Friedrich: "Social Context and Semantic Feature: The Russian Pronominal Usage", in Gumperz and Hymes (1972, 270ff.)

19. See Roger Brown and Marguerita Ford: "Address in American English", in Hymes (1964, 234ff.).

5. Semiotic Being

1. The first of Peirce's sign types – the *icon* – is said not to depend at all on the real existence of the object, for it to be able to signify. The example given is a pencil line representing a geometrical line, which is of course an imaginary construct. The icon, Peirce explains, is that which "excites analogous sensations in the mind for which it is a likeness" (1931-58, II, 168). This type of sign is thus closest to what most people mean by symbols, especially graphic symbols. Quite opposite in character is the second type – the *index* – which depends absolutely on its object, by virtue of its standing in relation to it: a symptom of a disease, for example, or a pattern of rock strata. The possibly even better known Saussurean concept of the sign is nearest to Peirce's third type: the *symbol*. The symbol is highly complex, and only incompletely within the grasp of our understanding. In one place, Peirce neatly characterizes the symbol as a sign (*representamen*) whose predominant feature consists in its being a rule that will determine its interpretant: a real enough entity, but only to the extent that existents will conform to it. Thus, for example, in the sentence *The table has collapsed* the noun subject can refer only to a level hard surface supported by uprights (or a single upright); it cannot refer to a tabulation, for instance. For someone who understands English and has heard well, Peirce's "dynamical interpretant" will be the actual effect this utterance has upon him, the totality and exact nature of this effect depending on its conjunction with other signs. Only with the symbol does habit or convention make its appearance, enabling the "rule" to be interpreted correctly. Even in a location in which tables are absent, or objects resembling tables, the effect of *The table has collapsed* will be no less felt, generating an appropriate interpretant; if not exactly the **same** interpretant to that which the recipient and interpreter of the message are accustomed. The complexity of the act of signification is well demonstrated by Peirce's own example: in *Ezekiel loveth Huldah*, both proper names Ezekiel and Huldah are indices; without them the statement would be devoid of reference. *Loveth* is a symbol. For its correct interpretation furthermore, the symbol needs to be represented in the mind of the interpreter as an icon: the image of a lover and beloved.

2. Binarism is the principle whereby two phenomena exist in collateral divergence, the one always accompanied by a manifestation, actual or implied, of the other.

3. See Barthes' essay "Myth Today" in (1972, 109-59, and in particular 114-5).

4. The most important of these is Nikolai Trubetskoy's monograph ([1949]1964).

5. See Jakobson, Fant and Halle (1952). Their work was further developed, but not fundamentally altered by Chomsky and Halle (1968).

6. The diagram below is taken from Jakobson, Fant and Halle's ground-breaking study (1952, 44). The phonemic transcription (American pronunciation) along the top row is of "Joe took father's shoe bench out". The bracketed signs in the columns represent redundant features:

	dʒ'o u	t' u k	f'a ə ð	ə z	ʃ' u u	b' e n tʃ	# 'au t
Vocalic	(-) + + (-) + (-)	(-)+ + (-) + (-)	(-) + +	(-) + (-)(-)		+ +(-)
Compact	+ + - (-) - +	(-)+ - (-) - (-)	+ - -	(-) + (-) +		+ - (-)
Grave	+ + - +	+ + + - + -	+ +	+ - -		+ + -
Nasal	(-) (-) (-)	(-) (-) (-) (-)		(-) + (-)		(-)
Tense	- + + +	- - +		- +	(-) +	
Optimal						
Constrictive	+ - - +	+ + +		- +		-
Stressed	+ - +	+ - -		+ -	+	+ -

7. In particular, William Labov's early studies, especially (1966, 1970 and 1972).

8. Not only the sensation of colour, but the "five senses" in general, are relatively recent in origin. At one time, "sense" meant only intelligence and ordinary common sense. The "five senses" meaning gained currency only in the late Renaissance, and even then, as C.S.Lewis (1961, 133) reminded us, the meaning belonged to the "bookish and abstract stratum of our vocabulary." By the time the meaning entered English it was already a scientific term. In the following century Locke ([1690], 1959) formulated a complete theory of sensation, at about the same time as Newton was expounding his "Optics" and the decomposition of light into the different wavelengths of the now classical colour spectrum.

9. See especially Goldstein (1948, 167-72).

10. This is incidentally borne out by the numerous place-names – especially in the names of hills, where in only a few instances could *Black* originally have signified "black".

11. See G. Lienhardt "Divinity and Experience: The Religion of the Dinka", in Douglas (1973, 65).

12. Interestingly, it appears that various other peoples of the Upper Nile, who are no longer dependent on cattle, retain and make use of a cattle-colour vocabulary.

13. Though it may be worth noting that colour terms are not a dominant feature of much literature. A preoccupation with varied shades of colour tends to occur in particular stylistic "periods" of a nation's literature.

14. Cited in Burnley (1976, 47)

15. "Nature is a temple, in which living pillars sometimes utter a babel of words, man traverses it through forests of symbols, that watch him with

knowing eyes." From the poem *Correspondances*. Prose trans. by F. Scarfe. *Baudelaire: Selected Verse*. (Harmondsworth: Penguin, 1961, 36)

6. Origins

1. From Blake's poem "Auguries of Innocence", in the "Pickering MS. (*ca.* 1800). *The Poems and Prophecies of William Blake*. London: Everyman (Dent) (1927,.337).

2. See (before proceeding, say, to Kathleen Coburn's *Collected Coleridge*) Owen Barfield's far from easy, but probably definitive, *What Coleridge Thought* (1971).

3. "All Religions are One" (1788). *The Poems and Prophecies of William Blake*. London: Everyman (Dent) (1927, 5)

4. Originally, Heidegger claimed (1959, 124ff.), *logos* signified gathering, bringing together, putting one thing together with another. Man, he went on to say, can be interpreted as both being, and the apprehension of being: infinite predication. Only through the category of the Word does anything come into being and **remain** in being. In very early times the *logos* principle appears to have set in train an independent philosophical tradition, known only from "pre-Socratic" fragments and citations in the work of the Classical philosophers. This tradition, poles apart from the "logic" of Aristotle, gathered momentum in the Neoplatonists, Plotinus especially, in whose work *logos* makes its appearance as the primary organ of sensation to which all the empirical senses are subordinate; culminating at last in Coleridge's Primary Imagination, "the living power and prime agent of all human perception." (1962).

5. See especially the first chapter of Barker (1985).

6. Sol Tax. "Primitive Man vs. *Homo sapiens*," in Montagu (1968, 83).

7. *Ibid.* p. 84: "Now extinct Tasmanian hunters and twentieth-century Englishmen are both equally characterized by living in self-identified communities with their different dialects, social structures, value systems."

8. The breakthrough came with the Gardners' now widely known work with a young chimpanzee Washoe (Alan and Beatrice Gardner. "Two-way communication with an infant chimpanzee," in Schreier and Stollnitz (1971).) The Gardners had suspected that earlier attempts to train chimpanzees to speak had failed on account of the erroneous assumption that vocalization was possible in a chimpanzee, and that perhaps sign language (American Sign Language) would be more appropriate in that chimpanzees obviously possess considerable gestural skill.

9. See Ward H. Goodenough: "Cultural Anthropology and Linguistics," in Hymes (1964, 36).

10. Stanley Diamond. "The Search for the Primitive," in Montagu (1968, 119).

11. *Ibid.* p. 127.

12. Bronislaw Malinowski. "The Problem of Meaning in Primitive Languages," in Ogden and Richards (1949, 316).

13. See Nikolaas Tinbergen (1989) for a definitive, as well as masterly, study of the complexity of instinctual behaviour over a wide range of species.

7. Words, People and Things

1. It was from Bacon's time onwards that logic and language appear to have parted company. Berkeley, a century later, is arguing for the need to be delivered from the deception of words. He compares verbal controversies to "weeds" that have sprung up in almost all the sciences: "a main hindrance to the growth of true and sound knowledge...We need only to draw the **curtain of words,**" said Berkeley, "to behold the fairest tree of knowledge." (My emphasis) (1910, 110).

2. Especially Barfield (1988).

3. I quote from Erwin Schrödinger, never a lone voice: "What we in our minds construct ourselves cannot, so I feel, have dictatorial power over our mind... But some of you, I am sure, will call this mysticism... We may, or so I believe, assert that physical theory in its present stage strongly suggests the indestructibility of Mind by Time" (1959, 87).

4. One is reminded of Alyosha Karamazov's personal discovery (in Dostoevsky's *The Brothers Karamazov,* Part III, Chapter 4, "Cana of Galilee").

5. See André Leroi-Gourhan (1964) who has put forward the view, well documented, that this early linear writing constitutes a highly developed ideography: "La main devenait ainsi créatrice d'images, de symboles non directement dépendants du déroulement du langage verbal, mais réellement parallèles. C'est dans cette étape que se constitue un langage que j'ai nommé, faute de mieux, 'mythographique' parce que la nature des associations mentales qu'il suscite est d'un ordre parallèle à celui du mythe verbal, étranger à une spécification rigoureuse des coordonnées spatio-temporelles" (1964, I, 290).

6. See Catherine H. Berndt: "The concept of primitive," in Montagu (1968, 17).

7. See Stanley Diamond: "The search for the primitive," in Montagu (1968, 113).

8. William Golding's *The Inheritors* is a convincing attempt to recreate the "languages" of two tribes, the one archaic by comparison with the other.

9. See Malcolm Crick (1976, 101).

10. *Mana* was originally a Polynesian (Maori) word.

11. "Its fundamental conception is identical with that of modern science; underlying the whole system is a faith, implicit but real and firm, in the order and uniformity of nature. The magician does not doubt that the same causes will always produce the same effects, that the performance of the proper ceremony, accompanied by the appropriate spell, will inevitably be attended by the desired result... Thus the analogy between the magical and scientific conceptions of the world is close. In both of them the succession of events is assumed to be perfectly regular and certain, being determined by immutable laws the operation of which can be foreseen and calculated precisely..." (p.49)

12. See Lévy-Bruhl ([1923]1965) and ([1927]1965); also (1949). Unhappily, Lévy-Bruhl's use of concepts such as "prelogical mentality" and "mystical participation" won him academic disfavour, by now however partly dispelled.

13. R.L.Sharp: "Notes on Northeast Australian totemism," in Coon and Andrews (1943,69).

14. R. Bulmer: "Why is a cassowary not a bird? A problem of zoological taxonomy among the Karam of the New Guinea Highlands," in Douglas (1973, 168-9).

15. S.J. Tambiah: "Animals are good to think and good to prohibit", in Douglas (1973, 163-5).

16. David Nash: "Linguistics and Land Rights in the Northern Territory," in McKay and Sommer (1984, 34-46).

17. See Berndt (1974, 8). Berndt describes the Dreaming as "a mythological and sacred time existing alongside secular time but not identical with it," and marking the paths along which mythic beings moved across the land, and across linguistically defined territories, leaving tangible expressions of their spiritual essence, in the form of a rocky outcrop, a waterhole, a tree, or an ochre deposit. See also the late Bruce Chatwin's *Songlines* (1987), written for a more popular readership.

18. Harry Hoijer (1951); reprinted in Hymes (1964, 146).

12. What is Meaning?

1. See their *The Meaning of Meaning* (1949, 186-7). The authors identify no less than twenty-two different meanings of "meaning".

2. See for example Louis Hjelmslev's version of "glossematics" which could be considered the ultimate in content-expression dualism (1961). Stephen Ullmann (1962, 56-7) proposes "a reciprocal and reversible relationship between sound and sense." This, Ullmann believes, is the "meaning" of a word. Challenged by a pre-publication reader to provide an example I reached, at random, for the formal-semantic contrast "down" /"up"

"Down" can of course be expressed by other terms such as *low* or *bottom* as well as by *down*, and "up" by *top* as well as *up*, and this fits satisfactorily with "reciprocal dualism". But soon the anomalies became apparent: *downland* is a kind of "upland", and *lowdown* is not a member of any formal/semantic pair.

3. Even in these enlightened days, language textbooks teem with semantically void sentences, which are not significant improvements upon specimens of the "la plume de ma tante..." type.

4. "The child who has learnt how to mean has taken the essential step towards the sharing of meaning, which is the distinct characteristic of social man in his mature state" (Halliday 1975, 36). This contrasts quite markedly with the approach of Chomsky where meaning is already (inchoately) known by the infant.

5. Barfield (1933, 137-8) claims there are more new words in Shakespeare's plays than in all the rest of the English poets put together: "Where the word which he employs is a new one, it has usually become so common in the course of years that we find it hard to conceive of a time when it was not."

6. See also Bakhtin (1973).

7. Colwyn Trevarthen: "Sharing Makes Sense: Intersubjectivity and the Making of an Infant's Meaning," in Steele and Threadgold (1987, 177-99).

8. "Even at two months an infant can act to regulate an exchange of states of conscious interest, and to do so the mind of an infant selects as "object" the mother's expressive face and voice, reacting to her eyes as windows of her interest. At the same time, the infant makes forms of expression that represent rudiments of verbal utterance, accompanied by gestural expressions of the hands that have the potentiality to link interests of the two subjects in the context of the reality they share." (ibid. p.179)

9. See Ransom ([1941]1979, 299): "indeterminate meaning [is] that part of the final meaning which took shape not according to its own logical necessity but under metrical compulsion; it may be represented by the poem's residue of meaning which does not go into the logical paraphrase."

10. It has been reported to me by one of his acquaintances, I do not know how reliably, that Boris Pasternak (himself a distinguished translator of Shakespeare) found the imprint of Shakespeare even in the Russian language.

9. Meaning and Symbol

1. My friend Charles Barham reports that, as a small child, he could not see rainbows (a not rare occurrence); but also that, even when taken to the zoo, he could not see elephants.

2. The confusion sometimes caused by the alternate use of "sign" and "symbol" has been recently surveyed by W. Terrence Gordon in "The Semiotics of C.K.Ogden," in Sebeok and Umiker (1990-91, 34ff.)

3. Jean Paul Russo (1989), cited in W. Terrence Gordon (See note 1, above), p.45: "Instead of one or even a dozen meanings, numberless shades of meaning fall across the spectrum of a word. Or perhaps it is better to withhold the idea of a word's meaning and say only that context has meaning."

4. The following diagram is taken from Ogden and Richards (1949, 11):

THOUGHT OR REFERENCE

CORRECT
(symbolizes a causal
relation)

ADEQUATE
(Refers to other causal
relations)

SYMBOL   (stands for an   REFERENT
                imputed relation)

TRUE

5. See Umberto Eco:: "A Logic of Culture" in Sebeok (1975, 16). See also Cesare Segre (1973, 31-2) on what he has called "unlimited semiosis": "We are in danger of smothering the real signs and symbols of our living world."

6. Cited in Eco (1976, 49ff.).

7. See Eco (1976, 125): "A code is commonly supposed to render the elements of two systems equivalent, term by term. But the study of semantic fields shows that (when speaking for instance of a 'language' as a code) it is necessary to consider a vast series of partial content systems (or fields) which are matched in different ways with the expressive units."

8. The word *code* has a long history, traceable to the beginnings of Roman Law. Only gradually did the word come to signify a system of rules, and only in the early years of the nineteenth century did it acquire the sense of a "system of signals" or cypher, until recent times its dominant meaning. *Code* has been ostensibly affected by morphosemantic (rhyming) contagion from other words of similar form. There is almost certainly contagion from *node*, something from *mode* and probably not a little from *electrode*.

9. See Alvin M. Liberman *et al*: "Language Codes and Memory Codes," in Melton and Martin (1972, 310).

10. A Manner of Speaking

1. See for example Keller (1994).

2. "All the artificial and figurative application of words eloquence hath invented, are for nothing else but to insinuate wrong ideas, move the passions, and thereby mislead the judgment; and so indeed are perfect cheats... they are certainly, in all discourses that pretend to inform or instruct, wholly to be avoided" (Locke [1690]1959, II, 146.)

3. Donald Davidson: "What Metaphors Mean," in Sacks (1979, 30).

4. "Order itself proceeds from the metaphorical constitution of semantic fields" (Ricoeur 1975, 22-3).

5. "No speaker ever completely exhausts the connotative possibilities of his words."

6. "A semantic motivation without status in the language as something already established with respect to either designation or connotation" (Ricoeur 1975, 98).

7. Willard V. Quine: "Afterthoughts on Metaphor (1): A Postscript on Metaphor," in Sacks (1979, 159). An impression that could remain with one after reading a recent survey appraisal of quantum theory (see John Gribbin *Schrödinger's Kittens.* London: Weidenfeld and Nicholson, 1995) might be that the whole of this sophisticated apparatus of knowledge, testable by experiment at every juncture notwithstanding, is about to dissolve into analogy and metaphor. Gribbin quotes a respectable physicist, who has claimed that rival interpretations of quantum theory are "like literary fiction in that they are free inventions of the human mind. In theoretical physics sometimes the inventor knows from the beginning that the work is fiction... When being serious... the theoretical physicist differs from the novelist in thinking that maybe the story might be true."

8. Nelson Goodman, cited in Ricoeur (1975, 233).

9. See note 7 above, (Quine, in Sacks 1979, 160).

10. Stephen Ullmann (1962, 179). But the matter is not quite so straightforward. Before dismissing a sentence like "This door is a door" as an obvious case of redundancy, we should consider the possibility that the second occurrence of "door" may be given the kind of spoken emphasis which would convert the sense into: "This door is a real door".

11. See Roman Jakobson: "Marginal Notes on the Prose of the Poet Pasternak," in Davie and Livingstone (1969, 145).

12. From Boris Pasternak's autobiographical *Safe Conduct*, in Pasternak (1959, 93).

13. See Note 11 above, (Jakobson, in Davie and Livingstone 1969, 141).

14. Jakobson, in Davie and Livingstone (1969, 141)..

11. Word, Meaning and Context

1. "It is the phenomenon which is characteristic of this language-game that in **this** situation we use this expression: we say we pronounced the word with **this** meaning and take this expression over from that other language-game" (Wittgenstein 1963, 216) (His emphasis).

2. "The meaning of a word is not the experience one has in hearing or saying it, and the sense of a sentence is not a complex of such experiences... The sentence is composed of the words, and that is enough" (Wittgenstein 1963, 182).

3. See P.F.Strawson: "On Referring," in Flew (1981, 32): "We are apt to fancy we are talking about sentences and expressions when we are talking about the uses of sentences and expressions... People use expressions to refer to particular things. But the meaning of an expression is not the set of things or the single thing it may correctly be used to refer to: the meaning is the set of rules, habits, conventions for its use in referring."

4. Gilbert Ryle: "The Theory of Meaning," in Mace (1957, 254ff.)

5. G. Ryle and J.N.Findlay: "Use, Usage and Meaning," in Zabeeh *et al.* (1974, 484). A distinction, Ryle argues, has to be maintained between linguistic problems that are philosophical problems and linguistic problems that belong to philology, grammar, rhetoric and so forth, since the former are strictly about the logic of the functioning of expressions. The present book should show that such a distinction is illusory.

6. "What a word means is the missing parts of the context from which it draws its delegated efficacy".

7. Firth willingly put his "operational linguistics", as he was tempted to call it, to good use during the Second World War as a consultant to the Air Ministry, when he studied the Japanese in the "limited situational contexts of war".

8. A sentence such as *I have not seen your father's pen, but I have read the book of your uncle's gardener* along with many thousands of like specimens would never find a use in real life (1957, 24). It is not that such sentences are ruled out as impossible but that they would never occur in a real-life situation.

9. In linguistics, and especially in British linguistics, the Firthian view has been influential, but not as influential as it might have been. Outside linguistics Firth's influence has been slight. Perhaps the time was, and still is, not ripe for the total approach Firth advocated. As Lyons (1969, 51) has put it: "Since no satisfactory formal theory of meaning has yet been proposed by anyone, the semanticist cannot afford to discount the insights and suggestions of someone like Firth."

10. Wittgenstein did however qualify his remark, claiming that this "definition" of "meaning" applies only to a "large class of cases" (1963, 20).

11. For a discussion of this and germane problems see Donald Davidson (1967, 304-325). In this frequently quoted paper Davidson, although he does not reach any definite conclusions, starts from the position that "a satisfactory theory of meaning must give an account of how the meanings of sentences depend upon the meanings of words" (p.304) and in a brief space reviews the problems facing the philosopher of language in this regard.

12. "In grasping a sense, one is not certainly assured of a reference" ([1892]1974, 58).

13. "By combining subject and predicate, one reaches only a thought. One never passes from sense to reference, never from a thought to its truth value. One moves at the same level but never advances from one level to the next. A truth value cannot be part of a thought, any more than, say, the sun can, for it is not a sense but an object"([1892] 1974, 64).

14. "All these completely new qualities and peculiarities belong not to the sentence that has become a whole utterance, but precisely to the utterance itself. They reflect the nature of the utterance, not the nature of the sentence" (1986, 74).

15. Richard Rorty (1979, 266) raises a similar point: "Was Aristotle wrong about motion being divided into natural and forced? Or was he talking about something different from what we talk about when we talk about motion? Did Newton give the right answers to which Aristotle had given wrong answers? Or were they asking different questions?"

16. "The world of objects that science knows, and from which it derives its own objectivity, is one of the relativities embraced by language's relation to the world. In it the concept of 'being-in-itself' acquires the character of a **determination of the will**. What exists in itself is independent of one's own willing and imagining. But in being known as being-in-itself, it is put at one's disposal in the sense that one can reckon with it – *i.e.* use it for one's own purposes" (Gadamer 1991, 450) (His emphasis).

17. See Lyons (1977, 204): "By analyzing or describing the sense of a word is to be understood its analysis in terms of the sense-relations it contracts with other words."

18. Roger Brown: "Languages and Categories," in Jerome S.Bruner (1956, 304).

12. Speaking and Writing

1. Dennis Tedlock's study (1983) and the more recent Glasgow Conference on the "Linguistics of Writing" (1987) have been significant milestones.

2. *Memoirs from a Dark Cellar* [1864] in Dostoevsky. *A Gentle Creature and Other Stories*. Trans. by D. Magarshack. London: Lehmann (1950).

3. Susan Peterson. *Lucy M.Lewis, American Indian Potter* Tokyo: Kodansha (1984, 44-5).

4. These songs and their "songlines" are well reported in the work of T.G.H.Strehlow (1971), and have been thrown into more dramatic relief in the late Bruce Chatwin's *The Songlines*. Harmondsworth: Penguin (1987).

5. "In the eyes of the natives these verses were magically efficacious because they had been composed and first put to ceremonial use by their own all-powerful totemic ancestors, who had passed them on to later human beings of their own totem" (Strehlow 1971, 244).

6. Schmandt-Besserat's work based on early pottery artefacts from the Near East used in accounting came to be generally known through her article in *Scientific American* (1978). There is also a brief account of her work in Coulmas (1989).

7. See the discussion in Manfred Bierwisch (1972)

8. M.A.K. Halliday, in Fabb *et al.* (1987, 148).

9. A logographic system of writing consisted of written "characters" or "hieroglyphs" that were either iconic ("pictograms") or symbolic ("ideograms"). The former were in their more archaic forms representations of object, which in later times is stylized (*e.g.* Archaic Chinese 𝕛 ,Modern Standard Chinese 日). Ideograms were abstract representations. In Chinese for example "east" was represented by 東 and "west" by 西 . By combining these two ideograms a further ideogram 東西 meaning "thing" was produced. A logographic system is most often made up of a "semantic" and a "phonetic" component. In Chinese the latter is nearly always in the right-hand segment of the character. The character "door""gate" 門 is pictographic in origin. But its pronunciation can be extended by means of rhyme or (less commonly) alliteration to create other words; and in combination with a different radical 悶 can give a different meaning "boredom" (in this instance the semantic radical "heart" is at the bottom, enclosed by a gate), resulting in very significant semiotic economy.

10. For a readable and informative introduction to the Phoenicians and alphabetic writing see Kristeva (1989, 93-7).

11. Jonathan Culler in Fabb *et al.* (1987, 174-5): "We are likely to go astray if we assume that the linguistics we have is a linguistics of speech and that the corrective to it would be a linguistics that took writing seriously. Certain aspects of writing – specifically writing as manifestation of an ideal, iterable linguistic object – have determined the linguistics which presents itself as a linguistics of speech; in relation to this linguistics, attention to the materiality of speech itself could be quite disruptive. A linguistics which sought to address all the contours of hesitation and of emphasis, the tones of voice that function as modal operators to indicate degrees of assurance,

aggressiveness, modesty, and so on, as well as the dialectal variations of speech that carry social information, would be distinctly more complicated than one which sought above all to assign the correct grammatical descriptions to sentences regarded as ideal objects."

12. J.R.Firth used this term to establish a distinction between it and the wider phenomenon of the speech community. A speech fellowship is described as "the speech of those whose sounds, intonation, grammar, idiom and usage are similar in structure and have similar function is a bond of fellowship based on the sharing of a truly common experience" (1957, 186).

13. This has recently been confirmed in a direct communication by Alain Peyraube.

14. M.A.K. Halliday, in Fabb *et al.* (1987, 148-9).

13. The Book

1. Roland Barthes: "To Write: An Intransitive Verb" in Macksey and Donato (1972, 140).

2. See Wellek and Warren (1976, 146): "Every experience of a poem... both leaves out something or adds something individual. The experience will never be commensurate with the poem: even a good reader will discover new details in poems which he had not experienced during previous readings, and it is needless to point out how distorted or shallow may be the reading of a less trained or untrained reader."

3. Barthes, influenced by Chomsky's linguistic theory, further speculated about the existence of a "literary faculty" in human beings, having nothing to do with genius, inspiration, or other mysterious imponderables, but with rules operating below the author's threshold of awareness. For a critical review of this approach see my paper "Linguistic Analogies" in Abbas and Wong (1981, 137-52).

4. M.A.K. Halliday: "Linguistic Function and Literary Style: An Inquiry into the Language of William Golding's *The Inheritors*", in Chatman (1971, 334).

5. J. R.Searle: The Logical Status of Fictional Discourse", in French *et al.* (1979, 241).

6. Searle, in French et al. (1979, 242).

7. "How to Do Things with Austin and Searle", in Fish (1980, 244-5)

14. Language in Literature

1. William Righter (1975, 87-8) puts it as follows: "Whatever form of

enquiry we undertake it is language which is primary and not the world which it describes – because we see things through it, it determines the nature of what we see. We can change the nature of our categories, our ways of organizing what we do with language, but we cannot escape it or the fact of seeing by means of it... Scientific hypotheses, logical and mathematical meta-languages, the explanations of historians, the concepts of Freudian psychology, the descriptions of novelists are all "fictions", constructions of the human intellect and imagination which we may put to the particular purposes for which they were designed."

    2. Jan Mukařovský: "Standard Language and Poetic Language"[1932], in Garvin (1964, 17ff.).

    3. Mukařovský, in Garvin (1964, 18)

    4. This calls to mind Virginia Woolf's essay "The Russian Point of View" in her *The Common Reader* (Harmondsworth: Penguin, 1938, 172-81).

    5. Paul Ricoeur: "What is a Text? Explanation and Interpretation", in Rasmussen (1971, 145).

    6. Several isolated examples are selected from writers as various as Milton, Browne, Donne and Pater, but Fish's argument that the separate praxis of these samples depends on what the reader makes of them, how the reader reacts to them, might have appeared less convincing if the samples had been given along with contexts in which they occur.

    7. It is only fair to mention that this material is not representative of the more recent work of Fish.

    8. The *I Ching* or *Book of Changes*. Translated into German by Richard Wilhelm and thence into English (London: Routledge and Kegan Paul, 1951). The *Book of Changes,* whether by chance or because of the awe it inspired, is the only one of the classics to have survived the "burning of the books" by the first emperor of Chin during the second century before our era (the remaining early literature had to be reconstructed from memory). Nowadays the *I Ching* tends to be dismissed as mumbo-jumbo, and Chinese fortune-telling has become a further debasement of it. The book would hardly have become known in the West had it not found favour among a "cult readership" during the nineteen-sixties and seventies.

    9. Wallace Stevens: *A Primitive like an Orb* (1964, 441)

    10. Wallace Stevens: *An Ordinary Evening in New Haven* (1964, 474).

15. Style and Being

    1. A selection of his more important writings is included in Garvin (1964).

    2. "Charles Baudelaire's *Les Chats*", reprinted in Lane (1970, 202ff.).

3. I am using "relevance" in Halliday's sense: "the notion that a linguistic feature 'belongs' in some way as part of the whole". See his "Linguistic Function and Literary Style: An Inquiry into the Language of William Golding's *The Inheritors*", in Chatman (1971, 359).

4. An unpublished analysis of a poem by Ella Wheeler Wilcox, presented by myself with tongue in cheek some years ago at a seminar. A prominent obituary notice in *The Times* (31 October 1919) describes the lady as "the most popular poet of either sex and of any age, read by thousands who never open Shakespeare." The poem itself is to be found in Richards (1926, 200-1).

5. Halliday, in Chatman (1971).

6. Halliday defines transitivity in a broader manner than would most linguists: "The set of options whereby the speaker encodes his experience of the processes of the external world of his own consciousness, together with the participants in these processes and their attendant circumstances" (Chatman 1971, 359).

7. Halliday, however, does not consider linguistics to be the whole of literary analysis, and believes the extent of the part played by linguistics in literary analysis can in the last resort only be determined by the student of literature, even though he adds the qualification that "a work of literature is meaningful only in the perspective of the whole range of uses of language" (Chatman 1971, 332).

8. In reference to Dolezel's "A Framework for the Statistical Analysis of Style", in Dolezel and Bailey (1969).

9. Aleksey Kruchenykh. *Selected Works* (in Russian) (Munich: Fink Verlag, 1973, 283ff.).

10. A re-expressed version of parts of my essay "Stylistics and Personality", in Lord (1970).

11. See my essay on and translation of the "Petersburg" version of *Stavrogin's Confession*, in Lord (1970, 102-7). The translation is mine, but it contains slight alterations.

16. The Word as Artefact

1. Until the seventeenth century, dictionaries were no more than glossaries. Mostly they took the form of interlinear glosses or, less commonly, bilingual listings for practical convenience of common words. The monolingual dictionary is relatively recent in origin. And it is a curious fact that the first such dictionary in English was published as late as the end of Shakespeare's lifetime. Cawdrey's *Table Alphabeticall* of 1604 was the first of a long series of such dictionaries, culminating in the eighteenth

century in Scott-Bailey's *New Universal Etymological Dictionary* and then in Dr. Johnson's *Dictionary of the English Language.*

2. Cited in Ullmann (1957, 223).

3. The citations from Eliot are from the poem *East Coker* in his *Four Quartets* (See *The Complete Poems and Plays of T.S.Eliot.* London: Faber and Faber, 1970, 177ff). The quotation from Longinus is from his *On the Sublime,* in T.S.Dorsch (ed.). *Classical Literary Criticism* (Harmondsworth: Penguin, 1965, 153).

4. Benveniste uses the term *merism* for the lowest hierarchical level (1971, 106).

5. An example of such a solution is the "lexeme". "Emic" solutions have played a formative role in structural linguistics. The main difficulty with the lexeme however is that, unlike other structural elements, it leads a shadowy non-empirical existence, its substance depending solely on its appearance-saving efficacy. The lexeme has been defined as the fundamental unit of the lexicon. As such a unit, the lexeme has been said to underlie all the different semantically and formally related variants (word-forms) that occur within a single word class. It has been proposed for example that *strong, strongly,* and *strength* are different (word-form) manifestations of a hypothetical lexeme STRONG.

6. My own surname for example, which in common with most other English surnames is opaque (having nothing to do with any aristocracy), becomes in Chinese: *luo* "gathering, spreading" + *de* "virtue, goodness".

7. Ernst Gombrich uses as illustrations, and discusses, two "different" photographs of Wivenhoe Park, Essex (Constable painted an earlier version of the same view) developed from the same negative (1977, 30).

8. Gombrich (1977, 277) in a reference to the work of the psychologist J.J.Gibson ("The visual field and the visual world", *Psychological Review* **59**: 148-51, 1951).

9. Cited in Gombrich (1977, 246).

10. See *Collins COBUILD* [Birmingham University International Language Database] *English Language Dictionary* (London: Collins, 1987, 404). The same dictionary however does cite the more traditional meaning.

11. The prefixes *in-* and *un-* are both negating prefixes in English and no doubt this has been an inherent weakness in the lexical item *uninterested.* It is an admittedly awkward term.

17. Words in Relation

1. Saussure, F. de. ([1915]1960, 123): "In discourse... words acquire relations based on the linear nature of language because they are chained

together. This rules out the possibility of pronouncing two elements simultaneously.

2. Saussure, F.de. ([1915]1960, 123): "Outside discourse... words acquire relations of a different kind. Those that have something in common are associated in the memory, resulting in groups marked by diverse relations."

3. Roman Jakobson: "Towards a Linguistic Typology of Aphasic Impairments", in Reuck and O'Connor (1964, 21ff.). See also Lesser (1978, 41-5).

4. Beatrice Warren: "Types, Distribution and Functions of Covert Semantic Relations in Complex Lexical Items and in Combinations of Lexical Items", in Hoppenbrouwers (1985, 55-62).

5. For "code-switching" see especially the extensive empirical investigations carried out in the 1960s and 1970s by William Labov (1966, 1972, and others), Peter Trudgill (1974, 1978), John Gumperz (in Gumperz and Hymes1964, and in Gumperz and Hymes 1971, and elsewhere), and other investigators.

6. The latter "feels" wrong. *Likes* in *likes and dislikes* is a unique idiomatic occurrence, a kind of back-formation, and hence provides no support for the noun *like* in the singular and in this particular sense.

7. A word class consists of all the forms belonging to a particular "part of speech". In English, for example, all nouns belong to a noun, or nominal, word class.

8. Cruse (1986, 278-85). Cruse has identified these restrictions as *selectional* and *collocational* restrictions, respectively. Selectional restrictions are those which have to do with the requirements of semantic co-occurrence as well as of truth-conditions.

9. The *Oxford Dictionary of Current Idiomatic English* (Cowie *et al.* (eds.). Oxford: Oxford University Press, 2 vols., 1983) confines itself to the indication that the sense "die" is informal, using illustrations from texts.

10. A typology has been proposed by Cruse (1986, 265ff.).

11. David Wiggins: "On Sentence-sense, Word-sense and Difference of Word-sense: Towards a Philosophical Theory of Dictionaries", in Steinberg and Jakobovits (1971, 14). Wiggins adds: "The practice and whole methodology of the relevant parts of linguistics are at present in too provisional and uncertain a stage of development."

12. Paul Ricoeur: "What is a Text? Explanation and Interpretation", in Rasmussen (1971, 44).

13. See Lord and Chang (1992, 349ff.).

14. It is known from studies in speech pathology that the brain does not treat words in the ways described (?prescribed) by much of modern linguistics. Indeed, there exists a certain amount of evidence that word categories can be separately disrupted by cerebral lesions. It appears that parts of the body, objects in a room, colours, and other aspects of a patient's

surroundings may possess independent neuropsychological status in the internal lexicon (See Geschwind 1973, 97ff.).

15. M.A.K. Halliday, in Halliday and McIntosh (1966, 19).

16. Angus McIntosh: "Patterns and Ranges", in Halliday and McIntosh (1966, 192).

17. McIntosh, in Halliday and McIntosh (1966, 189).

18. William Empson (1951, 34-5): "The emotion in a word, as I am treating it, is an extremely public object, practically as much as the Sense; there is a presumption that anybody would feel it under the circumstances, rather than that the speaker feels it...[The emotions of words] are comparatively permanent and simple, and they are used in building structures more elaborate and changeable than themselves. Normally they are dependent on a Sense which is believed to deserve them, and when they are detached from it the process is fairly easily recognised as some kind of playing or cheating."

19. Bloomfield used the term "**head** meaning" to distinguish between main and subsidiary senses while Cruse (1986, 49) has favoured a division into "primary" and "secondary".

18. The Lexicon

1. Uriel Weinreich: "Explorations in Semantic Theory", in Sebeok (1966, 443).

2. Chomsky (1965, 1965) characterizes the lexicon as "an unordered list of all formatives".

3. H.A.Gleason: "The Relation of Lexicon and Grammar", in Householder and Saporta (1967, 86).

4. Uriel Weinreich:"Lexicographic Definition in Descriptive Linguistics", in Householder and Saporta (1967, 26).

5. *The Shorter Oxford English Dictionary* (Oxford: Oxford University Press, 3rd. Edn. 1973, 91)

6. See David Wiggins: "On Sentence-sense, Word Sense and Difference of Word-sense: Towards a Philosophical Theory of Dictionaries", in Steinberg and Jakobovits (1971, 25).

7. See J.L. Austin: "The Meaning of a Word" in Urmson and Warnock (1970, 56); and Willard V. Quine: "Russell's Ontological Argument" in Schoenman (1967, 306): "The unit of communication is the sentence and not the word. This point of semantical theory was long obscured by the undeniable primacy, in one respect, of words. Sentences being limitless in number and words limited, we necessarily understand most sentences by

construction from antecendently familiar words. Actually there is no conflict here...we can say that knowing words is knowing how to work out the meanings of sentences containing them."

8. Uriel Weinreich, in Sebeok (1966, 450).

9. See for example P.H. Matthews (1974).

10. The tradition in China known as *sheng-xun* "etymological investigation through the study of sound" goes back at least to the 2nd. century A.D. when Liu Xi compiled a dictionary of etymology (*Shi Ming*) using the *sheng-xun* technique. Although most research in this area stopped in the Tang Dynasty, various more recent scholars have further developed the theory. Shen Jian-si (1894-1947) for example recognized that rhyming words may fall into more than one semantic category. The theory had some influence On Karlgren's *Word Families in Chinese* (1933). For further information see Lord and Chang (1987, 152-5).

11. As reported in Lord and Chang (1991).

12. Componential analysis has two different origins: one in linguistics, the second in anthropology. The former developed out of interest in semantic distinctive features (See Jakobson, 1971 and Hjelmslev,1961). See for example Greimas (1966), Katz and Fodor (1964) (but see also Bierwisch's (1969) critique as well as Bolinger's (1965) criticism, in a more satirical vein), and McCawley (1971). Perhaps the most elegant study is that of Pottier (1965) starting out from the French word *fauteuil*. Anthropological interest in semantic distinctive features originated in the investigation of tribal kinship systems. See in particular Goodenough (1956) and Lounsbury (1956), who pinpointed what he considered to be "those features of meanings or of situations, real or imported, of which the structure and usage of a language force recognition" – in his view "the distinctive features of meaning" (1956, 159).

13. In the tradition of Leibnitz's *Lingua Characteristica Universalis* Wierzbicka, by a stringent reduction, has concluded that the fundamental conceptual components – semantic "primitives" – in language which attain universality are no more than thirteen in number.

14. With subtlety and sensitivity to meaning in language Wierzbicka has pointed up the weaknesses of componential analyses based on syntactic or simplistic notions of the lexicon and not on the immanent character of words. But unfortunately the semantic primitives she has proposed do not touch the lexicon either inasmuch as they have to do only with the ways words behave in sentences.

15. The notion of semantic field was first systematically applied by Jost Trier, a German philologist ([1931], 1973; and 1934). Trier was fascinated by the way in which words fit together in mosaic-like patterns "each with different contours and in such a way that the contours fit" together within a single conceptual unity. If the semantic field is a reality it is a semiotic one.

16. "The decision as to what to put in each place also depends on the possibility of putting a different element there instead, so that each choice which is made will involve a complete reorganization of the structure, which will never be the same as one vaguely imagined nor as some other which might have been preferred to it" (1966, 19).

17. See for example Lehrer's approach to the semantic field embracing *hot* and *cold*, and terms relative to these (*warm, cool, lukewarm, burning, icy, frigid*, etc.) (1974, 110-1).

19. Words in Time

1. See Chomsky (1968, 36).

2. *Munt(e)* occurs mainly in the early part of the 13th century and in place-names (Mounts Olivet and Calvary). *Montaigne(s)* is the standard term by the time of Chaucer (latter part of the 14th century). The word occurs at least three times in The Monk's Tale, once with the accent on the first syllable, the other times with the accent of the second syllable (both occurrences are in rhyming endings).

3. Readers may wonder what has happened in my scheme to *fountain* (also from Old French), which of course rhymes completely with *mountain* except for the initial consonant (*fount* is a much later back-formation). The honest answer would be that, without a complete analysis being made of this morphosemantic region of the lexicon, one can only guess. *Fountain* may be found to be associated, but in an antonymic sense, with a final MSC which includes *mountain*. A fountain is of course as insubstantial as a mountain is solid and permanent.

4. All the following forms: (Greek) *lúkos* (Sanskrit) *vŕka-*, (Old Norse) *ulfr*, (Lat.) *lupus*, (Old English) *wulf* are derived by inference from the unlikely hypothetical **wl̥kʷos*.

5. Pierre Guiraud (1956), and Gordon (1982, 153).

6. C.S.Lewis (1960).

7. This latter option was passed over by William Tyndale in his Bible translation, when he translated the Greek *agapē* directly as *love*. (For this and a few comparable translatorial misdemeanours Tyndale was reviled by prominent fellow countrymen, and eventually a case was made against him while living abroad which led to his demise at the stake.[7]) See David Daniell: *William Tyndale: A Biography* (New Haven: Yale University Press, 1994).

8. *Outland*, a truly English word, has long since become a literary archaism; *outlander* had to be modelled on Dutch; and *outlandish* became semantically unrelated in Shakespeare's day.

9. It has been argued that English and French are so closely interrelated as to be dialects of a separate language (See Orr 1953).

10. See for example M.B.Emeneau:*India as a Linguistic Area* (University of California Publications in Linguistics 27. Berkeley: University of California Press, 1962), and John J. Gumperz: "Types of Linguistic Communities" and "Convergence and Creolization: A Case from the Indo-Aryan Dravidian Border in India", both articles reprinted in Gumperz (1971).

11. This can only partly be ascribed to social class differences. Poets of the stature of Chaucer or Shakespeare had key roles to play, not to mention Tyndale the great Bible translator.

12. The word *alien* – ironically itself a term of "alien" (Old French) origin – acquired its modern xenophobic meaning, interestingly enough, only towards the end of the seventeenth century (the word took on its secondary sense "repugnant" around 1720).

13. See for example Gorog (1981), and Witkowski *et al.* (1981).

12. On Being Human

1. It is clear from Aristotle's *De Anima* [*On the Soul*] that the question had preoccupied the Greeks since earliest Pre-Socratic times.

2. See R. McKeon (ed.). The Basic Works of Aristotle (New York: Random House, 1941, 546.)

3. "The roots and the developmental course of the intellect differ from those of speech – initially thought is nonverbal and speech nonintellectual... It is clear that ontogenetically thought and speech develop along separate lines and that at a certain point these lines meet" ([1934] 1962, 49-50).

Bibliography

Abbas, M.A. and Wong, T.-W. 1981. *Literary Theory Today.* Hong Kong: Hong Kong University Press.

Austin, J.L. 1962. *How to Do Things with Words.* London: Oxford University Press.

Bacon, F. [1606] 1876. *The Physical and Metaphysical Works of Lord Bacon.* Ed. by J. Devey. London: Bohn.

Bakhtin, M. M. [1929]1973. *The Problems of Dostoevsky's Poetics.* Trans. R.W.Rotsel. Ardis.

Bakhtin, M. M. 1981. *The Dialogic Imagination: Four Essays by M.M.Bakhtin.* Ed. by M. Holquist and trans. by C. Emerson and M. Holquist. Austin: University of Texas Press.

Bakhtin, M. M. 1986. *Speech Genres and Other Late Essays.* Ed. by M. Holquist and C. Emerson and trans. by V.W.McGee. Austin: University of Texas Press.

Barfield, O. 1933. *History in English Words.* 2nd edn.. London: Methuen.

Barfield, O. 1952 *Poetic Diction.* 2nd. edn. London: Faber and Faber.

Barfield, O. [1959]1988. *Saving the Appearances: A Study in Idolatry.* Middletown: Wesleyan University Press.

Barfield, O. 1971. *What Coleridge Thought.* Middletown: Wesleyan University Press.

Barfield, O. 1977. *The Rediscovery of Meaning and Other Essays.* Middletown: Wesleyan University Press.

Barker, G. 1985. *Prehistoric Farming in Europe.* Cambridge: Cambridge University Press.

Barthes, R. 1966. *Critique et Vérité.* Paris: Seuil.

Barthes, R. 1972a. *Mythologies.* Trans. A. Lavers. London: Cape.

Barthes, R. 1972b. *Critical Essays.* Trans. R. Howard. Evanston: Northwestern University Press.

Barthes, R. 1974. *S/Z: An Essay.* Trans. R. Miller. New York: Hill and Wang.

Bauman, R. and Sherzer, R.(eds.). 1974. *Explorations in the Ethnography of Speaking.* Cambridge: Cambridge University Press.

Beardsley, M. 1962. "The metaphorical twist," *Philosophy and Phenomenological Research* **22**: 293ff.

Benveniste, E. 1971. *Problems of General Linguistics.* Trans. M.E.Meek. Coral Gables: University of Miami Press.

Berkeley, G. [1710] 1910. *Berkeley: A New Theory of Vision and Other Writings.* Ed. by A.D.Lindsay. London: Dent (Everyman).

Berlin, B. and Kay, P. 1969. *Basic Colour Terms.* Berkeley and Los Angeles: University of California Press.

Berndt, R. M. 1974. *Australian Aboriginal Religion.* Leiden: Brill.

Berndt, R. M. and C. 1964. *The World of the First Australians.* Sydney: Angus and Robertson.

Berry, M. F. 1967. *Language Disorders of Children: The Bases and Diagnoses.* Englewood Cliffs: Prentice-Hall.

Bierwisch, M. 1969. "On certain problems of semantic representation", *Foundations of Language* **5**: 153-8.

Bierwisch, M. 1972. "Schriftstruktur und Phonologie", *Probleme und Ergebnisse der Psychologie* **43**: 21-44.

Birch, D. (ed.). 1985. *Style Structure and Criticism*. New Delhi: Bahri.

Bloch, B. and Trager, G. L. 1942. *Outline of Linguistic Analysis*. Baltimore: Linguistic Society of America (Special Publication).

Boas, F. [1940]1966. *Race, Language and Culture*. New York: Free Press.

Bolinger, D.W. 1965. "The atomization of meaning," *Language* **41**: 555-73.

Bolinger, D.W. 1977. *Meaning and Form*. New York: Longman.

Bonhoeffer, D. 1955. *Ethics*. Ed. by E. Bethge. Trans. N.H.Smith. London: SCM Press.

Brown, R. 1976. *A First Language:The Early Stages*. Harmondsworth: Penguin.

Bruner, J. S. *et al.*(eds.). 1956. *A Study in Thinking*. New York: Science Editions.

Bruns, G. L. 1974. *Modern Poetry and the Idea of Language: A Critical and Historical Study*. New Haven: Yale University Press.

Burnley, J.D. 1976. "Middle English colour terminology and lexical structure", *Linguistische Berichte* **41**: 39-49.

Cassirer, E. 1953. *Language and Myth*. Trans. S.K.Langer. New York: Dover.

Cassirer, E. 1953. *The Philosophy of Symbolic Forms*. 3 vols. Trans. R. Manheim. New Haven: Yale University Press.

Chafe, W. L. 1968. "Idiomaticity as an anomaly in the Chomskyan paradigm", *Foundations of Language* **4**: 109-27.

Chatman, S. (ed.). 1971. *Literary Style: A Symposium*. London: Oxford University Press.

Cherry, C. 1957. *On Human Communication*. Cambridge, Mass.: MIT Press.

Chomsky, N. 1965. *Aspects of the Theory of Syntax*. Cambridge,Mass.: M.I.T. Press.

Chomsky, N. 1966. "Linguistic theory". In Mead (1966).

Chomsky, N. 1968. *Language and Mind*. New York: Harcourt, Brace and World.

Chomsky, N. 1980. *Rules and Representations*. London: Oxford University Press.

Chomsky, N. and Halle, M. 1968. *The Sound Pattern of English*. New York: Harper and Row.

Coleridge, S. T. [1817]1962. *Biographia Literaria*. Ed. by J.Shawcross (with corrections). Oxford: Oxford University Press.

Collison, R.L. 1982. *A History of Foreign-Language Dictionaries*. London: Deutsch.

Conklin, H. C. 1955. "Hanunoo colour categories", *Southwestern Journal of Anthropology* **11**: 339-44.

Coon, C.S. and Andrews, J.M. (eds.). *Papers of the Peabody Museum of American Archaeology and Ethnology*. Cambridge, Mass.: Harvard University.

Coulmas, F. 1989. *The Writing Systems of the World*. Oxford: Blackwell.

Crick, M. 1976. *Explorations in Language and Meaning: A Semantic Anthropology*. London: Malaby Press.

Cruse, D.A. 1986. *Lexical Semantics*. Cambridge: Cambridge University Press.

Culler, J. 1975. *Structuralist Poetics: Structuralism, Linguistics and the Study of Literature*. London: Routledge and Kegan Paul.

Cusa, N. de [1450] 1979. *Idiota de Mente (The Layman: About Mind)*. Trans. C.L.Miller. New York: Abaris.

Cusa, N. de [1488] 1986. *De Ludo Globi (The Game of Spheres)*. Trans. P.M.Watts. New York: Abaris.

Davidson, D. 1967. "Truth and meaning," *Synthèse*, **7**: 304-25.

Davie, D. and Livingstone, A. 1969. *Pasternak*. London: Macmillan.

Deleuze, G. 1976. *Proust et les Signes*. Paris: Presses Universitaires de France.

Derrida, J. 1973. *Of Grammatology*. Trans. G.C.Spivak. Baltimore: Johns Hopkins University Press.

Derrida, J. 1977. *Glyph*. Baltimore: Johns Hopkins Press.

Derrida, J. 1988. *Limited Inc*. Evanston: Northwestern University Press.

Doležel, L. and Bailey, R.W. (eds.). 1969. *Statistics and Style*. New York: American Elsevier

Douglas, M. (ed.). 1973. *Rules and Meanings: The Anthropology of Everyday Knowledge*. Harmondsworth: Penguin.

Dufrenne, M. 1963. *Language and Philosophy*. Trans. H.B.Veatch. Bloomington: Indiana University Press.

Durkheim, E. [1915] 1961. *The Elementary Forms of the Religious Life*. Trans. J.W.Swain. New York: Collier.

Durkheim, E. and Mauss, M. [1903] 1963. *Primitive Classification.*. Trans. R. Needham. Chicago: Chicago University Press.

Eco, U. 1976. *A Theory of Semiotics*. Bloomington: Indiana University Press.

Elkin, A.P. 1954. *The Australian Aborigines: How to Understand Them*. Sydney: Angus and Robertson.

Empson, W. 1951. *The Structure of Complex Words*. London: Chatto and Windus.

Fabb, N. *et al.* 1987. *The Linguistics of Writing: Arguments between Language and Literature*. Manchester: Manchester University Press.

Firth, J.R. 1957. *Papers in Linguistics 1934-1951*. London: Oxford University Press.

Firth, J.R. 1966. *The Tongues of Men*. London: Oxford University Press.

Fish, S. 1980. *Is There a Text in this Class? The Authority of Interpretive Communities*. Cambridge, Mass.: Harvard University Press.

Flew, A. (ed.). 1981. *Essays in Conceptual Analysis*. Westport: Greenwood.

Fodor, J.A. and Katz, J.J. (eds.). 1964. *The Structure of Language: Readings in the Philosophy of Language*. Englewood Cliffs: Prentice-Hall.

Frazer, J. G. *The Golden Bough: A Study in Magic and Religion*. Abridged Edn. London: Macmillan.

French, P.A. *et al.*(eds.). 1979. *Contemporary Perspectives in the Philosophy of Language*. Minneapolis: Minnesota University Press.

Frye, N. 1971. *Anatomy of Criticism: Four Essays*. Princeton: Princeton University Press.

Gadamer, H.-G. 1991. *Truth and Method*. Trans. and revised by J. Weinsheimer and D.G.Marshall. New York: Crossroad.

Gadamer, H.-G. 1976. *Philosophical Hermeneutics*. Trans. and ed. by D.E.Linge. Berkeley and Los Angeles: University of California Press.

Garvin, P. L.(ed.). 1964. *A Prague School Reader on Esthetics, Literary Structure, and Style*. Washington, D.C.: Georgetown University Press.

Geschwind, N. 1973. "The varieties of naming errors", *Cortex* **9**: 97-112.

Giglioli, P.P.(ed.). 1972. *Language and Social Context*. Harmondsworth: Penguin.

Goldstein, K. 1948. *Language and Language Disturbances*. New York: Grune and Stratton.

Gombrich, E. 1977. *Art and Illusion: A Study in the Psychology of Pictorial Representation*. 5th. Edn. London: Phaidon.

Goodenough, W.H. 1956. "Componential analysis and the study of meaning", *Language* **32**: 195-216.

Goodman, N. 1982. "On thoughts without words", *Cognition* **12**: 211-7

Gordon, W.T. 1978. "Morphosemantics: A neglected chapter in linguistics", *Glossa* **12**: 3-15.

Gordon, W.T. 1982. *A History of Semantics* (Amsterdam Studies in the Theory and History of Linguistic Science III: 30). Amsterdam: Benjamins.

Gorog, R.P.de. 1981. "The application of onomasiology to synonymy, word formation, and etymology", *WORD* **32**: 99-108.

Greimas, A.J. 1966. *Sémantique Structurale*. Paris: Larousse.

Grossman, L. [1925]1965. *Poetika Dostoevskogo* [Dostoevsky's Poetics]. Moscow.

Guiraud, P. 1956. "Les champs morpho-sémantiques", *Bulletin de la Société Linguistique de Paris* **52**: 265-88.

Guiraud, P. 1960. "Le champ morpho-sémantique du verbe *chiquer*", *Bulletin de la Société Linguistique de Paris* **55**: 134-54.

Guiraud, P. 1966. "Le champ morpho-sémantique des noms du *chat*", *Bulletin de la Société Linguistique de Paris* **61**: 128-45.

Guiraud, P. 1975. *Semiology*. Trans. by P. Gross. London: Routledge and Kegan Paul.

Gumperz, J.J. 1971. *Language in Social Groups*. Stanford: Stanford University Press.

Gumperz, J.J. and Hymes, D. (eds.). 1964. *The Ethnography of Communication. American Anthropologist* **66**: 6, Part 2, vi.

Gumperz, J. J. and Hymes, D. (eds.). 1972. *Directions in Sociolinguistics: The Ethnography of Communication*. New York: Holt, Rinehart and Winston.

Habermas, J. 1978. *Knowledge and Human Interests*. 2nd Edn. London: Heinemann.

Halliday, M.A.K. 1975. *Learning How to Mean: Explorations in the Development of Language*. London: Arnold

Halliday, M.A.K. 1978. *Language as Social Semiotic: The Social Interpretation of Language and Meaning*. London: Arnold.

Halliday, M.A.K. 1985. *An Introduction to Functional Grammar*. London: Arnold.

Harris, R. 1980. *The Language-Makers*. Ithaca: Cornell University Press.

Harris, R. 1987. *The Language Machine*. Ithaca: Cornell University Press.

Heidegger, M. 1959. *An Introduction to Metaphysics*. Trans. R.Manheim. New Haven: Yale University Press.

Heidegger, M. 1962. *Being and Time*. Trans. J.Macquarrie and E. Robinson. London: SCM Press.

Heidegger, M. 1975. *Poetry, Language and Thought*. Trans. A. Hofstadter. New York: Harper and Row.

Hjelmslev, L. 1961. *Prolegomena to a Theory of Language*. Revised Edition. Trans. F.J.Whitfield. Madison: Wisconsin University Press.

Hoijer, H. 1951. "Cultural implications of some Navaho linguistic categories," *Language* **27**: 111-20.

Hoppenbrouwers, G.A.J. et al. (eds.). 1985. *Meaning and the Lexicon*. Dordrecht: Foris.

Householder, F.W. and Saporta, S. (eds.). 1967. *Problems in Lexicography*. Bloomington: Indiana University Press.

Humboldt, W. von. [1836] 1971. *Linguistic Variability and Intellectual Development*. Trans. G.C.Buck and F.A.Raven. Coral Gables: University of Miami Press.

Husserl, E. [1913] 1970. *Logical Investigations*. 2nd edn. Trans. J.N.Findlay. New York: Humanities Press.

Husserl, E. 1970. *The Crisis of European Sciences and Transcendental Phenomenology*. Trans. D.Carr. Evanston: Northwestern University Press.

Hymes, D. (ed.). 1964. *Language in Culture and Society: A Reader in Linguistics and Anthropology*. New York: Harper and Row.

Jakobson, R, Fant, G.C.M. and Halle, M. 1952. *Preliminaries to Speech Analysis*. Cambridge, Mass.: M.I.T.Press.

Jakobson, R. and Halle, M. 1971. *Fundamentals of Language*. 2nd. revised edn. The Hague:Mouton.

Jespersen, O. 1922. *Language: Its Nature, Development, and Origin*. London: Allen and Unwin.

Jones, A. I. 1978. "Form and meaning in a Australian language," *Language and Speech*, **21**: 278.

Karcevskij, S. 1929. "Du dualisme asymétrique du signe linguistique", *Travaux du Cercle Linguistique de Prague* 1: 33-8.

Katz, J.J. and Fodor, J.A. 1967. "The Structure of a Semantic Theory". In ed. L.Jakobovits and M.S. Miron. *Readings in the Philosophy of Language*. New York: Prentice-Hall, 398-431.

Keller, R. 1994. *On Language Change: The Invisible Hand in Language*. Trans.B. Nerlich. London: Routledge and Kegan Paul.

Kelly, L.G.(ed.). 1969. *The Description and Measurement of Bilingualism*. Toronto: University of Toronto Press.

Kluckhohn, C. 1949. *Mirror for Man: The Relation of Anthropology to Modern Life*. New York: McGraw Hill.

Kristeva, J. 1989. *Language the Unknown*. Trans. A.M.Menke. London: Harvester Wheatsheaf.

Kuhn, T.S. 1970. *The Structure of Scientific Revolutions*. 2nd. Edn. Chicago: Chicago University Press.

Labov, W. 1966. *The Social Stratification of English in New York City*. Washington DC: Center for Applied Linguistics.

Labov, W. 1970. "The Study of Language in its Social Context", *Studium Generale* **23**: 30-87.

Labov, W. 1972. *Sociolinguistic Patterns*. Philadelphia: University of Pennsylvania Press.

Lambert, W. E. 1972. *Language, Psychology, and Culture: Essays by Wallace E. Lambert*. Stanford: Stanford University Press.

Lane, M. (ed.). 1970. *Structuralism*. London: Cape.

Lehrer, A. 1974. *Semantic Fields and Lexical Structure*. New York: Elsevier.

Leibniz, G. W. 1934. *Philosophical Writings*. Trans. M. Morris. London: Everyman.

Leibniz, G. W. 1989. *Philosophical Essays*. Trans. R. Ariew and D. Garber. Indianapolis: Hackett

Leroi-Gourhan, A. 1964. *Le Geste et la Parole*. 2 vols. Paris: Albin Michel.

Lesser, R. 1978. *Linguistic Investigations of Aphasia*. London: Arnold.

Lévi-Strauss, C. 1966. *The Savage Mind*. Chicago: Chicago University Press. (Trans. of 1962. *La Pensée Sauvage*. Paris: Librairie Plon).

Lévi-Strauss, C. 1973. *Tristes Tropiques*. Trans. J. and D. Weightman. London: Cape.

Lévy-Bruhl, L. [1923] 1965. *How Natives Think*. Trans. L.A.Clare. London: Allen and Unwin.

Lévy-Bruhl, L. [1927] 1965. *The "Soul" of the Primitive*. Trans. L.A.Clare. London: Allen and Unwin.

Lévy-Bruhl, L. 1949. *Les Carnets de Lévy-Bruhl*. Paris: Presses Universitaires de France.

Lewis, C.S. 1960. *The Four Loves*. London: Bles.

Lewis, C.S. 1961. *Studies in Words*. Cambridge: Cambridge University Press.

Lieberman, P. 1985. *On the Origins of Language: An Introduction to the Evolution of Human Speech*. New York: Macmillan.

Locke, J. [1690]1959. *An Essay Concerning Human Understanding*. 2 vols. Ed. by A. Campbell-Frazer. New York: Dover.

Lord, R. 1966. "Complex homonymy in English lexical and semantic structure", *Studia Linguistica* **20**: 35-56.

Lord, R. 1970a. *Dostoevsky: Essays and Perspectives*. London: Chatto and Windus.

Lord, R. 1970b. "Lexico-semantic categories", *Studia Linguistica* **24**: 17-42.

Lord, R. 1974. "Learning vocabulary", *IRAL (International Review of Applied Linguistics)* **12**: 239-47.

Lord, R. and Chang, T.Z. 1987. "Morphosemantic categories in Chinese: An interim report", *Journal of the Atlantic Provinces Linguistic Association* **9**: 123-57.

Lord, R. and Chang T. Z. 1992. "How does the lexicon work?", *WORD* **43**: **3**: 349-374.

Lord, R. and T'sou, B.K.Y. 1976. *Studies in Bilingual Education: Sel;e4cted Papers from the 1976 International Symposium on Bilingual Education.* Hong Kong: Language Centre, University of Hong Kong-Heinemann.

Lorenz, K. 1987. *The Waning of Humaneness.* Trans. R.W.Kickert. Boston: Little, Brown & Co.

Lounsbury, F.G. 1956 "A semantic analysis of the Pawnee kinship usage", *Language* **32**: 158-94.

Lyons, J. 1969. *An Introduction to Theoretical Linguistics.* Cambridge: Cambridge University Press.

Lyons, J. 1977. *Semantics.* 2 vols. Cambridge: Cambridge University Press.

McCawley, J.D. 1971. "Prelexical Syntax", in R.J. O'Brien (ed.). *Report of the Twenty-Second Annual Round Table Meeting on Linguistics and Language Studies.* Washington, D.C.: Georgetown University.

McCune, K.M. 1985. *The Internal Structure of Indonesian Roots.* Nos. 21-22 *Linguistic Studies of Indonesian and Other Languages in Indonesia.* Jakarta: NUSA.

McIntosh, A. and Halliday, M.A.K. 1966. *Patterns of Language: Papers in General, Descriptive, and Applied Linguistics.* London: Longman.

McKay, G.R. and Sommer, B.A. (eds.). 1984. *Further Applications of Linguistics to Australian Aboriginal Contexts.* (Occasional Papers 8: Applied Linguistic Association of Australia). Melbourne: University of Melbourne.

Mace, C.E.(ed.). 1957. *British Philosophy in the Mid-Century.* London: Allen and Unwin.

Macksey, R. and Donato, E. (eds.). 1972. *The Structuralist Controversy: The Languages of Criticism and the Sciences of Man.* Baltimore: Johns Hopkins Press.

Mandelbaum, D. G.(Ed.). 1949. *Selected Writings of Edward Sapir in Language, Culture and Personality.* Berkeley and Los Angeles: University of California Press.

Matthews, P.H. 1974. *Morphology: An Introduction to the Theory of Word-Structure.* Cambridge: Cambridge University Press.

Mead, R.G..Jr.(ed.) 1966. *Language Teaching: Broader Contexts.* Northeast Conference Report.

Melton, A.W. and Martin, E. (eds.). 1972. *Coding Processes in Human Memory.* Washington D.C.: Winston.

Merleau-Ponty, M. 1962. *Phenomenology of Perception.* Trans. C. Smith. London: Routledge and Kegan Paul (International Library of Philosophy and Scientific Method).

Merleau-Ponty, M. 1964. *Signs.* Trans.R.C.McCleary. Evanston: Northwestern University Press.

Meschonnic, H. 1982. *Critique du Rhythme.* Paris: Verdier.

Misra, V. N. 1966. *The Descriptive Technique of Panini.* The Hague: Mouton.

Montagu, A (ed.). 1968. *The Concept of the Primitive.* New York: Free Press.

Morley, S. G. and Brainerd, G. W. 1983. *The Ancient Maya.* 4th. Edn., revised by R.J.Sharer. Stanford: Stanford University Press.

Mueller-Vollmer, K. (ed.). 1990. *The Hermeneutics Reader.* New York: Continuum.

Neisser, U. 1967. *Cognitive Psychology.* Englewood Cliffs: Prentice-Hall.

Ogden, C.K. and Richards, I.A. 1949. *The Meaning of Meaning.* 10th.edn. London: Routledge and Kegan Paul.

Orr, J. 1953. *Words and Sounds in English and French.* Oxford: Oxford University Press.

Pasternak, B. 1959. *Prose and Poems.* Ed. by S. Schimanski. Revised edn. London: Benn.

Peirce, C. S. 1931-58. *The Collected Papers of Charles Sanders Peirce.* Ed. by C. Hartshorne and P. Weiss. Cambridge, Mass.: Harvard.

Pottier, B. 1965. "La définition sémantique dans les dictionnaires", *Travaux de Linguistique et de Littérature* (University of Strasbourg) **3**: 33-9.

Preston, J. 1985. *A Language Not Our Own: The Language of Literature*. University of Hong Kong: Inaugural Lecture, Supplement to the Gazette, No.32.

Quine, W.V. 1969. *Ontological Relativity*. New York: Columbia University Press.

Ransom, J. C. [1941]1979. *The New Criticism*. Newport, Conn.: Greenwood Press.

Rasmussen, D.M. (ed.). 1971. *Mythic-Symbolic Language and Philosophical Anthropology*. The Hague: Mouton.

Reuck, A.V.S.de and O,Connor, M. (eds.). 1964. *Disorders of Language*. London: Churchill.

Richards, I.A. 1926. *Principles of Literary Criticism*. 2nd. Edn. Cambridge: Cambridge University Press.

Richards, I.A. 1936. *The Philosophy of Rhetoric*. London: Oxford University Press.

Ricoeur, P. 1975. *The Rule of Metaphor: Multi-disciplinary Studies of the Creation of Meaning in Language*. Trans. R. Czerny. Toronto: University of Toronto Press.

Riffaterre, M. 1959. "Criteria for Style Analysis", *WORD* **15**: 154-74.

Righter, W. 1975. *Myth and Literature*. London: Routledge and Kegan Paul.

Rossetti, A. 1947. *Le Mot: Esquisse d'une Théorie Générale*. Copenhagen: Munksgaard.

Russo, J.P. 1989. *I.A.Richards: His Life and Work*. Baltimore: Johns Hopkins University Press.

Sacks, S. (ed.). 1979. *On Metaphor*. Chicago: Chicago University Press.

Sapir, E. 1921. *Language: An Introduction to the Study of Speech*. New York: Harcourt, Brace and World.

Sapir, E. 1931. "Conceptual categories in primitive languages," *Science* **74**: 578.

Sarles, H. 1977. *Studies in Semiotics: After Metaphysics Toward a Grammar of Interaction and Discourse*. Lisse: Peter de Ridder.

Saussure, F. de 1916. *Cours de Linguistique Générale*. Ed. by C. Bally and A. Sechehaye. Paris: Payot. (English translation: *A Course in General Linguistics*. Trans. W. Baskin. New York: Philosophical Library, 1959).

Saville-Troike, M. 1982. *The Ethnography of Communication*. Oxford: Blackwell.

Schmandt-Besserat, D. 1978. "The earliest precursors of writing", *Scientific American* **238**: 50-59.

Schoenman, R. (ed.). 1967. *Bertrand Russell: Philosopher of the Century*. London: Allen and Unwin.

Schrier, A.M. and Stollnitz, F. (eds.). 1971. *Behaviour of Non-human Primates*. New York: Academic Press.

Schrödinger, E. 1959. *Mind and Matter*. Cambridge: Cambridge University Press.

Searle, J. R. 1969. *Speech Acts*. Cambridge: Cambridge University Press.

Searle, J.R. 1979. *Expression and Meaning*. Cambridge: Cambridge University Press.

Sebeok, T. A.(ed.). 1960. *Style in Language*. Cambridge,Mass.: M.I.T.Press.

Sebeok, T. A.(ed.). 1966. *Current Trends in Linguistics 3*. The Hague: Mouton

Sebeok, T. A. (ed.). 1975. *The Tell-tale Sign: A Survey of Semiotics*. Lisse: De Ridder.

Sebeok, T. A. and Umiker-Sebeok, D.-J (eds.). 1990-91. *The Semiotic Web*. Berlin: Mouton de Gruyter.

Segre, C. 1973. *Semiotics and Literary Criticism*. Trans. J. Meddemen. The Hague: Mouton.

Sollers, P. 1968. *Logiques*. Paris: Seuil.

Steele, R. and Threadgold, T. (eds.). 1987. *Language Topics: Essays in Honour of Michael Halliday*. Amsterdam: Benjamins. The Collected Poems of Wallace Stevens. London: Faber.

Steinberg, D.D. and Jakobovits, L.A. (eds.). 1971. *An Interdisciplinary Reader in Philosophy, Linguistics and Psychology*. Cambridge: Cambridge University Press.

Strehlow, T.G.H. 1971. *Songs of Central Australia*. Sydney: Angus and Robertson.

Stevens, W. 1964. *The Collected Poems of Wallace Stevens*. London: Faber and Faber.

Tedlock, D. 1983. *The Spoken Word and the Work of Interpretation*. Philadelphia: University of Pennsylvania Press.

Tedlock, D. 1986. *Popol Vuh: The Mayan Book of the Dawn of Life*. New York: Touchstone.

Terrace, H.S. *et al*. 1979. "Can an ape create a sentence?", *Science* **206**: 891-901.

Tinbergen, N. 1989. *The Study of Instinct*. Oxford: Oxford University Press.

Trier, J. [1931] 1973. *Der deutsche Wortschatz im Sinnbezirk des Verstandes: Die Geschichte eines spraclichlen Feldes*. Heidelberg: Winter.

Trubetskoy, N. S. [Troubetzkoy,N.S.] 1964. *Principes de Phonologie*. Trans. J. Cantineau. Paris: Klincksieck.

Trudgill, P. 1974. *The Social Differentiation of English in Norwich*. Cambridge: Cambridge University Press.

Trudgill, P. (ed.). 1978. *Sociolinguistic Patterns in British English*. London: Arnold.

Turner, V. 1967. *The Forest of Symbols: Aspects of Ndembu Ritual*. Ithaca: Cornell University Press.

Tyler, S. A. 1978. *The Said and the Unsaid: Mind, Meaning and Culture*. New York:Academic Press.

Ullmann, S. 1957. *Style in the French Novel*. Cambridge: Cambridge University Press.

Ullmann, S. 1962. *Semantics: An Introduction to the Study of Meaning*. Oxford: Blackwell.

Urmson, J.O. and Warnock, G.J.(eds.). 1970. *Philosophical Papers*. London: Oxford University Press.

Valéry P. 1956-75. *The Collected Works of Paul Valéry*. Ed. by J. Mathews and trans. P. Manheim. 15 vols. New York: Pantheon.

Vygotsky, L.S. [1934] 1962. *Thought and Language*. Ed. and trans. E. Hanfman and G. Vakar. Cambridge, Mass.: MIT Press.

Watts, P.M. 1986. *An Introduction to N. de Cusa* ([1488] 20-2). (See under Cusa, above).

Wellek, R. and Warren, A. 1976. *Theory of Literature*. 3rd. Edn. Harmondsworth: Penguin.

Whorf, B. L. 1962. *Language, Thought, and Reality: Selected Writings of Benjamin Lee Whorf*. Ed. by J.B.Carroll. New York: John Wiley, and Cambridge, Mass.: M.I.T.Press.

Wierzbicka, A. 1975. "Why 'kill' does not mean 'cause to die'", *Foundations of Language* **13**: 491-528.

Wierzbicka, A. 1980. Lingua Mentalis:*The Semantics of Natural Languages*. New York: Academic Press.

Witkowski, S.R. *et al*. 1981. "Where do tree terms come from?", *Man* 16: 1-14.

Wittgenstein, L. 1963. *Philosophical Investigations*. Trans. G.E.M.Anscombe. Oxford: Blackwell.

Zabeeh, F. *et al*. 1974. *Readings in Semantics*. Urbana: University of Illinois Press.

Subject Index

Personal Name Index